Islam in Southeast Asia

Series Editors
Nassef Manabilang Adiong
Institute of Islamic Studies
University of the Philippines Diliman
Quezon City, Central Luzon, Philippines

Imtiyaz Yusuf
College of Religious Studies
Mahidol University
Nakhorn Pathom, Thailand

Lily Zubaidah Rahim
Government and International Relations
University of Sydney
Sydney, NSW, Australia

Maznah Mohamad
Department of Southeast Asian Studies/Malay Studies
National University of Singapore
Singapore, Singapore

Nadirsyah Hosen
Faculty of Law
Monash University
Clayton North, VIC, Australia

The series publishes academic and policy research on historical and contemporary Muslim communities, both in the region and in the diaspora, and on all aspects of Islam in Southeast Asia. It concentrates on theoretical, methodological, empirical, religious, spiritual, and critical studies of Islam, including mundane praxes and lived Islam. We encourage interdisciplinarity and eclectic contributions from scholars and practitioners (e.g. preachers, spiritual/religious leaders, and policy makers) to facilitate a holistic approach towards the study of Islam. The series particularly welcome topics on: (1) Islam and Politics (2) Islam & Ethnicity; (3) Islam and Modernity; (4) MENA Influences in Southeast Asia; (5) pre-Modern and Contemporary Islamic Thought; (6) Sunni and Shia Relations; (7) Islamic Studies and Area Studies; (8) Canonical and Periphery Islam; and (9) Relations between Muslims and non-Muslims across the region. Contributions are welcome from across fields and disciplines including politics, international relations, sociology, humanities, the arts, anthropology, comparative religion, cultural studies, economics, history, law (jurisprudence), philosophy, mysticism (Sufism), and theology. The series will include original monographs, Palgrave Pivots, edited volumes/collections, and handbooks.

More information about this series at
http://www.palgrave.com/gp/series/16079

Jeffrey Ayala Milligan

Islamic Identity, Postcoloniality, and Educational Policy

Schooling and Ethno-Religious Conflict in the Southern Philippines

Second Edition

palgrave
macmillan

Jeffrey Ayala Milligan
Florida State University
Tallahassee, FL, USA

Islam in Southeast Asia
ISBN 978-981-15-1227-8   ISBN 978-981-15-1228-5 (eBook)
https://doi.org/10.1007/978-981-15-1228-5

Jointly published with De La Salle University Publishing House
The print edition is not for sale in the Philippines. Customers from the Philippines please order the print book from: De La Salle University Publishing House.
ISBN of the Co-Publisher's edition: 978-971-555-682-8

1st edition: © Palgrave Macmillan 2005
2nd edition: © The Editor(s) (if applicable) and The Author(s), under exclusive license to Springer Nature Singapore Pte Ltd. 2020
This work is subject to copyright. All rights are solely and exclusively licensed by the Publisher, whether the whole or part of the material is concerned, specifically the rights of translation, reprinting, reuse of illustrations, recitation, broadcasting, reproduction on microfilms or in any other physical way, and transmission or information storage and retrieval, electronic adaptation, computer software, or by similar or dissimilar methodology now known or hereafter developed.
The use of general descriptive names, registered names, trademarks, service marks, etc. in this publication does not imply, even in the absence of a specific statement, that such names are exempt from the relevant protective laws and regulations and therefore free for general use.
The publishers, the authors, and the editors are safe to assume that the advice and information in this book are believed to be true and accurate at the date of publication. Neither the publishers nor the authors or the editors give a warranty, express or implied, with respect to the material contained herein or for any errors or omissions that may have been made. The publishers remain neutral with regard to jurisdictional claims in published maps and institutional affiliations.

Cover image: © Tuah Roslan/Getty Images

This Palgrave Macmillan imprint is published by the registered company Springer Nature Singapore Pte Ltd.
The registered company address is: 152 Beach Road, #21-01/04 Gateway East, Singapore 189721, Singapore

For
The Muslim children of the Philippines,
and those who teach them.

FOREWORD

Islamic Identity, Postcoloniality, and Educational Policy: Schooling and Ethno-Religious Conflict in the Southern Philippines, Second Edition, Jeffrey Ayala Milligan.

The first edition captured a well-researched manuscript grounded in historical and ethnographical analyses regarding the evolution of Muslim education in the Philippines and its relations to educational policies created in various periods by various governmental bureaucracies. It proposes a postcolonial lens, despite its shortcomings, that speaks for the subaltern voice for the Muslim experiences of historical *pandita* schooling to modern formal schooling. Hindu ways of life have influenced pre-Islamic Moro culture and identity in Mindanao, but also to some greater extent, the entire Filipino nation as well. For examples, *Darangen* and *Radia Indarapatra* were Hindu legacies that represent the deepest souls of Maranao culture. Told to different generations for centuries, they symbolize the axial height of oral and performative literatures in Moro civilization. Home or community schooling, headed by the communal leader often viewed as the wise elderly man/woman, was the educational norm at that time (from pre-Islamic until pre-American colony) in Muslim Mindanao. Skills were taught that were imbued by cultural and religious norms, in this case Islamic education, which was passed down by Arab missionaries, Muslim traders, the Sufis (mystics), and steadfastly strengthened by marriages with the locals.

Spanish policy for more than 300 years was to inculcate Christianity, Catholicism in particular, in all aspects of Filipino lives. This resulted in two discriminating categories: one category for ordinary Filipinos and the other for the political elites. Muslim Moros were apprehensive of and resisted Spanish educational policy because, firstly, not all Moro lands were colonized, and secondly, Spanish treatment toward the Muslims was harsher than their treatment of Filipino Christians. Obviously, Spain's hatred toward the Moors was based on centuries of subjugation to Muslim rule during the existence of al-Andalus kingdoms. This Christianization policy changed with the arrival of another colonizer, the Americans. The difference with the Americans was their effort to educate the Filipinos, as well as the Muslims in Mindanao, through the pedagogy of imperialism. That is, instead of mutual integration, a direct and untoward assimilation was the educational policy implemented by the Americans. In other words, Muslims must forego their *muslimness* and accept and adopt secular modes of thinking and deeds. An American secular education was imposed, not only in various subjects, but most importantly in the enforcement of the English language. Contra American secular education, the wealthy Arabs (particularly Saudi Arabia) have provided petro-dollars to young male Moros (mostly Maranaos) in the 1980s to the present day in order to study Saudi orthodoxy and Arabic language and build mosques in Muslim Mindanao. This mendicant culture continued and has greatly Arabized most of the Moros and Filipino Muslim converts who label themselves as *balik-Islam* (or Muslim revert).

This assimilation policy continued under the Malolos congress, or in postcolonial Philippines, until early 2000s. The Jabidah massacre and the rebellion of MNLF and MILF members are some of the results of the failure of the assimilation policy, a policy in which nation-state (i.e., the statist Philippines) is the new religion that the Moros must adhere to. A sacred statist constitution, nationalistic story and personality (e.g., Rizal and his works), symbolic statist emblems and flag, material power of military and weaponry, and tyranny of the majority are the ingredients to establish the religion of the nation-state. However, gradual reforms took place in the early 2000s where Muslim holidays were incorporated in the national holidays and the creation of the ALIVE program, also known as "Arabic Language and Islamic Values Education" were institutionalized, a process of recognizing Muslim education by hiring Muslim teachers to teach Islamic subjects to Muslim grade school students nationwide.

Additional three chapters are presented in the second edition. They are all situated as the last chapters entitled "Islamization of Education in Muslim Mindanao," "Understanding the Past, Navigating the Future: Theorizing a Way Forward for Mindanao," and "Prophetic Pragmatism: Toward a Bangsamoro Philosophy of Education." Milligan identifies three goals for the Islamizing of the Project Madrasah Education: (1) to infuse Islamic teachings into the curricula, (2) to include secular subjects such as Western science, mathematics, English, and social studies into the curriculum, and (3) to establish pilot schools in the country. Chapter 6, *Theorizing a Way Forward for Mindanao*, reintroduces the pluses and minuses of postcolonial theory as an analytical tool to understand the impact of colonialism. However, Milligan argued for its insufficiency and proposes Dewey's pragmatic philosophy of education with "a future-oriented experimentalism in the pursuit of democratically determined moral ideals." The last chapter on Bangsamoro philosophy of education introduces us to two pragmatist philosophers, Cornel West and John Dewey, who differ on the importance of religious faith. Dewey is critical of supernatural religion as an impediment to thought while West "asserts the great good that has been and can be accomplished in the name of religious faith" by institutionalizing the importance of prophetic traditions (common to Abrahamic faiths), pragmatic epistemology (knowledge truths are coherence and must be accessible to everyone), and progressive Marxism (self-reflection).

The book ends with an examination of the philosophical challenge of reconciling religious faith (or pragmatic epistemology) and scientific method using "epistemic humility," an alternative approach to finding equitable balance between spirituality (faith) and rationality.

Manila, Philippines   Nassef Manabilang Adiong

Acknowledgements

A book such as this, which attempts to say something relatively coherent and useful about such things as Islamic identity, culture, history, and education in a place so far away from my own roots, is obviously collaborative in a fundamental sense. I simply could not have written it without the support—intellectual, personal, and financial—of a host of individuals and organizations. Whatever success it enjoys is due in large part to their insight, generosity, and wisdom. I take full responsibility for its faults.

Thanks go to Dr. Naseef Manabilang Adiong of the Institute for Islamic Studies at the University of the Philippines for his invitation to serve as a Fulbright Specialist there in November and December 2018. While at U.P. I enjoyed the warm hospitality of and stimulating conversations with Dean Macrina Morados, Dr. Nefertari Arsad, Dr. Jamael Cayamodin, Darwin Absari and many Muslim leaders, government officials, *madaris* administrators and teachers, and the graduate students of IIS. Their willingness to share their expertise and experiences aided immeasurably in bringing my research up to date for this second edition. I would also like to thank Neil Pacamalan of the US Embassy in Manila for facilitating my engagement with new and old colleagues in Mindanao in 2018.

I owe an especial debt of gratitude to Dr. Nagasura T. Madale, friend, scholar, and lover of all things Maranao for his invaluable assistance in my research for the first edition. His insight and support over the years have been indispensable and deeply appreciated. I am also deeply indebted to Dr. Aida Hafiza Macada-ag, whose help at the beginning and end of this project helped get it started and helped to bring it to a successful conclusion. I would also like to thank Dr. Datumanong Sarangani and his wife Dina, Dr. Benoni Omaca-an, Dr. Malawi Panambulan, Manaros B. Boransing, Dr. Mahad Mutilan, and so many others who have made me welcome in Marawi and Lanao del Sur and suffered my questions for these many years. And I must thank my family in the Philippines, my mother-in-law Wenceslawa Asi, Romeo and Olivia Balincongan, Solomon and Ruth Alfeche, David and Luningning Sarmiento, Tomong and Josefina Cortez, and all their children, for their hospitality, rides to and from airports, and always making me feel at home in the Philippines. And to them, I must add a whole host of friends and other relatives too numerous to mention.

My work here was also made possible by generous financial support. I would like to thank the Fulbright program for the Fulbright Specialist grant which enabled me to update my research at the University of the Philippines Institute for Islamic Studies in 2018, the United States Institute of Peace for the research grant supporting fieldwork in 2003 and 2004, the National Academy of Education for the Spencer Postdoctoral Fellowship supporting archival and fieldwork in 2000 and 2001, and the Philippine-American Educational Foundation for the Fulbright Senior Fellowship which supported preliminary work in 1999.

Finally, and most importantly, I thank my wife, Nenita Asi, and my sons, Ismael and Gabrial. My love for the Philippines began with my love for my wife and is sustained in my love for her and our sons. Their company has sustained me over the months and years of work in the Philippines. The critical love of the country, its people, its past, and its future represented, in part, in this book is a gift from her to me and a legacy, I pray, for them.

Parts of several chapters in this book have appeared as articles in a number of academic journals. They are reprinted here with the permission of their respective editors.

Milligan, J. A. (2010). The Prophet and the Engineer Meet Under the Mango Tree: Leadership, Education and Conflict in the Southern Philippines. *Educational Policy*, 24(1), 28–51.

Milligan, J. A. (2008). Islam and Educational Policy Reform in the Southern Philippines. *Asia Pacific Journal of Education*, 28(4), 369–381.

Milligan, J. A. (2006). Reclaiming an Ideal: The Islamization of Education in the Southern Philippines. *Comparative Education Review*, 50(3), 410–430.

Milligan, J. A. (2005). Faith in School: Educational Policy Responses to Ethno-Religious Conflict in the Southern Philippines, 1935–1985. *Journal of Southeast Asian Studies*, 36(1), 67–86.

Milligan, J. A. (2005). Postcolonial Pragmatism? Ethno-Religious Conflict and Education in Postcolonial Spaces. *Philosophy of Education*, 287–295.

Milligan, J. A. (2004). Islamization or Secularization? Educational Reform and the Search for Peace in the Southern Philippines. *Current Issues in Comparative Education*, 7(1), 1–8.

Milligan, J. A. (2004). Democratization or Neocolonialism? The Education of Muslims Under U.S. Military Occupation, 1903–1920. *History of Education*, 33(4), 451–467.

Milligan, J. A. (2003). Teaching Between the Cross and the Crescent Moon: Islamic Identity, Postcoloniality and Public Education in the Southern Philippines. *Comparative Education Review*, 47(4), 468–492.

Milligan, J. A. (2002). Religion, Diversity and Public Education: Challenges for Teacher Education in the U.S. and Philippines. *Silliman Journal*, 42(2), 12–37.1.

Milligan, J. A. (2001). Religious Identity, Autonomy, and National Integrity: Implications for Educational Policy from Muslim-Christian Conflict in the Philippines. *Islam and Christian–Muslim Relations*, 12(4), 435–448.

Milligan, J. A. (2000). Rethinking the Ideal of the Educated Person: An Alternative from the Maranao-Filipino Oral Epic "Darangen". *Journal of Thought*, 35(3), 67–79.

Contents

1. Education and Ethno-Religious Conflict in Postcolonial Spaces — 1

2. Precolonial Culture and Education in the Southern Philippines — 23

3. Pedagogical Imperialism: American Education of Muslim Filipinos, 1898–1935 — 55

4. Faith in School: Educational Policy Responses to Muslim Unrest in the Philippine Republic — 105

5. We Sing Here Like Birds in the Wilderness: Education and Alienation in Muslim Mindanao — 141

6. Reclaiming an Ideal: The Islamization of Education in Muslim Mindanao — 183

7. Understanding the Past, Navigating the Future: Theorizing a Way Forward for Mindanao — 215

8 Prophetic Pragmatism: Toward a Bangsamoro
  Philosophy of Education   239

Bibliography   269

Index   285

CHAPTER 1

Education and Ethno-Religious Conflict in Postcolonial Spaces

From the passing wake of the colonial era and the Cold War, ethnic and religious conflicts have reemerged as one of the most significant threats to the internal stability of many states as well as peaceful relations between states. The last decade of the twentieth century and the first decade of the twenty-first have borne witness to a renewed emphasis on expressions of nationalism defined in terms of religious and ethnic identity. In the rubble of the former Yugoslavia, Serbian nationalists slaughtered Bosnian Muslims as both sides attempted to carve out independent states based on ethnic, and to some degree, religious differences. In the Russian Republic of Chechnya, a war of independence took on a religious dimension as Chechen Muslims sought support from radical Islamic movements and the Russian government attempted to portray its engagement there as one of the fronts in the worldwide "war on terrorism." Violence between Hindu nationalists and Muslims in India has claimed thousands of lives in terrible spasms of ethno-religious hatred. The world's most populous Muslim nation, Indonesia, was troubled for decades by its own Islamic insurgency in Aceh, Muslim–Christian violence in the Moluccas, and the threat of Islamic extremism in Java. Meanwhile, resistance among the Muslim Uighur people of China's Xinjiang province to government policies make the international news.

Each of these conflicts is, of course, different. Each one emerges from and responds to its own complex historical, political, cultural, and religious context. However, there are important similarities. Many of them, for instance, have emerged in ethnically diverse states that are themselves artifacts of colonialism, either of the West or the former Soviet Union. That imposition of colonial power established hierarchies of the colonizer and the colonized, the powerful and the powerless, the oppressor and the oppressed that inspired, dialectically, nationalist aspirations in subject peoples throughout the twentieth century.[1] During the Cold War, these anticolonial struggles were often expressed within a Marxist-inspired ideological framework that saw imperialism as the inevitable culmination of Western capitalism. However, the disappointments of national independence and Marxism's erosion of credibility after the collapse of the Soviet Union have led many in formerly colonized countries to turn to alternative ideological frameworks for the expression of legitimate grievances and the struggle to realize communal aspirations. In many instances, this has meant a turn to religious and ethnic identities long suppressed by postindependence nationalisms premised on the meaningfulness of states defined by colonial borders.[2] While it would not be accurate to say that any of these conflicts are purely religious in nature, it is fair to say that in each of them, religious differences are mapped onto ethnic, political, linguistic, and class differences in ways that seem to make them more virulent and perhaps intractable. In 1903, at the height of the colonial era, the great African-American sociologist W.E.B. DuBois declared that the problem of the twentieth century would be the "color-line," a problem intimately intertwined with colonialism, as he and later anticolonial intellectuals would come to recognize.[3] One century on, it seems reasonable to ask whether the problem of the twenty-first century will be the religion-line.

The Role of Education

What, we might ask, has education to do with such matters? Surely armed rebellions and terrorism are military and law enforcement problems, not the responsibility of schools. Surely political questions of independence, democratization, or human rights are the purview of political leaders, not teachers. Economic policy makers are surely better equipped to address matters of poverty, economic underdevelopment, and unemployment than educational policy makers. And questions of religious belief and attitudes are widely seen as off-limits for public education in many modern democratic states. What does education have to do with any of this? A lot. Education and educational policy, while certainly not the only or even the main factor, are nevertheless significant players for good or ill in such conflicts.

The significance of education in such contexts stems from its function and location in society. Along with families and religious institutions, the school is an institution charged with the socialization of the young into the life of the larger community and society. It sits at the nexus between the private world of the family and the public world of the state and holds within its walls that which is most precious to us—our children. Thus, education is inevitably a contested terrain. Because of this, it offers a unique window to the fears and aspirations of a society. It offers insight into what a community wants to change in itself, what it aspires to be, and the nature of the disagreements over just what these points are. As an institution of the state, public education is an instrument for the expression of state authority, the inculcation of national identity and loyalty, and the implementation of state policies designed to effect social control and change. The school is as ubiquitous an outpost of the state as the military camp in most nations.[4] It is an outpost largely occupied, however, by local people, and thus, its impact is influenced as much by their aspirations as by the intentions of the state. And local intellectuals—educators—who face the challenge of mediating, transmitting, and translating between the political center and periphery and from the present to the future, staff it. While it is no sole cause or panacea, education can play an important role in exacerbating or mitigating social conflicts. Thus, inquiry into the role of educational policy and its relationship to ethno-religious conflict is relevant to understanding and responding to them.

THE CASE OF THE MUSLIM PHILIPPINES

The southern Philippines provides a uniquely illustrative case of the challenges faced at the intersection of postcoloniality, ethno-religious conflict, and educational policy. Spain arrived in the Philippines in the mid-sixteenth century and proceeded to establish its colonial rule over what had been up to that time an archipelago of more than 7000 islands and dozens of distinct cultures and languages. Spain's colonial rule lasted for more than 300 years and led to the dominance of Catholic Christianity in most of the islands and the profound influence of Spanish culture on indigenous cultures. Spanish territorial claims and administrative policies in the region, in effect, defined the territorial identity of the modern Philippine state; it, in effect, created the Philippines.[5] As Spanish power and influence were spreading westward around the globe, Islam had been spreading for centuries beyond the Middle East and into Southeast Asia, including the southern Philippines. Therefore, when Spain arrived in the Philippines, it encountered what it perceived as an old enemy—Muslims—whom it promptly dubbed "Moros." Thus began three centuries of conflict between a Christianized, Spanish-controlled colonial government bent on extending its control throughout the Philippines and the Islamized ethnic groups of Mindanao and the Sulu Archipelago equally bent on preserving their independence. The resulting dichotomization of the country between Christian and Muslim bedevils Philippine society to this day.[6]

Spanish colonization did more to give birth to the modern Philippine state than simply define its territorial boundaries. It also contributed, dialectically, to the emergence of a sense of Filipino identity and nationalism that would struggle to transcend ethnic and linguistic difference and inspire a struggle for independence that had been largely won by 1898. This nascent Philippine state was crushed, however, by the US invasion and occupation of the islands during the Spanish–American War. This new colonization came at the expense of Philippine independence and hundreds of thousands of Filipino lives. However, what is more important for this study is, perhaps, the fact that the US colonization included the military muscle necessary to make good Spain's territorial claims in Muslim Mindanao and Sulu. In a series of military engagements that, according to one contemporary observer, exceed the Indian Wars of the American West in terms of frequency and severity of combat, the United States largely subdued Muslim Filipinos by the first decade of the twentieth century and brought them under the effective rule of a Manila-based government for the first time in their history.[7] Thus, what had by then become known as "the Moro Problem" became a perennial problem for the successive Philippine governments. Muslim Mindanao became, in effect, an internal colony, and Muslims became a subordinated and largely despised minority within the emerging Philippine nation.

The legacy of this colonial experience—frequently described as 300 years in a Spanish convent and 50 years in Hollywood—is in part the reification of the Muslim–Christian dichotomization of the

Philippine society and its mapping onto long-standing class and cultural divisions in ways that have often added to the conflicts emerging from such differences the fuel of religious zealotry. The consequence has been almost a century of on-again, off-again armed conflict. Long after colonial officials declared an end to Muslim resistance, armed "bandits" and "uprisings" continued in Muslim Mindanao into the 1920s. Muslim guerillas fiercely resisted the Japanese occupation during World War II. Thereafter, since the late 1960s, a succession of Muslim secessionist movements has come into existence, such as the Bangsamoro Liberation Organization in the late 1960s, the Moro National Liberation Front in the 1970s, and the Moro Islamic Liberation Front (MILF) from 1978 to date.[8] The resulting conflicts have claimed more than 100,000 lives, displaced hundreds of thousands more, and severely hobbled the economy of Mindanao and the entire country. The conflict continued into the twenty-first century with numerous Philippine Army and marine units fielded against 12,500 MILF mujahideen and the Abu Sayyaf terrorist group and talk of US military involvement in what was characterized as a front in the so-called war on terrorism.

But there is more to the colonial legacy than armed conflict, for educational policy has figured prominently in efforts to solve the Moro Problem for at least a century. American rule in Muslim Mindanao, for instance, was described by one contemporary scholar as "a notable example of colonization that gets its theory and justification from the principles of modern pedagogy."[9] Another observer, writing toward the end of the American occupation, noted: "The day of the fighter was past. The day of the teacher had come."[10] Subsequent commonwealth and independent Philippine governments would largely continue this policy of integration through education into the 1990s when it was supplemented, but not superseded, by a relatively ineffective policy of educational autonomy. Thus, education and educational policy have not been the only tools, but they have been major tools by which successive Philippine governments have tried to solve the Moro Problem. Thus, the Filipino Muslim educational experience provides a useful, perhaps unique, case through which to study the potential and the pitfalls of educational policy as a tool for addressing ethno-religious tensions both in the Philippines and in other societies.

While such a study might usefully employ any number of theoretical perspectives from the fields of education, economics, human resource development, sociology, anthropology, and others, Filipino Muslim experience, as I noted above, is "triply" postcolonial. It is a legacy of Spanish and American imperialism as well as an internal colonialism imposed by independent Philippine governments enmeshed in a more or less neocolonial relationship with the United States. Thus, postcolonial theory offers a useful, if not necessarily comprehensive, lens on Filipino Muslim educational experience.

Postcolonial Theory

Postcolonial theory represents a multidisciplinary, methodologically diverse scholarly and political project aimed at uncovering the history and continuing legacy of colonialism and incorporating the perspectives of colonized peoples.[11] It is, according to Leela Gandhi, "a disciplinary project devoted to the academic task of revisiting, remembering, and, crucially, interrogating the colonial past."[12] It emerges from a sense of dissatisfaction with traditional popular and scholarly accounts of colonialism and recognition of the ways in which such accounts furthered relations of domination and subordination to the benefit of the colonizer and the detriment of the colonized.[13] Thus, it critically engages the historical amnesia that not only obscures the realities of the colonial period but also erases the history of colonized peoples outside their relationship with the colonizer and masks the continuation of neocolonial relations after formal independence. Given the Philippines' approximately 400-year experience as a colony of first Spain and later the United States, postcolonialism represents the most useful theoretical framework for understanding the relationship between Muslim Filipinos and the mainstream of Philippine society as well as the role educational policy has played in it.

The term postcolonial addresses, however, more than the time of colonialism and subsequent independence; it also names a mode of critical inquiry into the lasting and pervasive consequences of the colonial encounter.[14] A central assumption of postcolonial theory is that colonialism shaped not only the existing structures of the colonized and the colonizing societies at a given moment in history but that it has left a lasting and indelible mark on both, which continues to shape neocolonial relations of dependency and control between them and within a global system of relations that Ania Loomba defines as imperialism.[15] While the term colonialism is most often associated with the direct political control of the territory of one country by another, Ashis Nandy argues that such colonization of land required for its success and perpetuation the colonization of minds as well.[16] Thus, the psychology of colonialism, what Franz Fanon described as an inferiority complex of the soul, continues after formal independence in a condition Gandhi terms "postcoloniality."[17]

Drawing on Hegel's idea of the acquisition of identity and self-consciousness through the recognition of others, Fanon and Albert Memmi recognized the relationship of the colonizer-colonized as a historical manifestation of Hegel's master-slave narrative.[18] The inequality of this relationship creates enduring, dichotomous hierarchies of knowledge, value, and identity defined in binary opposites such as colonizer-colonized, civilized-primitive, scientific-superstitious in which the left-hand term describes the ideal embodied in the colonizer and the right-hand term the failings of the colonized that justify his subordination. The colonized, however, have not been passive partners in this relationship. Many resist; therefore, it is necessary for postcolonial theory to inquire into the modes of psychological resistance as well as acquiescence to the colonization of minds.[19] I argue later that the distinction of Christian–Muslim in the Philippine context is mapped onto these hierarchies of knowledge, value, and identity in ways that make postcolonial theory relevant to the understanding of Muslim–Christian relations and the educational policy in postindependence Philippines as well as during the period of American colonialism.

Postcolonial theory situates itself in a rather uneasy, but nevertheless creative tension between Marxist thought and poststructuralism.[20] While earlier critics of colonialism such as Memmi and Fanon drew on Marxism's account of imperialism as the logical result of capitalism to both explain colonialism and conceptualize the resistance to it, more recent postcolonial theorists have recognized that experience is dissected by determinants other than class. Differences of race, ethnicity, gender, and, as I argue in the Philippine case, religion also define inequitable distributions of social power.[21] As Foucault has shown, power is everywhere.[22] It is fluid and is not necessarily contained in the neat distinctions of the powerful and the powerless implicit in much of Marxist thought. This insight is crucial to the recognition of inequitable relations within colonized societies. Yet, at the same time the Marxist contribution to postcolonial theory preserves the recognition of the powerful-powerless hierarchy as a meaningful description of "constellations" of power that do represent broad inequities in colonized societies.

Again, this creative tension is crucial to understanding Muslim Filipino relations with Americans and Christian Filipinos: the colonizer-colonized, powerful-powerless dichotomy does describe the relative political and economic disempowerment of Muslim Filipinos. However, it fails to account for differences of class and gender within Muslim Filipino society that, in some contexts, reverses the larger power relationship between Muslim and Christian Filipinos. Poststructuralist conceptions of power offer this insight. It is also helpful in understanding theoretically the cooperation and collaboration of some of the colonized with the colonial project. Thus, poststructuralist complications of overly tidy dichotomies between colonizer-colonized and powerful-powerless foreground the internal divisions within colonized societies, raising the question of whether and to what extent local elites were ever really victims of colonialism and the possibility that anticolonial struggles benefited these elites while maintaining the colonial subordination of significant segments of ostensibly independent states.[23] Important aspects of such continuing relations of domination and subordination within postcolonial states—the hierarchical ordering of broad ethno-religious differences in the southern Philippines, for instance—are usefully illuminated by the concept of internal colonialism.

The internal colonial model was proposed by two Mexican sociologists in the mid-1960s as an explanation for relations between postindependence states and Amerindian populations.[24] While the concept was open to criticism for not fitting neatly with the dichotomous conceptual framework of early Marxist-inspired postcolonialism, it has proved useful in analyzing forms of oppression such as apartheid, caste, and the plight of indigenous peoples within settler colonies, which are of interest in native and ethnic studies and are highlighted by those versions of postcolonialism influenced by poststructuralist conceptions of power.[25] Thus, it is particularly relevant to understanding relations in postcolonial states composed of ethnic groups with quite different languages and social structures and unequal access to social power, a description that fits Muslim–Christian relations in the Philippines quite well.

Internal colonialism occurs within the political and economic context of neocolonialism. It is "applied to the double bind of the national state after independence: on the one hand, to enforce the colonial politics toward indigenous communities and, on the other, to establish alliances with metropolitan colonial powers."[26] According to

Silvia Rivera Cusicanqui (1993), the concept of internal colonialism calls attention to a particular form of domination.

> [A] form of domination grounded in a colonial horizon of long duration… although underground and invisibly. To this horizon has been added—but without totally superseding or modifying it—the most recent cycles of liberalism and populism. These more recent horizons were only able to rework the colonial structures of long duration by converting them into modalities of internal colonialism, and these older structures remain crucial when an explanation of the internal stratification of Bolivian society is needed and when the fundamental social contradictions have to be explained, when particular mechanisms of exclusion and segregation, distinct from the political and state structures of the country, need to be revealed, since they are the very foundation of the most pervasive forms of structural violence.[27]

While Cusicanqui's account of internal colonialism is articulated in terms of Bolivian postcolonial experience, it is, I believe, applicable to Muslim–Christian relations of stratification, exclusion, segregation, and structural violence in the southern Philippines as well.

John Liu (1976/2000) identifies a number of characteristics shared by the internal colonial model and classical colonialism, characteristics that highlight the relevance of this model to the case of Muslim Mindanao.[28] One of these common characteristics is the forced entry of the colonized into the colonial relationship. As I discuss at greater length in subsequent chapters (Chapters 1–5), Muslim Mindanao was appended to the Philippine state by force of American arms between 1898 and 1920, a political condition Muslim Filipinos had resisted for centuries and which many continue to resist today. A second common characteristic is the economic dependency of the internal colony, a situation in which labor markets and the exploitation of natural resources benefit the colonizer at the expense of the colonized. Many Muslim Filipinos recognize and critique a contemporary form of economic dependency in which the wealth generated by agricultural production, logging, fishing, and electrical generation benefits large corporations and a tiny local elite rather than local farmers and poorly paid workers and in which the local tax receipts generated by these industries are cycled through the central government before reallocation to local political entities.

A third important characteristic shared by the internal colonial model and classical colonialism is a condition of political dependency that institutionalizes inequities between the dominant society and the subordinated minority. Despite formal legal equality in the independent state, political dependency is maintained by force and intimidation, by measures diluting the voting strength of the minority, by the co-optation of selected individuals in order to deprive the minority of leadership and maintain the illusion of social mobility between classes, and the provision of severely constrained local political autonomy.[29] These are, again, common characteristics of contemporary Muslim Filipino experience. While Muslim Filipinos theoretically enjoy equality under the law, the presence of a significant percentage of the Philippine armed forces, corrupt law enforcement officials, and the private armies of local elites, conspire with the fact of their economic dependency to severely curtail the enjoyment of their political and human rights. Years of officially supported Christian Filipino migration into traditional Muslim areas has reduced Muslim Filipinos to a numerical minority in all but four provinces, a fact Philippine governments exploited in their insistence that the question of autonomy or independence be put to a popular vote. And Muslim Filipinos have come to recognize the illusion of a political autonomy granted to majority-Muslim provinces in which financial control remains with the central government.

Yet another similarity Liu (1976/2000) identifies between the internal colonial model and classical colonialism is the presence of racial and/or cultural subordination justified by and reinforcing hierarchies of knowledge, value, and identity captured in social dichotomies of civilized-savage, peaceful-violent, developed-underdeveloped, modern-backward, and so on.[30] In the Philippine context, the Christian–Muslim dichotomy maps directly onto these distinctions in ways that locate the problems of Muslim–Christian relations in the failings of Muslims, congratulate the mainstream elite for its greater proximity to the ideal, and absolve it of any responsibility for the problems. Thus, relevant categories marking the broad frontier between power and powerlessness in the southern Philippines become religion and culture rather than race and culture, though once again it must be remembered that class and gender complicate and even occasionally reverse this relationship in particular local contexts. Nevertheless, the broad hierarchies of knowledge, value, and identity remain salient, constructed through a variety of mechanisms, including the virtual erasure of the unique history and humanity of Muslim Filipinos and the cultural-political marginalization of local languages that, according to Memmi, furthers cultural dependency. As I argue later, educational policy and practice in Muslim Mindanao constitute one of the primary means of effecting this cultural-religious subordination.

"The essence of both classical and internal colonialism," writes Liu, "is the colonizers' monopoly on political, economic and military power. In both situations, racism provides the rationale for the colonizer's dominance."[31] In the Philippine case, I believe, religious and cultural bigotry, kindled from the religious and cultural bigotry of centuries of colonial rule by Spain and the United States, provide this rationale. And the particular response to the social tensions engendered by this internal colonialism, what Liu calls the assimilation/integration model, was quite specifically inherited from US colonial policy toward Muslim Filipinos prior to 1920. This model, resting upon the hierarchies of knowledge, value, and identity discussed above, offers the subordinated minority the opportunity to conform to majority norms and justified the minority's subordination by its inability or unwillingness to do so. The internal colonial model, however, interrogates such hierarchies as products of biases built into the social fabric and reads conflict in the majority–minority relationship—such as that between the Muslim minority and the Philippine state—as a form of anticolonial resistance.[32]

Antonio Gramsci argued that the ideological hegemony of these ideas of domination-subordination is achieved through a combination of coercive force and consent. The first, Althusser points out, is carried out through "repressive state apparatuses" such as the military and police, while the second is enacted through "ideological state apparatuses" such as the media, churches, families, and schools.[33] While I will attempt to address the way military force has figured in the colonization of Muslim Filipinos, my central purpose will be to attempt to account for the ways in which the peculiarly pedagogical nature of American colonial rule in the Philippines and in particular Muslim Mindanao led to a postcolonial reality in which educational policy would become and remain a key mechanism in the internal colonization of Muslim Filipinos and, hence, a potential site for the transformation of that condition.

A key assumption, then, of postcolonial theory is that understanding of present conditions in postcolonial states requires an understanding of the colonial legacy.[34] And one of the most enduring legacies of colonialism is formal systems of schooling.[35] In many colonized societies, the colonial period saw the first introduction of widespread formal schooling. Such schools were frequently oriented toward what was seen as practical agricultural and vocational training designed to train indigenous populations for a role as agricultural and low-skilled laborers in the colonial economies. Such schooling often also included instruction in the colonizer's language, culture, and history in order to prepare locals for subordinate bureaucratic positions in colonial government and businesses.[36] Thus, colonial schooling was designed to educate colonized peoples within the framework of a center–periphery relationship, which defined the colonizing power as the epitome of civilization and the repository of advanced knowledge and the colonized as an antithesis more or less distant from this ideal and more or less capable of aspiring to it through education. This dichotomy was frequently expressed in and justified by appeals to Darwinian evolutionary theory, which obscured obvious prejudice beneath a veneer of quasi-scientific objectivity. While such explicitly biased dichotomies have been softened in the rhetoric of development-underdevelopment, the dichotomous, hierarchical relationships tend to persist to the benefit of the colonizer and the detriment of the colonized.[37]

The effects of formal schooling in the colonies were also buttressed by both academic and popular discourses in the colonizing societies. Said (1979), for instance, has demonstrated how the colonial encounter gave rise to areas of academic expertise in which experts in the colonizing societies claimed a privileged knowledge of the colonized, knowledge that was used to define the colonizer-colonized relationship in terms of civilization and barbarism, modern and backward, and so on.[38] Such academic discourses were reinforced and complemented by popular discourses such as travel writing and journalistic reporting.[39] They in turn shaped pedagogy and curriculum of schools in the colonizing societies.[40] Thus, the term "colonial education" describes not only the education provided to the children of colonized societies, but it describes as well the education of those in colonizing societies. Moreover, social and economic inequities in the postcolonial period have tended to perpetuate such inequities in knowledge production and distribution, inequities which often mean that scholars of former colonies must seek knowledge of their own societies from their colonizers and which leave unexamined the epistemological claims of the colonizer formed within the colonial encounter.[41]

Formal school systems constitute one of the enduring legacies of the colonial period, leading some critics of colonialism to argue that "the continuation of the educational system erected by the colonial regime is by far the most powerful instrument for perpetuating the concepts, the outlook, and the value on which the privileged classes' power is built."[42] The continuation of colonial systems of schooling is frequently reflected in the language policies of postcolonial education as well as the content of school curricula. The colonizer's language is often retained in postcolonial educational systems in the belief that maintenance of a "world language" will improve the colonized society's chances for economic development and access to scientific and technological language. Continuation of the basic structure and content of colonial curricula is justified on similar grounds. This continuity is often reinforced by a sense of inertia in the postcolonial period on structural and curricular matters as educational policy makers focused on linear expansion of access to education to more and more of the local population.[43] The effects of international aid and the role of expatriates in postcolonial development have also tended to reinforce the continuity of colonial educational structures, language policies, and curricula.[44] This emphasis on the linear expansion of colonial schooling in the postcolonial period neglected the fact that the purpose of such schooling was the production of a local elite supportive of the colonial relationship and that the maintenance of such systems, combined with the high attrition rates of the poor, tends to confer advantages on the already advantaged, thus perpetuating and reinforcing the inequitable class structures formed in the colonial period.[45]

In spite of this, however, education remains a crucial and contested segment of postcolonial societies. It is seen as central to economic development: "The main engine of growth is accumulation of human capital—of knowledge—and the main source of differences in living standards among nations is differences in human capital," the formation of which "takes place in schools, in research organizations, and in the course of producing goods and engaging in trade."[46] Education is also seen as instrumental in the maintenance of political stability and the development of national identity. According to Wilson (2001), the school, as an instrument for the communication and implementation of state policy, has in many places replaced the military outpost as a marker of the state's presence and influence. And the teacher, as local intellectual, becomes both the instrument of transmission and translation of state policy to the local citizenry. However, as local institutions and local intellectuals, the school and its teachers also constitute a site of translation and possibly contestation of the state's agenda. Thus, schools occupy a crucial intermediate location between the center and periphery, between the postcolonial state and its internal colony.[47]

In constructing this reading of Muslim Filipinos' colonial and postcolonial educational experience, I draw on a variety of sources, including indigenous myths, colonial and postcolonial government reports, field observations, and interviews with Muslim Filipino educators and parents, as well as a broad spectrum of secondary source materials. The result is a shifting analytical focus between the level of national educational policy targeting Muslim Mindanao and local responses to those policies as expressed in the educational experience of the Maranao people of the Lake Lanao region. While I do not intend by this to diminish the diversity within a Muslim Filipino community composed of more than a dozen different ethno-linguistic groups, the Maranao do constitute the first or second largest of these groups and are closely related culturally, historically, and linguistically to one of the other three largest Muslim groups, the Maguindanao. Moreover, as one of the centers of historical and contemporary resistance to successive Philippine governments, Lanao illustrates as well as any other region the shortcomings of colonial and postcolonial educational policy as a tool in mitigating ethnoreligious tensions. I believe, therefore, that a focus on the specific tensions between national educational policy and Maranao religious and cultural aspirations is justified.

In the following chapters, I attempt to draw a historical and contemporary sketch of the conflict between Muslims and Christians in the southern Philippines, a conflict variously known as the "Mindanao Problem" or the Moro Problem. Drawing upon the limited contemporary and historical literature as well as local myth, I attempt to offer some—admittedly tenuous and imperfect—insight into the educational structures and values of the Maranao prior to their effective colonization by the United States at the end of the nineteenth and the beginning of the twentieth century, in order to understand how and where colonial educational changes clashed with indigenous practices. Subsequent chapters describe the peculiarly pedagogical character of US imperialism in Muslim Mindanao and the continuation of that colonial pedagogy in the postcolonial educational policies of the Philippine state. In these chapters, I attempt to highlight how the Christian–Muslim distinction in the southern Philippines maps onto other hierarchies of knowledge, identity, and value forged in the colonial encounter with Spain and the United States and sustained in the postcolonial period in what constitutes an internal colonial relationship between the Christian center and the Muslim periphery in the Philippine state. I return, in the final chapters, to the contemporary educational experiences of the Maranao, particularly their responses to national policies and efforts to initiate reforms consistent with local needs and values. In doing so, I focus in particular on the role education and educational policy have played in exacerbating this long-running ethno-religious conflict and what role its transformation might possibly play in mitigating it.

Limitations

Before embarking on such a project, however, it is important to acknowledge the subjectivities peculiar to this particular inquiry that may, in spite of the best of intentions, lead to the omissions, silences, alternative interpretations, and so on that make any inquiry, at best, a contribution to the conversation on a particular topic rather than the last and definitive word on it. I realize that it has become almost a parody of postmodern scholarship to list the particulars of an author's positionality—in my case white, male, non-Muslim American academic of mixed Anglo-Puerto Rican heritage. However, I think it is an important gesture in acknowledging the perspective that inevitably conditions one's analysis of data, history, or culture and avoiding, insofar as it is possible, the danger of "the first world intellectual masquerading as the absent nonrepresenter who lets the oppressed speak for themselves."[48] While it is not possible to step outside the particularities of my own identity to assume the old persona of the disinterested, objective observer of unmediated reality, it is necessary to be honest with readers by identifying wherever possible the points of an inquiry that define its peculiar perspective and which constitute potential sites of critical engagement by readers with the text.

My first experience of the Islamicized regions of the southern Philippines came as a US Peace Corps volunteer assigned to Lanao del Sur to train provincial high school teachers in English language instruction. I arrived there with largely a blank slate in terms of my previous knowledge of the Philippines. However, that slate had been formatted—if I may mix my metaphors—by the intellectual and cultural experiences fairly typical of growing up in the American South during the 1960s and 1970s and a university education in British and American literature. I arrived in a Philippines, however, that was anything but a blank slate in terms of Filipinos' knowledge of the United States and Americans. Filipinos' memory and dispositions had been shaped by almost a century of colonial and postcolonial relations. For many, this meant a warmth and respect for Americans that led them, and me, to assume that I had something to contribute to the betterment of Philippine education in Mindanao, an assumption that gave me privileges I would have never enjoyed in the United States. For others, this meant a deep suspicion of another "Kano" furthering the neocolonial domination of the Philippines.

I arrived in the Philippines in 1985, the last year of the crumbling Marcos dictatorship, and stayed through 1987, the first year of the return of an imperfect democracy under Corazon Aquino. It was a period in which the Communist Party of the Philippines and its New People's Army reached its peak, helping to create an intellectual and political climate on the university campus where I was based crisscrossed by discourses of colonialism and neocolonialism, revolution, and repression. Situated, as it was, in Muslim Mindanao, the university also occupied the contact zone between Muslims and Christians, and so the climate was also profoundly affected by the historic tensions and hope of that relationship as well as the continuing threat of the then simmering secessionist movement of the Moro National Liberation Front. This was also a period in which I met and married my wife. Thus, this brief period marked the beginning of a lifelong interest in and connection to this region and its problems and prospects. In a rather strange sense, much of what I hold dear today is ultimately an artifact of the Spanish–American War.

That particular time and place was a simmering stew of postcolonial baggage, neocolonial entanglements, anticolonial struggle, cultural misunderstanding and understanding, political repression, and change that led directly and indirectly to the academic interests and the academic position I currently occupy. I have, in a sense, spent the last 35 years trying to understand that experience and at the same time coming to understand how much of it I do not and will never understand. My experience and my intellectual preoccupation with it eventually led to the roughly five years of research that informs this book, research supported by the US Fulbright Program, the National Academy of Education's Spencer Postdoctoral Fellowship, and the US Institute of Peace. Given this history, I must acknowledge that this book is enabled by and written from a position of postcolonial privilege unavailable to equally able Muslim Filipino scholars. It represents, however, an attempt to turn a critical eye on the colonial legacy that underpins that privilege and continues to marginalize them. Thus, it may in some small way open up the conversation on this topic to their indispensable voices.

For, as I noted above, even the most careful and conscientious of inquiries on such a topic from such a particular perspective runs the risk of falling into the well-worn intellectual ruts of colonial knowledge production, which produced hierarchies of knower-known, subject-object, colonizer-colonized that buttressed colonial and neocolonial privilege. As Philip Altbach (1978) argued, "as long as knowledge about the nature of society in developing countries is mediated through Western sources, it is suspect for all the possible methodological and ideological biases, misrepresentations, and other problems such mediation may entail."[49] Watson (1982) goes even further to suggest that such mediation enhances the role of the foreign expert and international aid in perpetuating neocolonial dependency.[50] While this book is on one level a critique of the legacy of US colonial influence on Muslim Filipino education, it is also inevitably a critique of Philippine postcolonial education by an outsider occupying a position of some institutional privilege within the former colonial power. Thus it, in some ways, retraces the very trajectory of knowledge production it attempts to critique.

One might seek intellectual cover for such a project by appealing to the poststructuralist conceptions of power that complicate the simplistic dualisms of colonizer-colonized, oppressor-oppressed that inform much postcolonial discourse. Power, as Foucault (1990) teaches us, is fluid; hence, it is incorrect to simply assume that the American observer possesses it always and in all circumstances and Filipinos, Muslim or Christian, do not. Moreover, one might argue that the inquiry attempted here is in fact a "genealogy" of power as it has worked through educational policy in the southern Philippines. There is no outside of power; it has us rather than we it. Therefore, the sort of knowledge production represented in this book is not really the sort of simplistic conception of knowledge production criticized in more Marxist-inspired postcolonialism. However, I must concur with Spivak (1988) when she argues "that the substantive concern for the politics of the oppressed which often accounts for Foucault's appeal can hide a privileging of the intellectual and the 'concrete' subject of oppression that, in fact, compounds the appeal."[51] The differences of relative power and privilege are real and must be acknowledged.

Yet another danger inherent in such an inquiry is what Loomba (1998) refers to as "nativism" or what Bruckner (1986) criticized as "third worldism."[52] Both point to a tendency among First World intellectuals to romanticize the native "Other" and claim solidarity with them by criticizing the "West" or "imperialism" and thus claim a kind of moral redemption for the perceived sin of being a white Euro-American. Such a move is inherently patronizing and a thinly disguised attempt to portray oneself as the "good white guy" by vociferously attacking those "bad white guys." Yet, at the same time, colonialism and the colonial legacy are historical facts that impinge upon contemporary reality in ways that demand the criticism of both its "victims" and those it privileges. Thus, the taint of self-serving sentimentality for the oppressed Muslim Filipino is a risk this book must run even as it attempts to avoid such a trap.

Given the inevitable distortion caused by the various lenses of power, colonial privilege, positionality, and so on that stand between the observer and the observed in an inquiry such as this, one is tempted to suggest that the only viable response is silence. Since it is impossible for me—or any observer for that matter—to entirely extricate myself from these determinants of my location and achieve an unmediated encounter with the reality I attempt to describe here, it might perhaps seem better to say nothing than run the risk of contributing to the perpetuation of neocolonial relationships. However, such a response assumes the existence of a privileged perspective on educational policy for Muslim Filipinos unmediated by the distorting lenses of culture, history, ideology, class, gender, and so on. There is no such perspective. There are only other, more or less interesting or compelling, perspectives distorted by their own point of view. This is one. I hope that it offers something useful to the conversation.

Moreover, if, as postcolonial theory suggests, the fact of colonization shaped the consciousness of both the colonized and the colonizer, then the colonial legacy in the southern Philippines is an American legacy too. The privileged academic has an equal responsibility to understand its effects and work, where they have promoted injustice, to change them in the future. The postmodern recognition that there is no outside of power does not rescue the First World academic from the network of unequal relations that continue to privilege his or her work, often at the expense of scholars in formerly colonized societies; nor does silence answer the responsibility that follows from one's involvement in that network. The only response is, as Spivak (1988) suggests, "to read and write so that the impossibility of such interested individualistic refusals of the institutional privileges of power bestowed on the subject is taken seriously."[53] This means, I think, that the postcolonial inquirer must eschew the epistemological pretensions of the objective observer even as he attempts to make his inquiry as accurate, complete, and objective as possible and acknowledge the places where his inquiry may fall short of that ideal.

Therefore, this inquiry does not pretend to be the last and definitive word on the "truth" regarding educational policy and Muslim Filipino educational experience in the southern Philippines. It does not rest upon a conception of inquiry as the search for and setting down of truth. Rather, it rests upon a conception of inquiry as conversation in which participants from a variety of specific and limiting subject locations endeavor to understand a given topic as thoroughly, as responsibly, and as respectfully as possible. So, while it is a contribution to the conversation as careful, thorough, and accurate as I can make it, it is also an Emersonian provocation to other readers to agree, extend, critique, or revise; in short, to engage in the conversation on a topic that, I believe, has too often been neglected. It is written in the belief that arguments about the past, or even the present, are not so much disagreements over what is happening or has happened, but rather discussions about what we hope the future will be. This is the spirit in which this book is written and, I hope, the spirit in which it will be read.

Notes

1. Anderson, *Imagined Communities*, 113–140.
2. Kepel, *The Revenge of God*, 1–12.
3. DuBois, *The Souls of Black Folk*.
4. Wilson, "In the Name of the State?" 313–344.
5. For a general account of this phenomenon in colonized societies, see Anderson, *Imagined Communities*.
6. Majul, *Muslims in the Philippines*.
7. Gowing, *Mandate in Moroland*.
8. Lucman, *Moro Archives*.
9. Torrance, "The Philippine Moro," preface.
10. Jones, "Our Mandate Over Moroland," 609.

11. Brydon, *Postcolonialism*, 1.
12. Gandhi, *Postcolonial Theory*, 4.
13. Brydon, *Postcolonialism*, 2.
14. Ibid., 4.
15. Loomba, *Colonialism/Postcolonialism*, 6.
16. Gandhi, *Postcolonial Theory*, 15.
17. Ibid., 4; Fanon, *Black Skin, White Masks*.
18. Gandhi, *Postcolonial Theory*, 16; Memmi, *The Colonizer and the Colonized*.
19. Gandhi, *Postcolonial Theory*, 17.
20. Loomba, *Colonialism/Postcolonialism*, 42.
21. Gandhi, *Postcolonial Theory*, 168–169.
22. Foucault, *The History of Sexuality, Vol. 1*, 93.
23. Loomba, *Colonialism/Postcolonialism*, 9.
24. Mignolo, *Local Histories/Global Designs*, 104.
25. Ibid., 104, 197; Brydon, *Postcolonialism*, 19.
26. Mignolo, *Local Histories/Global Designs*, 97, 104.
27. Silvia Rivera Cusicanqui, "La raiz: colonizadores y colonizados," in Albo et al., eds., *Violencias Encubiertas en Bolivia*, Vol. I (La Paz: CIPCA-Aruwiyiri, 1993), 31; cited in Mignolo, *Local Histories/Global Designs*, 199.
28. John Liu, "Towards an Understanding of the Internal Colonial Model," in Brydon, ed., *Postcolonialism*, Vol. 4, 1347–1364.
29. Liu in Brydon, *Postcolonialism*, 1353.
30. Ibid.
31. Ibid., 1359.
32. Ibid., 1360.
33. Loomba, *Colonialism/Postcolonialism*, 32–33.
34. Foster, "The Educational Policies of Postcolonial States," 3–26.
35. Watson, "Educational Neocolonialism—The Continuing Colonial Legacy," in Watson, ed., *Education in the Third World*, 181–200.
36. Osterhammel, *Colonialism: A Theoretical Overview*, 100–103.
37. Maybury-Lewis, *Indigenous Peoples, Ethnic Groups, and the State*, 11–13.
38. Said, *Orientalism*.
39. Pratt, *Imperial Eyes*.
40. Willinsky, *Learning to Divide the World*.
41. Altbach, "The Distribution of Knowledge in the Third World: A Case Study in Neocolonialism," in Altbach and Kelly, eds., 301–330.
42. T. Mende, *From Aid to Recolonisation* (London: Harrap, 1973), 99; cited in Watson, *Education in the Third World*, 183.
43. Watson, *Education in the Third World*, 184.
44. Altbach, "Distribution of Knowledge"; Watson, *Education in the Third World*, 193–196.

45. Watson, *Education in the Third World*, 184; James, "The Role of Education in ASEAN Economic Growth: Past and Future," 215–238.
46. Robert E. Lucas, "Making a Miracle," *Econometrica* 61, no. 2: 270; cited in James, "The Role of Education," 217.
47. Wilson, "In the Name of the State?"
48. Spivak, "Can the Subaltern Speak?" 292.
49. Altbach, *Education and Colonialism*.
50. Watson, *Education in the Third World*.
51. Spivak, "Can the Subaltern Speak?" 292.
52. Loomba, *Colonialism/Postcolonialism*, 18; Bruckner, *The Tears of the White Man*, 3–9.
53. Spivak, "Can the Subaltern Speak?" 280.

CHAPTER 2

Precolonial Culture and Education in the Southern Philippines

Almost every written account of the Philippines begins with a description of it as an archipelago of 7100 islands. While this has become something of a cliché in the literature on the Philippines, it is useful in that it does point to the extensive geographic, cultural, and linguistic diversity of the country. While roughly four centuries of colonization have more or less established the geographical identity of the Philippines, the combination of colonial experience and cultural diversity has rendered any sense of common national identity quite tenuous. This is particularly the case in the cultural and geographic margins of Philippine society: among the poor, in the remote rural areas, among the tribal minorities known collectively as the "Lumad," and particularly among the Islamized ethnic communities frequently lumped together under the name bestowed upon them by the Spanish: Moros. In such a context, with such a history, it is perhaps unsurprising that a relatively weak Philippine state has been unable to assert the effective control of the rule of law into every corner of such a sprawling and diverse nation.[1]

This challenge of the Philippine state is nowhere more evident than in Mindanao, the second largest island of the archipelago and home to a population of approximately 25 million people. Its population is perhaps the most diverse in the country, including indigenous tribal communities and millions of immigrants from every region of the country who were resettled during the American colonial regime and after World War II in what was billed as the "land of promise."[2] The resettlement policies of both colonial and independent governments quickly displaced the indigenous Lumad from their ancestral homelands and brought increasing cultural and economic pressure on the 13 Islamized ethnic groups that constituted a majority of the inhabitants of the western half of the island of Mindanao. Today, in spite of a population in the region of approximately five million, Muslims comprise a numerical minority in all but five provinces of their traditional homeland.[3] This region, however, lies at the periphery of state power, with its back to the Muslim states of Malaysia and Indonesia, and united by a common faith and common historical experiences. The combination of culture, geography, and experience has conspired to produce and sustain often violent struggles between successive Philippine governments bent on extending effective state control throughout the national territory and Muslim communities fighting to maintain political, cultural, and religious independence. It is a struggle that has been known for more than a century as the Moro Problem.

The stakes for both sides are significant. Mindanao today is home to a large number of domestic and multinational industries in agriculture, fishing, mining, and manufacturing. Much of the food consumed in the Philippines as well as a large portion of the country's exports is produced in Mindanao. It is an island rich in natural resources and vital to the economic health of the nation. It is simultaneously, however, a land of grinding poverty as well, and some of the worst of this poverty is found in the predominately Muslim regions of the island. According to official government statistics from the late 1990s, the five Muslim majority provinces which comprised the Autonomous Region in Muslim Mindanao (ARMM) displayed the highest indices of social stress in the country. More than 62 percent of the population lived below the official poverty line, double the national rate. The region experiences the highest or next to highest rates of infant and maternal mortality and the lowest rates of literacy and life expectancy. Together, the five provinces of the ARMM exhibited the lowest figures in the entire country on the state's Human Development Index—a combination of social indicators designed to measure people's ability to achieve a decent standard of living and lead a long and healthy life.[4]

The continued existence of such poverty in a setting of such great potential wealth is sustained by a number of factors, chief among them a tradition of class relations, frequently described as feudal, which leads to the extraction and transfer of wealth from Mindanao to Manila and abroad by "a Manila-based [and expatriate] elite who have continued to construct a set of national policies which conform most closely to their own prejudices and interests."[5] This extraction and transfer of wealth is indicative of an internal colonialism that has devastated Mindanao environmentally, socially, and economically, exacerbating social tensions and contributing to the rise of what Matsura (1992) has described as a "politics of subnationalism" born of exploitation and neglect.[6] While these are problems that plague all of Mindanao, they have become particularly volatile in relations between the Christian majority of the Philippines and the Muslim minority centered in western Mindanao for they tend to intersect with and exacerbate tensions between the two religious communities—tensions with a long and troubled history.

I would like to begin this account of the colonial and postcolonial marginalization of Muslim minority peoples in the Philippines by attempting to draw a rough sketch of the precolonial cultural and educational structures of one of these communities. Some sense of these structures is necessary in order to better understand the cultural, political, and educational tensions of the colonial and postcolonial periods. Insight into the precolonial past of the Muslim Philippines is difficult, however. The effort is hampered by the sheer length of time of Spanish colonization—beginning in the mid-sixteenth century, a dearth of written accounts of this period, and the likelihood that such written accounts as do exist are narrated from the perspective of more or less hostile observers. It is possible, however, to begin to piece together a necessarily incomplete picture of Mindanao outside Spanish control by reading such accounts against the grain of their bias. And I propose, moreover, to seek further insight into this period by focusing to a significant extent on the social structure and cultural production of one of the 13 Muslim ethno-linguistic communities, the Maranao people of the two Lanao provinces. While the Maranao were among the last of these groups to adopt Islam, they were perhaps the least disturbed by Spanish pressure right up to the end of the nineteenth century. Spanish forces succeeded in penetrating Lanao briefly only twice in 250 years, once in the early seventeenth century and then again in the 1890s. Thus the Maranao are perhaps most likely to have preserved social structures and cultural attributes that reflect, albeit dimly, the cultural and educational values of pre-Islamic and precolonial Mindanao.

Mindanao and the Coming of Islam

Perhaps unsurprisingly, the history of Muslim Mindanao parallels in broad terms the history of insular Southeast Asia. Like its Malaysian and Indonesian neighbors, contemporary Muslim Mindanao manifests the cumulative cultural influences of the ancient Malay, India, Islam, and Western colonization. Some insight into the continuing legacy of these cultural and historical influences is essential to understanding the contemporary dimensions of the ethno-religious conflict long known as the Moro Problem as well as the role of educational policy in it.

The first demonstrable outside influence on the cultural development of Mindanao came as a result of the Indianization of much of Southeast Asia between the first and fourteenth centuries, a period that saw the rise of influential Hindu civilizations such as Funan, Srivijaya, and Majapahit.[7] While Mindanao lay at the periphery of such influence, historical accounts of Southeast Asian trade demonstrate the presence of Filipino ships across the South China Sea as early as the third century and well-established trade routes between the Indianized state of Funan in the delta region of southern Vietnam and a country that the Chinese sources called Chu-po, located variously in north Borneo or the Sulu Archipelago.[8] The geographic and cultural proximity of these two regions would be illustrated later by the claim of suzerainty over north Borneo by the sultan of Sulu. Whatever the source, however, the fact of early Indian influence is supported by the presence of Sanskrit loan words in Muslim Filipino dialects dating to as early as the tenth century and artifacts dating from the twelfth to fourteenth centuries. Moreover, the greater frequency of such evidence in the languages and cultures of western Mindanao and Sulu reflect the region's geographic proximity to the Indianized areas of Southeast Asia.[9]

Perhaps the most dramatic and lasting legacy of Indian influence in Mindanao, however, is found in the oral traditional literatures of some of the Islamized ethno-linguistic groups of the southern Philippines. The Maranao, for instance, one of the largest of these groups, trace their identity as a people through two mytho-poetic sources—the *Radia Indarapatra* and the oral-epic *Darangen*—that display apparent parallels to the Hindu Ramayana and provide further evidence of early Indian influence on the cultures of western Mindanao.[10] Before the introduction of the Qur'an, these traditional literatures provided a source of wisdom, entertainment, cultural identity, and education in the history, values, customs, and behavioral norms of the Maranao.[11] And they are still occasionally recited today as *anonen a rawaten*—an inspiration for appropriate behavior worthy of emulation—despite being branded in some quarters as un-Islamic.[12] These narrative legacies of pre-Islamic, Indian-influenced culture still constitute, along with Islam, a foundation of Maranao culture and offer important insights into imagery and ideology that inform Maranao behavior.[13]

Anthropologists describe this combination of pre-Islamic and Islamic influences as "a Malay sultanate structure grafted onto an organizational structure of cognatic kinship."[14] In other words, underlying the profound cultural and religious influences of Islam lies a social structure based on kinship ties rather than territory, a social organization that profoundly reinforces religious ties idealized in the concept of the Muslim *ummah*. Among the Maranao, membership in this extended kin-group is defined by one's ability to document one's blood ties to preceding generations of Maranao via genealogies, known as *salsila*, which claim to trace the lineage of the Maranao to both the mythic progenitors of the *Radia Indarapatra* and *Darangen* as well as the Prophet Muhammad. Thus anyone outside the *salsila* is not a Maranao.[15] The *salsila*, moreover, define status relations between families and communities, and, together with custom—*adat*, govern interpersonal relations in Maranao society. In addition, kinship relations as documented in the *salsila* provided the organizational structure of Maranao society into four "encampments of the lake," called *pengampong* and their subdivision into districts, villages, and *agama*, a small group of closely related kin groups with a defined territory and its own mosque, the presence of which marks its distinction from other *agama*.[16] Membership, it is important to remember, is based on kinship rather than residence. Even the traditional Maranao concept of nation, *bangsa*, is premised on kinship ties.[17] While the larger Maranao social structures have waned somewhat in their contemporary significance, the *agama* remains an important organ of collective decision-making and organized action.[18]

At least one aspect of this social structure's relevance to education in the context of the Moro Problem is the centrality of kinship groups that "interlock persons and places in a network of ceremonial and legal obligations" and thus serve as a marker of Maranao identity.[19] Thus Spanish, US, and even independent Filipino governments have been widely considered *gobirno a sarawang tao*: a government of foreigners.[20] Because these governments were and are grounded in histories, cultural assumptions, and values quite different from the Maranao's, they introduce conceptions of group identity based on citizenship and political organization grounded in territory that cut across and potentially undermine the kinship ties central to Maranao identity. The laws of the state may conflict with the dictates of *adat*—customary law or *shariah*—Islamic law. The values and needs of the modern state offer routes to social status—via education, business, or politics, for instance—that often contradict the traditional status hierarchies encoded in the *taritib*.[21] Academic observers of the Maranao note that Maranao owe their allegiance first to their indigenous sociopolitical organization and only second to the government and that *adat* is more important than the law.[22] Thus, even under the best of circumstance such differences are bound to elicit tensions between a community so constituted and an outside legal authority. In the case of the Islamized communities of Mindanao, however, such differences are reinforced by religious differences and rendered potentially explosive by a long and bitter history of conflict. The Maranao, Tawagon (1990) claims, generally do not distinguish between what is Maranao and what is Islam. Therefore, "telling these people to abandon things Maranao is equivalent, first, to telling them to lose their identity as Maranao and as Muslims and, second, to asking them to accept what they refuse to accept."[23] Such a demand and resistance to it has lain at the heart of the Moro Problem for centuries.

By the late thirteenth century, the spread of Islam through insular Southeast Asia began to influence the cultures of the Sulu Archipelago and Mindanao, initiating a gradual process of Islamization that would profoundly change, though not entirely replace, the cultural identity of the region's inhabitants over the subsequent six centuries. Perhaps the earliest datable evidence of Islam's presence in the Sulu area is the tomb of Sayid Alawi Balpaki in the Tawi-tawi island group. It bears a date corresponding to the year 1310 in the Western calendar, suggesting the presence of a Muslim community in the area as early as the last quarter of the thirteenth century.[24] Through the second half of the fourteenth century, Sulu genealogies—*tarsila*—point to the arrival of Muslim missionaries, known collectively as *makhdumin*, in the Sulu region. One of the most famous of these missionaries, Sharif Auliya Makhdum reportedly arrived in Sulu around 1381. He was followed almost ten years later by a Rajah Baguinda, thought to be an aristocratic Malay Muslim from north Borneo. The first sultanate was founded in Sulu in 1450 by Abu Bakr. After that, the process of Islamization quickened through the sixteenth century via increasing contact with the Malay Muslim world and was further strengthened in the seventeenth century through alliances with neighboring Muslims against Western and Christian colonization efforts.[25]

Islamization of Mindanao is commonly dated to the middle of the fifteenth century with the appearance of Muslim missionaries and the establishment of Muslim settlements in the Pulangi River basin of west-central Mindanao. One of these individuals, Sharif Muhammad Kabungsuwan, is most often credited with bringing Islam to Mindanao around 1515. It is to him, for instance, that Maguindanao and Maranao sultans trace their ancestry in order to assert the legitimacy of their claims. Over the next century, marriage alliances were forged among the royal families of Maguindanao, Sulu, and Ternate, in modern-day Indonesia, cementing the Islamization of the datu classes in the Cotabato region. As with their Sulu brethren, contact with the Spanish toward the end of the sixteenth century tended to strengthen the Islamic identity of Muslim inhabitants of Mindanao.[26] From Cotabato, Islam gradually spread into the isolated interior of the Lake Lanao region via the coastal city of Malabang in the seventeenth century. Reports from a Spanish military expedition, which first penetrated the lake region briefly in 1645, described the local datus as Muslim but suggested that many of their followers had not yet converted. The Spanish would not return to the region until the last decade of the nineteenth century. By that time, the Maranao were thoroughly Islamized.[27]

Historians generally describe the Islamization of the southern Philippines as a peaceful process initiated by traders and missionaries from Muslim Southeast Asia and Arabia who settled in the region, married into local ruling families, and thereby gradually converted the ruling classes to the new religion. Because Islam did not come at the head of a foreign army but through the influence of traditional leaders, it was considered less foreign and less of a threat than the Christianity that arrived backed by Spanish naval power in the late sixteenth century.[28] In addition, the version of Islam brought into the region was in all probability Sufi, a mystical expression of Islam that may have been more amenable to the spiritual traditions of the local cultures.[29] Thus, Islam spread gradually and peacefully through the Sulu Archipelago and much of western Mindanao, profoundly reshaping the cultural landscape of the region. Majul (1973/1999) described its impact as follows:

These people in the Philippines gained from Islam a high sense of religious community, new laws, a more developed political organization, a new system of writing, and, above all, a new ethical outlook on life. Having adopted values that transcended their race and particular culture, they began to consider themselves as an historical people, yet assuming all the time that their history was not the result of their own making and efforts. Without their consciousness as well as all the benefits that Islam brought to the peoples of Sulu and Mindanao, they would have easily been swept away by Western colonialism and relegated to the limbo of conquered peoples.[30]

By the time Spain arrived in the Philippines in the mid-sixteenth century, Islam had been spreading unmolested for as much as two centuries, putting down deep roots in the Tausug, Maguindanao, and Maranao ethnic communities. On a foundation of ethnic identities constructed by kinship, common language, and common culture, Islam erected a more sophisticated political structure and a powerful spiritual bond that reinforced kinship ties even as it introduced a new layer of identity as Muslims that would begin to forge a sense of kinship with other Muslim groups and lead to the development of a proto-nationalist identity.[31] Thus, when Muslim Filipinos encountered Spanish colonists for the first time they encountered a radically different culture with an alien sociopolitical structure, a system of laws inconsistent with *adat* and *shariah*, conceptions of social status that ignored the protocols of the *taritib*, and an alien religion introduced more or less at gunpoint. And when the Spanish colonists encountered Muslims in the Philippines in the sixteenth century, they saw another version of the hated Moors, whom they had ejected from the Iberian Peninsula less than a century before, and dubbed them Moros. The conflicts that ensued over the next three centuries were, essentially, hostilities between rival independent powers. By the end of the Spanish regime at the close of the nineteenth century, most Christian Filipinos would come to consider the Moros a separate race, thus establishing the distinction between Muslim and Christian as the "most critical level of ethnic segmentation in Mindanao."[32]

Pre-Islamic Educational Values in Mindanao

Insight into indigenous educational values in Mindanao is limited for the reasons mentioned above and is further obscured by the cultural influences of both Islam and Western educational practices over the intervening centuries. Though both of these outside influences—particularly Islam—can be seen, in all fairness, as an integral part of the educational landscape in Mindanao today, an accurate understanding of their indigenous expression requires some sense of the genealogy of those values and how the succession of cultural influences interact, modify one another, or conflict. I attempt to gain some basic insight into these earliest educational values by once again focusing on the cultural production of the Maranao prior to their adoption of Islam and their experience of Western colonialism. My window into this early period of Maranao culture is the *Darangen*.

The *Darangen* is the epic poem of the Maranao. It narrates the origins of the Maranao people among heroic characters of spiritual as well as human descent. Its chapters relate events in the lives of the mythic progenitor of the Maranao, Diwata Ndaw Gibon, and his descendents, principally the heroic prince Bantogen. The general character of the *Darangen* and its importance in Maranao culture has been compared to the *Iliad* and *Odyssey* of Greece, the *Ramayana* and the *Mahabharata* of India, and the Anglo-Saxon *Beowulf*.[33] Though often frowned upon by Maranao religious leaders as un-Islamic, the *Darangen* nevertheless represents one of the most important artifacts of early Maranao society and reflects significant aspects of contemporary Maranao culture.

To a significant extent, the *Darangen* reflects Maranao culture as it was prior to the coming of Islam and Western colonialism.[34] It is an example of originally oral, traditional literature passed down from generation to generation. It is not, however, a dead cultural artifact, but rather a living part of traditional Maranao culture. It is still used for special purposes such as marriage negotiations, the investiture of royal titles, and rural festivities. Possession of a complete *kirim* version of the tales is a jealously guarded family heirloom considered evidence of royal descent. It also served an educative purpose in that the heroes of the tales were held up as models of ideal behavior for Maranao youth.[35] Given this educative function and its representation of early indigenous culture, the *Darangen* provides a unique window on the precolonial and pre-Islamic educational values of the Maranao.

Though not a traditional or common approach to educational inquiry, the use of literary sources is nevertheless well established in the philosophy of education. As the contemporary philosopher of education Jane Roland Martin (1985) has observed, "the general expectation that any educational theory worth recording is readily accessible in books or academic journals becomes unreasonable when the objects or subjects of educational thought are considered marginal. Thus, we will have to look to sources of data that the history of educational thought regards as far from standard: to personal letters, diaries, pamphlets, pieces of fiction, and to oral sources as well."[36] The educational theories of Muslim Filipinos have not just been considered marginal; they have been ignored and disparaged over a century and a half of colonial and postcolonial rule, thus contributing to the exacerbation of ethno-religious conflict in the southern Philippines. In order to try to understand that educational theory, its tensions with American and Christian Filipino theory, and to begin to theorize how changes in educational policy and practice might mitigate these tensions, I turn to a far from standard source, the Maranao oral-epic *Darangen*.

The Concept of the Educated Person in the *Darangen*

With the exception of references to courage and prowess in battle, the epithet "educated" is perhaps the most common and laudatory term used to describe the major heroes of the *Darangen*. Though many characters are praised as educated, those most commonly described in such terms are the central figure of the narrative, Bantogen, his half-brother, Madali, Bantogen's son, Sayana, and Bantogen's wife, Princess Paramata Gandingan. The qualities of these characters and their actions, which elicit in the text the description "educated," point to a well-defined conception of the educated person. They define a conception of the educated person more existential than epistemological, a conception expressed in the quality and nature of the individual's being rather than the quantity or quality of knowledge possessed.

Two separate passages specifically enumerate the attributes of the educated man.[37] The first says the educated Maranao man controls his temper and displays the qualities of honesty, reason, prudence, intellect, wisdom, and honor. The second passage adds to this list clear thinking, good conduct, compassion, gratitude, and justice leading to peace, patience, sympathy, and bravery. Each of these attributes is linked metaphorically to the other as parts of a boat, suggesting that the individual "sinks" or "floats" in Maranao society precisely to the extent that one exhibits these characteristics. Interestingly, both lists include attributes that are consistent with a Western tradition of the educated person emphasizing the quality of thought: reason, intellect, wisdom, and clear thinking. However, most of the attributes describe the quality of the educated person's interactions with others. They suggest a conception of the educated person that is defined as much by the quality of one's behavior as by one's intellect. It is a status one lives rather than merely possesses. It is, in effect, a form of social intelligence.

This suggestion is apparently born out by frequent passages in the *Darangen* where the epithet educated is attached to characters who are enacting some approved behavior. For instance, the curriculum described in both accounts of the training of Diwata Ndaw Gibon's sons stresses behavior. They are advised by their father in the art of ruling their people. They are told to set an example for their people by being brave and strong, tolerant of the poor who are "ignorant and cannot learn proper manners," and to safeguard the important artifacts of their people.[38] The emphasis of their instruction is on the proper behavior of a ruler.

The education of Sayana, the "model of the future generations of the Asalan i Gibonen," displays a similar emphasis on external behavior.[39] These passages state explicitly that he is instructed in the proper ways to behave in relation to others, in the art of personal combat, in the dancing of the *sagayan*, a war dance, in playing small bells attached to the warrior's shield and sword to convey messages, and in the etiquette used in communicating with the royal ladies housed in the *lamin*. While some of his lessons stress a destructive form of behavior—the art of personal combat, for instance—most others emphasize conduct in interpersonal relations designed to exhibit and preserve the dignity of both parties and thus maintain the relationship.

This emphasis on the maintenance of smooth interpersonal relationships—social intelligence—is also exhibited in the high value placed on verbal eloquence in the world of the *Darangen*. In fact, the most common characteristic of the educated person in the *Darangen* is skill in the art of using language effectively, a quality that earns the individual respect and praise from friends and enemies alike. Speech, whether before a group or between individuals, is highly stylized and formal. It is characterized by elaborate introductory remarks and is extremely allusive. At times, there seems to be more interest in how something is said rather than in what is said. Lively verbal jousts are common in conversations between men and women, especially lovers. Even conversations between enemies are strictly couched in the conventions of polite discourse, thus there is no loss of face—*maratabat*—by either party, and at least a semblance of smooth interpersonal relations maintained. All interpersonal relations are thus characterized by very strict forms of address, speech, and behavior that, when adhered to, are hallmarks of the educated Maranao man. When these codes are violated, it is seen as, at best, the mark of ignorance, at worst, a prelude to violence.

Yet another distinctive attribute of those characters described as educated is their mastery of the art of walking properly. More than just physical grace, this quality refers to the individual's mastery of a highly stylized, almost exaggerated gait accented by a large square handkerchief, called a *mosala*, which is draped over the shoulder or swayed gracefully as one walks. Like the rhetorical formalities prized as a hallmark of the educated person, walking properly draws the attention and admiration of others in society and distinguishes the individual as a well-educated Maranao. Along with the arts of physical combat, this art suggests the value of physical intelligence in the Maranao conception of the educated person.

An additional attribute of the educated person in the cultural milieu of the *Darangen* is the knowledge of tradition, or cultural intelligence. Characters described as educated are familiar with the "book of prophecy," a system of choosing the proper dates for important events, and the "four ways of doing good": telling the truth, keeping promises, giving what is due, and following tradition and custom. The educated Maranao's knowledge of tradition includes genealogy; he must know his relationship with other members of his clan as well as the relationship between his clan and others in order to determine the proper course of action in any given situation. Thus, tradition is, and is a framework for, moral education. To go against tradition is the mark of an ignorant person. To be forced by an enemy to do what is against tradition is often described as a fate worse than death.

Though male characters are most often described as educated, wise, or well taught, female characters do earn similar praise. The most conspicuous example of such a woman is Paramata Gandingan, the wife of Bantogen and mother of Sayana.[40] With the exception of training in combat, she displays the same attributes common to the educated man. She too displays a high degree of verbal eloquence, a graceful walk, refined manners, a strong sense of tradition, and a form of aesthetic intelligence expressed in her unparalleled talent in playing the *kolintang*, the focal instrument in the Maranao musical ensemble of brass gongs. Instead of skill with the *kampilan*, the Maranao warrior's weapon of choice, she is skilled in weaving and embroidery, producing the special costumes that are the mark of a warrior's social status. Her attributes are as worthy of praise as those of the educated man and as much a source of pride to her clan. In a society that so clearly prizes prowess in battle, it is perhaps inevitable that the qualities of the educated woman would be prized less than those of the educated man to the extent that she does not engage in combat. However, the educated Maranao woman embodies almost all of the characteristics of the educated man and is clearly valued as a member of her society.

A Maranao man or woman becomes educated by emulating the behavior of his or her "teachers." Teaching is not, however, an institutionalized profession. It is carried out by relatives of the same gender as their students and of the same social class. To be taught by someone outside one's family is considered shameful and an indication that one's family was a failure in the training of its children.[41] Therefore, there are no schools, as such, in the world of the *Darangen*. Children are taught at home or in the community to practice the skills they are supposed to learn. Once a child has been properly educated, it is expected that the student will one day pass on the same instruction to subsequent generations.[42]

In the cultural milieu of the *Darangen*, educated means knowing and following the rules of one's society. Conversely, "uneducated" or "ignorant" means not knowing or not following those rules. When Diwata Ndaw Gibon, the mythic progenitor of the Maranao people, instructs his sons in the art of ruling, he defines "ignorance" as the inability to learn proper manners.[43] Thus, the uneducated Maranao is one who does not know or practice the formalities of polite conversation. He does not know how to walk properly. He lacks honesty, reason, prudence, compassion, gratitude, patience, sympathy, and bravery. He is incapable of clear thinking and good conduct. He is ignorant of the four ways of doing good. In short, the uneducated person does not know who he is. He does not know what it means to be a Maranao, an identity that is determined by one's knowledge of and conformity to a set of culturally defined behaviors that create and sustain smooth interpersonal relations.

This emphasis on behaviors that create and sustain smooth interpersonal relationships is seen in the shortcomings of Boroboro sa Ragat's education. The half-brother of Sayana, the boy who is held up as the model for future generations, Boroboro sa Ragat is said to miss being perfect to the extent that he does not learn to show consideration for others.[44] In his training as a warrior, he is taught to be ferocious by being allowed to cruelly beat other children who, by virtue of their lower status, cannot defend themselves. The attitude developed by this method is said to promise the collapse of Bembaran should Boroboro sa Ragat ever ascend to throne. Thus, consideration for others as expressed through culturally sanctioned behaviors that create and maintain smooth interpersonal relations is the glue that holds Maranao society together and is the hallmark of the educated person.

The conception of the educated person implicit in the *Darangen* suggests that the early Maranao did not distinguish between socialization and education. Learning in the *Darangen* is not fragmented into social skills that the individual learns at home and in community and "knowledge" that is acquired through formal education in institutions. Learning is a seamless process that takes place through activity rather than passive study and is designed to promote participation in the cultural life of the community and thus the perpetuation of the culture. There is no such thing as mere possession of knowledge; the educated person *lives* his/her knowledge. It is clearly demonstrated in one's overt behavior in social interaction with others. If it is not demonstrated through proper behavior, then one is not recognized as an educated person regardless of the training one may have had.

This suggests a conception of the educated person that is somewhat analogous to our contemporary conception of a talented person: Neither is recognized if not used. Knower and known are not separate. Therefore, the educated person is forced to continually deploy his or her learning through culturally sanctioned behavior. One's status as an educated person is not something one lays claim to once and for all with the possession of a diploma or some other certification; it must be reclaimed daily through one's socially constructive behavior.

Pre-Spanish Islamic Education in Muslim Mindanao

The Islamization of the southern Philippines is generally thought to have been gradual and largely peaceful. Thus, Islam and Islamic education in all probability settled into indigenous communities as a new layer of cultural and educational practice resting upon pre-Islamic values in a mutually adaptive, syncretic fashion. This process continued and was undisturbed by as yet nonexistent colonial pressures from the beginning of Islamization in the fourteenth century to the arrival of the Spanish in the mid-sixteenth century. In this period, Islam had ample time to put down deep roots in the ethno-linguistic groups of western Mindanao and the Sulu Archipelago. These deep roots would enable the Islamized cultures to preserve themselves largely intact and politically independent right up to the end of Spanish rule in 1898. Sulu and Maguindanao *tarsila*—genealogical narratives in which the earliest accounts of Muslim Filipino culture and history have been handed down—offer important insights into the beginnings of Islamic education in the southern Philippines.[45] Later, accounts of Muslim Filipino culture and education written by Western observers—increasingly common toward the end of Spanish rule—lend further insight into Muslim Filipino educational values and practices prior to their successful colonization by the United States at the dawn of the twentieth century.

Given the gradual and peaceful process of Islamization in Mindanao and Sulu, it would not be inaccurate to say that the religion was brought by teachers and spread through education. The *makhdumin*—a term describing a series of individuals credited with introducing Islam to the region—were respected for their piety and acted as teachers of the faith. At least one account in Sulu traditions describe a *makhdum* teaching children to read and write by drawing letters in the sand on the seashore.[46] With the establishment of the first sultanate in Sulu by Abu Bakr—Sharif al-Hashim—came the first recorded organized instruction in the *Qur'an* and *Hadith* in the *madrasah* established by the sultan. This first sultan is credited in the Sulu *tarsila* with having "taught others to teach," thus discharging the responsibility of the sultan to maintain an adequate number of Koranic schools in his realm to serve the needs of his subjects.[47] The extent of such organized education in Mindanao and Sulu was documented by William Dampier, a British traveler who visited Maguindanao in 1686.

> They have Schools, and instruct their Children to read and write, and bring them up in the Mahometan Religion. Therefore, many of the Words, especially in their Prayers, are in Arabick; and many of the words of civility the same as in Turkey.[48]

Over the centuries of Muslim Filipino independence prior to American colonization, formal education in Mindanao and Sulu was more or less institutionalized in what came to be known as the pandita school. *Pandita*, a Sanskrit word meaning "learned man" corresponding to the Arabic *alim*, was a name given to individuals who, regardless of social standing, had distinguished themselves by acquiring a superior knowledge of Islam.[49] But, in a cultural context in which Islam was believed to govern all aspects of social and individual life, the pandita's knowledge was extensive. In addition to serving as religious functionaries, they served as courtiers of the sultan, judges, scribes, and medical experts. In effect, they constituted a class of indigenous intelligentsia that was a precursor of the contemporary *ustadh* and *ulama*.[50] The pandita was a figure of considerable importance in Muslim Filipino society. One British observer noted in the 1890s that the pandita seemed "to be almost the chief in his district—not in the warlike sense, like the Datto; but his word has great influence."[51] He was often, in the opinion of many Spanish and American observers, a key figure in inspiring and leading Muslim Filipino resistance to the colonial designs of Spain and the United States.[52] One Maranao pandita wrote the following defiant note to Moro Province Governor Tasker Bliss in 1907.

> The Lion of God to the District Governor, Tomas, and Baltazar:
>
> Do not come in the night, pigs. If you do I will crush you. Come in the daytime so that the Moros can see the dead Americans. Ashamed be God. All of you that come I will give as Sungud [marriage portion] to the Virgin. Durum pacal [the kris that cuts fast] is ready.[53]

The pandita school—more appropriately called *makatib*, from the Arabic *kataba*, "to read"—typically consisted of small tutorial classes conducted in the mosque or at the home of the pandita.[54] Pupils would live with or visit the teacher daily, supported by the more prosperous families who wanted their children to learn the fundamentals of the faith.[55] Soon after the US occupation of Mindanao and Sulu on the eve of the twentieth century, American observers reported that pandita schools were a common feature of many Muslim Filipino communities.[56] In the act of dismissing the pandita schools as "valueless" from the standpoint of the US colonial regime, Frank Carpenter, governor of the Department of Mindanao and Sulu from 1914 to 1920, wrote the following account.

> These schools are conducted by men, generally more or less learned Mohammedans called "panditas," who are distinguished in communities in which they live by reason of some knowledge of the Koran, writings by commentators thereon, and other books deemed sacred or authoritative

by Mohammedans. These panditas are also generally persons credited with the ability to read the Arabic version of the Koran. The instruction given by them relates to the forms and principles of the Mohammedan religion as practiced in Mindanao-Sulu, reading the Koran, reading and writing the local dialect in modified Arabic script, and some elementary principles of arithmetic.[57]

While Spanish and American accounts of pandita schools are generally dismissive, it is clear that the institution, largely unhampered by 300 years of Spanish colonialism in the northern and central Philippines, was firmly rooted in Mindanao and Sulu by the dawn of US colonial rule in 1898.[58] It was relatively widespread and important in the social life of Muslim Filipino communities where the *pagtamat* [completion ceremony] was an important event in the lives of the Muslim children.[59] In the introduction to his *Sulu Reader*, Najeeb Saleeby, the first Superintendent of Public Instruction in the Moro Province, testified to the importance of the pandita schools to Muslim Filipinos.

> They have a written language of their own and a system of education of which they are very jealous, and which they prize as dearly as their religion. No matter how inadequate this system may be they will keep it as long as they are Mohammedans and it will keep their preference for many years to come.[60]

While most American observers in the Moro Province judged the pandita schools inadequate, disparaging the knowledge claims of the panditas and dismissing the learning that went on there, some commented favorably on the remarkable achievements of this wholly indigenous system of education. Charles Cameron, for instance, Superintendent of Public Instruction in the Moro Province after Saleeby, wrote in 1910:

> The remarkable influence of the pandita schools may be learned from the fact that during the early days of the American occupation the literacy of the Moros was estimated at 8% of the total population in the Cotabato valley, 4% among the Sulus, and 2% among the Samals. Considering the fact that the census of 1903 shows that but 14% of the total Christian population of the Philippines were able to read and write, this is a truly remarkable showing ...

> The students who attend these [pandita] schools learn only to read and write their native dialect, but this is by no means an insignificant accomplishment. The mental development in learning to read and write—the spanning of the gulf between literacy and illiteracy—represents probably the most important and difficult step in the education of an individual of any race. The pandita schools, as they have been denominated, are praiseworthy ...[61]

Well into the twentieth century, the writing of Muslim Filipino dialects continued in Arabic script. Arab cultural influences survived in the customs and practices of Muslim Filipinos.[62] The practice of Islam, often disparaged by American observers as a corruption of the religion of the Prophet, remained strong and at the center of Muslim Filipino identity. These facts suggest the effectiveness of pandita schools in helping to preserve the cultural and religious identity of Muslim Filipinos against three centuries of Spanish attempts to transform both.

Spain's Moro Wars

The long history of Spain's colonial rule in the central and northern Philippines from 1565 to 1898 is a story of the gradual transformation of a Malay culture organized into independent villages, called *barangay*, and closely related linguistically and socially with the rest of insular Southeast Asia into a hispanicized colony with perhaps as much in common with Central America as it had with its Asian neighbors. Spain's introduction of the *encomienda* system, a policy granting economic and social control of vast areas of the Philippines to favored individuals, led to a form of feudalism that would profoundly shape Filipino society. The exercise of colonial control through the Catholic religious orders ensured that Catholic Christianity would constitute, perhaps, the most lasting and profound influence on the nation that would emerge from Spanish rule in 1898.[63] Thus, by the end of Spanish rule, the Philippines was composed of a populace still, in many respects, culturally Malay though largely Catholic and an indigenous, increasingly nationalist, elite that looked to Europe for cultural and political ideals.

This story is not the story of much of Mindanao, however. For, when the Spanish began their colonization of the archipelago in 1565 they soon encountered the extreme eastern boundary of Islam, the despised religion that they had succeed in expelling from their own homeland only 75 years before. The encounter, perhaps inevitably, quickly became a continuation of their war against Muslims in southern Spain.[64] For the next three centuries, Spanish relations with Muslim Filipinos would be punctuated by repeated military expeditions against the Moros launched by successive governors-general with the aim of claiming fame and fortune for themselves and effecting the subjugation of Muslim Mindanao to Spanish rule. And for the next three centuries, despite some successes, they would largely fail in their efforts due to lack of resources, corruption, lack of military zeal, and, most importantly, an indefatigable resistance mounted by Muslim Filipinos.[65] It was, according to a contemporary observer, "a continual campaign [that] may be qualified as a religious war."[66] It was a period Cesar A. Majul (1999) aptly named in his seminal history of Muslims in the Philippines the "Moro Wars."[67] It was a period that defined, and continues to shape, what would come to be called the Moro Problem.

The dichotomization of Philippine society between Moro and Christian began with the process of Spanish colonization. A Papal Bull issued in 1537 had declared the "Indios" of the Spanish empire capable of a degree of rationality that enabled them to understand and therefore accept Catholicism. Therefore, they were not to be stripped of their liberty or property. Such ideas apparently influenced Spain's Laws of the Indies and led to a more conciliatory policy, which sought to ensure that Spain's Asian possessions would not be subject to the bloody conquests suffered by its American colonies.[68] This policy did not apply, however, to those who were Moros "by birth and choice," as the instructions of Phillip II to Miguel Lopez de Legazpi stated in 1566. Muslims who remained Muslim and attempted to either spread their religion or resist Spanish aims could be enslaved. Thus, one of the first official documents of Spanish colonial rule in the Philippines divided indigenous cultures into two categories: Indio and Moro.[69] This dichotomization of Philippine cultures, combined with Moro resistance to Spanish designs, led to a policy of reduction whereby Spanish authority in the Philippines sought to reduce the sultanates of Sulu and Maguindanao to vassal status, control the trade and commerce of Mindanao and the Sulu Archipelago, stop Moro raids against Spanish controlled territories, stop the spread of Islam, and convert Muslims to Christianity.[70] The very first iteration of the Moro Problem, therefore, was defined as the political, economic, and religious subjugation of the Islamized ethno-linguistic communities of the southern Philippines.

The Moro Wars that punctuated Spain's colonial rule in the Philippines reflected slightly different policy objectives over time, but the overall objective—the subjugation of Muslim Filipinos to the rule of Manila—remained the same, right up to the end of that rule. The first stages of the conflict between 1565 and 1663 focused on ending the influence of Bornean Muslims, connected via kinship ties to the Sulu sultanate, over events in Sulu. Emphasis then shifted to reducing the Sulu and Maguindanao sultanates to vassalage and facilitating the conquest of Muslim territories in the region by establishing a fort at the tip of the Zamboanga peninsula in 1635. The twin priorities of Spanish efforts in this period were conquest and Christianization.[71] The Muslim response was devastating: "In meddling with the Mohametan territories the Spaniards may be said to have unconsciously lighted on a hornet's nest," a move that "brought woe upon their heads for many generations."[72] The series of Moro raids on Luzon and the Visayas that ensued over the next two centuries profoundly affected the residents of the Spanish controlled islands economically and psychologically, uniting them in opposition to and hatred of the Moros.[73] Eventually, the difficulties of Moro resistance led to the abandonment of Zamboanga in 1663 and a period of relative peace for the next 50 years.[74]

The Spanish position at Zamboanga was refortified in 1718, inaugurating a renewed attempt to expand Spanish influence in Mindanao via commercial and trading relationships rather than outright force. Spanish treaties with Sulu essentially treated the sultanate as an independent, sovereign power. By 1751, however, Spain turned once again to force to effect the subjugation of the Muslim territories, authorizing the governor-general in Manila to deploy additional resources to make war on the Muslims, destroying settlements and crops, enslaving prisoners, and branding captives in order to forever distinguish them from non-Muslim Filipinos. Visayan "corsairs" were enlisted in the campaign in exchange for the right to keep war booty. In 1752, a Spanish squadron sailed with 1900 men. Though it launched several assaults in the Sulu region, the campaign met with little lasting success. It did, however, succeed in eliciting Sulu reprisals against Samar and Panay that, along with Maranao raids on Leyte and other islands, furthered the social and economic dislocation of the Visayas and Christian Filipino fear of Muslims.[75]

The late eighteenth century saw increasing political and commercial relations with Sulu as well as slow but steady Spanish inroads in the Maguindanao territories of central Mindanao. By the mid-nineteenth century, however, Spain's need to check the inroads of rival colonial powers in the region led to yet another military campaign in 1851 designed to establish a physical presence in support of Spanish political claims to Mindanao and Sulu. This led to the establishment of a mild protectorate over Sulu, albeit a protectorate the Tausug refused to recognize as an acceptance of Spanish sovereignty. A subsequent campaign launched in 1876 and utilizing steam-powered gunboats finally settled the question of Spanish control, which was ratified by treaty in 1878. Guerilla resistance continued, however, including the use of *juramentado*, a forerunner of the modern suicide bomber in which individual Muslim fighters launched religiously sanctioned suicide missions against superior Spanish military force. Because of this continuing resistance, the Spanish garrison in Sulu remained on a war footing until it was surrendered to American forces in 1899.[76]

Meanwhile, in the Muslim regions of Cotabato and Lanao resistance continued. The Spanish colonial regime was forced to send military expeditions against the Maguindanao under Datu Utto, who led a successful armed resistance to Spanish forces for several years in the 1880s. And in 1891, Governor-General Valeriano Weyler launched the first Spanish effort to penetrate the Lake Lanao territory of the Maranao since 1640. Weyler's campaign met fierce resistance from Maranao fighters such as Amai Pakpak and, though it succeeded in capturing Marawi, it failed to establish any effective control over the region.[77] Attacks on Spanish and Christian Filipino forces continued, eliciting a second Spanish campaign, in 1895, by 3000 Spanish troops and Christian Filipino volunteers. However, Maranao resistance continued, and the Spanish garrison at Marawi remained in a virtual state of siege. Thus, by the time Spain was forced to abandon its garrisons in Muslim Mindanao as a consequence of the Philippine Revolution underway in Luzon, it exercised little effective political control of Muslim Filipinos and had made almost no headway in their conversion to Christianity. Muslim datus quickly stepped into the vacuum created by the Spanish withdrawal.[78]

In spite of the tenuousness of their foothold in Muslim Mindanao, Spain continued to claim sovereignty over all of Mindanao and the Sulu Archipelago. And even as it continued its policy of reducing Muslim Mindanao to Spanish authority through military means, it embarked on a "civilization" policy in the nineteenth century that encouraged the migration of Christian Filipinos from Luzon and the Visayas to Spanish-controlled areas along the northern coast of Mindanao.[79] This policy, continued in the ensuing decades by the US colonial regime and independent Philippine governments, would gradually shift the population balance in much of Mindanao from Muslim to Christian dominance. By the demise of the Spanish regime in 1898, however, little other than the northern Mindanao provinces of Caraga and Misamis, the settlement at Zamboanga, and the garrison at Jolo were (more or less) controlled by Spain. Writing in 1846, one foreign observer noted, "the rest is independent" and "the interior of the country is little known."[80] Almost 60 years later, another contemporary observed that Spain had "failed to subjugate the Mohametans or to incorporate their territory in the general administrative system of the colony after three centuries of intermittent endeavor."[81]

The three centuries of Spain's Moro Wars and Muslim Filipino counterattacks had succeeded in creating a poisonous relationship between Muslim and Christian Filipinos. The depth of the mutual hatred is captured in the public comments of two Spanish friars in support of the 1876 campaign against Sulu: "The war against Jolo is now a just war, a holy war in the name of religion." Another wrote, "war and war without quarter or rest for the wicked sons of the Qur'an; war to the death with blood and fire. Go brave Spanish soldier to the combat in the fiery arena without fear because you are supported and protected by the fury of the God of armies ..."[82] Muslim *ulama* declared a *jihad*.[83] Though Spain had largely succeeded in ending Muslim raids on Christian islands by 1848, accounts of licentious Moros prone to rape and incest remained common and some residents of Manila reportedly believed that people with tails inhabited Mindanao.[84] And, well into the twentieth century, in the Visayas the Moro remained a figure to frighten disobedient children with or censure the conduct of a young person for behaving "like a Moro."[85] For their part, Muslim Filipinos had come to hate and despise the Christians of the North.

> But for all their efforts the Spaniards still failed to eradicate Islam from the Muslim South, although they succeed in causing enmity between the peoples of the Philippines on the basis of religious differences. The crusading spirit of the Spaniards coupled with the fear of and hatred for the Muslims which they inculcated among the Christians in the Philippines is still evident today. On the other hand, the Muslim response of sheer hatred and contempt for the natives utilized to fight them has generated the suspicions Muslims invariably hold for all Christians.[86]

Thus, Spain's government in the Philippines largely failed in its effort to reduce the Moros to colonial control. Thus, the Moro Problem became a part of the colonial inheritance passed on to the new masters of the Philippines in 1898: the United States of America.

Spanish Education and Muslim Filipinos

The history of Spanish education in the Philippines is, of course, almost as long as the history of Spanish colonial domination: almost 400 years between 1521 and 1898. This history has been well documented by both Filipino and foreign historians of education.[87] However, most histories of education in the Philippines pay little, if any, attention to the education of Muslim Filipinos since, from the perspective of the Filipino majority, the history of education in the Philippines is the history of the Spanish education of Filipinos as well as Filipino attempts to claim access to the elite education long reserved for Spaniards and their offspring in the islands. Spanish education had little impact on Muslim Filipinos other than confirming in them the long-held belief that colonial education, intended to Christianize and Hispanicize native Filipinos, was something to be avoided at all costs.

From the very beginning of European contact with the Philippines, travelers took notice of indigenous schools and evidence of education. The letter of a bishop, for instance, attached to a Spanish expedition in 1588 mentions Koranic schools in the province of Maguindanao and observes that many natives were able to read and write in Arabic-like script, "an art … unknown in other tribes."[88] In very short order, however, Spanish priests began establishing schools; one of the first was established by Father Pedro Chirino on the island of Panay in 1593. These first schools were largely devoted to the teaching of the Catholic catechism and enough reading and writing for natives to be aware of their obligations to the faith.[89] A few others offered some training to natives in music and basic arithmetic, but the most were largely focused on the Christianization of the country.[90] They were typically established by members of the Augustinian, Franciscan, Dominican, or Jesuit religious orders, located in or near the local church or convent, and taught by the parish priest.[91] Their primary aims were to inculcate Catholic Christianity, impose Spanish cultural dominance, and teach Spanish language, though this latter goal was often deliberately thwarted by the religious orders, who were often the only representatives of Spanish colonial rule in most Filipino communities.[92]

Such catechism schools at the village level gradually expanded through the seventeenth and eighteenth centuries until, by the beginning of the nineteenth century, outside observers note that almost every town had a school.[93] While their expansion throughout Luzon and the Visayas is no doubt attributable to the missionary zeal of the Catholic friars, the extension of education was also official colonial policy. In 1686, for instance, Charles II issued a royal decree encouraging the teaching of Spanish in order to facilitate conversion to Christianity, and again in 1792 Charles IV ordered the establishment of schools in order to teach Spanish and thus supplant local dialects.[94] Though the friars largely ignored the monarchs' decrees regarding the teaching of the Spanish language, they vigorously pursued the propagation of the faith in the Philippines. Thus, by the beginning of the nineteenth century schools of various types were quite widespread. One French observer commented in 1846 that "the education of the Indios is far from backward, if it is compared to that of the lower classes in Europe ... One sees that in the Philippines, education of the sons of the country as well as of mestizos and Indios of both sexes is not as neglected as certain persons claim."[95] Others noted, however, that such education remained almost exclusively in the hands of the friars.[96]

While schools were becoming more common into the nineteenth century, it was not until the issuance of the Education Decree of 1863 that the Spanish colonial administration established the first public system of primary education in the Philippines.[97] The Education Decree of 1863 created a Commission of Public Instruction headed by the governor-general of the Philippines, the archbishop of Manila, and other appointed officials charged with overseeing a system of public elementary schools. It also established provincial commissions chaired by the provincial governor and the bishop of the local diocese.[98] Local schools remained under the supervision of the parish priest.[99] The decree also established normal schools under the supervision of the Society of Jesus and charged them with the training of Christian Filipinos in the art and science of teaching as well as religion, morality, and sacred history.[100]

While the Education Decree of 1863 ushered in a new era of education in the Philippines marked by an effort to curtail church control, Catholic Christianity remained a major topic in school curricula throughout the nineteenth century.[101] Parish priests remained responsible for the inspection of schools and were charged with teaching Christian doctrine, morality, and sacred history as well as seeing that "nothing was taught contrary to Christian doctrine and morals."[102] As Bazaco (1953) noted, Spanish governments were united in the opinion "that it was not possible to give to the Filipino youth a complete and solid education without including in it the tenets of Christian religion and morality."[103] This heavy Catholic influence continued right up to the end of Spanish rule when the royal decree of Queen Regent Maria Cristina asserted in 1892 that "the two principal objects of primary education in Filipinas is to inculcate in the heart of the studious youth love for religion and the Castilian language."[104]

Almost from its beginning, Spanish educational policy created a dual system of education typical of colonial societies.[105] So-called catechism schools provided for the natives' Christianization and Hispanicization while other schools, modeled on those available to the elites in Spain, catered to the needs of resident Spaniards and their mixed race descendents. As early as 1611, with the opening of the University of Santo Tomas in Manila, Spanish colonial authorities began to establish a small number of elite schools for the education of Spanish residents as well as the upper classes of colonial society.[106] Through most of the Spanish colonial period, native Filipinos had little, if any, access to these schools. They responded to Spanish racism in educational policy by establishing, especially during the nineteenth century, private schools designed to duplicate the education available to Spaniards and the social elites of the colony. Thus, over the course of the century, attendance at catechism schools waned as more people sought social advancement via the superior education offered in private schools and the elite institutions increasingly open to them toward the end of Spanish rule. By this time, however, Spanish education had become increasingly associated with Spanish colonial domination and the demand for social and intellectual equality an expression of growing nationalism.[107] By the end of Spanish rule in 1898, therefore, education in the Philippines remained deeply influenced by Catholic Christianity and had begun to be an issue in a growing nationalist sentiment increasingly articulated by members of the Filipino educated elite such as Jose Rizal, the intellectual godfather of Filipino nationalism.[108]

While Spanish education—particularly the religious instruction of the catechism schools—exercised an important impact on the cultural evolution of Filipinos in the Visayas and Luzon, it is almost certain that it had little or no impact on the Muslims of Mindanao and Sulu. Spain's relations with the Muslims in the south had been one of intermittent war and mutual animosity for 300 years. By the latter half of the nineteenth century, Spanish control in Mindanao was limited primarily to areas with large Christian populations or was barely tolerated in Muslim areas such as Sulu and Cotabato. As late as the 1890s, colonial officials were still mounting military expeditions against the Maranao Muslims in the Lake Lanao region. This legacy of conflict, when combined with the avowed aims of Spanish education—Christianization and Hispanicization—undoubtedly limited the numbers of Muslim Filipinos participating in Spanish education even in those few areas where it might have been available to them.

This likely lack of Muslim Filipino interest in Spanish education is supported by Spanish census figures from 1818 and 1866, which document the percentage of provincial populations enrolled in school. In provinces with large Christian populations—Caraga and later Misamis, Surigao, and Davao—the percentage of the population in school ranged from 14 to 31 percent. In traditionally Muslim regions such as Zamboanga and Cotabato there are no figures from 1816, likely reflecting rather tenuous Spanish control in those areas early in the nineteenth century. By 1866, however, 4 and 5 percent, respectively, of the population of these provinces is reported to be enrolled in school, figures that compare favorably with most provinces in Luzon and the Visayas. However, the population figures reported—8932 in Zamboanga and 3913 in Cotabato—undoubtedly refer to the Christian population of the provinces.[109] Thus, it is clear that only a very tiny proportion of the Muslim population—if any at all—were enrolled in Spanish schools in the latter half of the nineteenth century. Later figures in 1870 report 22 schools for boys and 19 for girls in Mindanao with an enrollment of approximately 7500 pupils. The 1892 statistics on national schools report six schools in Cotabato, 11 in Davao, and 15 in Zamboanga.[110] Again, it is likely that these figures represent areas of the heaviest Christian settlement.

CONCLUSION

One striking characteristic of Christian and Muslim Filipino education prior to the successful colonization of Muslim Mindanao by American forces in the early twentieth century is the similarity of purpose and technique. The pandita schools of Muslim Filipinos and the catechism schools available to the Christian Filipino masses were focused on the inculcation of religious belief, Islam or Christianity. They were typically located in or associated closely with the dominant religious institution of the community, the mosque or the church. They were typically taught by individuals in the community respected for their religious knowledge and authority, the pandita or the priest. Literacy and numeracy skills were occasional adjuncts to the main purpose of the school: induction into the religious life of the community. Both institutions reportedly emphasized rote learning. The education increasingly available to Christian Filipinos, however, was distinguished by the gradual evolution of a system of education still steeped in religion but with a modernizing and increasingly secular curriculum that opened onto a larger world. Muslim Filipinos, by virtue of their faith and history, were almost entirely cut off from this system. Moreover, the legacy of conflict and isolation severely hampered any attempt by Muslim Filipinos to develop a comparable system of advanced education based on Muslim models. Thus, on the eve of American intervention in the southern Philippines, Muslim Filipinos were culturally, politically, and religiously separate from the rest of the country. Mostly untouched by Spanish influences, their system of education must have remained largely what it had been for centuries.

Glimpses into the precolonial educational values of Muslim Filipinos offered through windows like the *Darangen* of the Maranao or the *pandita* schools suggest that precolonial Muslim education in the Philippines was focused on cultural reproduction through the socialization of Muslim youth into the traditions and values of Muslim Filipino ethnic communities. These traditions and values likely varied somewhat among Maranao, Maguindanao, and Tausug ethnic communities; however, they apparently shared a conception of ethnic identity rooted in kinship. Identification as Maranao, for instance, meant that one could locate oneself vertically through genealogical relationships extending back, theoretically, to Radia Indarapatra and the Prophet Muhammad and horizontally in a network of kinship relations that defined one's immediate community, its relations to other communities, and its relation within the larger community called Maranao. Thus, identity as a Maranao was not defined by residence within a particular geographic region or formal citizenship within a defined state. Maranao identity resulted from being born into the network of kin called "the Maranao" and learning to enact the traditions and values expected of members of that community.

A central tenet off that value system was the importance of the extended family, the clan. The Maranao conception of *maratabat*, for instance, suggests the primacy of the family over the individual. The *maratabat* of the individual, while reflective of the actions and accomplishments of the individual, derived from and at the same time enhanced or tarnished the dignity and social status of the extended family. This suggests that the most important social unit is not the individual, as it increasingly became in modern liberal democracies, but rather the extended family, the *bangsa*, which together are constitutive of the *agama* or village. The individual members of the *bangsa*, however, possess the capacity of embodying or failing to embody the early Maranao's conception of the educated person and thus enhancing or detracting from the *maratabat* of the clan. This conception of the educated person was both an expression of the knowledge and experience of the early Maranao as well as a manifestation of the cultural and religious ideals to which the individual aspired. Pre-Islamic and Islamic traditional education was thus focused on the inculcation of knowledge and behaviors constitutive of Maranao identity among those born into Maranao kinship networks.

The introduction and spread of Islam reinforced intra-ethnic identity by adding another layer of commonality—a common faith—that all members of the ethnic community shared. But the adoption of Islam also introduced a nascent inter-ethnic identity that bridged the gaps between the various kinship networks and traditions defining Maranao, Maguindanao, Tausug, and so on in a sense of common identity as Muslims, which twentieth-century Muslim separatists would later cultivate as a nationalist *bangsamoro* identity opposed to assimilation into the Philippine state. Spanish colonial aggression, when it came, reinforced this sense of ethnic and religious identity in defense of outside threats to its very existence. While the values and practices of informal and formal education in Muslim Filipino communities has not been recorded in the genealogies and histories of the period with the same detail as family histories or the military confrontations of the Moro Wars, education no doubt played as important a role in preserving the cultural cohesion of Muslim Filipinos as their prowess with the *kampilan* did on the battlefield.

After the United States displaced the Spanish in 1898, the Americans' bamboo schoolhouses and well-intentioned teachers would introduce a radically different conception of the educated person. It would be a conception of the educated person that stressed practical skills in farming or handicrafts, forms of practical intelligence no doubt valued by precolonial Maranao because of their necessity but secondary at best to an indigenous conception of education that prized social, cultural, physical, and religious intelligence. In some respects, the American conception of the educated person would turn the Maranao's on its head. Knowledge of and conformity to custom and tradition would suddenly become an indication of ignorance and backwardness rather than intelligence. Knowledge of Islam and its deep relevance to all aspects of life would suddenly become irrelevant, at best, and an impediment, at worst, to becoming educated in the American system. Whether intended or not, this radical transformation of the dominant conception of the educated person would prove as much a threat to the survival of Muslim Filipino culture as the Americans' Krag-Jorgensen rifles and Stokes mortars did to the physical survival of Muslim Filipinos themselves.

NOTES

1. Turner and Turner, "Introduction: Images of Mindanao," 2.
2. Ibid.
3. National Statistical Coordination Board, *1999 Philippine Statistical Yearbook* (Makati City: National Statistical Coordination Board, 1999). I have estimated the Muslim population of the region based on the population of the Autonomous Region in Muslim Mindanao, which exceeds 2 million, and the percentages of Muslims in majority Christian provinces given in Costello, "The Demography of Mindanao," in Turner, et al., *Mindanao*, 41.
4. National Statistical Coordination Board, 1–35.
5. Costello, "The Demography of Mindanao," 54.
6. Matsura, "Contemporary Politics in Mindanao," in Turner, et al., *Mindanao*, 149.
7. Coedes, *The Indianized States of Southeast Asia*.
8. Walters, *Early Indonesian Commerce*.
9. Francisco, "Sanskrit in Maranao Language and Literature," 23–48.
10. Tawagon, "The Darangen as a Pre-Islamic Oral Tradition," 6–56.
11. Ibid., 20.
12. Madale, "A Socio-Cultural Analysis of Radia Indarapatra."
13. Tawagon, "The Darangen," 34, 40.
14. Bentley, "The Evolution of Muslim–Christian Relations," 137.
15. Tawagon, "The Pengampong," 66.
16. Ibid., 68.
17. Ibid., 64.

18. Saber and Tamano, "Decision-Making and Social Change in Rural Moroland," 62.
19. Tawagon, "The Pengampong," 63.
20. Saber and Tamano, "Decision-Making and Social Change," 17.
21. Tawagon, "The Pengampong," 42; Baradas, "Ambiguities in Maranao Social Rank Differentiation," 273–278.
22. Tawagon, "The Pengampong," 71.
23. Ibid., 124.
24. Sarangani, "Islamic Penetration in Mindanao and Sulu," 49–73; Majul, *Muslims in the Philippines*, 68.
25. Majul, *Muslims in the Philippines*, 68.
26. Ibid., 76.
27. Ibid., 77–78.
28. Ibid., 50.
29. Sarangani, "Islamic Penetration," 61–62.
30. Majul, *Muslims in the Philippines*, 84.
31. Ibid., 54.
32. Mednick, "Encampment of the Lake," 129, 139.
33. Saber, "Foreword," *Darangen, Vol. 1*, 4.
34. Ibid.
35. Coronel, "Introduction," *Darangen, Vol. I*, 6–16 and personal communication, 1992.
36. Martin, *Reclaiming a Conversation*, 180.
37. *Darangen, Vol. VIB*, 9.
38. *Darangen, Vol. 1*, 43–53.
39. *Darangen, Vol. VIA*, 141–144.
40. *Darangen, Vol. VIA*.
41. *Darangen, Vol. VIB*, 21.
42. *Darangen, Vol. VIA*, 144.
43. *Darangen, Vol. VIA*, 141–143.
44. *Darangen, Vol. VIB*, 2.
45. See Majul, *Muslims in the Philippines*.
46. Ibid., 45, 105.
47. Ibid., 64, 395.
48. Cited in ibid., 105.
49. Ibid., 114, 441.
50. Mastura, "Assessing the Madrasah," 6–7.
51. Foreman, *The Philippine Islands*, 148.
52. Majul, *Muslims in the Philippines*, 108–109.
53. Bliss, *The Annual Report of the Governor*, 28–29.
54. Boransing, Magdalena, and Lacar, *The Madrasah Institution*, 10.
55. Ibid.; Majul, *Muslims in the Philippines*, 115.

56. Gowing, *Mandate in Moroland*, 63.
57. Cited in ibid., 302.
58. Boransing et al., *The Madrasah Institution*, 12.
59. Mastura, "Assessing the Madrasah," 7.
60. Saleeby, *Sulu Reader for the Public Schools*, ii.
61. Cameron, "The Schools of Moroland," 35–36.
62. Majul, *Muslims in the Philippines*, 105.
63. Constantino, *The Philippines*.
64. Michael O. Mastura, "Administrative Policies Towards the Muslims in the Philippines: A Study in Historical Continuity and Trends," *Mindanao Journal* 3, no. 1 (July–September, 1976): 98–113.
65. Foreman, *The Philippine Islands*, 133; Dery, *The Kris in Philippine History*, 131–133.
66. Foreman, *The Philippine Islands*, 133.
67. Majul, *Muslims in the Philippines*, 121.
68. Mastura, "Assessing the Madrasah," 99.
69. Ibid.
70. Ibid.
71. Majul, *Muslims in the Philippines*, 182.
72. Foreman, *The Philippine Islands*, 131.
73. Dery, *The Kris in Philippine History*, 142.
74. Majul, *Muslims in the Philippines*, 183.
75. Ibid., 280–285.
76. Ibid., 320–321, 354.
77. Esteban, "Amaipacpac: 19th Century Maranao Hero," 14–25.
78. Majul, *Muslims in the Philippines*, 368–370.
79. Mastura, "Assessing the Madrasah," 105.
80. Mallat, *The Philippines*, 206–207.
81. Foreman, *The Philippine Islands*, 162.
82. Quoted in Majul, *Muslims in the Philippines*, 346.
83. Ibid., 347.
84. Mallat, *The Philippines*, 29, 39.
85. Dery, *The Kris in Philippine History*, 143.
86. Majul, *Muslims in the Philippines*, 408–409.
87. See, for instance, Bazaco, *History of Education in the Philippines (Spanish Period, 1565–1898)*, or Estioko, *History of Education*.
88. Bazaco, *History of Education in the Philippines*, 3; Estioko, *History of Education*, 163.
89. Schwartz, "Filipino Education and Spanish Colonialism," 203.
90. Bazaco, *History of Education in the Philippines*, 49, 54.
91. Ibid., 39, 59.
92. Estioko, *History of Education*, 166.

93. Schwartz, "Filipino Education," 204.
94. Zaide and Zaide, eds., *Documentary Sources of Philippine History*, Vol. 6, 134–136 and *Vol. 7*, 240–241.
95. Mallat, *The Philippines*, 434.
96. Foreman, *The Philippine Islands*, 192.
97. Zaide and Zaide, *Documentary Sources in Philippine History*, Vol. 7, 178.
98. Bazaco, *History of Education in the Philippines*, 198–199.
99. Isidro, *The Philippine Education System*, 10.
100. Ibid., 15.
101. Schwartz, "Filipino Education," 202.
102. Bazaco, *History of Education in the Philippines*, 224.
103. Ibid., 339.
104. Zaide and Zaide, *Documentary Sources in Philippine History*, Vol. 8, 158.
105. Schwartz, "Filipino Education," 203.
106. Bazaco, *History of Education in the Philippines*, 158.
107. Schwartz, "Filipino Education," 206, 215, 217.
108. Estioko, *History of Education: A Filipino Perspective*, 186.
109. Manuel Buzeta, *Diccionario Geografico, Estadistico, Historico de las Islas Filipinas*, Vols. 1 and 2 (Madrid, 1851); J.P. Sanger, *Census of the Philippines, 1903, Vol. 3* (Washington, DC, 1905), 591 cited in Schwartz, "Filipino Educatiion," 205.
110. Bazaco, *History of Education in the Philippines*, 228–229.

CHAPTER 3

Pedagogical Imperialism: American Education of Muslim Filipinos, 1898–1935

For at least several decades now, scholars of the history of American education have documented how education was deployed in the early twentieth century to complete the destruction of Native American cultures begun by military means in the nineteenth century. Much of that literature goes on to account for the ways in which that legacy of destruction continues to shape the educational experience of Native Americans today.[1] But the tide of US westward expansion did not stop with the "closing" of the American frontier in the 1890s. As a result, partly, of US involvement in the Spanish–American War, the tide of American expansionism swept across the Pacific, engulfing Hawaii, Guam, and the Philippines and marking the US arrival on the world stage as an international imperial power.[2] Tension, however, between the US national origins in resistance to colonialism and its sudden acquisition of its own colonial possessions caused considerable controversy at the time and led to a certain degree of ambivalence over American involvement in colonialism as well as the nature of American colonialism. That ambivalence, experienced in the context of the progressive movement in US domestic society, contributed to the evolution of a colonial policy for the Philippines in which schooling would play a central role.[3]

Educational historians in both the United States and the Philippines have extensively documented American involvement in establishing, expanding, and shaping Philippine public education.[4] Comparatively little has been written, however, on one highly distinctive element of

© The Author(s) 2020
J. A. Milligan, *Islamic Identity, Postcoloniality, and Educational Policy*, Islam in Southeast Asia,
https://doi.org/10.1007/978-981-15-1228-5_3

US educational involvement in the Philippines: the American education of Muslim Filipinos on the southern islands of Mindanao and the Sulu Archipelago. Most references to this unique chapter of American education in the Philippines are contained in more general accounts of US colonial policy toward the Moros.[5] However, a careful analysis of American educators' deployment of orientalist discourses in the formulation and implementation of educational policies for Muslim Filipinos offers important insights into the evolution of American education for cultural minorities.[6] Such an analysis suggests that the application of attitudes and experiences formed in the encounter between American educational thought and subordinated cultures in the United States to a religious minority in an explicitly colonial setting partially transformed the basis of American educational oppression from differences of race and culture to differences of religion and culture. Thus, it highlights religious identity as a site of cultural oppression and resistance in the Philippines. Furthermore, such an analysis reveals the pedagogical character of American imperialism in the Philippines and the role of education in shaping American colonial policy. This pedagogical colonialism represents a crucial intermediate step in the evolution of colonial relations from explicit economic exploitation and religious evangelization to a discourse of social development that masks the continued subordination of religious and cultural minorities behind the benevolent face of the teacher and the democratic ethos of the public school. Thus, the critical examination of American educational policy and practice for Muslim Filipinos in this important period of both the United States and Philippine history not only provides crucial insights into the critical interrogation of contemporary Muslim–Christian relations in the Philippines, but also provides an important insight into the role of religious identity in American conceptions of social and educational development as well.

DISCOURSES OF AMERICAN ORIENTALISM

The United States arrived in the Philippines in 1898 as a result of its general assault on Spanish possessions in the Spanish–American War. At the moment of Admiral Dewey's arrival in Manila Bay, Filipino insurgents had been engaged in a two-year struggle to claim their independence from Spain and had succeeded in bottling up most Spanish forces in urban garrisons like the Intramuros in Manila. Professing support for the Filipino cause while awaiting reinforcements from the United States, Dewey persuaded Filipino forces to permit Americans to occupy positions in Manila. Two months after the Philippines was ceded to the United States in the Treaty of Paris in December of 1898 fighting erupted between US troops and forces of the newly declared Philippine Republic. The fighting would continue long after hostilities concluded in the other theaters of the war, raging on for at least four more years and claiming the lives of up to 600,000 Filipinos and more than 5000 Americans.[7] The war bitterly divided Americans into imperialist and anti-imperialist camps and saw the use of tactics and levels of brutality by US forces that drew congressional hearings.[8]

Preoccupied with Filipino resistance in the northern Philippines, American forces did not occupy Spanish garrisons in Mindanao and Sulu until later in 1899, quickly signing a treaty with the sultan of Sulu to ensure a measure of peace in the region while they dealt with the fighting in the north.[9] The region remained under direct military rule until July 1903, when the Moro Province was organized under General Leonard Wood as its first governor. The Moro Province was administered separately from the rest of the Philippines under successive military governors until it was reorganized as the Department of Mindanao and Sulu under American civilian leadership in 1913.[10] By 1920, the department was abolished and the region incorporated into the administrative machinery of the Philippines as separate provinces.[11] Thus, it was not until 1920 that Filipino Muslims came under the direct administrative control of Christian Filipino government.

Given the proximity in time between the closing of the American frontier and the opening of a new frontier in the Philippines, it is perhaps inevitable that American soldiers, civilians, and colonial officials would carry with them social, intellectual, and psychological lenses shaped by previous experience with African-Americans and Native Americans in the United States. Many officers were veterans of the military campaigns against Native Americans and quite consciously used that experience to interpret their experience in the Philippines and shape colonial policy.[12] Common soldiers brought with them prejudices formed in the context of American racism.[13] Many colonial officials, in preparing for their new duties, studied the writings and experiences of British imperial officials and scholars.[14] Attitudes were further shaped by a large body of journalism and travel writing as Americans attempted to understand this new colonial possession that few knew anything about. Thus, as postcolonial scholars have demonstrated in other contexts, the lens through which Americans regarded their imperial adventure was shaped by a combination of prior experience with US minorities and both academic and popular discourses.[15] These discourses would help shape the pedagogy of American colonialism.

The Pioneer Discourse

One of the most obvious, and perhaps inevitable, discourses shaping American perspectives and policy in the Philippines was the pioneer experience. In this *pioneer discourse*, American soldiers saw themselves as direct heirs to the troops who won the West. Many had direct combat experience against Native Americans. In this discourse, Muslim Filipinos were cast as "Indians." "The inhabitants are the Mohammedan Moros, only now removed a slight step from a savagery akin to that of our North American Indians of a century ago."[16] Scholars and journalists of the period looked to the experience of the American West to put the fighting into an intelligible context for American audiences.

> Never during the continental expansion of the United States were armed encounters between the Indians and American troops so frequent and so serious as the conflicts that took place between the Moros and American forces from 1904 to 1914.[17]

Experience or expertise with Native Americans was an evident qualification for duties in the new colony. David Prescott Barrows, for instance, one of the first colonial officials appointed to oversee Muslim Filipinos, wrote his doctoral dissertation on the ethnobotany of the Cahuilla people and looked to the experience in land allotment and education of the Indian Bureau for ideas for the administration of his agency.[18] Other writers saw differences, but the difference was one of American desires and interests rather than American perceptions of Muslim Filipinos. "The manifest destiny of the red man has been and is either assimilation with the white race or with the ashes of his ancestors ... On the other hand ... their [the Moros'] lands are at present neither needed nor desired for homes by the white race ..."[19] The implication was, however, that if the white race needed their land—as it would later decide it did—then the destiny of Muslim Filipinos would be similar to that of the Native Americans.

In this *pioneer discourse*, colonists were seen as contemporary versions of the white pioneers who settled in the American West. Commenting on the rich possibilities for agricultural development in Mindanao, General Leonard Wood, first governor of the Moro Province wrote, "What is needed here is an influx of such people as built up the West."[20] Such a perspective helped to shape colonial policies on land ownership and immigration from the United States. Officials noted the low population density of Mindanao as compared to the Visayas and Luzon and implemented policies to transform the communal land-owning traditions of Muslim and tribal Filipinos by fixing individual families on homesteads.[21] These policies encouraged migration of small farmers from the Christianized Visayas and Luzon into territory claimed by Muslim Filipinos as well as the establishment of large agricultural plantations by white immigrants. Such policies directly exacerbated long-standing tensions between Muslims and Christians in the region.

Discourses of "Civilization"

In interpreting their contemporary drama through the lens of the pioneer discourse, American officials and immigrants did much more than recast themselves and Muslim Filipinos in the roles of cavalry, settlers, and Indians. Though the settling of the West and the "Indian Wars" were relatively recent history, their contemporary social and cultural milieu was increasingly characterized by the application of scientific ideas to theories of individual and social progress. Evolutionary theory, for example, was applied to the understanding of how children learn and cultures evolve.[22] The educator G. Stanley Hall, for instance, was so profoundly influenced by the application of evolutionary theory to the psychology of learning that he defined education as "conscious evolution" and its goal as "fitness for life."[23] Hall's analysis of human behavior in the context of evolutionary theory led to the development of what he called "genetic" psychology, the notion that the human mind evolved in the same manner and in tandem with the evolution of the body, and his "Law of Recapitulation," a belief that the mental development of the individual progressed through the same evolutionary stages as the "race."[24] Applied to religions and cultures, Hall's "law" could locate any individual or group on a spectrum defined by the poles of primitive "savagery" and the pinnacle of intellectual, physical, and cultural evolution: white, Western, male, Christian culture.[25] The role of the teacher and education, then, was to direct and facilitate this process of evolution toward the desired ends or at least as far along the path as any particular individual or culture was "fit" to travel.

This social Darwinism provided the quasi-scientific underpinning to a *civilization discourse* that permeated the writings and policies of officials in the Moro Province. This is most explicitly stated in an analysis of the problems of government of the province written by General Tasker Bliss, a medical doctor and second governor of the Moro Province.

> There are certain evolutional channels through which society must pass in its onward march from barbarism to civilization. One of these stages has always been some form of despotism, such as feudalism, servitude or despotic paternal government, and we have every reason to believe that it is not within the bounds of possibility for humanity to leap over this transition epoch and pass at once from pure savagery to free civilization. If we apply our own system of government to these wild peoples we demoralize, we extirpate, and we never really civilize. We cannot compress the work of ten centuries into one, and whatever system we eventually adopt, one founded on nature as a guide is more likely to succeed than by suddenly thrusting upon these people a form of government adapted to a race that has reached a higher plan of civilization.[26]

The governor's analysis defined a cultural continuum in the Philippine context anchored on one end by the primitive and savage Moros and "wild tribes" and modern, white, Christian American civilization on the other. The Christian Filipino, who "already has the highest form of religion" and therefore has "considerable culture," was thought to be much further along that continuum and thus, in spite of his racial difference, much closer to the ideal epitomized by white, Christian, American culture.[27]

The great bulk of writing on Muslim Filipinos in the period between 1898 and 1925 reinforced this conception of culture as a continuum between barbarism and civilization with Moros and Americans at opposite ends. Muslim Filipinos were routinely described as violent, ignorant "savages."

> It is manifest that the Malanaos (one of the 13 Muslim ethno-linguistic groups) are savages. To reach our civilization they must pass a great gulf. In its crossing they may, like the Indian, be lost. Why, then, try to make them cross it? Why open their country and try to civilize them?

Because civilization has better things for them. Because many of them are not only ready to receive it themselves, but are helping to fetch it to their whole country. Because they are part of us; we cannot leave them behind. Because savagery and civilization cannot exist side by side; either all Mindanao must be turned over to the savagery of the aggressive Moros, or all taken over to civilization. Because, finally, the Moros stand in the way of our destiny, and we cannot permit that.[28]

Official reports of the time reinforced this distinction between civilization and savagery by categorizing various ethno-linguistic groups in the Philippines into the "civilized" and "non-civilized" tribes. Muslim Filipinos were categorized in official documents among the non-civilized.[29] Prior to the organization of the Moro Province in 1903, responsibility for Muslim Filipinos was vested in the Bureau of Pagan and Mohammedan Tribes in the Interior Department. Later, the name was changed to the Bureau of Non-Christian Tribes. After the abolishment of the Department of Mindanao and Sulu in 1920, responsibility for the administration of Muslim Filipinos' affairs returned to the Bureau of Non-Christian Tribes, where it remained until the 1930s.[30] Thus, Islam was officially synonymous with a lack of civilization well into the 1930s.

Muslim Filipinos' location in the evolution of civilization and their description as savages served to reinforce the *pioneer discourse* in other ways as well. Throughout the popular literature published from the turn of the century into the 1940s, Muslim Filipinos are routinely depicted as both an exotic and threatening Other. Foreign writers regularly emphasize their "gaudy" dress, practice of slavery, and polygamy. "Savages all, their smile is infectious, even though it discloses filed teeth, stained and reddened by the constant chewing of the betel nut, which runs like blood from their lips."[31] Other authors emphasize the dangers of Muslim Filipino violence, highlighting their fighting prowess and the *juramentado*, a ritualized, suicidal attack on non-Muslim invaders.

> He is still the same undersized brown devil who files his teeth, kills best with a knife, and knows that he goes with glory to Allah if he slays a single Christian.
>
> A people who lie among the heaps of the dead after a fight and spring to their feet to murder you as you pass to look for their wounded, who cut you down in the back from the grass after you have gone by, who give their first warning on an outpost by ripping up your stomach with a yard of cold steel—that is the race with which the Regular is now contending.[32]

Such accounts served two purposes: They positioned the American soldier or civilian in Mindanao as a courageous defender of civilization and American honor and the Muslim Filipino as an exotic, dangerous, not-quite-human Other incapable of understanding or being understood by civilized Americans.

The portrait of the Muslim Filipino as a dangerous, uncivilized Other was given a tincture of moral disgust via accounts of Moro sexual "degeneracy." In their frequent justifications for the necessity of continued US governance of the Moro Province, American officials pointed to the "chaos" that had reigned in the region in the period between the withdrawal of Spanish forces and the implementation of American rule when Christian Filipino women were allegedly stripped of their clothes and forced to walk naked before crowds of Muslim men in Cotabato.[33] Official reports and popular accounts also reported frequently on some Muslim Filipinos' practice of polygamy, viewing it as a form of sexual slavery that revealed the degeneracy of the Moro and called for the chivalrous actions of the American to liberate Muslim women from their bondage. In a section of his annual report for 1913 entitled "Slavery of Polygamy," Governor John J. Pershing wrote "The first wife taken is the legal spouse, while the other so-called wives are merely concubines." He goes on to describe the custom of dowries as the selling of women and concludes that "These so-called wives, except for the first one, are in reality slaves who are compelled by the laws of Islam to submit to their masters."[34] Pershing's disgust in this passage and others is palpable, as is his steadfast refusal to examine what was, in fact, a relatively infrequent practice within its cultural context.

The portrait of the Muslim Filipino as an exotic, morally degenerate, dangerous Other was not and could not be the only theme in the web of discourses defining his position on the continuum of civilization and his relationship to the American ideal. To do so would, in effect, constitute a case for the kind of genocidal violence unleashed upon Native Americans in the previous century. Though American colonial officials harbored many of the attitudes and biases they had developed in their encounter with Native Americans, times had changed and there was a recognition that what had been done to the Native Americans was morally problematic as well as some sympathy for the Native American even as their fate was seen as a necessary, though unfortunate consequence of the march of civilization.

> The fact that the changes he [the Native American] is called upon to make are contrary to the laws of nature as revealed in the history of human development, that at best he cannot expect to become more than an inferior imitation white man, may add a touch of pathos to his destiny, but cannot alter it.[35]

> The lamented fate of the noble red man has long since ceased to inspire our bards ... We are in hearty sympathy with the irresistible spirit of the age, but we pause long enough to record a lingering regret for the vanishing point of ancient customs and laws, wholly inconsistent with our method of thought, but fraught with much of the simple joy of living.[36]

This paternalistic combination of an unquestioned sense of cultural superiority and an abstract sympathy for the subordinated other emerges in an infantilizing discourse: The Muslim Filipino is portrayed as an irrational, emotional child. "The Moro['s] Mohammedanism is a veneer of which he is distinctly proud, as of a little lad dressed for the first time in a sailor's suit, with long trousers and stripes of authority on his coat sleeve."[37] Tasker Bliss's account of the problems of government in the Moro Province in 1909 offers the most explicit rendering of this infantalization discourse and its implications for colonial policy.

> What would we think of a man who should advocate principles of perfect freedom in a family or school? We should say that he was applying a good principle to a case in which conditions rendered it inapplicable—a case in which the governed are in an admitted state of mental inferiority to those who govern them and are unable to decide what is best for their permanent welfare ... Children would never grow up into well-behaved and well-educated men if the same absolute freedom of action that is allowed to men were allowed to them. Under the best of education, children are subjected to a mild despotism for the good of themselves and society... Now this is not merely an analogy, *there is in every respect an identity of relation between master and pupil or parent and child on the one hand and an uncivilized race and its civilized rulers on the other.* (emphasis added)[38]

Along with this conception of the Muslim Filipino as a child, comes the claim that he is capable of improvement: "These Moro people, with all their faults, are brave and industrious, and have in them material out of which to make a good people."[39]

Portrayed as a primitive, uncivilized, child-like people, Muslim Filipino culture then was of little value and worthy of little respect. Whatever respect accorded it was simply a result of the need to advance American colonial aims while engendering as little resistance as possible.[40] Muslim Filipinos' Islamic identity was not seen as something worthy of respect or recognition, but rather as a "veneer," a sailor suit with long trousers and stripes worn by a child. In short, they are not "real Muslims" and know very little about their faith in American eyes. "The Mohammedan religion ... is no more than skin deep among the Moros."[41] Even the religious leaders know little of their faith, and the enterprising American officer can acquire enough knowledge of Islam to amaze and disarm them in a few hours of study. "I primed myself at once and was soon astonishing the panditas (teachers of Islam), who were themselves really ignorant of their religion."[42] Governor Leonard Wood summarized the American view of the seriousness of Islam as an aspect of cultural identity in his first report as governor of the Moro Province.

> The Moros are, in a way, religious and moral degenerates. They profess Mohammedanism, but practice only those precepts of the Koran which suit their individual tastes. They have no written laws worthy of the name. Evidently the first Mohammedan priests brought with them to the Islands the teachings of the Koran in more or less purity, and also certain of the Mohammedan laws, but since that time, so far as can be gathered from the traditions of these people, they have gradually fallen away from the religious teachings and most of the laws ...[43]

Islam is generally seen as an impediment to American policy, something to be gotten around, undermined, and eventually sidelined while avoiding any perception of a Spanish-style frontal assault on the faith that would only heighten Muslim Filipino resistance.

The collective effect of these official, academic, and popular discourses regarding Muslim Filipinos and the Moro Problem was to firmly fix in the minds of Americans and Filipinos alike the idea of an evolutionary continuum of civilization. On one end of that continuum was the Moro—uncivilized, savage, and morally degenerate—and on the other was the American—civilized, modern, peaceful, and morally upright. On one end of the continuum was Islam and on the other Christianity. But this schematic conceptualization of civilization did more than simply locate cultures along the evolutionary scale; it also defined the direction of progress. Progress lay in the direction of becoming more like the American, even if it was generally believed that Filipinos—particularly the Muslims—would never quite attain that ideal. Furthermore, in spite of American claims of religious neutrality, moral and cultural progress clearly lay in the direction of moving from Islam toward Christianity. While American colonial officials never really expected Muslim Filipinos to abandon Islam—they were often in fact wary of missionary efforts for fear they would stir up trouble—they did attempt to "modernize" Muslim Filipinos out of most of the values and customs that had come to express their adherence to Islam over the centuries. Christian Filipinos, because they "already had the highest religion" and had, at least among the educated, adopted more of Western cultural values, became honorary white men, allies, and apprentices in the grand project of civilizing and Filipinizing the Moro. Thus, in Mindanao at least, religious difference trumped racial difference in demarcating the line between ruler and ruled, power and powerlessness, center and margin. Though the Americans came upon the scene in Mindanao confident that it would not repeat the mistakes of Spain in dealing with Muslim Filipinos, they ended up reinforcing the social dichotomy between Muslims and Christians, but this time hiding the religious bias behind a patina of science and social progressivism. In so doing, American colonialism armed itself and its Christian Filipino apprentices with an analytical framework guaranteed to preserve their position of cultural superiority and a sense of moral justification which protected them from any doubts as to the morality of their cause.

The analytical framework constructed by these discourses contained within it clear implications for colonial policy. These policy alternatives were spelled out by Najeeb Saleeby, a Lebanese-born American physician who served as the first Superintendent of Public Instruction in the Moro Province and who was among the first to seriously study the history and culture of Muslim Filipinos.

> In conclusion it may be briefly said that in our conduct of Moro affairs we are bound to follow one of two courses. We have to either be tolerant and accept present conditions and institutions as they are and gradually reform them, or be intolerant and introduce radical changes from the start. The first course begins with enmity and proceeds with patience and makes slow but permanent progress with telling effect. The second course is bound to begin with enmity and proceed with opposition every step

of the way. The latter course has been tried for over three hundred years. History has declared its failure and humanity has condemned its principles...Reformation can be fostered by patient instruction and good example, but it cannot be forced into being by commands and threats. A few evil national customs may have to be checked by force, but force applied as the sole agent of national reform is cruel and harmful.[44]

In short, the choices were to repress through military means or to civilize. While military muscle may from time to time be required to facilitate the achievement of colonial policy, the only morally defensible policy within the moral and conceptual geography defined by the discourses discussed here was to "civilize" the Moro.

Thus, the civilization—the development—of Muslim Filipinos became the primary aim of and justification for American colonial rule in Mindanao. And the instruments of that civilizing mission were to be the great hallmarks of American civilization: capitalism, the small farm, Christianity, and education. The Americans were, in the words of one writer, "making men out of savages ... by teaching to them the benefits of labor and industry."[45] Five years later, the same author, writing about the success of a commodity exchange established for Muslim Filipinos in Zamboanga, described US policy as a "unique and unprecedented experiment of turning savages into citizens by business methods."[46] The individual ownership of land and the fixing of Muslim Filipino families on small, single-family farms would awaken in them "a sense of thrift and business" and make him "conscious of his rights and awake to his interests, tak[ing] a new pride in his township and work[s] for its advancement."[47] Though American officials claimed neutrality on religious matters and professed their fealty to the principle of separation of church and state, they nevertheless valued the educative example of good Christian men and women. In his official report for 1913, Governor Pershing wrote:

> Charitable persons at home who desire to aid in the rescue of benighted people from the darkness of superstition and savagery may find them here living under the American flag. The Philippine Islands occupy a very important position as an outpost of Christian civilization in the Orient, but it must be remembered that the Islands themselves contain a non-Christian population numbering probably a million souls ... The Moro Province extends a cordial welcome and proffers its every earnest support to individual or societies willing to engage through these channels in the uplift of its wild people.[48]

The chief instrument of civilization, however, would be education, for the portrait of the Muslim Filipino as an uncivilized, misbehaving, and ignorant child—albeit a child with some potential—established the Moro Problem as essentially a pedagogical problem. Thus, colonial policy drew on contemporary educational ideas and established public schools in order to implement those policies. One contemporary academic observer described American colonialism in Mindanao as a "new experiment in colonization, an experiment that has been, and still is, the story of a great modern advance in race pedagogy … a notable example of colonization that gets its theory and justification from the principles of modern pedagogy."[49] The American experiment in colonialism, an experiment they were preparing Christian Filipinos to one day take over through the policy of "Filipinization," was not simply another adventure in the economic exploitation of a colonized people, it was an effort to radically transform the language, economy, culture, and *religion* of a people in the name of development. Writing in 1920, one American observer succinctly described the aim of the US pedagogical imperialism: "Seventeen years ago Leonard Wood undertook to disarm a savage people and to establish among them a respect for Christian law and democratic institutions … The day of the fighter was past. The day of the teacher had come."[50]

The Pedagogy of Imperialism: Public Education in the Moro Province

American involvement in Philippine education began almost before the fighting had stopped. Existing schools were reopened as quickly as possible, and, in some cases, American soldiers were assigned to serve as teachers.[51] This was the case as well for schools in Mindanao and Sulu, where the first schools were established in January 1900, just two months after the US Army began replacing Spanish garrisons.[52] However, since the existing schools were almost exclusively within the areas previously controlled by Spain, they included few, if any schools serving Muslim children. The establishment of the Moro Province in July 1903, however, included provision for a Department of Public Instruction with direct responsibility for the organization, administration, and expansion of public education throughout the region.[53] In the years of its existence, the department experienced the least turnover of upper administrative personnel of any department within the provincial government.[54] Between 1903 and 1914, the Department of Public Instruction had only two superintendents: Najeeb M. Saleeby, an Arab American physician whose knowledge of Arabic enabled him to complete the first extensive study of Muslim Filipino history and culture, and his deputy, Charles R. Cameron, a graduate of Cornell University who served in the department for more than ten years.[55] As part of the colonial policy of Filipinization, the Department of Public Instruction in the Moro Province was merged into the Bureau of Education of the insular government in 1915. Though it remained for a few years after that as a distinct administrative unit within the Bureau of Education, it was gradually absorbed into the educational bureaucracy of the insular government as individual provinces within the overall government of the Philippines. By 1922, Mindanao and Sulu had ceased to exist as a distinct geographic-administrative entity within the insular Bureau of Education.[56]

The dominant theme of educational reports from this period is the expansion of the public educational system, providing more schools and teachers and increasing enrollments. Given the challenge of providing access to free public education in a region where it had been hitherto absent, it is perhaps natural that colonial administrators measured and reported their successes in terms of numbers of schools, enrollments, etc. This raw quantification of educational progress has generally led historians of the period to see the growth of public education between 1903 and 1920 as an unadulterated boon to Mindanao and Sulu during this period of direct American administrative control.[57] The data from the period support such a picture. The total number of schools grew from 52 in 1904 to 366 in 1920, while the total number of teachers rose from 74 to 239 between 1904 and 1914.[58] Enrollment also grew steadily and substantially in the 17 years of American administration. Soon after the establishment of the Moro Province in 1903, enrollment in provincial schools stood at 2114.[59] By 1920, enrollment in the province had grown to more than 33,000.[60]

The facts behind the numbers, however, depict a more complex picture, revealing patterns that temper the overall image of educational progress and skew the benefits of what progress there was rather heavily toward the Christian inhabitants of the province. Enrollment, for instance, was largely confined to the first two grades of primary school, with the highest enrollment by far in first grade. In 1910, approximately 75 percent of total enrollment in the province was in first grade. By 1914, first-grade enrollment had climbed to 85 percent of total enrollment and remained at approximately 65 percent of total enrollment in 1920.[61] Enrollment after second grade dropped precipitously and continued to drop through higher grades. Thus, the vast majority of children enrolled in American colonial schools from 1903 to 1920 did not attend beyond the first or second grade; therefore, it is quite unlikely that they retained much of what they learned in the way of literacy and other skills for any significant period of time thereafter.

Some of the most revealing details behind the overall growth of public education in the province were the locations of schools, who taught in them, and who they tended to serve. As late as 1914, schools in the Moro Province were almost entirely located in predominately Christian areas such as Zamboanga or near military sites in Muslim areas. This was due in part to unsettled conditions in areas beyond immediate American military control and the unwillingness of teachers to work in schools in such areas. For example, 200 of the 231 teachers in service in the province in 1914 were Christian Filipinos who were generally reluctant to serve in rural Muslim communities. Only 15 of the teachers were American and 16 Muslim Filipinos, numbers that had remained relatively stable since 1904.[62] Not surprisingly, then, enrollments were heavily skewed toward the Christian population, a relatively small minority of the total population of the province. In 1904, only 240 of the 2114 children enrolled were Muslim.[63]

By 1907, Superintendent of Public Instruction Charles R. Cameron reported that Muslim Filipinos constituted 17 percent of school enrollments, yet they comprised 90 percent of the total population of the Moro Province. That year Cameron reported "37 Yakan and Maranao students." Given the population, at the time only about one in 5000 Maranao were in school. In 1909, he reported that 8 percent of the total Christian population was enrolled in school while only about one-tenth of one percent of the Muslim population was enrolled.[64] By 1913, the total Muslim student enrollment had grown to 1825, approximately 12 percent of total enrollment, but still only one-half of 1 percent of the Muslim population of the province while approximately 10 percent of the total Christian population was enrolled in the schools.[65] After 1915, when the schools in the Department of Mindanao and Sulu were absorbed into the insular Bureau of Education, reports do not distinguish Muslim and Christian enrollment in the figures reported for the provinces that comprised the department. However, extrapolating from the Muslim enrollment in 1914, it is apparent that Muslim enrollment in 1920 in all likelihood remained below 10 percent of the Muslim school-age population. Therefore, beneath the surface picture of steady growth in public education between 1903 and 1920 in Mindanao and Sulu lies a reality in which public schools, overwhelmingly staffed by Christian Filipino immigrants, serve primarily Christian Filipino children living in Christian-dominated areas or near military installations. And they, along with the tiny minority of Muslim children attending, are highly unlikely to attend beyond the first or second grade. Thus, the widely held notion that Americans brought the benefits of public education to Muslim Filipinos is far more myth than reality.

While one of the avowed aims of US policy in the Philippines was to prepare Filipinos for self-government, educational policy for Muslim Filipinos stressed their cultural transformation into small farmers and workers within a "modern civilization." According to Tasker Bliss, second governor of the Moro Province, the schools were "government agencies for civilization" charged with preserving the social order so recently won and tenuously maintained by the US Army and conveying "certain fundamental modern ideas ... common to the civilized world."[66] To this end, schools were established, boarding schools for Muslim girls set up, and "promising" Muslim youth sent to Manila and even to the United States to imbibe the knowledge, values, and outlooks of modern civilization.

The conception of civilization conveyed by educational policy in the Moro Province was one modeled on a mid-nineteenth-century American ideal that was rapidly disappearing in the United States. This model was one that idealized the individual small farmer and craftsman as the moral center of modern democratic society. Industrial and agricultural education, then, with this model as its regulative ideal, became the "beginning [of] our attack upon Moro and pagan savagery."[67] Industrial and agricultural education were seen as tools to counteract the "lassitude of mind and idleness of body" that characterized Muslim Filipinos and "occidentalize and modernize [their] Mohammedan and Oriental modes of thought."[68] Superintendent of Public Instruction Charles R. Cameron summed up the purpose of industrial education in the schools of the Moro Province in 1910:

> The purpose which inspires all the industrial work in the schools of this province is that of providing education for the eye and the hand in conjunction with the mind. We cannot separate industrial training from academic training without causing one-sided development. Purely academic education tends to make the student *visionary and impractical* [emphasis added], while industrial training narrows the mind, develops commercialism and prevents the acquisition of high ideals ... It is believed that true education consists in an harmonious mingling of the two and this is the principle followed in the schools of the Moro Province.[69]

In short, the purpose of American education was to produce small farmers and semiskilled craftsman imbued with a protestant work ethic and untroubled—and therefore not troublesome—by any "vision" of their own of what they or their society might be, different from what their American teachers had for them.

This vocational emphasis of educational policy was focused from the beginning of the colonial regime to prepare Muslim children for "useful callings" and vocations suited to the practical life for which they were destined.[70] To prepare for these useful callings, industrial education began by "teaching the Moro children the useful arts of their own people." Such arts included hat making, mat making, beadwork, wood carving, and weaving of articles valued as "curios" characteristic of "the work of the race" as well as "work of more civilized design" made from "patterns selected and explained by the American teachers" such as doilies, table covers, napkin rings, hammocks, bamboo furniture, and so on.[71] The agricultural curriculum had "for its specific objective the training of boys to be efficient, practical small farmers and the girls to be farmers' wives and mothers. That is, it is proposed to educate toward the soil rather than away from it."[72] But agricultural and industrial education was aimed at more than just producing small farmers, it helped disabuse boys of the "idea of earning their living by some other means than manual labor" and provided "a large number of well-trained natives" possessing a "reasonable knowledge of English, arithmetic and kindred subjects, [and] a thorough knowledge of wood-working, iron-working, and agricultural methods." In short, the need of the Moro Province was for workers on American plantations, craftsmen to produce the various items needed by Americans, and individual farmers fixed on small plots of land to free up land for American commercial agriculture.[73]

A third important aim of American educational policy in the Moro Province was to prepare the province for its eventual integration with the rest of the Philippines. For 25 years, the fundamental policy of American and Filipino policy was the "ultimate incorporation of that area [Mindanao and Sulu] into a united Philippines."[74] To this end, educational leaders saw the schools, with their preponderance of Christian Filipino teachers and students, as a means of bringing Muslim Filipinos into association with Christian Filipinos.[75] It was assumed that such association would lead to the erosion of prejudices among both Christian and Muslim Filipinos. "Promising" Muslim boys were sent to schools outside the area "where they are trained as prospective teachers and at the same time imbued with the culture of the Christian Filipinos."[76] Thus, American educational policy for Muslim Filipinos was aimed at moving them along the "evolutional channels of civilization" toward the attainable ideal epitomized by Christian Filipinos and integrating them into a unified Philippines as a subordinated class of workers and farmers. In short, Muslim Filipinos were not being educated for self-government; they were being educated for government by Christian Filipinos.

The formal curriculum of the public schools in the Moro Province generally mirrored the curriculum in use in the schools administered by the insular Bureau of Education except for a greater emphasis on vocational education. These schools offered three and later four years of primary instruction, which included three years of English, three years of arithmetic, one year of geography, and the "rudiments of a useful occupation." This was followed by an intermediate course of elementary instruction for three years that offered courses of study in teaching, farming, housekeeping, trade, business, and general education characterized by a "great emphasis on vocational training."[77] Schools continued to offer a curriculum consisting of English, arithmetic, geography—particularly of the Philippines—science, and colonial and American government. Intermediate schools were also expected to have a laboratory, a shop, a garden, and a model Filipino home for instruction in housekeeping. High school courses of study for durations between two and four years included programs in literature, history and science, teaching, commerce, agriculture, and arts and crafts. "Body training" in singing, drawing, handiwork, and physical exercise was offered throughout the curriculum.[78]

The primary differences in the formal curriculum of schools in the Moro Province were the lengthening of primary education to four years to provide for more industrial work and ambivalence on the language to be used as a medium of instruction. Industrial education accounted for as much as 25 percent of the curriculum for Muslim children with one hour per day devoted to it in first and second grades and one and a half hours per day in the higher primary grades.[79]

> Work begins in the first year with stick laying, block building, paper folding and other kindergarten occupations. In the second year, hat weaving and mat weaving, as well as in some instances bead work and needlework are taken up. In the third and fourth years the work of the sexes is divided–the boys taking up rattan working, while the girls devote their entire time to needlework. The girls continue needlework and dress making through the intermediate course, while upon entering the Provincial school the boys take up carpentering. *It will thus be seen that every school in the Province is, in a sense, a trades school, and it is the intention of the authorities to increase still further industrial work.* [emphasis added][80]

Older boys received training in woodworking and ironworking using simple hand tools since it was assumed that they were unlikely to ever be called upon to use power tools. Older girls, in both regular public schools and the boarding schools, which were viewed as one of the only ways to entice their parents to send them to school, were offered training in "personal cleanliness, housekeeping, sewing, cooking, embroidery making and speaking, reading and writing English."[81]

The second major difference in the curricula of the Moro Province schools reflected shifting attitudes toward the most appropriate medium of instruction for the schools. The first governor of the Moro Province, Leonard Wood, found little value in the local languages.

> There is no object whatever in attempting to preserve the native dialects as they are crude, devoid of literature, and limited in range ... and not believed to present any features of value or interest other than as a type of savage tongue ... We cannot expect to continue the many different dialects of the island, and any attempt to do so would be unwise, but we can hope, with a reasonable degree of assurance, to make English the main language and the medium of transacting all official and most business affairs in the comparatively near future.[82]

However, Superintendents of Public Instruction Najeeb Saleeby and Charles R. Cameron, as well as Governor Tasker Bliss, later favored teaching children through the medium of their own languages. They believed that this was a more efficient and effective means for teaching American ideas and achieving literacy.[83] To this end, Saleeby created readers in Tausug and Maguindanao using Arabic script. They contained a phonetic primer as well as a translation of the Arnold Primer exactly the same as the English version to facilitate translation.[84] In spite of these differences, however, the underlying language policy was to eventually make English the common language of the entire country.

In spite of its faults and shortcomings, there was much about formal American educational policy and curricula that was laudable. While a contemporary educator might quibble with some aspects of the policy or curriculum—the emphasis on industrial education, for instance—it seems apparent that educational policy makers in Mindanao and Sulu at the time were exercising their best judgment and motivated by what they saw as noble intentions. However, there was a significant gap between intentions and reality. Two aspects of this gap are important. First, the data on enrollment from the period demonstrate that only a small minority of children ever attended school beyond the first or second grade. Furthermore, the enrollment data show that the large majority—80 percent or more—of those children enrolled in Mindanao and Sulu were Christian Filipinos. Therefore, despite the best of intentions, only the tiniest of minorities among Muslim Filipino children ever received even a primary school education from the American public school system let alone the whole scheme of education from primary through secondary school. Second, the gap between overt intentions and reality in the Moro Province is one of the sites where the various discourses analyzed above worked to create a *hidden* curriculum that shaped the educational experience of Muslim Filipinos as much as the formal curriculum did.[85] The experience of this hidden curriculum is what Muslim Filipinos actually reacted to, not the educational experience American officials said they were offering.

The two main aims of this hidden curriculum were the deculturalization of Muslim Filipinos and their political-economic subordination to a Philippine government dominated by Christian Filipinos. The aim of deculturalization in turn included two objectives: the transformation of cultural practices and social relations and the emptying out of Muslim Filipinos' religious identity. The American scheme of public education for Muslim Filipinos addressed the first of these two objectives at several levels. For instance, education within a colonial context offered alternative routes to social status and power that undermined ancient cultural traditions. A young man of humble origins might use his American education to acquire status within the colonial regime—one of the avowed purposes of schooling in the province—and his familiarity with local culture to become a kind of intermediary between colonial and indigenous centers of political power.[86] Thus, alternative routes to and centers of social power are established, inevitably undermining the traditional power of the sultan, the datus, and the aristocratic families. A commonly told story today in Mindanao is that Muslim families refused to send their sons and daughters to the American schools for fear that they would be converted to Christian. They sent their slaves instead, thus hastening the erosion of their traditional social and political power.[87]

Educational policies also served to implement other colonial policies that struck at the heart of the traditional economic structure. Among Islamicized and non-Islamicized ethnic groups in Mindanao, land was traditionally owned in common by interconnected networks of extended families. The datu, the traditional leader of this network, exercised authority over the right to use the land. Thus, the concept of land as an individually owned, alienable commodity was foreign to Muslim Filipinos.[88] The tradition of slave-raiding among Muslim Filipinos, which was one cause of Christian Filipino fear and hatred, had emerged historically as a consequence of Muslim Filipinos' need to work large areas of land with a relatively small population.[89] The policy of the Americans, many of whom had direct experience with American slavery, was to abolish slavery. Moreover, noting the low population density, which had led to the tradition of slavery in Muslim Mindanao, Americans encouraged migration of Christian Filipinos from Luzon and the Visayas as well as farmers from the United States to Mindanao to take up and farm "public" land that was divided up and allocated to individuals in the Torrens system.[90] The primary aim of agricultural training, especially the farm schools where students boarded, was to replace the traditional conception of land use and ownership with a system that placed individual farmers on fixed plots of land that they owned and farmed themselves.[91] The second aim was to produce knowledgeable agricultural workers for the large, foreign-owned plantations that the transformation of land ownership practices enabled.[92] Thus, educational policy attempted to reconcile Muslim Filipinos to colonial policies that struck at the very foundations of traditional political and economic power.

Another avenue of attack in the deculturalization of Muslim Filipinos involved the transformation of gender relations within Muslim Filipino society. Traditionally, marriages in Muslim Filipino society were arranged and viewed as a mechanism for establishing or reinforcing relationships between different clans. Part of the marriage negotiation involved the negotiation and exchange of a dowry that was determined at least partly in reference to the social status of the two families and which was collected from the groom's extended family and distributed among the bride's extended family. Thus, marriage was, and is, much more than a union between two individuals, and it constitutes a social bond between two extended families and comes with the expectation of mutual support and protection. As Muslims, Muslim Filipino men were permitted to have as many as four wives, provided they could meet the requirement in the Qur'an that they be able to provide equally and adequately for each wife. Given this restriction, and the poverty of the area, polygamy was not, and is not, nearly as common as many outsiders presume.[93]

Most American observers and colonial officials looked upon such practices with barely concealed disgust. They looked upon the arrangement of marriages and the exchange of bride price as nothing more than a form of sexual slavery that cemented their image of Muslim Filipinos as moral degenerates. Governor John J. Pershing wrote, "These so-called wives, except for the first one, are in reality slaves who are compelled by the laws of Islam to submit to their masters."[94] And Pershing was clear in his view that such traditions were impediments to progress and would have to be cast aside in the march toward civilization. "Unless he can be induced to relinquish some of his most vicious customs ... the Moro faces the future with very little of promise ... He cannot progress far while he is bound down in the chains of polygamy and female slavery."[95]

One of the ways of "freeing" Muslim Filipinos from the "chains" of "female slavery" and polygamy was through the education of Muslim girls in boarding schools. American educational officials discovered very early that Muslim Filipino families were extremely reluctant to send their daughters to school, fearing their conversion to Christianity or other deviation from social expectations and the important role they played in Muslim Filipino society. Boarding schools, in which "the handicaps of the home and environment of the whole life are removed," were seen as the only "practical way to reach the Mohammedan and pagan girl."[96] Though only a handful of girls ever actually attended these schools, those who did were usually the daughters of datus and other prominent families and thus seen as having an important future role in shaping gender roles in Muslim Filipino society. The object of these boarding schools was made explicit in Pershing's 1913 annual report.

> An endeavor is being made to bring them [Muslim girls] up to womanhood under the elevating moral influence of the American Christian woman. Although it is well understood that Christianity as a religion is not mentioned in the school, yet it is lived by the teachers, and it may, in some measure, influence the lives of these young girls who, under Moro customs and traditions, could only hope to become polygamous wives or concubines of the datus who offer the greatest sum of money for their purchase. To secure for them the honorable position of wife, it should be the eventual purpose of our officials to find similarly trained husbands for them, if possible, when they reach womanhood.[97]

Thus, one rather explicit moral aim of the hidden curriculum of the colonial schools was the substitution of a Western, Christian model of marriage for customs that were central to the constitution and preservation of Muslim Filipino culture.

Perhaps the most profound element of this hidden curriculum of the United States' pedagogical imperialism in the Moro Province reflected American attitudes toward Islam. American officials, as well as civilian observers, generally did not take Muslim Filipinos seriously as Muslims. They dismissed Muslim Filipinos' practice of Islam as shallow and ignorant, a pretense. They certainly saw it as an impediment to progress. They differed somewhat, however, in the stance toward Islam they advocated, basically vacillating between a tolerance born of expedience and out-and-out hostility. Tolerance was limited, however, by supposedly civilized Christian norms.

> The fundamental principle of a righteous colonial policy should be unquestioning respect for the beliefs, the customs, and the traditions of the subjugated or the protected peoples, *so far as such consideration is not repugnant to the requirements of human good, as measured by the judgement of the Christian nations of the earth.* [emphasis added][98]

The Superintendents of Public Instruction, first Najeeb Saleeby and later Charles R. Cameron, were less inclined to see Islam as an impediment. Saleeby did not think it should stand in the way of colonial policy, and Cameron actually instituted a policy of donating books and materials to

Islamic schools in an effort to earn the trust of Muslims and because he believed that they were, in teaching Muslim children to read, contributing to the overall goal of educating Muslim Filipinos.[99] Even here, however, the underlying principle was expediency, the recognition that any perceived threat to Islam would generate more opposition to colonial policy than it was worth.

Other officials were much more explicit and hostile in their attitudes toward Islam. General John Pershing, last military governor of the Moro Province, invoked the principle of separation of church and state in his denunciation of support for Islamic schools. His denunciation of this policy, however, went beyond a concern with the constitution to an explicit denunciation of Islam.

> It has been seriously suggested that Islamic preceptors be brought into the Province to teach Mohammedanism through the medium of the public schools. That such a radical departure from the theory of independence of the public school system should be proposed is almost beyond belief. To anyone who has even casually investigated the character of the proselytizing Arabian and other Mohammedan teachers who have hitherto cursed this Province, there appears every reason to oppose the suggestion. Their presence here has been detrimental to good government, and there is little doubt that to their occult inspiration may be charged much of the opposition that we have met among the Moros during the last ten years. The provincial government could not consistently approve any plan for the propagation of Mohammedanism through the prostitution of the public schools.[100]

Pershing's hostility toward Islam was also reflected in his policy toward Muslim Filipinos' fulfillment of their duty as Muslims to make the pilgrimage to Mecca at least once in their life. In his official report, he disparaged "these poor, ignorant people [who] annually spend thousands of pesos which should to go the improvement of their farms, or for the benefit of their families in other ways" who contract "loathsome diseases," which they spread in the community, and who come back "with an exalted idea of their own importance." In 1913, he gave instructions to district governors in the province to discourage Muslims from making the pilgrimage unless they could prove to the satisfaction of the district governor that they could afford the trip, that they had in no way burdened their families financially, and that they had not borrowed the money or mortgaged property. In effect, the district governor was to decide who could make the haj. In the very next section of his annual report, however, Pershing solicited "charitable persons at home who desire to aid in the rescue of benighted people ... in this outpost of Christian civilization" to come to Mindanao. To such people, "the Moro Province extends a cordial welcome and proffers its very earnest support."[101]

While not nearly so blatant as Pershing, Frank Carpenter, civilian governor of the Department of Mindanao and Sulu, evinced a similar bias against Islam and in favor of Christianity in spite of American constitutional principles. In his first report, he wrote disparagingly of Muslim teachers in Islamic schools as inclined to "mysticism and a pretense to magic" and dismissed the instruction Muslim children received in schools as "valueless from the standpoint of the government." In that same report, he reports quite favorably on the good work of Catholic schools and "the beginning of the establishment of relations of coordination and cooperation" between Catholic and Protestant mission schools and the government of the department. This agreement allowed private schools to draw on public schools for advice and assistance and shifted emphasis for new public schools from areas served by Christian schools to Muslim areas.[102] While on the one hand such a policy might be seen as a laudable effort to put public resources to the greatest benefit for Muslim Filipinos, it also reveals a congruence of aims between Christian and public schools in Mindanao and Sulu.

Taken together, this more or less hostile disposition toward Islam, coupled with a relatively unapologetic preference for Christianity as the religion of civilized humanity, meant that this hidden curriculum was aimed at "educating" Muslim Filipinos away from Islam and toward Christianity. Colonial officials, however, never really expected Muslim Filipinos to convert to Christianity; they realized that any overt effort to bring this about would engender the same sort of resistance that had been marshaled against the Spaniards. But they were attempting to, in effect, "empty out" the cultural expression of Islam in Mindanao by prohibiting or interfering with everything Christians found repugnant. In essence, it was tolerable to call oneself Muslim so long as one conformed to the values and practices of Christian civilization. Thus, while the policy of Filipinization was usually expressed in terms of Filipinos taking over the reins of government, the policy of Filipinization was also cultural. The objective of the hidden curriculum was to transform the "Moro" into a mirror image of his Christian Filipino "brother."

Both the overt and hidden curricula of the US pedagogical imperialism in Mindanao and Sulu grew out of Americans' effort to interpret what they encountered there through the lenses of the discourses discussed above. In particular, prevailing Western conceptions about the evolution of civilization, the tendency within that discourse—shaped by genetic psychology and social Darwinism—to infantilize non-Western peoples, and Americans' ambivalence toward its participation in colonialism all combined to frame the United States' approach to colonial rule in Mindanao and Sulu as a pedagogical problem. Conceiving American imperialism in the Philippines in such terms was one way, perhaps the only way, to reconcile Americans' perception of themselves as a democratic people with the profoundly undemocratic business of imperialism in which they were engaged in the Philippines. As Governor Tasker Bliss said in 1910: "What would we think of a man who should advocate principles of perfect freedom in a family or school? We should say that he was applying a good general principle to a case in which the conditions rendered it inapplicable."[103]

Thus, American colonial rule in Mindanao and Sulu was fundamentally pedagogical. Given this orientation, public education played a profound role in implementing both the formal and hidden curricula of colonial policy. However, all other aspects of the colonial government—health and sanitation, infrastructure development, commerce, and so on—were seen as providing educative models for the edification of Muslim Filipinos. And, just as good parents and teachers were expected to be firm when necessary in bring children into adulthood or savages into civilization, corporal punishment, in the form of frequent punitive military expeditions, remained a necessary component of the pedagogy carried out in the little red schoolhouse that was Mindanao and Sulu.

WILLFUL CHILDREN AND IDLE SCHOOLBOYS: MUSLIM FILIPINO RESISTANCE TO PEDAGOGICAL IMPERIALISM

Muslim Filipinos' resistance to American colonial aims took a variety of forms, but the most obvious and unmistakable was armed resistance. Armed resistance to the US civil and military presence in Mindanao and Sulu was almost constant. Though government reports frequently proclaimed the return of peaceful conditions, they inevitably included reports of "banditry" and "outlawry" that had to be put down by US or Philippine Constabulary troops. One American officer described the situation in 1904: "Even under the mailed fist he rebels. All the time there is blazing fitfully a warfare that shows how red the embers are beneath the ashes."[104] During Bliss's tenure as governor a "disturbance" in the Zamboanga peninsula "spread over approximately six hundred square miles ... and affected twenty thousand natives," requiring the district governor to mount 14 expeditions to quell it.[105] In 1906, Muslim Filipino resistance in Sulu culminated in the Battle of Bud Dajo, which claimed the lives of more than six hundred men, women, and children.[106] A few years later, the governor of the Moro Province described Bud Dajo as "to modern civilization a regrettable incident, but ... a severe but necessary *lesson* [emphasis added] that has borne most excellent fruit."[107] In Sulu, again in 1913, as many as 10,000 Muslim Filipinos gathered on Mount Basak to resist US troops and were attacked after "most" of the noncombatants were persuaded to leave. Pershing reported that the effort to disarm Muslim Filipinos between 1911 and 1913 had collected a "surprising" 7000 weapons.[108] The next year Frank Carpenter, governor of the newly established Department of Mindanao and Sulu, announced the surrender of Datu Alamada with 500 armed followers and 3000 supporters.[109] Writing as late as 1928, one American observer noted the willingness of Muslim Filipinos to fight even in the face of certain death from the "high powered rifles, Stokes mortars, and gas bombs of the Philippine Constabulary."[110] Interspersed between these accounts of major engagements are dozens of accounts of smaller punitive expeditions against "outlaws" and "bandits" in almost every district as well as chilling accounts of *juramentados* charging fixed American positions with a spear or running themselves on an American bayonet to get within striking distance of the soldier at the other end.[111] Muslim Filipino resistance lasted longer than direct American administration of Mindanao and Sulu. It is an open question whether their American "benefactors" killed more Muslim Filipinos than they educated.

Muslim Filipino resistance to American objectives was not confined to armed conflict. Resistance to educational objectives was common as well, though less obvious since the accounts of American observers at the time were predisposed to view the limited success of public schools in attracting Muslim Filipino children as due to their ignorance and backwardness rather than resistance to colonial policy. However, such direct resistance to American schooling is evident. The fact that only a tiny fraction of the Muslim Filipino population was ever served by the public schools of the Moro Province and Department of Mindanao and Sulu was generally attributed to the remoteness of most villages and the reluctance of American or Christian Filipino teachers to serve outside the Christian-dominated cities or far from military installations. This was of course true; however, it is also an indication of the general hostility of people in those areas toward Americans and their Christian Filipino allies while the low Muslim enrollment in those areas served by schools clearly suggests resistance to American educational policy. Even after the passage of compulsory education laws, Muslim Filipinos sent the children of servants and slaves, hid their own children, and particularly avoided sending their daughters to American schools. In 1926, in a period of a few months, more than 20 schools were burned to the ground in the area around Lake Lanao. One observer wrote in 1928: "There are school districts in Lanao today which the division superintendent of schools, an American, cannot safely visit without an escort of soldiers."[112]

Despite American comments disparaging the depth of their understanding and commitment to Islam, Muslim Filipino resistance was largely rooted in their faith and their recognition that the hidden curriculum of American educational and administrative policies constituted an attack on their religious identity. Official American reports confirm this fact in their repeated attribution of the cause of unrest to religious leaders. Leonard Wood wrote in 1904 that "the people [of Lanao] are densely ignorant and very suspicious and are easily played upon by the Arab priests, who, it is believed, are responsible very largely for the attitude of the people."[113] Bliss's report of 1907 quotes a letter from Uti, "a fanatical priest, from the Masiu area of Lake Lanao:"

> The Lion of God to the District Governor, Tomas, and Baltazar:
>
> Do not come in the night, pigs. If you do I will crush you. Come in the daytime so that the Moros can see the dead Americans. Ashamed be God. All of you that come I will give as Sungud [marriage portion] to the Virgin. Durum pacal [the kirs that cuts fast] is ready. (29)

The following year too Bliss placed blame for "lawless elements" in Zamboanga on the "Salip, the Mohammedan bishop" of the region.[114] American officials also recognized that resistance to public education was also rooted in a defense of Islam: "The real school problem of this

Province is the development of the Moro and Pagan tribes, but their peculiar religious prejudices and their barbaric state makes school progress a difficult task."[115] Pershing too attributed much of the opposition to public schooling Americans encountered to the "occult inspiration" of "Mohammedan teachers."[116] Evidence for religiously inspired resistance to American schooling can also be seen in the continued popularity of "pandita schools," whose primary purpose was the inculcation of Islam.[117] American colonial officials recognized that the first and most difficult impediment to their program of civilization and "educational development" was Islam.[118] Therefore, in spite of their claims of religious neutrality, the hidden curriculum of American public education, as well as American policy in general, in Mindanao and Sulu constituted a direct assault on the cultural, and thus religious, identity of Muslim Filipinos.

The Policy of Filipinization

In 1916, the US Congress passed the Jones Act declaring American intentions regarding the future political status of the Philippines.[119] The Act established a bicameral Philippine Legislature that assumed the power to make laws throughout the country. Its intent was to authorize the gradual transfer of authority to Filipinos in a process that would culminate ultimately in total independence. The Act also ended the separation of administrative authority over Christian and non-Christian Filipinos, phasing out the Department of Mindanao and Sulu for a newly established Bureau of Non-Christian Tribes headed by former department governor Frank Carpenter, who reported to a Filipino Secretary of the Interior.[120] By 1918, Carpenter was turning over day-to-day operations to his Filipino deputy, Teopisto Guingona, who would soon replace Carpenter as director. Most of the Bureau's staff were Christian Filipinos who had been trained under Carpenter's tutelage as governor of the Department of Mindanao and Sulu. In very short order, the only high ranking positions in Mindanao occupied by Americans were, rather tellingly, the governorship of Sulu, command of the Philippine Constabulary, and superintendent of schools.[121]

While Americans and Filipinos officially agreed upon the eventual goal of colonial policy—independence—there was considerable disagreement over the timetable and the geography of an independent Philippine state. Many Americans pointed to ongoing tensions between Muslims and Christians as evidence of Filipinos' inability to govern an independent

Philippines that included Mindanao and Sulu. While some of this concern no doubt reflected very real problems as well as concern for the welfare of Muslim Filipinos, much of it was also motivated by American self-interests. Mindanao's extensive natural resources and economic potential led some Americans to call for the separation and continued colonization of Mindanao and Sulu, a move seriously contemplated in a bill introduced in the US Congress in the mid-1920s.[122]

Filipino advocates of independence, needless to say, vigorously opposed any partitioning of the Philippines as well as any delay in the granting of independence. This overriding concern with independence led most Christian Filipino officials to downplay Muslim–Christian tensions, supporting their contentions with very public rhetoric regarding their "Muslim brothers" in Mindanao and Sulu. The leadership of the emerging Philippine nation recognized the importance of Mindanao to the economic viability of the new nation and the internal and external threats to national security posed by instability in the region.[123] Thus, the Philippine Legislature vigorously opposed any separation of Mindanao and Sulu from the rest of the archipelago and attempted to dismiss arguments—the supposed inability of Christian Filipinos to govern Muslim Filipinos, for instance—that were marshaled in support of such separation.

The voices of Muslim Filipinos were largely unheard in this debate between Americans and Christian Filipinos over the future of Mindanao.[124] The sentiments of many of them were expressed by a young Maguindanaoan datu, Gumbay Piang, at a predominately Christian Filipino gathering called to express opposition to the Bacon Bill, which proposed separating Mindanao and Sulu and was then before the US Congress. Datu Piang noted that Filipino Muslims only heard "loud talk of brotherhood for the Moros" from the Philippine Legislature when there was some threat for the Philippines of losing Mindanao. He was, he said, "inclined to believe that the Filipinos were treating the Moros as their colonial subjects with no real interest for the progress of the subject people." He described the Moros' predicament as being positioned "between two fearful and objectionable daggers, Americans at one side and Filipinos at another," charging that the Filipinos' policy of colonization would result in the extermination of Muslim Filipinos just as the US colonization of the American West had led to the virtual extermination of the American Indian.[125] Though Datu Piang ultimately supported independence, his comments eloquently expressed the disappointment of many Muslim Filipinos with the policy of Filipinization and their very real fears about their likely status in an independent state dominated by Christian Filipinos. Their concerns were largely unheard, however, and the process of Filipinization continued.

While Christian Filipinos assumed greater and more widespread roles in the administrative structure of the colony, key elements of the educational bureaucracy remained in the hands of the United States right up to the establishment of the Philippine Commonwealth in 1935. That this was the case testifies to the central importance of education in what I have termed here the pedagogical imperialism of American rule in the Philippines. Even in 1935, the secretary of Public Instruction, one of six departments under the governor-general, was appointed by the president of the United States and served as vice governor-general of the Philippines. The director of the Bureau of Education was appointed by the governor-general upon the recommendation of the secretary and the approval of the Philippine Senate and exercised authority over all public schools in what was a highly centralized system of education. Well into the mid-1930s, these positions remained in American hands, though Christian Filipinos had recently occupied the post of assistant director. Divisional superintendents, who were appointed by the secretary of Public Instruction on the recommendation of the director of the Bureau of Education, appointed the municipal and supervising teachers in charge of individual school districts.[126]

While Filipinos held numerous positions further down the educational hierarchy, American educators continued to hold key posts, particularly in Mindanao and Sulu. In the late 1920s, for instance, though a Filipino occupied the post of assistant director of the Bureau of Education, American educators served as superintendents of all seven of the provinces comprising the former Department of Mindanao and Sulu. Americans also served as principals of the general course high schools in the Muslim-dominated provinces of Sulu and Lanao, while Filipinos occupied those positions in the provinces of Cotabato, Davao, Agusan, and Bukidnon, provinces with large or majority Christian populations. The principals of agricultural and farm schools were American in Muslim provinces and Filipino in majority Christian provinces. Academic and industrial supervisors in all seven provinces, however, were Christian Filipinos.[127] Thus, the administration of education in Muslim Mindanao and Sulu remained a largely American and Christian Filipino affair right up to the inauguration of the Philippine Commonwealth in 1935.

While the administration of education in Muslim areas was dominated by Americans and Christian Filipinos, the teacher core did include a growing minority of Muslim Filipino educators. The Director of Education reported in 1915, for instance, a total of 273 teachers in Mindanao and Sulu, the great majority of whom were Christians. There were "only a few Mohammedans."[128] This would remain the case for at least the next decade as hundreds of Christian Filipino teachers were sent south to Mindanao to staff a growing educational system. By 1919, 600 Christian Filipinos had gone to Mindanao.[129] By 1921, there were 1694 Christian Filipino teachers in so-called non-Christian schools.[130] These teachers were encouraged to take up homesteads in the communities where they taught, so they would continue to serve as role models for non-Christians after they left the teaching profession. Moreover, the common understanding of their role continued to be dominated by the civilization and pioneer discourses. Their activities were repeatedly described in annual reports as "pioneer work" aimed at "placing all elements of the population on the same cultural level."[131]

As more Muslim Filipinos participated in the educational system and acquired the credentials necessary for appointment to the colonial schools, more were appointed as teachers. They remained, however, a relatively small minority of the teacher core in most Muslim provinces. In 1932, this situation led the Mindanao-Sulu Mohammedan Students Association to lodge a protest with the governor-general over discrimination against Muslim teachers in Sulu. The discrimination was blamed on the American superintendent King Chapman. After Chapman was replaced in 1932 by Edward M. Kuder, an educator with long experience in Mindanao and pro-Muslim sympathies, the percentage of Muslim teachers in Sulu grew from 24 percent in 1932 to almost 47 percent in 1936. By the end of Kuder's administration of Sulu schools in 1939, the percentage of Muslim teachers was approaching 70 percent.[132] This was not the case, however, in the schools of other predominately Muslim provinces. Thus, the education of Muslim Filipinos continued to be carried out largely by American administrators and Christian Filipino teachers who saw themselves as pioneering agents of civilization to the uncivilized Moros. Frank Laubach, an American missionary active in education in Lanao, described what was taking place in the schools as "stepping out of barbarism and into civilization." He summed up the process as "the most wonderful tale in Mindanao … for the first time in the history of Islam a Mohammedan nation is going to school to Christian teachers."[133]

In terms of gross enrollment and number of schools, education in Mindanao and Sulu appeared to grow steadily between 1903 and the beginning of the commonwealth. Between 1903 and 1932, for instance, enrollment in the schools of Mindanao and Sulu grew from 1936 to 63,023. The enrollment figures for 1932, however, only represented 24.44 percent of the school-age population in the region. But these figures obscure enrollment rates for Muslim children since they include Christian Filipino populations in Mindanao who tended to have a larger proportion of their school-age children actually enrolled in schools. Based on enrollment figures, school-age populations, and reports of the non-Christian percentage of enrollment in the predominately Muslim provinces of Cotabato, Lanao, and Sulu in the early 1920s, it appears that fewer than one in five school-age Muslim children were actually enrolled in school.[134]

For the following six years—coinciding with the transfer to Filipino authority—enrollments decreased steadily among non-Christian students, especially in Lanao, which lost 2027 students. In 1925, non-Christian enrollments decreased in Cotabato, Davao, Lanao, and Zamboanga. Only Sulu reported increases in enrollment. Government reports in this period blame the decrease on the non-enforcement of compulsory attendance laws, the attitudes of parents, and unrest in Lanao. By 1927, the percentage of the school-age population enrolled in school in the majority Muslim regions of Cotabato, Lanao, and Sulu ranged from a low of 12.7 percent to a high of 20.35 percent.[135] The relatively low attendance rates as well as the decline in enrollment in response to the dropping of compulsory attendance laws would seem to suggest that many Muslim families, given a choice, chose not to send their children to government schools.

Enrollment figures imperfectly reflect the extent of participation and the impact of American supported education in Mindanao and Sulu between 1903 and 1941. As late as 1926, attendance was highly irregular, with the average child attending school only one to three times a week. Added to this were high drop out rates, particularly in Lanao where roughly 40 percent of the children enrolled in each of the first five grades did not continue on to the next grade level. The effect of this was that total enrollment was heavily concentrated in the first three grades. From 78 to 91 percent of total enrollment in Cotabato, Lanao, and Sulu was concentrated in the first three grades in 1926.[136] Enrollment picked up again after this period. However, given the low participation rates and high drop out rates, it is clear that the vast majority of Muslim children received little or no exposure to the American run educational system in Mindanao before World War II.

Those children who did attend school beyond the first grade were exposed to a curriculum that placed a heavy emphasis on industrial and agricultural education. The American and Christian Filipino administrators in charge of education in Mindanao and Sulu saw the emphasis on industrial and agricultural education, particularly agricultural and settlement farm schools, as the most appropriate means of adapting to the needs of the local communities. In industrial education and home economics, children produced crafts and crops that were then sold, presumably to teach them the value of a marketable skill but also to generate funds for the support of the schools. The academic curriculum stressed literacy-related subjects such as language, conversational English, reading, phonics, and writing as well as physical education, music, number work, civics, hygiene and sanitation, and "good manners and right conduct." Intermediate grades added geography, Philippine history, and government to this list. The high school, which was "imported from the United States with few changes," offered academic, normal, trade, agricultural, and home economics courses of study.[137]

Widely used reading texts of the time attempted to incorporate material deemed relevant and interesting to Filipino schoolchildren. They depict a version of Filipino experience, however, in which Muslim Filipinos are non-existent. Readers for younger children include numerous stories with animal characters, Christmas stories, "typical" Filipino children with names like Pedro, Rita, Juan, and Clara, as well as patriotic stories about Jose Rizal and Abraham Lincoln.[138] The author of the series, Camilo Osias, a future education official and senator of the Philippine Republic, announced in the preface to one of the readers that "the nationalization of our education system has been definitely adopted, and the *Philippine Readers* have been written with this policy in view ... the author has, however, avoided anything that makes for race feeling, petty sectionalism, or narrow nationalism."[139] The content thereafter includes stories about "our heroes ... Bonifacio, Mabini, and Rizal," as well as Bible stories, British and American poetry and patriotic songs, as well as stories from other countries. The sixth and seventh books in the series include "The Story of Bantugen" and a "myth from Mindanao" about King Indarapatra and Sulayman, both of which are based on stories from the *Darangen* of the Maranao.[140] The seventh book also includes a story entitled "Mohammad," which describes Islam as "the most warlike religion of all, one that has forced its way by fire and sword." The Muslim statement of faith—"there is no God but God"—is portrayed as the "war cry" of the "Mohammedans."[141] These readers, copyrighted in 1922 and reprinted into the 1950s, offer a vision of Philippine experience in which Filipino Muslims are but a dim historical memory and Islam itself a violent but geographically remote faith followed by Arabs but not Filipinos.

As the end of direct American rule in the Philippines approached in the late 1920s and early 1930s, the overtly racist rhetoric of the civilization discourse gradually softened as the language of development began to displace the stark dichotomies of civilization and savagery that characterized much of the rhetoric of officialdom in the old Moro Province. In 1925, for instance, W.W. Marquardt, a former director of the Bureau of Education, advised American teachers considering service in the Philippines to stay home if they harbored racist attitudes.

> If you possess racial prejudices, or if you cannot sympathize with the endeavor of a small nation to prepare itself for independent national existence, you are lacking in at least two of the elements essential to your own peace of mind and to your future success in the Philippine teaching service.[142]

In that same year, the Monroe Commission Survey criticized the type of education offered to Muslim Filipinos as irrelevant to their needs, paternalistic, and externally imposed, thus justifying the resistance to schooling displayed by many Muslim Filipinos, especially for their girls. The Commission went on to recommend a greater attention to Muslim educational needs in the context of their cultural traditions and aimed at improving the community and not just enabling the privileged few to attain greater status in the broader Philippine society.

> It cannot be too strongly emphasized that any school which prepares a few individuals to escape from the limitations of the restrictive life of their people does these people harm rather than good. In removing prospective leaders an injury is done to the people as a whole. Prolonged attempts should be made through the schools to build upon and improve these traditional activities. This can only be done through long, continued study, through experimentation, and patient effort.[143]

Other American officials who began their colonial careers in Mindanao in educational positions assumed, in some cases, broader responsibilities, bringing with them a measure of sympathy for Muslim Filipinos. James R. Fugate, who served for years as the principal of the Indanan School for Moro Boys in Jolo, became governor of Sulu in 1928. In his annual report, he criticized the tendency to see Moro resistance to modern advancement as evidence of their ignorance. "Too many of us are unwilling to grant the Moro a single virtue," he wrote. "To unjustly blame and kill for pretended lack of reception of these [roads, schools, modernization] is but to unction our own guilty conscience, excuse our stupidity."[144]

While the rhetoric softened, however, the overall policy of integration into an independent Philippine state governed from Manila remained the same, and the discursive frameworks that shaped and directed the policy remained intact. Muslim Filipinos were less likely to be portrayed as dangerous savages with filed teeth stained red as blood, but the aim of American education remained "to bring non-Christians up to the same cultural plane and closer union with Christians."[145]

> The interrelation of the social and economic development of the people is clearly recognized, each in turn being the cause and effect in the progressive march of the people to a higher plane of living.[146]

Thus, the civilization discourse remained intact in the gentler vocabulary of development, positioning Muslim Filipinos as uncivilized and defining the direction of civilization as conformity with Christian Filipino models. Muslim Filipinos were expected to adopt Western, Christian civilization without necessarily becoming Christians.[147]

The aim of American education among Muslim Filipinos continued to be the transformation—destruction—of all those aspects of Muslim Filipino culture inconsistent with the values of the civilized nations of the earth. "One of the first tasks of the public schools," wrote former Mindanao-Sulu Superintendent of Public Instruction Glenn Caulkins in 1931, "was to break down the class distinctions."[148] In other words, education was intended to break down the traditional social structure and replace it with something closer to an American or at least Christian Filipino model. The original harsh discourse highlighting the supposed sexual degeneracy of the Moro is softened but kept in place in a continuing concern for the emancipation of Muslim Filipino women, some of whom are sent to boarding schools in Manila to associate with Christian Filipinos and gain "a broader view of the social position of women," which will eventually "help to break down objectionable features of the Moro social system."[149]

> The problem of securing for Moro women a position in the home comparable to that Christian Filipino women enjoy is one of the most perplexing that faces the schools. The solution is sought through the education of the girls, many thousands of whom are attending the public schools. Also groups of Moro girls are sent to Manila and in the provincial capitals of Mindanao-Sulu where they live with Christian Filipino girls—an association that is designed to give them actual living experiences that will point the way to the emancipation of Moro women.[150]

The paternalism inherent in these aims of American education continued to position the Muslim Filipino as a child, extending the infantilizing discourse just as surely as the explicit descriptions of him as a child in a sailor suit did two decades before. Thus, the aims and discursive structure of the Americans' pedagogical imperialism remained firmly in place even as the more benign rhetoric of development and education masked this fact and served, as Fugate wrote, to "unction our own guilty conscience."[151] Well intended as it may have been, the aim of pedagogical imperialism was the destruction of traditional Muslim Filipino culture, and so it remained, as the American administration drew to a close, poised "between two fearful and objectionable daggers" as Datu Piang described it, facing a fate not unlike that of the American Indian.[152]

Caught between the horns of such a dilemma, Muslim Filipino leaders exhibited somewhat contradictory attitudes toward the place of their people in the emerging Philippine Republic. Often their attitude toward integration depended on which side of the issue they perceived their self-interest lay. Those who had been appointed to offices under Christian Filipino administrations or who maintained positive working relations with Christian Filipinos tended to favor independence, while those without such relations or appointments were more likely to resist any sort of cooperation more than absolutely necessary.[153] Adaptation to the emerging political order was most evident in areas with the longest exposure to Spanish and American influences—Jolo and the urbanized areas of Cotabato and Zamboanga—but vast rural areas of Cotabato and Lanao remained relatively unchanged by government pressures into the 1930s.[154]

Even in areas with the longest exposure to Muslim–Christian interaction, however, Muslim Filipino attitudes toward their Christian countrymen were characterized by a general contempt for people they saw as weak. Many saw the rising population of Christian Filipinos in traditionally Muslim areas as an invasion of interlopers who were robbing them of their patrimony and making them second-class citizens in their own land. "The Moros," wrote Governor-General Leonard Wood in 1923, "look upon the Christian Filipinos who fill most of the government offices a good deal as the people of the [U.S.] South looked upon the so-called carpet baggers."[155] The rapid resettlement of Christian Filipinos from Luzon and the Visayas, encouraged by official government policies, increasingly put Muslims in direct competition with Christian immigrants over land, economic and political opportunities, and even education on a playing field that, given the waxing political power of their traditional enemies, was increasingly uneven.

The ensuing resentment translated into deep suspicion on the part of Muslim Filipinos toward independence. Governor-General Wood claimed in 1921 that "the Moros are a unit against independence."[156] In 1930, the director of the Bureau of Non-Christian Tribes reported to a pro-independence meeting in Manila that "the majority of the Mohammedan Filipinos do not feel, or do not realize, that they are part of the Filipino people."[157] In 1934, 200 Maranao datus addressed a letter to Governor-General Murphy to be read before the constitutional convention demanding that Islam and Maranao traditions be protected in the constitution, that Muslims be appointed to government posts, and that they be given 20 years to secure titles to their lands. If their demand for protection was not included in the constitution, then they asked to remain under American colonial rule until they were ready for a separate independence. Their letter was never read before the delegates of the constitutional convention.[158] Though the Muslim provinces eventually voted for independence, it is clear that the overwhelmingly favorable Christian vote swamped Muslim ambivalence on the question.[159]

While it is clear that by 1935, Muslim Mindanao had been administratively and politically integrated into the Philippine Commonwealth, Muslim Filipinos themselves were not integrated socially. Joseph Ralston Hayden, a political science professor at the University of Michigan who later became secretary of Public Instruction and vice governor-general in the 1930s, framed the situation in the rhetoric of the civilization discourse for the journal *Foreign Affairs* in 1928.

During the past quarter century the cruder manifestations of such a backward civilization have been forcibly curtailed. Upon it has been superimposed an alien system of government and education embodying American, Filipino, and Spanish concepts and practices, but the belief that the Moro has been fundamentally changed during this brief period is simply self-deception. The old Moro civilization is still deeply rooted among this proud, ignorant, stubborn and highly courageous people.[160]

The accuracy of Hayden's assessment is borne out by Muslim Filipino actions at moments when the American and Filipino political grip was loosened. When compulsory attendance laws were not enforced, enrollment by Muslim children dropped. After the Japanese invasion in 1941 drove Americans and Filipinos from power in Mindanao Muslim traditions and, to some extent, traditional political institutions rapidly reasserted themselves. Indeed, traditional political institutions—the sultanate and datu system—remained a relatively intact and influential parallel political structure alongside American and Filipino government well past independence.[161]

Muslim Filipino resentment of the cultural, political, and economic pressures they were increasingly subjected to erupted repeatedly, if sporadically, into armed resistance. While the overwhelming military power of the US Army had effectively crushed large-scale resistance by the time the Moro Province was turned over to civilian rule in 1914, armed outbreaks typically dismissed as outlawry by government officials continued almost continuously from the abolition of the Department of Mindanao and Sulu right up to the eve of the Japanese invasion in December 1941. Between 1921 and 1928, Joseph Ralston Hayden reported that several hundred Maranao had been killed in guerilla warfare with colonial authorities. The constabulary, he wrote, "acts as an army in hostile occupation. In many of its battles with the Moros no quarter has been granted by either side."[162] In 1926, romantic overtures of Christian Filipino schoolteachers toward Muslim girls in Marawi led to the deaths of the teachers, the removal of girls from the school system, and the destruction of 50 buildings—including 26 schoolhouses—in Lanao.[163] "There are school districts in Lanao today," Hayden reported in 1928, "where the division superintendent of schools, an American, cannot safely visit without an armed escort of soldiers."[164]

In 1931, an editorial in *The New Republic* reported on "another year of bloodshed in Lanao," where the presence of 500 *cottas*—Maranao bamboo fortifications—demonstrated that "twenty five years of guerilla fighting have not solved the Moro Problem." The editorial goes on to disparage the effectiveness of colonial education policy in overcoming Muslim Filipino hostility and resistance.

> Bamboo versions of the Little Red Schoolhouse exist in the villages where military force is heaviest, and in them a few Moro children parrot the assignments of ill-prepared Filipino teachers. They learn—or half learn—the three R's, and write essays about Abraham Lincoln, the Battle of Bunker Hill, and a pale little boy with a hatchet who cut down some foreign kind of tree, and who was not ingenious enough to tell a necessary lie—a trait of character foreign to the Oriental nature, which not even their Christian teacher can understand. The medium of expression used by teacher and pupils is "bamboo English." The fine native arts, the poetry, the mythology, and the dramatic history of their race they may learn at home, in the shelter of their cotta walls. And here they also learn the lessons of hate and contempt. The medium of expression is Arabic script and the local dialect.[165]

In the same year, another outbreak of violence in Sulu escalated from the public humiliation of a prominent Tausug datu disarmed of his *kris* by an overly zealous constabulary officer into armed disorder in the province. Over the next two years, clashes between "outlaw bands" and the constabulary led to "great loss of life on both sides." One local official wrote to an advisor of the governor-general that "the Moros in the eastern end of the island are all restless. Indirectly, all of them are in sympathy with the outlaws."[166]

In 1936, violence erupted again in Lanao in response to the Military Training Act. Maranao fighters reoccupied several *cottas*, prompting commonwealth officials—with President Manuel Quezon's approval—to order an attack. Twenty-three Maranao were killed in the initial attack, after which Philippine Army units and three military aircraft reinforced constabulary troops for a four-month campaign to destroy ninety-one more Maranao *cottas*. During the campaign, enrollment in the schools of Lanao dropped by half.[167] As late as December 1, 1941, exactly one week before the Japanese invasion of the Philippines, *Time* magazine reported in an article entitled "Terror in Jolo" that *juramentado* attacks had averaged one every other day for the previous two months: "Through the Isle of Jolo spread a familiar, deadly-chilling fear ... the Moros were going juramentado again."[168] In a single column on a single page, the article managed to deploy almost every image of the Moro that had been used since 1898 to locate him discursively as an uncivilized, dangerous, sexually deviant Other with "filed teeth" and an irrational penchant for killing Christians as a ticket to a heaven filled with beautiful virgins.

One week later Muslim Filipino resistance to the *gobirno a sarawang a tao* would turn toward the Japanese occupiers. The feared image of the Moro fighter would, briefly, merge into that of the courageous ally in the guerilla struggle against the Japanese. The underlying discourses that had framed colonial attitudes and policies toward Muslim Filipinos since 1898 remained firmly fixed, however, in the psyche of most Americans and Filipinos. For their part, Muslim Filipinos continued their long history of violent resistance when possible and grudging accommodation as necessary in the face of external threats to their cultural, religious, and political independence. Thirty-seven years of pedagogical imperialism had succeeded in making the Muslims of the southern Philippines more or less unwilling citizens of an independent Philippine state, but sociocultural integration was just about as far off as it had been when the American soldiers and schoolteachers arrived in 1898.

The Legacy of Pedagogical Imperialism in the Philippine South

The period of direct American administration of Mindanao and Sulu from 1898 to 1920 marked both a continuation of the three-century-long conflict between Muslims and Christians and an important transformation in the way the conflict was read by many Filipinos and their new colonial rulers. The United States inherited the so-called Moro Problem from Spain as well as Spain's policy of turning to Christian Filipinos as allies in the implementation of colonial policy in the Philippine south. However, in reinterpreting the conflict as a pedagogical problem—the civilization of a "savage race"—instead of a political, economic, and religious confrontation between enemies, the American colonial regime was able to soften both its own and the world's perception of its occupation of Mindanao. Casting the occupation in pedagogical terms, Americans were able to hide their cultural and religious bigotry behind a veil of modern social science scholarship, mask oppressive colonial policy in the rhetoric of modern education, and thus obscure its assault on the cultural and religious identity of Muslim Filipinos behind the benevolent mask of the American and Christian Filipino schoolteacher.

The consequences of this re-visioning of the Moro Problem were profound, particularly since it created an interpretive framework in which resistance could be read as justification of the policy. Muslim Filipinos' resistance of American efforts to lift them out of their "darkness" into the "light" of the modern, civilized, Christian world was seen as confirmation of their ignorance and backwardness. Viewed through the pedagogical lens, the use of military repression was not war against an enemy but rather a form of corporal punishment required to reinforce "lessons" in appropriate behavior to hard-headed, unruly students. Repeated instances of "misbehavior" elicited repeated "punishment." Thus, the Americans' pedagogical imperialism represented a vast social experiment in cultural transformation along lines similar to the psychological theories of behavior modification—utilizing similar tools of positive and negative reinforcement—then gaining prominence in the United States.[169] Mindanao became a vast schoolhouse in which Muslim Filipinos were cast as dull, though educable, students and Christian Filipinos as the new teachers being groomed—not without some misgiving and doubts about their competence—to take over the noble task of "civilizing" the Moro. In effect, the Christian Filipino became an honorary white man, the designated successor to their American mentors as the representative of modern, Western, white, Christian civilization in Mindanao, Sulu, and the other "non-Christian tribes" of the Philippines. In taking up that mantle, they also took up the two tools their mentors used in their work: military muscle and education.

Pedagogical imperialism was the logical consequence of a cultural discourse on civilization that framed white American relations with subordinated peoples of color in the United States itself as well as in Puerto Rico, Hawaii, the Philippines, and its other colonial possessions. The trope of the pioneer, the infantilization of the subordinated Other, the threatening sexual subtext of gender relations so radically different from those sanctioned by Western, Christian morality, and the discourse of scientific modernity lent the civilization discourse a missionary zeal and a sense of historical certainty. The agents of pedagogical imperialism—American and Filipino—were confident that development would lead to integration with the Christian majority, that association between the former enemies would lead to mutual tolerance, and that Muslim Filipinos would gladly surrender traditions that had defined them as distinct peoples for centuries in the interest of progress. And they assumed, moreover, that the religion of Muslim Filipinos could be bracketed out of the whole process, that they could be goaded along the road to civilization without threatening an Islamic identity inextricably bound to cultural traditions and defined historically in opposition to their Christian neighbors to the north.

By the end of direct American rule in 1935, all the regions of what had been the relatively independent territories of the Moros had been thoroughly penetrated by American colonial power. They had been divided into provinces and incorporated into the political and administrative structure of the new Philippine Commonwealth. Muslim Filipinos, however, did not enter the new state as equals but as socioeconomic subordinates in an ostensibly democratic political system that in fact masked a long tradition of semifeudal elite-masses relations that remained more or less untouched by several decades of American egalitarian rhetoric. In this sense, the Muslim masses were no worse off than their Christian counterparts. However, 300 years of ethnic and religious hatred radically intensified the marginalization of the Muslim peasantry from the centers of cultural, economic, and political power in the emerging Philippine state. The growing migration of Christian Filipinos from Luzon and the Visayas into Mindanao made it increasingly impossible for Muslim Filipinos to ignore this fact.

In effect, the colonial mantle that had passed from Spain to the United States was passed on to the Christian Filipino. With their vision blurred by centuries of mutual hostility, their American mentors bequeathed to their Filipino apprentices the twin lenses of feigned objectivity and progressive benevolence rooted in the application of social science to understand the Moro Problem and modern pedagogy to solve it. Wearing these lenses and perhaps intoxicated with their newfound status as representatives of modern civilization, the Christian Filipinos who took over the reigns of government in Mindanao and Sulu as a result of the policy of Filipinization were unable to see that Filipinization—or integration as it would later come to be called—within the framework of pedagogical imperialism meant assimilation and the cultural and religious extinction of Muslim Filipinos. Muslim Filipinos who chose to adopt the values and habits of modern, Western, Christian civilization would be, theoretically, welcomed into the mainstream provided they remained only nominally Muslim. Those who struggled to preserve their religious and cultural distinctiveness justified their social and economic marginalization by their willful rejection of progress.

Many Muslim Filipinos, on the other hand, though with their own vision blurred by centuries of conflict, nevertheless saw clearly the choice pedagogical imperialism offered them, whether it was administered by Americans or Filipinos. Many recognized clearly the choice offered them. Many resisted it. Many would continue to resist it. While widespread Muslim resistance had been effectively crushed by superior American military might in the first decade or so of the century, it sputtered in fits and starts right up until 1941, when it was temporarily redirected toward the Japanese occupation. Less than three decades after the end of the war, however, it would roar back to life. But, by that time the Moro Problem was no longer an American, colonial problem. It was an internal colonial problem of a sovereign Philippines.

NOTES

1. Adams, *Education for Extinction*; Spring, *The Cultural Transformation of a Native American Family and Its Tribe, 1763–1995: A Basket of Apples.*
2. Karnow, *In Our Image: America's Empire in the Philippines.*
3. Brands, *Bound to Empire: The United States and the Philippines*, 60–84.
4. Lardizabal, *Pioneer American Teachers and Philippine Education*; Pecson and Racelis, *Tales of the American Teachers in the Philippines*; Suzuki, "American Education in the Philippines"; Gleeck, *Americans on the Philippine Frontiers*, 42–100.
5. The 13 Islamicized ethno-linguistic groups of the southern Philippines were dubbed Moros by Spanish colonizers in the sixteenth century after the Muslim "Moors" of north Africa whom the Spanish had only recently driven from their homeland. For general accounts of American policy toward Muslim Filipinos, including brief accounts of educational policy, see Gowing, *Mandate in Moroland*; Thomas, "Muslim but Filipino."
6. By "orientalist discourses," I am referring to the complex set of social and academic lenses through which the West regarded and attempted to understand the Muslim world and Asia. See Said, *Orientalism.*
7. Constantino, *The Philippines: A Past Revisited*, 203–236, 251.
8. Bain, *Sitting in Darkness.*
9. Gowing, *Mandate in Moroland*, 26–37.
10. Carpenter, *Report of the Governor of the Department of Mindanao and Sulu (Philippine Islands), 1914*, 325.

11. Gowing, *Mandate in Moroland*, 27–275.
12. Gowing, "Moros and Indians," 1–4.
13. Early on some American soldiers referred to Filipinos as "niggers." See Karnow, *In Our Image*, 140.
14. Gowing, *Mandate in Moroland*, 109.
15. Said, *Orientalism*. See also Pratt, *Imperial Eyes*.
16. Brownell, "What American Ideas of Citizenship May Do for Oriental Peoples: A Moro Experiment," 975.
17. Hayden, "What Next for the Moro?" 638.
18. Barrows, "The Memoirs of David Prescott Barrows," 47–48.
19. Townsend, "Civil Government in the Moro Province," 148.
20. Cited in Gowing, "Moros and Indians," 8.
21. Charles R. Cameron, "Memorandum on Schools of the Moro Province, Zamboanga, Moro Province, July 20, 1907," C-88.1-023-80, Charles R. Cameron Papers, Xavier University Museum and Archives, Cagayan de Oro, Philippines, 2; Cameron, "The Schools of Moroland," 1–2; Brig. Gen. Pershing, *The Annual Report of the Moro Province for the Fiscal Year Ended June 30, 1913*, 3.
22. See, for instance, Herbert Spencer, *Education: Intellectual, Moral, and Physical*.
23. Partridge, *Genetic Philosophy of Education*, 15–31, 91–98.
24. Ibid., 15, 21, 27, 31.
25. Hall, *Educational Problems, Vol. II*, 69–72.
26. Tasker Bliss quoted in Ralph W. Hoyt, *Annual Report of Colonel Ralph W. Hoyt*, 29–30.
27. Bliss, *Annual Report of Brig. General Tasker H. Bliss, U.S. Army, Governor of the Moro Province, 1906*, 81.
28. Bullard, "Road Building Among the Moros," 819.
29. See, e.g., Brig. Gen. Pershing, *The Annual Report of the Governor of the Moro Province for the Fiscal Year Ended June 30, 1913*, 51–52.
30. Barrows, "Memoirs of David Prescott Barrows," 47; Gowing, *Mandate in Moroland*, 326; Teopisto Guingona, "Historical Survey of Policies Pursued by Spain and the United States Toward the Moros in the Philippines," unpublished manuscript report to the Japanese government of the Philippines, 1943, 56.
31. Brownell, "What American Ideas of Citizenship May Do for Oriental Peoples," 979.
32. Lieut. L.B., "The Regular and the Savage," *Lippincott's Magazine* 74 (December 1904), 731, 736.
33. Wood, *First Annual Report of Major General Leonard Wood, Governor of the Moro Province*, 5.
34. Pershing, *Annual Report of the Governor, 1913*, 71.

35. Townsend, "Civil Government in the Moro Province," 148.
36. "District of Lanao," *The Mindanao Herald*, 79.
37. Torrance, "The Philippine Moro," 120.
38. Bliss, "The Government of the Moro Province and Its Problems," 29–31.
39. Wood, *Third Annual Report of Major General Leonard Wood, U.S. Army, Governor of the Moro Province, July 1, 1905 to April 16, 1906*, 27.
40. See, e.g., Saleeby, "The Moro Problem," 7–42.
41. LeRoy, "The Moro and Pagan Question," 1766–1767.
42. Bullard, "Preparing Our Moros for Government," 388.
43. Wood, *First Annual Report of Major General Leonard Wood, Governor of the Moro Province, Zamboanga, Mindanao, P.I., September 1, 1904*, 9.
44. Saleeby, "The Moro Problem," 42.
45. Brownell, "What American Ideas of Citizenship May Do for Oriental Peoples," 975.
46. Brownell, "Turning Savages into Citizens," 921.
47. Saleeby, "The Moro Problem," 35.
48. Pershing, *The Annual Report of the Governor of the Moro Province, 1913*, 59.
49. Torrance, "The Philippine Moro," preface.
50. Jones, "Our Mandate Over Moroland," 609.
51. Barrows, "Memoirs."
52. Cameron, "The Schools of Moroland," 35.
53. Carpenter, *Report of the Governor of the Department of Mindanao and Sulu (Philippine Islands) 1914*, 325.
54. Pershing, *Report of the Governor of the Moro Province*, 81.
55. Saleeby, "Studies in Moro History, Law and Religion."
56. The Government of the Philippine Islands, Department of Public Instruction, *Twenty-Third Annual Report of the Director of Education*.
57. See, for instance, Gowing, *Mandate in Moroland*.
58. Wood, *First Annual Report of Major General Leonard Wood*, 14; Carpenter, *Report of the Governor of the Department of Mindanao and Sulu, 1914*, 351.
59. Wood, *First Annual Report*, 14; Carpenter, *Report of the Governor of the Department of Mindanao and Sulu, 1914*, 351.
60. The Government of the Philippine Islands, Department of Public Instruction, *Twenty-First Annual Report*, 82–83. It must be noted, however, that a substantial increase in numbers of schools, teachers, and enrollments resulted from the addition of the provinces of Bukidnon and Agusan, both predominately Christian, to the Department of Mindanao and Sulu in 1914.

61. Charles R. Cameron, "Seventh Annual Report of the Superintendent of Schools of the Moro Province, School Year 1909–1910," C-88.1-025-80, Charles R. Cameron Papers, Xavier University Museum and Archives, Cagayan de Oro, Philippines; Carpenter, *Report of the Governor of the Department of Mindanao and Sulu*, 352; The Government of the Philippine Islands, *Twenty-First Annual Report of the Director of Education*, 85.
62. Carpenter, *Report of the Governor*, 349, 351.
63. Wood, *First Annual Report*, 14.
64. Cameron, "Sixth Annual Report" and "Seventh Annual Report" in Cameron Papers.
65. Pershing, *The Annual Report of the Governor of the Moro Province, 1913*, 51–52. My estimates here are based on a combination of Pershing's figures for public schools and Carpenter's figures for private schools in the same year. See Carpenter, *Report of the Governor of the Department of Mindanao and Sulu*, 353.
66. Bliss, *Annual Report 1906*, 80.
67. Ibid., 83.
68. Torrance, "The Philippine Moro," 139.
69. Cameron, "Seventh Annual Report of the Superintendent of Schools," Cameron Papers, 21–22.
70. Bulletin No. 7-1904, *Courses of Instruction for the Public Schools of the Philippine Islands Prescribed by the General Superintendent of Education, Manila, P.I., June 15, 1904* (Manila: Bureau of Printing, 1904), 3–4.
71. Bulletin No. 6-1904, Bureau of Education, *Report of Industrial Exhibits of the Philippine Schools at the Louisiana Purchase Exposition* (Manila: Bureau of Public Printing, 1904), 28–29.
72. Charles R. Cameron, "Conditions in Mindanao and Sulu, 1913," C-22.2-028-80, Charles R. Cameron Papers, 9.
73. Wood, *First Annual Report*, 15; Wood, *Third Annual Report*, 15; Bliss, *Annual Report, 1908*, 14.
74. Hayden, "What Next for the Moro?" 637.
75. Torrance, "The Philippine Moro," 152.
76. Jones, "Our Mandate Over Moroland," 612.
77. The Government of the Philippine Islands, Department of Public Instruction, "A Statement of Organization, Aims and Conditions of Service in the Bureau of Education" (Manila: Bureau of Printing, 1911), 2.
78. Bulletin No. 7-1904. "Courses of Instruction for the Public Schools of the Philippine Islands," 3, 6, 9.
79. Cameron, "Sixth Annual Report of the Superintendent of Public Instruction," 10.

80. Cameron, "Memorandum on Schools of the Moro Province," 2.
81. Cameron, "Sixth Annual Report of the Superintendent of Public Instruction," 12–13; Pershing, *The Annual Report of the Governor of the Moro Province 1913*, 32.
82. Wood, *First Annual Report, 1904*, 14–15.
83. Bliss, *Annual Report, 1906*, 82.
84. Saleeby, *Sulu Reader for the Public Schools of the Moro Province*.
85. I take this notion of a hidden curriculum from Jane Roland Martin, *Changing the Educational Landscape: Philosophy, Women and Curriculum* (New York: Routledge, 1994), 154–169.
86. A Muslim Filipino scholar advocated education for just this reason. See Saber, "Marginal Leadership in a Culture-Contact Situation," 1–55.
87. Isidro, *The Moro Problem: An Approach Through Education*, 34.
88. Jaime Dumarpa, "An Exploratory Study of Maranao Muslims' Concepts of Land Ownership," 7–72; Rodil, "Ancestral Domain," 233–248.
89. McKenna, *Muslim Rulers and Rebels*, 70–71.
90. Rodil, "Ancestral Domain," 236–237. See also Cameron, "Conditions in Mindanao and Sulu," 10.
91. Jones, "Our Mandate Over Moroland," 612.
92. Carpenter, "Report of the Governor, 1914," 350.
93. Disoma, *The Meranao*, 18–53.
94. Pershing, *The Annual Report of the Governor, 1913*, 71.
95. Ibid., 72.
96. Torrance, "The Philippine Moro," 171.
97. Pershing, *The Annual Report of the Governor, 1913*, 31.
98. Finley, "The Development of the District of Zamboanga," 63.
99. Saleeby, "The Moro Problem," 34; Cameron, "Schools of Moroland," 35.
100. Pershing, *Report of the Governor, 1913*, 33.
101. Ibid., 58–59.
102. Carpenter, *Report of the Governor, 1914*, 354, 388–390.
103. Bliss, "The Government of the Moro Province and Its Problems," 4.
104. Lieut. L.B., "The Regular and the Savage," 732.
105. Brownell, "Turning Savages into Citizens," 930–931.
106. Gowing, *Mandate in Moroland*, 161.
107. Hoyt, *Annual Report, 1909*, 29.
108. Pershing, *Report of the Governor, 1913*, 62–63.
109. Carpenter, *Report of the Governor, 1914*, 338.
110. Hayden, "What Next for the Moro?" 636.
111. The juramentado was an individual who had undergone a religious ritual in preparation for a suicide attack on the enemies of Islam in the Philippines. Lieut. L.B., "The Regular and the Savage," 736.

112. Hayden, "What Next for the Moro?" 642.
113. Wood, *First Annual Report*, 21.
114. Bliss, *Annual Report, 1908*, 25.
115. Hoyt, *Annual Report, 1909*, 20.
116. Pershing, *Annual Report, 1913*, 33.
117. Cameron, "The Schools of Moroland," 35–36.
118. Torrance, "The Philippine Moro," 201.
119. Gowing, *Mandate in Moroland*, 268.
120. Thomas, "Muslim but Filipino," 328.
121. Ibid., 82, 88.
122. Ibid., 140.
123. Ibid., 260.
124. Ibid., 154.
125. Ibid., 132–133.
126. Cook, "Public Education in the Philippine Islands," 24.
127. The Government of the Philippine Islands, Department of Public Instruction, *Twenty-Seventh Annual Report*, 94–100.
128. The Government of the Philippine Islands, Department of Public Instruction, *Sixteenth Annual Report of the Director of Education*, 57.
129. The Government of the Philippine Islands, Department of Public Instruction, *Nineteenth Annual Report*, 72.
130. The Government of the Philippine Islands, Department of Public Instruction, *Twenty-First Annual Report*, 50.
131. Bureau of Education, *Nineteenth Annual Report*, 72.
132. Thomas, "Muslim but Filipino," 205–210.
133. Laubach, "A Literacy Campaign Among the Moros," 41; Laubach, "Moslems Under the American Flag," 347.
134. The Government of the Philippine Islands, *Twenty-Seventh Annual Report*, 60; Caulkins, "Public Education in Mindanao-Sulu Philippine Islands Under the American Regime," 12, 22–23.
135. The Government of the Philippine Islands, *Twenty-Seventh Annual Report*, 61–62, 122.
136. Ibid., 62, 126, 135.
137. Caulkins, "Public Education," 26–30.
138. Osias, *The Philippine Readers, Book II, III*.
139. Osias, *The Philippine Reader, Book IV*, iii.
140. Osias, *The Philippine Reader, Book VI*, 187; Osias, *The Philippine Reader, Book VII*, 91.
141. Ibid., 257, 260.
142. The Government of the Philippine Islands, Department of Public Instruction, *The Philippine Islands: Information for Americans Thinking of Entering the Philippine Teaching Service*, 28.

143. Board of Educational Survey, *A Survey of the Educational System of the Philippine Islands*, 101–103.
144. Cited in Thomas, "Muslim but Filipino," 175–176.
145. The Government of the Philippine Islands, Department of Public Instruction, *Twenty-Second Annual Report*, 40.
146. Caulkins, "Public Education," 108.
147. Thomas, "Muslim but Filipino," 34.
148. Caulkins, "Public Education," 96.
149. Ibid., 98.
150. Ibid., 102.
151. Cited in Thomas, "Muslim but Filipino," 176.
152. Ibid., 133.
153. Ibid., 79, 243.
154. Ibid., 80.
155. Ibid., 80, 102, 120.
156. Ibid., 96.
157. Ibid., 241.
158. Ibid., 252–255.
159. Ibid., 257.
160. Hayden, "What Next for the Moro?" 637.
161. Thomas, "Muslim but Filipino," 156.
162. Hayden, "What Next for the Moro?" 642.
163. Laubach, "A Literacy Campaign Among the Moros," 38.
164. Hayden, "What Next for the Moro?"
165. "Americanizing the Moros," *The New Republic* 65 (January 21, 1931), 260.
166. Cited in Thomas, "Muslim but Filipino," 190.
167. Ibid., 275–279.
168. "Terror in Jolo," *Time* 38 (December 1, 1941), 18.
169. Thorndike, *Education: A First Book*.

CHAPTER 4

Faith in School: Educational Policy Responses to Muslim Unrest in the Philippine Republic

By the time Filipinos finally regained self-government with the inauguration of the Philippine Commonwealth in 1935, faith in education as an indispensable tool in the achievement of social cohesion and economic modernization had been firmly established among politicians, educational policy makers, and ordinary citizens. This faith, moreover, generally included a belief in the effectiveness of education in helping to resolve the ethnic and religious tensions that continued to plague the Philippine south. However, the ongoing nature of these tensions revealed this assumption of education's efficacy in resolving such a conflict as in fact a form of faith, a belief held in the absence of or in spite of evidence regarding its warrantability. Guided by this faith, policy makers would tend to continue the general policies established by the American colonial regime, leaving unexamined the fundamental assumptions about civilization, progress, and the nature of Muslim Filipino relations with the emerging state that had shaped American policies since 1898. Thus, trusting to the efficacy of schooling to resolve the so-called Moro Problem in the fullness of time, Filipino leaders could turn to what was perceived to be the more pressing problems of the reborn Philippine Republic. In doing so, they not only failed to attend to a continuing chronic problem in the Philippine body politic, they also missed an opportunity to rethink the sorts of educational policies that might have been more likely to further the goal of mitigating ethno-religious tensions in Mindanao and Sulu.

Educational Policy in the Philippine Commonwealth

In 1935, the Philippines began what was planned as a decade of self-rule under a commonwealth government in preparation for the reestablishment of full independence in 1945. After centuries of colonial rule, after the brutal suppression of the Filipino independence struggle by American troops between 1898 and 1902, and after more than three decades of peaceful, but persistent, agitation for independence, Filipinos embarked upon complete self-government and eventual independence determined to forge a free, independent, and prosperous Philippine state from the northernmost extremes of Luzon to the last islands of the Sulu Archipelago. One of the greatest challenges to building this new nation on the foundations of colonial borders would be the tremendous geographic, cultural, and linguistic diversity contained within those borders. And nowhere in the archipelago was this challenge greater or more pressing than in Mindanao. For here, where much of the natural resources crucial to the economic success of the nation lay, was also where some of the greatest threats to the security of the new state festered. Mindanao was farthest from the centers of political power. It contained a large and restive Muslim minority and growing Japanese economic concerns. Measures had to be taken to ensure the future of a unified Philippine state.

The Commonwealth government's response to this challenge was to cultivate and promote the spirit of Filipino nationalism that had begun to develop in response to colonial domination toward the end of Spanish rule. It pursued this goal primarily through the medium of the school. No less a person than the president of the Commonwealth, Manuel Quezon, took an active interest in educational policy, seeing in it the means to a national spiritual reconstruction that would reorient Filipino identity and values from their primary affiliation with family and province toward loyalty to the emerging Philippine state. According to Quezon, the primary purpose of education was to make the individual a better servant of the state.[1] "The schools teach nationalism," wrote one educational leader of the period, "not only through the textbooks, but through every activity that may inculcate patriotism."[2]

Camilo Osias, Quezon's technical assistant on educational matters and later education leader and senator in the Philippine Republic, recommended in 1940, for instance, that all students be taught to revere a "patriotic shrine" consisting of a "trinity of objects" to include a portrait of Jose Rizal, the father of the independence movement against Spain, the president of the Philippines, and a map of the country.[3] Thus, nationalism became a central value to be inculcated through education in a concerted effort to subordinate provincialism, ethnolinguistic identity, and familism to national identity and loyalty to the state. In doing so, Quezon was effectively trying to radically reorient Filipino cultural values along lines that he believed were necessary for the success of an independent Philippine state and were, not coincidentally, in the interests of the social elites who would govern it.

While patriotism was "the keynote of this educational policy," religious faith was a second broad goal of educational policy in the Philippine Commonwealth. Though this objective was never stated in anything more specific than a broad monotheism, its implementation in an overwhelmingly Catholic country ruled for more than three centuries through Catholic religious orders could hardly avoid being interpreted in explicitly Christian terms. From the commonwealth period to the present, the inculcation of a monotheistic faith in God and nationalism have been at or near the top of the list of values to be inculcated through Philippine education. Quezon's Code of Civic and Ethical Principles, which by executive order supplemented educational goals stipulated in the commonwealth constitution, listed "faith in Divine Providence that guides the destinies of men and nations" as the first of sixteen ethical principles which should be promoted among Filipinos through the medium of the schools. Love of country was a close second.[4] While Philippine constitutions would include language almost identical to that of the US Constitution guaranteeing church-state separation, other language within them would make clear that the nation might aspire to neutrality between monotheistic faiths, but not to neutrality between such faiths and secularism.[5]

In this aspect and many others, Quezon's Code represented a mix of Philippine historical experience, long-standing sociocultural biases, and political hope. By the end of the nineteenth century, a nascent Filipino identity had emerged out of the colonial experience, expressing itself in a struggle for independence from Spain inspired by Jose Rizal and led by Andres Bonifacio, Emilio Aguinaldo, and others. While American intervention in 1898 thwarted this initial effort to establish an independent state, the desire for independence continued, increasingly expressing itself in an American-inspired democratic discourse. Democratic political discourse, however, obscured a cultural and historical reality in which the marriage of religious and civil authority in the Spanish regime had given rise to a semifeudal society in which a handful of elite families dominated the political and economic life of the emerging nation.[6] Thus, nationalism, interpreted as loyalty to a state defined by colonial borders and reverence for a pantheon of heroes, largely from Luzon, who led the independence movement against Spain, was to be erected upon a cultural foundation of Filipino Catholicism, effectively defining Filipino identity as a dialogical product of the encounter with Spanish imperialism. In textbooks, this would be frequently expressed in the observation that the Philippines is the only Christian nation in Asia.[7] An intimate relationship between religious and political authority, therefore, was of long standing in the Philippines and unlikely to be supplanted by an American rhetoric on church-state separation continually contradicted by its own Protestant Christian biases.

The principles of the Quezon Code, moreover, reflected democratic aspirations, loyalty to the state, and elite contempt for the masses. The Code counseled Filipinos to love their country and to be prepared to sacrifice for it, to live a clean and frugal life, and to respect the dignity of manual labor, among other maxims.[8] Elsewhere Quezon condemned the "easy going parasitism" and "social inefficiency" of the common Filipino.[9] Thus, the Code, in setting out ideals, also contained an implicit critique of the masses as being *not* clean, frugal, or hardworking. Reading beyond the veneer of democratic principles, Quezon's Code and the educational policies designed to promote its objectives defined Quezon's agenda for "national spiritual reconstruction." In drawing on a more or less common religious identity to help bring about a national identity defined in terms of loyalty to a state ruled by traditional elites, it more or less successfully obscured—at the policy level if not the practical—the competing class interests of the elite and the masses and inadvertently reinforced the long-held sense among ordinary Muslims and Christians that Moro and Filipino were separate national identities.

The overall policy of the Philippine government toward Muslim Filipinos remained more or less what it had been through the Spanish and American colonial period: the full and complete integration of Muslims and their traditional territory into a Philippine state geographically defined by Spanish territorial claims and administered by a Manila-based sociopolitical elite. Though the Spanish efforts to Christianize the Moros were dropped in favor of constitutional guarantees of religious freedom, the discursive framework of Filipino national identity into which Muslims were to be integrated was largely defined in terms of the political, cultural, and religious experience of the Manila-based elite and the Christian majority. The power and privilege of this elite, in turn, rested historically upon their embrace of the basic values and fundamental assumptions of their former colonial masters, thus perpetuating the discursive patterns that had shaped government policies toward the Muslims since 1898 and colored Christian attitudes toward them since the sixteenth century. The basic contours of what was essentially an internal colonial relationship, as well as the explicit policy of integration, would frame the government's responses to the Muslim minority through at least the first four decades of independence.

Initially, and through the first few decades of independence, Philippine governments' responses to what had long been known as the Moro Problem were broadly twofold: to downplay the significance of the problem and to assume that education would solve what remained of it. In his address to the first national assembly of the new commonwealth government, President Manuel Quezon stated: "The so-called Moro Problem is a thing of the past. We are giving our Mohammedan brethren the best government they ever had and we are showing them our devoted interest in their welfare and advancement."[10] And since the Moro Problem was a thing of the past, the Philippine government could proceed with its plans for dealing with the economic and national security challenges it faced in Mindanao: colonization by Christian Filipinos.

> The time has come when we should systematically proceed with and bring about the colonization and economic development of Mindanao ... If, therefore, we are resolved to conserve Mindanao for ourselves and our posterity, we must bend all efforts to occupy and develop it and guard it against avarice and greed ... Every cent spent for the purpose will mean increased national wealth and greater national security.[11]

Quite explicit in Quezon's language is a dichotomization of "us" and "them" or "they" that corresponds with the historic dichotomization of Christian and Muslim in Philippine society. Their land is to be the object of our colonization, and by implication, they are to be our colonial wards. Thus, from the first presidential address of the first national assembly, the internal colonial relationship between Manila and Muslim Mindanao is established.

The effort to homogenize cultural and religious differences that might impede the promotion of nationalism seemed to require a centralization of educational decision-making in which, it was assumed, a unified curriculum and educational policies imposed throughout the country would gradually unify the disparate ethnic and linguistic communities of the archipelago into a single Filipino identity. This meant, in part, denying the educational significance of such differences. Camilo Osias, chairman of the National Council of Education, suggested this in 1940:

> The education of minority groups and other special classes is simplified by the absence of deep-seated racial divisions or prejudices and of social castes in the Philippines. There is now a wonderful homogeneity of the population—racial, political, economic, social, and cultural.[12]

Somehow the cultural and religious differences that had fueled more than three centuries of Muslim–Christian conflict had disappeared in less than 20 years.

In the context of such an effort to create a common national identity, differences, as they were during the American regime, tended to be recast as deficiencies if they were seen as undermining of the nationalist project. In this way, the erasure of differences and assimilation of minorities into a mainstream defined by the traditional elite were redefined as economic and cultural uplift. This had been expressed in the Jones Law, which had created a Philippine Legislature in 1916 and ultimately led in 1920 to the direct administration of Muslims by Christian Filipinos through the Bureau of Non-Christian Tribes. It also clearly articulated the policy to be followed toward these "tribes."[13]

> Foster by all adequate means, and in a systematic, rapid, and complete manner, the moral, material, economic, social and political development of those regions, always having in view the aim of rendering permanent the mutual intelligence between, and complete fusion of, the Christian and non-Christian elements populating the provinces of the Archipelago.[14]

Commonwealth policy toward Muslims represented, essentially, a continuation of the American policy of integration, albeit with a greater emphasis on speed of that integration than most American officials had thought wise. This was, no doubt, partly driven by the threats to the national and economic security of the Philippines that unrest in

Mindanao represented, but it is likely that it also reflected a tendency on the part of national leaders to neglect Muslim Filipino concerns unless they were confronted with open conflict.

MUSLIMS, EDUCATION, AND INTEGRATION IN THE PHILIPPINE REPUBLIC

This pattern of reaction in the absence of a proactive policy toward Muslim Filipinos continued throughout the first decades of Philippine independence. After the incredible devastation of World War II, the attention of the first two presidents of the Philippines—Manuel Roxas and Elpidio Quirino—was largely focused on postwar reconstruction and recovery. The old Moro Problem, quiet at the moment, was placed on a back burner. This inattentiveness was further exacerbated by the Hukbalahap rebellion in central Luzon, an armed peasant revolt that continued well into the 1950s.[15] With a Marxist inspired uprising on their doorstep, a war-ravaged national infrastructure to attend to, and a tendency to dismiss Muslim Filipino alienation from the mainstream as an artifact of the past gradually being erased by education and development, government leaders, perhaps inevitably, paid little attention to Muslim Filipino concerns.

This inattentiveness and insensitivity to Muslim concerns were exhibited in the governments' response to the Hukbalahap rebellion, an uprising of landless peasants in the heavily populated agricultural regions of central Luzon. The insurgency reached its height in the administration of President Elpidio Quirino, whose defense minister and successor to the presidency, Ramon Magsaysay, established the Economic Development Corps, a plan to resettle surrendered Huk guerillas on ancestral Muslim lands in Lanao and Cotabato.[16] Thus, the government reacted to population and land ownership problems in the north in precisely the same way the American colonial authorities had reacted: government-supported emigration of Christian peasants to government-claimed land in the Muslim regions of Mindanao. This inevitably exacerbated growing tensions between Muslims and Christians in the region over land ownership. And the introduction of significant numbers of Christian immigrants with a history of armed anti-Japanese and anti-government action into a Muslim region with its own long history of armed resistance would prove an explosive mix in the early 1970s.

Educational policy in the new Philippine state generally continued the trends established under the colonial and Commonwealth governments. The National Council of Education, drawing on the educational aims stipulated in the Philippine Constitution, listed the educational system's primary goal as "impress[ing] upon our people that they are citizens of the Republic" and the second as promoting among Filipinos "an abiding faith in Divine Providence." In 1950, the Philippine Congress, in a concurrent resolution, reversed the order of these overall aims in charging education with teaching Filipinos to live a "moral life guided by faith in God and love for fellow man" and "to love and serve the Republic of the Philippines." Then again, in 1957, the Board of National Education defined the schools' aims as inculcating "moral and spiritual values inspired by an abiding faith in God" and producing an "enlightened, patriotic, useful and upright citizenry."[17]

While nationalism and religious faith continued to be expressed as the first or second broad goal of Philippine education, other policies addressed more concrete objectives, revealing the practical challenges the educational system faced in a newly independent country just emerging from a devastating war. Educational policy makers faced the challenge of extending access to elementary and secondary education to more children and providing the teachers, facilities, and books to accommodate them. Educators needed to find ways to keep children in school once they started. There were deep concerns about the training and compensation of teachers. Adult education and vocational training also absorbed policy makers' attention.[18] But the values explicitly articulated in the goal of fostering a common Filipino identity consistently posited that identity in essentialist terms: *the* Filipino way of life, *our* culture, *the* Filipino personality, *the* Filipino language, *the* philosophy of Filipino life, and the *true* Filipino.[19] While the religious values to be inculcated were not generally articulated in such explicit terms, there can be little doubt that, where that objective was explicitly implemented, it was most likely expressed within a Christian framework.

While educational policy makers were not blind to the challenge religious and ethnic diversity posed for their social and economic agendas, they had considerable faith in the power of a centralized educational system and a unified curriculum to subordinate, if not entirely erase, that diversity to a common Filipino identity. The particular challenge posed by a largely unintegrated Muslim minority was not entirely ignored. However, it was widely assumed that education would solve that and just about all other problems.

> We underline the imperative necessity of developing among the non-Christian elements a spirit of dynamic Filipinism, love of country, and loyalty to the government and free institutions. Exceptional care and attention should be paid to insulating them from subversive propaganda and preventing borers from within … Widespread education, sound and liberal and patriotic, is the best defense against ideological fifth elements.[20]

As long as the old Moro Problem was not an active revolt, it could be safely regarded as just another element of the diverse cultures lumped together under the label "non-Christian tribes" in need of benevolent modernization and assimilation.

The Moro Problem was still festering, however. The collapse of governmental authority in Mindanao during the war had facilitated the reassertion of former attitudes and habits toward external authority.[21] Among these attitudes were a sense of identity rooted in Islam and ethnicity and a profound mistrust of government education. One Filipino educator of the period wrote that 50 years of American education had had little effect on the life of common folk, who still identified themselves as Muslims rather than Filipinos.[22] Many Muslims continued to eye government schools with deep suspicion, believing that their purpose was to convert their children to Christianity. The curriculum, standardized throughout the country by a Manila-centered bureaucracy, was widely dismissed as "basically Christian" and hence anti-Muslim. Textbooks were criticized for content that was either offensive or culturally unfamiliar to Muslim students.[23] The situation was compounded by the shortage of resources and poor facilities that plagued other areas of Philippine education. The result, for instance, in Lanao province was extremely low participation rates among school-age children. And where children did attend school, Muslims and Christians tended to self-segregate.[24] One Muslim educational scholar laid much of the blame for the sad state of Muslim Filipino education at the time on "a highly centralized bureaucracy and non-flexible curriculum which doesn't reflect local culture."[25]

One result of Muslim Filipino mistrust and dissatisfaction with government education was a growing tendency to send their children to Islamic schools.[26] While Islamic instruction had been a feature of Muslim Filipino society ever since the arrival of Islam in the fourteenth century, the early 1950s saw an Islamic revival among the new generation of Muslim leaders educated in secular Filipino schools. One consequence of this resurgence was the establishment of formal Islamic schools such as the Kamilol Islam Institute in Marawi City in 1954, which expanded to collegiate level in 1959 under the name Jamiatul Philippines Al-Islamia. Muslim missionaries from the Middle East as well as Filipino Muslims educated in Islamic countries contributed to the growing network of *madaris* in the region throughout the 1950s and 1960s.[27] This network provided educational alternatives for those Muslim Filipinos suspicious of government educational objectives and desirous of fostering their identity as Muslims rather than Filipinos. Thus, the continued development of two parallel educational systems—Islamic and governmental—with the contradictory aims of orienting Filipino Muslim identity either toward an essentialized Filipinism or a purified Islamism contributed to the division of Muslim and Christian Filipinos.[28]

Muslim Filipino dissatisfaction in the early 1950s was not confined to the development of Islamic educational alternatives, however. Between 1952 and 1953, the so-called Kamilon rebellion peaked in Sulu, tying down up to 3000 troops in a campaign that lasted four years. During the same period, the Datu Tawantawan uprising in Lanao del Norte further refocused government attention on the Moro Problem.[29] During the Sulu rebellion, the House Committee on National Minorities of the Philippine Congress appointed a commission of three Muslim congressmen to investigate the causes of the turmoil. The committee's report to Congress in 1954 stated:

> More than any other factor involved which had given rise to the so-called Moro Problem is the educational phase. For if the Muslims had been prepared and their ignorance, which is the root cause of the problem, had been wiped out by education ... little if any at all would be such problems as economic, social, and political which now face the government ... *Education could have nipped the whole problem in the bud* ... (emphasis added)[30]

The Moro Problem, the committee reported, was a problem of "inculcating into Muslim minds that they are Filipinos and this government is their own and that they are part of it." The solution was "integration of the Muslim Filipinos into the Philippine body politic in order to effect in a more complete measure their social, moral and political advancement."[31] Thus, into the mid-1950s the discursive framework of government policy toward the Muslim minority perpetuated the civilization discourse of the American colonial regime. Though the language deployed is shifting from the overtly racist rhetoric of civilization and savagery to the language of development-underdevelopment, it nevertheless continues to position Muslims rhetorically as socially and morally backward, that is, savage. At the same time, government efforts to route all international trade via Manila cast the ancient Muslim Filipino trade via Sulu and Zamboanga to the rest of insular Southeast Asia as smuggling.[32] Thus, though the language is softened somewhat, the discourse continues to portray Muslim Filipinos as the dangerous, backward, violent, and morally degenerate pirates they had been seen as since the Spanish regime. Furthermore, as the committee's report demonstrates, the government's response to Muslims' continuing refusal to be Filipino and recognize the government as their own is to deploy the same two instruments of colonial policy deployed and perfected by the American regime: military pacification against overt resistance and educational assimilation against cultural resistance. After five decades of effort to resolve the Moro Problem, the Philippine government still had faith in education as a means of resolving ethno-religious conflict, augmented, as necessary, by the periodic application of corporal punishment of these recalcitrant pupils by the Philippine armed forces.

One of the first official government responses to the Alonto Report was the passage of Republic Act No. 1387 in 1955, which provided for the establishment of a state university at Marawi City in the Muslim-dominated province of Lanao del Sur. The Philippine Congress created the university "to serve primarily as a vital government instrument in promoting greater understanding between Muslims and Christians."[33] Aside from providing higher educational opportunities to local Muslim students, the university's objectives included the economic development of Mindanao, the preservation of indigenous cultures, and, most importantly, promoting the integration of Muslims into the Philippine mainstream. At least at the level of its mission statement, the government's charge to the university to study and preserve Muslim Filipino culture suggested a softening of the long-lived civilization discourse which quite clearly postulated the surrender of Muslim religious and cultural identity as the price of civilization. However, as Edward Said (1979) demonstrated in his genealogy of academic orientalism in Europe, such cross-cultural study carried out within a discursive framework of civilization-savagery, modernity-tradition, and development-underdevelopment continues to position the object of such study as exotic Other and present culture as a degenerate shadow of past glories.[34] The effect of such orientalist academic discourses can be to privilege the scholar, whether a cultural outsider or an insider who has assimilated himself to majority expectations, while leaving relatively unexamined the distortions of power and privilege in contemporary majority–minority relations. The continuing power of such discourses to perpetuate age-old Christian Filipino stereotypes of Muslim Filipinos presented the university with the challenge of recruiting and retaining faculty to come to an area whose image had long been shaped by a colonial pioneer discourse that cast life there as a frontier existence threatened by cattle rustlers, petty outlaws, and the dreaded *juramentado*.[35]

Another serious problem was the lack of Muslim students ready for college work. By the time the university began operation in 1961, for instance, only 17.7 percent of school-age children in the province were in school, and only 2 percent of these were in high school.[36] The university responded by establishing its own network of feeder schools, but by the late 1970s, the university had only managed to graduate a little over 300 local Muslim students.[37] In addition, the university faced from the beginning the challenge of retaining the character of a national university from the pervasive influence of a local culture whose values were often powerfully at odds with the fundamental values of a modern, western university. Thus, the survival of a strong sense of Maranao cultural identity as well as Islamic religious identity in the surrounding society tended to frustrate the integration agenda behind the university's establishment. Today, while the university can claim numerous successes, it has clearly not lived up to the goal of integrating Muslim Filipinos into the national mainstream: Lanao del Sur remains today one of the centers of Muslim resistance to the national government.[38] In fact, it might be fair to say that the university has in fact been assimilated into the local Maranao Muslim culture rather than serving as the instrument for integrating Maranao Muslims into the mainstream of Philippine society.

Two years after passing the legislation establishing Mindanao State University, the Philippine Congress passed Republic Act 1888 creating the Commission on National Integration, the latest of a line of government entities—the Moro Province (1903–1913), the Department of Mindanao and Sulu (1914–1917), the Bureau of Non-Christian Tribes (1917–1937), the Commissioner for Mindanao and Sulu (1937–1950), and the Office of the President (1950–1957)—tasked with fostering the development and integration of Muslim Filipinos.[39] This succession of government bureaucracies charged with resolving the Moro Problem was, in effect, merely name changes for a government policy toward Muslim Filipinos that remained virtually indistinguishable from American colonial policy. American policy toward Muslim Filipinos was articulated in the Jones Law of 1916.

> To foster by all adequate means, and in a systematic, rapid, and complete manner, the moral, material, economic, social and political development of those regions, always having in view the aim of rendering permanent the mutual intelligence between, and complete fusion of, the Christian and non-Christian elements populating the provinces of the Archipelago.[40]

Philippine government policy toward Muslim Filipinos, as articulated in the enacting legislation of the Commission on National Integration (CNI) was a paraphrase of the American policy articulated in the Jones Law.

> To effectuate in a more rapid complete manner the economic, social, moral and political advancement of the non-Christian Filipinos or national cultural minorities and to render real, complete and permanent the integration of all said national cultural minorities into the body politic, creating the Commission on National Integration charged with said functions.[41]

Forty years on, after colonization, Japanese occupation, and a decade of independence, government policy toward the Muslim minority remained the same as it had been under American colonial rule. Development-related activities remained largely consistent as well, though the Commission's objectives were somewhat more comprehensive, focusing attention on economic and agricultural development, land reform, legal assistance, infrastructure development, and more. Only two of the Commission's fifteen objectives were explicitly educational. The education division, however, soon became the most active and well funded of the five divisions.

> The Commission considers education as one of the powerful forces that can accelerate the efforts toward national integration. After the National Cultural Minorities have been properly schooled, they will find it easy to adapt themselves to our ways and customs.[42]

Tellingly, the language of the Commission recapitulates the dichotomization of Christian and non-Christian—read Muslim—identity established under Spanish colonization and perpetuated through American colonial discourses right up to the late 1950s. "They" are not quite real Filipinos. Integration-adaptation to differences is one way: "they will find it easy to adapt themselves to our ways and customs." Expressed in a context where difference is expressed largely in terms of religion and where national identity is conceived practically, albeit unofficially, against a foil of Christian identity, this adaptation to "our" ways strongly implies religious conversion as part of that adaptation. And the instrument of this adaptation is, as it had been since 1903, the school.

The activities of the education division, however, were focused largely on providing scholarships for minority students to attend university. Approximately 70 percent of its funding was devoted to this purpose.[43] But even the effectiveness of this effort was severely limited by corruption revealed in government investigations in the early 1960s, which found that many scholarships had gone to relatives, as political favors, and to "ghost students."[44] By the time the Commission was disbanded in 1975, it had enabled 3000, mostly Muslim, students to obtain a college education but had achieved little else.[45] Writing just a few years before the dissolution of the Commission in a retrospective report of its impact, Clavel (1969) reported that few CNI scholars had made use of their educations and that "the Commission has ... not permanently improved the socio-economic conditions of the minorities."[46] Two years later, the Filipinas Foundation (1971) reported "an embarrassing lack of concern on the part of the national government and private sector to understand Muslims as Filipinos, much less to contribute toward their social and economic uplift."[47] Clearly, by the early 1970s, the effort to promote integration via educational policy had not accomplished much.

Aside from the obvious problems of inadequate funding, corruption, and mismanagement that often plague development efforts, the Commission's integration effort was further complicated by a conceptual framework with origins in the earliest days of the US colonial regime. The US effort to develop and integrate Muslim Filipinos was framed in a discourse regarding civilization, which drew on social Darwinism and political progressivism to place cultures on a continuum of civilization running from savagery on one end—epitomized by Muslim Filipinos—and civilization on the other—epitomized by white, Euro-American,

Christian culture. Education was the progressive means of moving cultures as far along that continuum as they were naturally capable of moving. While the civilization discourse represented a considerable improvement over the genocidal violence carried out against Native Americans, it remained fundamentally racist.

By the 1950s and 1960s, proponents of integration had largely dropped the rhetoric of civilization, but had more or less retained the framework of the civilization discourse in the language of development. In attempting to define who and what constituted the National Cultural Minorities that were to be the target of CNI integration efforts, the Commission defined its clients largely in terms of their proximity to modern, Western culture.

> It is a Cultural Minority in that its culture differs from that of most natives of the Philippines whose original native, or Asian-influenced culture has been strongly modified for many generations of contact and changes in ethical, cultural, and religious beliefs, practices, law, customs, government, education ... from Euro-American sources. The Native Asian basis has been thoroughly mixed and fused with Occidentalism or Westernized so that the modern Filipino majority culture while still physically Asian and tropical is heavily weighted ethnically and psychologically by Euro-American and North Atlantic influences.[48]

Thus, development and modernity continued to be defined in a civilization discourse defined in Western terms, and integration via education was the means of bringing minorities, particularly Muslim Filipinos, into conformity with that ideal. This view is rather clearly articulated in the conclusion of Clavel's (1969) report on the first decade of the CNI.

> If the minorities are to become active members of the national community, they should abandon, as the price they have to pay, their backward ways and adopt those that are in consonance with modern living. Inevitably, they have to observe some values upheld by the majority group...in the process of helping them attain a higher degree of civilization, they have to discard some of their traditional values and customs. It is suggested that they retain those [values and customs] [that] do not constitute a barrier to national progress and an irritant to their relations with one another or with the members of the majority group.[49]

Here, in language almost identical to that deployed by the American governors-general of the Moro Province—Leonard Wood, Tasker Bliss, and John Pershing—was the old civilization discourse. Modernity and civilization are embodied in our—Christian Filipino—values because, as the definition of National Cultural Minority cited above clearly states, they are closest to the white, Christian, Euro-American epitome of civilization. They must abandon their backward ways as the price of civilization. In short, they should stop being Moros and be like their Christian Filipino brethren. They may retain those values—perhaps the exotic dances and costumes the majority finds entertaining—so long as they, to borrow a phrase from one American colonial official, are "not repugnant to the requirements of human good, as measured by the judgment of the Christian nations of the earth."[50] Though expressed, no doubt, with the best of intentions, the statement reads like an invitation to cultural suicide.

This was precisely the invitation offered to Muslim Filipinos by the American military governors of the Moro Province 60 years before, terms that had been largely resisted. While a few individual Muslims had achieved enough success in the larger society to perpetuate the illusion of the permeability of the Muslim–Christian cultural divide, such terms often meant that "the educated Muslim all too often becomes a part of a rootless intelligentsia, unable to go back wholeheartedly into his own traditional culture, but unwilling because of his religion to assimilate himself completely in the Christian society."[51] Thus, while education had still not succeeded in the wholesale assimilation of the Muslim minority into the Philippine mainstream, it did alienate some Muslim individuals who, tempted by the widespread faith in education, willingly occupied marginal positions in the gap between the majority and minority communities in hopes of carving out some sense of personal agency, for either self-serving or altruistic reasons.[52] Most Muslims, however, continued to lack access to the resources that would enable them to pursue integration on these terms or any others. In Lanao del Sur, for instance, 80 percent of children dropped out of school before completing the sixth grade.[53] The situation was somewhat better in other Muslim provinces, but they still lagged behind the rest of the country.

Meanwhile, the pages of educational journals increasingly gave voice to hopeful—most often non-Muslim—voices on the issue of Muslim integration. Other studies, however, suggested that the effort to achieve integration through uniform educational policies and curricula left ethno-religious differences untouched if they did not in fact exacerbate them.[54] In fact, more than 65 percent of Muslims surveyed in 1971 identified themselves as Muslim rather than Filipino and significant majorities held unfavorable views of government education.[55] Many continued to reject integration in favor of an Islamic education at home or abroad. Many others accepted the education, but put it to use resisting integration. The outbreak of an armed secessionist movement led by Western-educated Muslim intellectuals in the early 1970s demonstrated as definitively as anything else the inadequacy of education alone to diffuse this conflict.[56] As Filipino historian Cesar Majul noted in retrospect, "the fact that the secessionist movement among the Muslims began to germinate in the late 1960s shows that it [the Commission on National Integration] failed to integrate the bulk of the Muslim population into the body politic."[57]

By the late 1960s, despite ten years of CNI education programs and roughly five prior decades of education for integration, the long-festering Moro Problem was about to boil over once again into armed rebellion. Decades of alienation from the Philippine mainstream, resentment toward government policies that reinforced their sense of second-class citizenship, and escalating tensions over land ownership resulting from the government's policy encouraging Christian migration into traditionally Muslim areas had created explosive conditions by 1968–1969. In fact, violence between paramilitary groups—the Christian Ilaga (rats) and the Muslim Blackshirts and Barracuda—was already an increasingly common occurrence in Cotabato and Lanao.[58] It was, however, the so-called Jabidah Massacre that lit the fuse of Muslim secessionism and all-out war.

For decades, the Philippines claimed the Malaysian state of Sabah in North Borneo on the grounds that it was the successor state of the old Sulu sultanate, which had supposedly included North Borneo. Under President Ferdinand Marcos, the Philippine armed forces began secret training of a small band of Muslim guerillas who were to infiltrate Sabah and spark unrest that the Philippines might use to make good its claim. For reasons that remain unclear to this day, the plan was aborted, and all but one of the Muslim recruits killed at their base on the island of Corregidor in Manila Bay. The lone survivor managed to escape, reporting the massacre to the public and setting off a storm of Muslim protest over the government's apparent contempt for Muslim Filipino lives.[59] The controversy quickly gave birth to the Mindanao Independence Movement (MIM), which was led by several nationally prominent Muslim politicians.

While the MIM was short-lived, a second, much more formidable secessionist movement was emerging under the leadership of a former University of the Philippines political science instructor, Nur Misuari. Misuari's Moro National Liberation Front (MNLF) quickly emerged as an umbrella organization that united disparate Muslim paramilitary under a political ideology of Moro nationalism and secession. The MNLF viewed the Moro Problem as a legacy of Spanish and American imperialism and characterized its struggle as "a jihad for national salvation from colonialism."[60] It expressed and sought solidarity with other third world, anticolonial struggles throughout the Muslim world. The escalating unrest in Mindanao and the plight of the Filipino Muslims there quickly drew the attention of Muslim governments, particularly Libya, which poured millions of dollars of military training and equipment as well as international political support into the MNLF's cause.

The reemergence of the Muslim secessionist struggle coincided with the rebirth of a communist insurgency throughout the country in the late 1960s and early 1970s led by the Communist Party of the Philippines and its armed wing, the New People's Army. Citing the combined threat, President Ferdinand Marcos declared martial law in late 1972.[61] Contrary to Marcos' intent, martial law may well have contributed to the growing influence of the MNLF as it further eroded Muslim political power at the national level by centralizing power in exclusively Christian hands—Marcos and his cronies. It also presented Muslims with two stark options—cooperation with the martial law regime or resistance—and rendered the choice urgent through a program of disarmament.[62] The result was a rapid expansion of the movement, which grew into a guerilla army numbering in the tens of thousands by the mid-1970s. In response, the Philippine government increased military spending by 700 percent and quadrupled the size of the Philippine armed forces from 60,000 to 250,000. It also established the paramilitary Civilian Home Defense Forces, which came to number more than 60,000. By 1975, three-quarters of the entire armed forces of the Philippines were engaged in Muslim Mindanao.[63]

Between 1972 and 1976, large-scale fighting raged between the MNLF and Philippine government forces in Muslim Mindanao. The results were horrific: 50,000 killed, 2 million refugees, 200,000 homes destroyed, 35 cities and towns destroyed, and 1 million hectares of land vacated by Muslim occupants.[64] While the signing of the Tripoli Agreement in late 1976 brought large-scale fighting to an end, it ultimately failed in addressing Muslim concerns and left a tense standoff in Mindanao between the MNLF and the Philippine government.[65]

As the Marcos regime waged all-out war against the MNLF, it also launched a series of policies designed to bring about what it called the New Society and to convey the impression to its Muslim citizens and the world that the war in Mindanao was not a genocide against Muslim Filipinos. Thus, it responded to Muslim unrest with two of the same weapons deployed by the US colonial regime: confrontation and conciliation, military assaults and education. The Marcos dictatorship increasingly oriented educational policy in the New Society toward economic development. While the long-standing objective of promoting moral values through religious faith did not disappear from official policy statements, Marcos educational policies gave top billing in its lists of objectives for Philippine education to economic development, nationalism, and the promotion of the goals of the New Society.[66] In addition, specific policies attempted to target Muslim concerns in order to mitigate hostility toward the government and facilitate the continuing policy of integration.

In 1973, for instance, Marcos issued Letter of Instruction No. 71-A allowing the use of Arabic as a medium of instruction "in schools and areas where the use thereof permits."[67] Any meaningful implementation of the policy, however, was severely limited by the lack of teachers capable of teaching Arabic. Moreover, the presence or absence of Arabic instruction in public schools had never been one of the top concerns of Muslim Filipinos regarding the public schools. Consequently, few significant steps were taken toward the implementation of the order until the early 1980s when Mindanao State University began a formal program to train Arabic language teachers.[68] In spite of this effort, Arabic language instruction remained limited and largely ineffectual. Regional Departments of Education in Mindanao also launched small-scale literacy projects, awarded scholarships to MNLF rebels who had "returned to the fold of the law," prepared new textbooks with basic information about Muslim culture, and attempted to foster the "integration" of Islamic schools by introducing public school curricula into the *madaris* and helping them seek official government recognition.[69]

Most of these efforts were seen as ineffective and insincere attempts on the part of an increasingly brutal dictatorship to improve the lot of Muslim Filipinos, mere window dressing rather than substantive educational reforms. Thus, by the mid-1970s, after 40 years of government policies designed to effect the integration of Muslim Filipinos through education into the mainstream of Philippine society, most Muslims still lacked confidence in the government, and less than one-fifth of Christian and Muslim Filipinos had favorable attitudes toward each other.[70] In a 1975 study of relations among nine Filipino ethnic groups, the Filipinas Foundation found that Filipino Muslims were consistently ranked last by other groups in terms of their desirability as neighbors, employers, employees, friends, or marriage partners. "Muslims are regarded above all as unreliable, hostile and proud people, and lead all other ethnic groups in being extravagant, non-progressive, lazy, hostile, unreliable, poor, proud, conservative, and stingy."[71] The most common reasons listed for disliking Muslims were listed as "fierce" (24.8 percent), "treacherous" (19.9 percent), "killers" (11.8 percent), "warlike" (10.9 percent), and "religious difference" (10.9 percent). Interestingly, the charge that Muslims were "anti-government" was cited by only 5.4 percent of non-Muslim respondents as a reason to dislike them.[72]

Thus, the savage image of the Muslim Filipino posited in the American civilization discourse had survived 70 years of education for integration largely intact. The fact that it did was no doubt due in part to the continuation of conflict between Muslims and Christians in the 1950s and then again in the late 1960s and 1970s. However, it also points to the failure of educational policy and curricula over the previous six or seven decades to eradicate these popular stereotypes or to convince Muslims to embrace integration into a society that held them in such obvious contempt. Moreover, the Filipinas Foundation study showed that each ethnic group tended to rank itself as the most desirable-admirable, while later research demonstrated the continuing importance of the extended family as "the most central and dominant institution in the life of all individuals."[73] Thus, not only was the dream of Muslim integration into Philippine society as far off as it had ever been, the provincialism and familism Manuel Quezon had railed against 40 years before had largely survived the long effort by nationalist educators to replace them with a new "Filipino" identity.

Studies by Muslim educational scholars in the late 1970s and early 1980s continued to claim that government textbooks contained little or nothing relevant to Muslim Filipino experience or useful in counteracting negative images of Muslim Filipinos in the Christian mainstream.[74] Madale's (1983) surveys of Muslim Filipinos found that 97 percent of his respondents believed that the "educational system in Muslim areas failed in its goals and objectives as evidenced by its inability to effect observable changes in local people's culture and society." Common Muslims, he reported, were still suspicious of government education because it tended to alienate them from their identity as Muslims, which superseded any sense of identity as citizens of the Philippines.[75] Schools in Muslim areas were dilapidated and lacking in textbooks, supplies, and highly qualified teachers. A unified curriculum still failed to adequately include Muslim culture. After 50 years of Filipino rule, the Philippine government was still seen by many Muslims as a *gobirno a sarawang a tao*, a "government of foreign people."[76] The MNLF refused to accept the "false autonomy" implemented by the Marcos administration and continued—albeit at a lower level of intensity—its armed struggle against the Philippine government.[77] By 1985, Filipinos' long-standing faith in education as the tool that would finally resolve Muslim–Christian tensions and bring about national integration had borne little fruit.

It is, therefore, reasonable to conclude that the policy of integration pursued by successive Philippine governments between 1935 and the demise of the Marcos dictatorship in 1986 was largely a failure. The policy no doubt contributed here and there to the social mobility of individual Muslims and led some non-Muslim Filipinos to a better understanding of their fellow citizens. However, it is important to understand the reasons that such a well-intentioned policy failed to meet its objectives. One obvious cause was the failure to effectively implement the policies articulated. The objectives of the Commission on National Integration, for instance, which targeted economic development, land reform, legal assistance, agricultural development, and more, if successfully carried through, might have had a significant impact on Muslim Filipinos' sense of belonging to the Philippine Republic. But lack of resources, inefficiency, and corruption—often, it must be said, by Muslim leaders themselves—troubled the CNI and other efforts, such as the Southern Philippines Development Authority.[78] Filipino policy makers recognized the fact, which the failure of integration does not contradict, that economic development and political reform were essential to integration. Filipino Muslims had to feel that the country cared about their plight and that they had a future as citizens of the Philippines. Educational policy was necessary, but insufficient.

However, it also seems clear that the educational policies pursued were problematic conceptually as well as practically. And these flaws had roots in the US colonial period when American colonial officials first deployed educational policy as a tool for integrating Muslim Filipinos and repeatedly used the history of Muslim–Christian relations and the supposed inability of Christian Filipinos to govern the Muslims as a justification for delaying Filipino rule of Muslim Mindanao. This helped create a tendency among Filipino officials to minimize the differences between Muslims and Christians and to adopt the same policy tools used by the Americans in dealing with Mindanao. Thus, Philippine government officials continued the Americans' civilization discourse, in no small measure because it flattered them as already possessing "the highest form of religion," continuing the tendency to see deviation from the ideal as deficiencies to be corrected.[79] The only change in this discourse in the post-independence period was rhetorical, substituting words like modern and development for civilization and undeveloped for savagery. The underlying biases and objectives remained unchanged. Neither the American nor Filipino governments ever seriously considered, for instance, granting Muslim Filipinos the independence they fought so long to preserve and have fought so long to regain.

Educational policy, pursued within the conceptual framework of civilization-development, gave integration a veneer of benevolence that masked a long tradition of "prescription," which Freire (1990) claims is "one of the basic elements of the relationship between oppressor and oppressed" and which marked both the colonial relationship between the colonizers and the colonized and internal colonial relationship between the elite—Christian and Muslim—and the masses.[80] This false generosity preserved the moral-epistemic and therefore cultural-political privilege of the Filipino mainstream behind a mask of benevolent concern for their "Muslim brothers" and cast Muslim resistance to an essentially oppressive pedagogy as evidence of ignorance and ingratitude.

The Manila-centered educational elite continued to hold the power to define national identity in terms of colonial borders and their own historical experience. This nationalism, moreover, was profoundly colored by a Christian foil deeply rooted in mainstream culture by four centuries of Catholic political domination and explicitly authorized by educational goals charging schools with producing citizens with an "abiding faith in God." Authorized by a centralized government bureaucracy and the nationalist ideal to compose and impose a unified curriculum from "Aparri to Jolo," this educational elite was positioned to define the ideological framework within which integration would occur. Therefore, when Muslim Filipinos rejected the offer on the grounds that it constituted assimilation into a "basically Christian" culture via a "basically Christian" school system, their rejection could be read as further evidence of their ignorance, backwardness, and parochialism. The proponents of nationalism via a unified curriculum did not stop to consider that different groups might experience the same curriculum in different ways and that, as Jane Roland Martin (1992) has suggested, a unified curriculum may not be a unifying curriculum.[81]

A New-Old Idea: Educational and Political Autonomy for Muslim Filipinos

By the mid-1980s, the Marcos dictatorship was crumbling under the combined weight of an ever-growing political opposition alienated by years of corruption and repression and an increasingly effective insurgency led by the New People's Army and the Communist Party of the Philippines. Sparked by the assassination of Marcos's chief political rival, Benigno Aquino, a broad coalition of opposition forces emerged by 1985 led by Aquino's widow, Corazon, and representing a route to political change between the two extremes embodied in the communist insurgency and a dictatorial political status quo. Corazon Aquino's election to the presidency after the snap elections of 1986 and the so-called People Power Revolt that enforced the election results ushered in a hopeful period promising a return to democratic government after 20 years of martial law and dictatorship. Amid such tumultuous times, the long-festering Moro Problem receded once again to the back burner of Philippine political consciousness.

Aquino entered the presidency with the goals of reestablishing democratic, constitutional rule and pursuing peace talks with both the communist and Muslim insurgents. To this end, the Aquino administration entered into talks with Nur Misuari and the MNLF soon after assuming office. Her administration's approach to solving the Moro Problem, however, represented in essence a throwback to American and Marcos administration approaches to the reconciliation of a Muslim minority bent on preserving a separate political and religious identity and the territorial integrity of a Philippine state defined by colonial borders. The new-old solution to the problem would be political autonomy for the Muslim regions. The political segregation of Muslims from the Philippine mainstream had, of course, been one of the justifications for the establishment of the Moro Province and the Department of Mindanao and Sulu at the beginning of the century. And prior to the handover of political authority to the Commonwealth government, some American and Muslim observers had advocated the separation of Muslim Mindanao under an autonomous political structure, continued American colonization, or outright independence.

In 1976, the Marcos administration resuscitated the notion of autonomy to secure the MNLF's signature on the Tripoli Agreement, which promised autonomy to 13 provinces with Muslim populations in Mindanao. The policy of autonomy, however, faced two difficult challenges. The first was demographic. The MNLF demanded autonomy for all of what they saw as traditionally Muslim areas. But, decades of resettlement programs under colonial and independent governments had shifted the population balance from majority Muslim to majority Christian in all but a handful of Mindanao provinces. The vast majority of Christian inhabitants refused to join a Muslim-dominated autonomous region. The second challenge was the difficulty of defining a level of autonomy that met Muslim leaders' demands without acquiescing to a de facto independent state. The Tripoli Agreement ultimately failed to reconcile the MNLF with the government on just these issues.

The Aquino administration's talks with the MNLF foundered as well on the MNLF's insistence on the strict implementation of the 1976 Tripoli Agreement.[82] The Aquino administration pressed on with their own autonomy agenda, however, organizing a plebiscite in 1991 in which only the four majority Muslim provinces of Lanao del Sur, Maguindanao, Tawi-Tawi, and Sulu opted to join the new Autonomous Region in Muslim Mindanao (ARMM).[83] Soon after the establishment of the ARMM, the national Department of Education, Culture, and Sports devolved authority for public and private elementary and secondary education in the four provinces to a Regional Department of Education, Culture, and Sports (RDECS) headed by a secretary appointed by the ARMM government.[84] Ostensibly, the creation of an autonomous region with an autonomous educational system constituted the first time since Muslim Mindanao lost its independence in the late nineteenth century that Muslim advocates of the Bangsa Moro—the Moro nation—had had direct responsibility for the administration of public and private schools in the region.

The educational policies formulated by this regional educational authority in its early years exhibited a basic continuity with national educational policy since it was largely formulated and implemented by Muslim educators who had long been part of the national educational establishment. However, the policies of the RDECS did initiate a deliberate move toward the Islamization of public education in Muslim Mindanao.[85] Responding to language in the 1987 Philippine Constitution that charged public schools with the spiritual development of Filipino children as well as the cultural needs and aspirations of Philippine ethnic minorities, the RDECS promulgated new educational policies designed to infuse Islamic cultural values throughout the public school system. Arabic instruction was increasingly emphasized as a second language.[86] The Values Education Program was also reinterpreted from an Islamic perspective, and a program to reevaluate and rewrite textbooks to more accurately reflect the role of Islam in the history and culture of the Philippines was undertaken.[87]

The RDECS also took steps to rationalize the curricula of the madaris by broadening their course of study from a focus on Islam and Arabic to include subjects like mathematics, science, social studies, English, and so on.[88] Right up to the end of the 1990s, most Muslim children who opted to pursue their education through the madrasah system were unable to switch to the public educational system or enroll in Philippine universities since the curricula of their madrasah education typically did not include subjects at the core of the public school curriculum. Thus, they were cut off from the social and economic advancement that public education theoretically made possible. The madrasah reconciliation effort was designed to enable students to move back and forth between the madrasah and public educational systems by ensuring that their curricula were comparable while retaining their Islamic orientation.[89]

The major thrust of RDECS policy in the mid-1990s seemed to be to bring what had in the past been two distinct, unconnected systems of education closer together: The public schools would become more Islamic, and the Islamic schools would include the core subjects of the public school curriculum. Thus, the creation of the RDECS within the ARMM was intended to enable the evolution of a system of education which respected and responded to the place of Islam in Muslim Filipinos' lives and, hopefully, contribute to the resolution of Muslim–Christian conflict in ways that a Manila-centered or purely secular system of education had failed to do. There was little evidence, however, that this continued faith in schooling had any more impact on Muslim–Christian relations or even on the more immediate educational problems of Muslim Filipinos.

The limited impact of more autonomous educational policy-making was hampered by at least three factors. First, to a significant extent, RDECS policy-making was constrained by the necessity to remain largely consistent with the policy directions established by the national Department of Education, Culture, and Sports (DECS). This tendency was no doubt exacerbated by the fact that educators affiliated with the RDECS tended to be individuals who had come of age professionally in the highly centralized, top-down, Christian-dominated culture of the national DECS bureaucracy. This surely had a negative effect on the degree of policy experimentation allowed or even imagined by policy makers in the ostensibly autonomous RDECS. Second, the ARMM and its Department of Education remained largely dependent on the national government for funding. Unsurprisingly, adequate funding was a perennial problem, particularly for madrasah reconciliation efforts, since public funds could not be used for religious schools. This meant that few madaris were financially able to hire the teachers to expand their curricula as envisioned in the reconciliation effort. Finally, the age-old problem of corruption continued to plague education in the autonomous region as it had for years and as it long had in Philippine education in general. Kickbacks and shady contracts siphoned off badly needed funds, both qualified and unqualified teachers were often forced to buy positions from corrupt administrators, political cronyism often counted for more than qualifications in the appointment of teachers and administrators, and ghost schools, teachers, and students drained resources from the system.[90]

Even if RDECS policy decisions had been perfectly tuned to meet the educational needs of Muslim children and thus supportive of the nation's faith in education as an effective tool for the integration of its Muslim minority, such problems would have severely limited their effectiveness. However, in key respects, particularly its effect on the reconciliation of Muslims and Christians, the autonomy policy had serious flaws. The so-called Moro Problem, for instance, was never a problem simply for Muslim Filipinos of Mindanao. It was a Filipino problem. The bias, ignorance, and stereotypes that fueled it were a national problem that required changes in the curricula and attitude of all Philippine schools, not just those of Muslim Mindanao. While RDECS-ARMM policies may have had a positive impact in those contact zones where Muslim and Christian Filipinos interacted on a face-to-face basis, they could not address this part of the problem.

Even as the government tinkered with autonomy as a solution to Muslim aspirations for self-rule and the maintenance of Islamic identity, the armed struggle for independence continued. Five years after the establishment of the ARMM, a new Philippine government under Fidel Ramos finally concluded a peace treaty with the MNLF and brought its chairman, Nur Misuari, into the government of the ARMM.[91] By that time, however, many long-time observers of the Moro Problem had concluded that the MNLF was a spent force politically and militarily.[92] While the talks and ultimate peace treaty revived Misuari's political fortunes briefly, the military muscle of the Muslim secessionist movement had long since passed to the Moro Islamic Liberation Front (MILF), a faction that had broken away from the MNLF in 1984. The MILF was led by Salamat Hashim, a Maguindanaoan who had received an Islamic education in the Middle East, whose break with Misuari and the MNLF was in part over the quasi-secular, nationalist character of MNLF ideology that had evolved from Misuari's leftist-oriented student activism in the 1960s. Salamat advocated a more strictly Islamist expression of Bangsamoro aspirations.[93]

The shift in the character of the Muslim secessionist movement in the Philippines from a predominately nationalist to a more Islamist orientation followed similar shifts in other Muslim revolutionary movements throughout the Middle East. In the late 1960s and early 1970s, political movements throughout the Muslim world, inspired by leftist political ideologies, pursued what Gilles Kepel (1994) termed "Islamization from above," articulating their struggles through anticolonial and nationalist discourses like that articulated by Nur Misuari. By the mid-1970s, however, a growing disillusionment with the supposed modernism embodied in failed Arab governments led many to seek radical social change through a process of "Islamization from below," an increasingly fundamentalist orientation that sought to reorganize societies on a strictly Islamic foundation.[94]

The MILF pursued their version of this process of Islamization from below, in part, by establishing communities, rather than the purely military camps established by the MNLF, which sought to put into practice the sort of Islamic community they envisioned for the entire Bangsamoro homeland. By the end of the 1990s, there were 13 of these communities-military camps. The two largest, Camp Abubakar in Maguindanao and Camp Bushra in Lanao del Sur, contained schools, mosques, post offices, stores, rice mills, sharia courts, and military academies—even a drug rehabilitation center in Bushra. Their inhabitants included women, children, and the elderly as well as 15,000 mujahideen.[95] Under the administration of President Fidel Ramos, these communities remained relatively free from military assault so long as the MILF refrained from offensive actions. The character of these communities, however, suggested that even as the Ramos administration concluded a peace treaty with Misuari and the MNLF and established the ARMM in response to the Muslims' secessionist sentiments, key segments of the Muslim Filipino community were embracing an Islamist orientation less interested in adapting itself to the Philippine mainstream.

INTEGRATION AND AUTONOMY: RECYCLING COLONIAL POLICY IN THE POSTCOLONIAL

A historical review of colonial and postcolonial educational policy as it has been deployed in response to the so-called Moro Problem in the southern Philippines highlights two broad policy experiments tried by American and Filipino governments: integration and autonomy. Both regimes have tried their own versions of both policies. The Americans began with the notion of a separate government for the Muslims in order to put them on their feet politically and thus facilitate their eventual integration into the Philippine mainstream. Independent Philippine governments started with the goal of rapid and complete integration of the Muslim minority until the violent resistance of that minority in defense of their distinctive cultural and religious identity forced the government to again experiment with some version of separate, autonomous administration for Muslim regions. In many respects, postcolonial policy regarding the Muslim minority constitutes a mirror image of colonial policy, thus supporting reading of the conflict as an internal colonial relationship.

Both the integration and autonomy projects represent reasonable, if somewhat predictable, responses to the challenge posed by the Muslim minority given Philippine cultural and historical conditions. Both policies appear problematic, however, since neither has yet been entirely successful in resolving the conflict. Yet, the shortcomings of both experiments can offer useful insight into the most effective educational responses to such ethno-religious conflicts. The integrative project, for instance, is clearly the oldest experiment in educational policy designed to address

Muslim–Christian tensions in the Philippines. It has been deployed in one form or another since the first decade of the last century. The American architects of Philippine colonial education clearly had great faith in education as a tool for integrating Muslim Filipinos into the larger body politic of the country. Later, educational officials of successive independent Philippine governments exhibited the same faith. Both also conceived the problem of integration as a matter of misinformed suspicion—ignorance—on the part of Muslim Filipinos toward the benevolent intentions of government and a lack of access to education that perpetuated the social, cultural, and economic isolation of Muslim Mindanao.

To the extent that this represented an accurate reading of the problem, educational interventions were somewhat successful. By the late 1990s, many thousands of Muslim and non-Muslim Filipinos enjoyed positive and productive social relationships. And, though the education of Muslim Filipinos continued to face serious problems, the quality of that education and access to it were undoubtedly better than they were even 20 or 30 years before. However, the rapid growth of Islamic schools, the still frequent assertion of an Islamic before a Filipino identity by many Muslim Filipinos, and the continuing presence in the field of up to 15,000 MILF mujahideen strongly suggest that the integration project had failed in part because it had not adequately appreciated the extent to which the conflict was a struggle to maintain the religious and cultural identity of Muslim Filipinos.

The policy of integration appears to have been problematic in other ways as well. For instance, in defining the impediments to integration in terms of Muslim misunderstanding and access to government schools, the policy failed to adequately understand that it was in fact seeking to integrate Muslim Filipinos into an educational system in which the fundamental purposes, goals, values, etc. were already defined by the cultural values of Christian Filipinos. Many Muslim Filipinos, on the other hand, were acutely aware of this fact. Integration was successful only to the extent that Muslim Filipinos were willing to conform to those values. Many were. But many others continued to resist. They saw integration into a system dominated by the unexamined philosophical assumptions of a culture that had been openly hostile to them for centuries as assimilation, as an unacceptable surrender of a religious and cultural identity of which they were justifiably proud. Thus, to the extent that the Muslim–Christian conflict in Mindanao had been a struggle to preserve that identity, the policy of integration perhaps exacerbated tensions rather than resolved them. The tens of thousands of children enrolled part-time and full-time in the madaris, the thousands of mujahideen, and the ordinary Muslim citizens who support both represent a more than symbolic rejection of the policy of integration.

The limited autonomy of the Autonomous Region in Muslim Mindanao and its Regional Department of Education, Culture, and Sports represented, theoretically, a distinct shift in policy, both politically and educationally. Given the historical concern of Manila governments to forge a sense of national identity out of incredible cultural, linguistic, and geographic diversity—a concern that reinforced the colonial centralization of educational policy-making in Manila—this tentative step toward decentralization was significant. While this policy experiment remains relatively new, continued problems of funding, political disarray, corruption, and insufficient freedom—politically and mentally—for genuine experimentation do not bode well for its success.

An important unspoken assumption of the policy of integration was that the so-called Moro Problem was a problem located among Muslim Filipinos. It would be solved as they adapted the mainstream's ways. The policy represented, in effect, an attempt on the part of the majority to fix that problem for Muslim Filipinos through education. The autonomy experiment, on the other hand, seemed to constitute an admission that the majority could not fix the problem for them, that Muslim Filipinos would have to solve the problem themselves. To the extent that this was true, the autonomy policy leaves in place the assumption that the Moro Problem is the Moro's problem. However, it was never just their problem, for it was driven in large part by the centuries-old stereotypes, bigotry, fear, and mistrust of Christian Filipinos for Muslim Filipinos. The autonomy project did not—indeed could not—address this aspect of the problem. Therefore, to the extent that the autonomy project simply facilitated the creation of schools and curricula that addressed Muslim needs by reinforcing the religious and cultural pride of Muslim Filipinos while leaving intact Christian Filipino prejudices, then the policy may also have strengthened the centrifugal forces that had been separating Muslim and Christian Filipinos for centuries.

It is reasonable to assume that both the policies of integration and autonomy pursued by colonial and postcolonial administrations did not vindicate Americans' and Filipinos' faith in education as the tool that would bring about the integration of Muslims and Christians in a single Filipino identity. Both policies no doubt contributed here and there to the social mobility of individual Muslims and led some non-Muslims to a better understanding of their fellow citizens. However, as late as 1997, an analysis of interethnic relations between Muslim and Christian Filipinos found that the "perceptions and understandings that Muslims and Christians have of each other lack objectivity and are colored by strong biases and prejudices; but especially strong are the biases Christians have against the Muslims."[96] The continued alienation of so many Muslim Filipinos and the ongoing secessionist movement suggest that the policies had indeed failed as mechanisms for mitigating the ethno-religious differences that separated Muslim and non-Muslim Filipinos. In fact, the conflict would reach new levels and extremes of violence by 2000 as elements of the secessionist movement became increasingly linked with international terrorist organizations.[97]

Thus, the Philippine experiment in the use of educational policy to mitigate ethno-religious tensions and effect national integration seemed to reinforce educational insights gained in other multicultural democracies: Imposition of a single, authorized point of view is inherently oppressive and can only be accomplished through the application of both symbolic and real violence. Such an imposition inevitably incites resistance. Genuine integration, the opposite of such imposition, is a two-way street; it requires the mutual adjustment of both the minority and the majority communities. In the Philippine context, for instance, this would mean majority Filipinos learning more about their Muslim fellow citizens and critically interrogating the deep bigotry bequeathed to them by their colonial and neocolonial experience. The Philippine experience in deploying education as a tool to mitigate ethno-religious conflict after 1935, however, offers a cautionary tale for those who would subscribe to such a faith in schooling: Educational policies that posit, implicitly or explicitly, contemporary Euro-American civilization as the ideal to which the education of Muslim Filipinos must aspire are likely to fail. Educational policies that presume essentialist notions of national identity and blithely ignore the Christian bias in that identity are doomed to fail.

Notes

1. Gripaldo, "Quezon's Philosophy of Philippine Education," 40.
2. Isidro, *Education in the Philippines*.
3. Osias, "Notes on Education."

4. Elevazo and Villamor, *Educational Objectives and Policies*, 12.
5. Constitution of the Republic of the Philippines, Article III, Section 5; Department of Education, Culture, and Sports, *Values Education for the Filipino*, 10.
6. Constantino, *The Philippines: A Past Revisited*.
7. See, for instance, Zaide, *Philippine History and Government*.
8. Elevazo and Villamor, *Educational Objectives*.
9. Gripaldo, "Quezon's Philosophy," 43.
10. Cited in Thomas, "Muslim but Filipino," 263.
11. Ibid.
12. Osias, "Notes on Education," 172.
13. Gowing, *Mandate in Moroland*, 267–268.
14. Osias, "Notes on Education."
15. Angeles, "Islam and Politics," 150–152.
16. Ibid., 152–154.
17. Elevazo and Villamor, *Educational Objectives and Policies*, 16–19.
18. Aldana, *The Educational System of the Philippines*, 369–389.
19. Ibid., 162–163; Osias, *Speeches on Education*, 3–4.
20. Osias, "Notes on Education," 175.
21. Mednick, "Encampment of the Lake," 38.
22. Soriano, "Our Moro Problem and the Community School in Mindanao," 428.
23. Mangadang, "The Educational Problems of the Muslims in Lanao," 125–130; Madale, "Ghost Schools and the Maranaw."
24. Mednick, "Encampment of the Lake," 36, 40; Soriano, "Our Moro Problem."
25. Tamano, "What of Education in the Muslim Provinces," 141.
26. Ibid.
27. Mastura, "Assessing the Madrasah as an Educational Institution," 9–10.
28. Boransing, "Oplan Bangsa Pilipino," 17.
29. Clavel, *They Are Also Filipinos*, 15; Salgado, "Development Policies," 106–107.
30. Isidro, "Education in the Muslim Regions," 100.
31. Salgado, "Development Policies for Muslim Mindanao," 107.
32. Angeles, "Islam and Politics," 157.
33. Isidro, *Muslim–Christian Integration*, 376.
34. Said, *Orientalism*.
35. Isidro, *Muslim–Christian Integration*, 373. The *juramentado* was the term for a Muslim who has sworn an oath to carry out a suicide attack on those considered to be infidels.
36. Isidro, "Education in the Muslim Regions," 103–104.
37. Van Vactor, "Education for Maranaos," 29.

38. Vitug and Gloria, *Under the Crescent Moon: Rebellion in Mindanao*.
39. Clavel, *They Are Also Filipinos*, 17–18.
40. Osias, "Notes on Education," 172.
41. Cited in Clavel, *They Are Also Filipinos*, 84.
42. Clavel, *They Are Also Filipinos*, 19–21.
43. Filipinas Foundation, *An Anatomy of Philippine Muslim Affairs*, 162.
44. Ibid., 27–28.
45. Salgado, "Development Policies," 110.
46. Clavel, *They Are Also Filipinos*, 71.
47. Filipinas Foundation, *An Anatomy of Philippine Muslim Affairs*, 192.
48. Ibid., 4.
49. Clavel, *They Are Also Filipinos*, 71.
50. Finley, "The Development of the District of Zamboanga," 63.
51. Peter G. Gowing cited in Tamano, "The Educational Problems of the Muslims in the Philippines," 126. On the importance of model minorities in supporting myths of social mobility see John Liu, "On the Internal Colonial Model," in Brydon, *Postcolonialism* (New York and London: Routledge, 2000).
52. See, for instance, Saber, "Marginal Leadership in a Cultural-Contact Situation."
53. Isidro, "Education of the Muslims," 8–12.
54. See, for instance, Ante, "Muslim–Christian Integration in the Notre Dame Schools of Sulu," 48–50; Arong, "Schooled in Conflict."
55. Filipinas Foundation, *An Anatomy of Philippine-Muslim Affairs*, 116–117.
56. Nur Misuari, the chairman of the Moro National Liberation Front, was a former political science professor at the University of the Philippines. On the outbreak of the armed secessionist struggle see George, *Revolt in Mindanao*.
57. Cesar Majul cited in Salgado, "Development Policies," 110.
58. For a detailed account of these events see George, *Revolt in Mindanao*.
59. Vitug and Gloria, *Under the Crescent Moon*, 2–23.
60. Nur Misuari, cited in Angeles, "Islam and Politics," 238.
61. Karnow, *In Our Image*, 439.
62. Angeles, "Islam and Politics," 186.
63. Ahmad, "The War against the Muslims," 25.
64. Ibid., 27.
65. Che Man, *Muslim Separatism*, 149–151.
66. Navarro, "Curricular Directions in the New Society," 22–38; "Schoolyear 76–77 Sees More Reforms in RP's Educational System," 1–3; Elevazo and Elevazo, *Philosophy of Philippine Education*, 61–78.

67. Department of Education and Culture, *A Year of Progress Under Martial Law*, 48.
68. Hassoubah, *Teaching Arabic as a Second Language in the Southern Philippines*, 24–25.
69. MEC, *Report on Educational Development in the Seventies*, 82–85; MEC, *Annual Report 1980*, 227–235; MECS, *Annual Report 1983*, 3; MECS, *Annual Report 1984*, 194–196, 218–224.
70. Filipinas Foundation, *An Anatomy of Philippine Muslim Affairs*, 124; Filipinas Foundation, *Philippine Majority–Minority Relations and Ethnic Attitudes*, 158–159.
71. Filipinas Foundation, *Philippine Majority–Minority Relations*, 137.
72. Ibid., 159.
73. Ibid., 118; Lacar, "Familism Among Muslims and Christians in the Philippines," 42–65.
74. Madale, "Educational Implications of Moro History," 89–97.
75. Madale, "Educating the Muslim Child," 15–42.
76. Madale, "Educational Goals and the Search for National Identity," 248–255.
77. Vitug and Gloria, *Under the Crescent Moon*, 34–35.
78. Salgado, "Development Policies."
79. Bliss, *Annual Report of Brigadier General Tasker H. Bliss, 1906-Aug. 27*, 86.
80. Freire, *Pedagogy of the Oppressed*, 46.
81. Martin, *The Schoolhome*, 81–83.
82. Vitug and Gloria, *Under the Crescent Moon*, 39.
83. Ibid., 40.
84. Macalinog I. Saligoin, "The DECS-ARMM and Its Mission," 3, 11.
85. Tamano, "Islamic Education and Its Direction in the ARMM," in Tamano, *Educational Visions*, 82–87.
86. Ibid.; Houssabah, *Teaching Arabic as a Second Language*.
87. Tamano, "Islamic Education."
88. See, for instance, Damonsong-Rodriguez, *A Madrasah General Education Program for Muslim Mindanao*; Tamano, "Islamic Education."
89. Rodriguez, *A Madrasah General Education Program*.
90. Van Vactor, "Education for Maranaos," 2–38; Chua, *Robbed: An Investigation of Corruption in Philippine Education*.
91. Vitug and Gloria, *Under the Crescent Moon*, 58.
92. Ibid., 37, 44–45.
93. Abuza, *Militant Islam in Southeast Asia: Crucible of Terror*, 39–40.
94. Gilles Kepel, *The Revenge of God: The Resurgence of Islam, Christianity and Judaism in the Modern World* (University Park: Pennsylvania State University Press, 1994), 13–46.

95. Jinnati Mimbantas, interview with the author, Camp Bushra, July 1999; Vitug and Gloria, *Under the Crescent Moon*, 109–110.
96. Tolibas-Nunez, *Roots of Conflict*, 84.
97. Abuza, *Militant Islam in Southeast Asia*, 89–120.

CHAPTER 5

We Sing Here Like Birds in the Wilderness: Education and Alienation in Muslim Mindanao

More than a century on from the establishment of the US military government of the Moro Province, Muslim Mindanao remains a region apart from the rest of the Philippine Republic. Despite a century of political, social, and educational efforts to assimilate Filipino Muslims into the mainstream of Philippine society, they remain a collection of more or less distinct ethno-linguistic communities bound together by a widespread sense of alienation from the Philippine government and the Christian majority and a determination to preserve their distinctive identity as a Muslim community, part of *dar-ul Islam*. As an effort to integrate Muslim and Christian Filipinos into a unified Philippine society, the Moro Province failed. The Jones Law failed. The Commission on National Integration failed. Education for integration has failed. The policy experiment of political and educational autonomy embodied in the Autonomous Region in Muslim Mindanao failed as well.

A century of American, Japanese, and Philippine military efforts to extinguish armed resistance to cultural, political, and religious assimilation have failed to stamp out violent separatist movements. Efforts to initiate peace talks between the MILF and the Philippine government in 1999 foundered in early 2000 amidst an "all out war" against the MILF declared by the administration of President Joseph Estrada. Philippine military assaults over a period of months were successful in driving the MILF from all of the community-camps it had established throughout western Mindanao, including the two largest, Camp Abubakar and Camp Bushra. However, while the Philippine armed forces were successful in occupying MILF camps, they were not successful in destroying the MILF's ability to wage war. Over the next decade elements of the MILF engaged in a series of offensive and defensive military actions that led to many more deaths and thousands of new refugees. Meanwhile, a series of devastating bombings rocked cities throughout the region.

From the mid-1990s to the present the conflict has taken on disturbing international implications. As early as 1980, the MILF had begun sending mujahideen for training and combat experience in Afghanistan. One result of this effort was the establishment of ties with the Al-Qaida network of Osama bin Laden, which began funding Islamic charities in Mindanao and recruiting soldiers for the war in Afghanistan.[1] Abuza (2003) asserts that Al-Qaida had "thoroughly penetrated" the Philippines by the late 1990s and that "every major plot by Al-Qaida against the United States had some ties to the Philippines."[2] Just as ominously, a new armed group, the Abu Sayyaf, emerged on the scene in the mid-1990s, gaining international attention with attacks on Filipino civilians and a series of high-profile abductions of foreign tourists from resorts in Malaysia and Palawan in 2000 and 2001.[3] By 2003, the Philippine government was accusing the MILF of providing training for operatives of the Indonesian terrorist group Jemaah Islamiyah as well. After the Al-Qaida attacks on New York and Washington on September 11, 2001, these international ties led the United States to focus increased attention on the conflict in Mindanao as a significant front in the worldwide war against terrorism.

Despite the ongoing problems, there are grounds for some hope. Formal peace talks between the MILF and the Philippine government began in mid-2004 in Malaysia and finally bore fruit in 2015 with the signing of a peace accord which was ratified by the Philippine legislature in 2018 and approved by the voters of Muslim Mindanao in early 2019. The ratification by voters established a new Bangsamoro Autonomous Region in Muslim Mindanao, replacing the old ARMM and marking the transition of the MILF from an armed secessionist movement into a governing political organization. And the United States, a little over a century after it established the Moro Province, has displayed renewed interest in Muslim Mindanao, delivering tens of millions of dollars in aid to the region. According to a joint communiqué issued after US President George W. Bush's visit with Philippine President Gloria

Macapagal-Arroyo in Manila in 2003, significant portions of that aid were to be targeted toward educational development for Muslim Mindanao. A century later, American and Filipino faith in education as a useful tool against ethno-religious conflict in Mindanao remains undimmed.

Children of the Lake: Educational Faith and Despair in Lanao del Sur

Muslim Filipinos' continuing struggle to negotiate a place in Philippine society that affirms their cultural history and Islamic identity, claims their full rights as citizens of a democratic Philippines, and offers the hope of a better future for themselves and their children is illustrated no more forcefully than in the educational experience of the Maranao, the "people of the lake" in the province of Lanao del Sur. Among the last of the 13 Muslim ethno-linguistic communities to receive Islam, Lanao del Sur today is, with the possible exception of Sulu, the most thoroughly Islamized and the most traditional province of Muslim Mindanao. The history and geography of the province explain the paradox. At the heart of the Maranao's ancestral lands is Lake Lanao—the second largest body of fresh water in all of the Philippines—lying at 700 meters above sea level.[4] The lake is surrounded by forested, volcanic mountain ranges that rise many hundreds of feet above the lake, forming a highland bowl roughly 40 kilometers from the coast of Iligan Bay to the north and Ilana Bay to the southwest.[5] This geographic isolation, coupled with the historic martial prowess of the Maranao people, helped ensure that the heart of the Maranao country remained relatively untouched by colonial governments until the American occupation of the region in the first few years of the twentieth century. Thus, the people of the lake have retained to this day a fierce sense of pride and independence along with a powerful loyalty to Islam and their own cultural traditions.

For many of the same reasons, Lanao del Sur remains one of the most impoverished and violent regions of the country as well, even among the other provinces of the Bangsamoro Autonomous Region in Muslim Mindanao. And both problems have profound effects on the schools in the province. Most public schools are typically overcrowded, physically unattractive and dilapidated, and grossly ill-equipped in terms of books, materials, desks, and so on. Local feuds, called *rido* in Maranao, occasionally disrupt the schools, as has the fighting between Philippine government forces and the MILF, whose second largest camp, Bushra, was located in the province. Schools are often used to house refugees from the fighting. It is no surprise, therefore, that absentee rates among pupils as well as teachers are often quite high and that the academic achievement of graduates is most often too low to allow them to succeed at the nearby Mindanao State University.

The children of the lake, however, as well as their families and teachers, have not entirely lost faith in education as a path to a better life. Their efforts to forge such a path while preserving their identity as Muslims illustrate the chronic problems of education in Muslim Mindanao and at the same time constitute important experiments in educational reform designed to reconcile the Philippine government's century-long faith in education as a tool for mitigating ethno-religious conflict and the Maranao's faith in education as a route to a better future. Chapter 4, therefore, draws upon an ethnographic study conducted over a ten-month period in 2000–2001 of 15 public high schools in Lanao del Sur and neighboring provinces in order to examine some of these educational problems and experiments within the context of the larger political and cultural trends shaping Muslim Mindanao.

Late one afternoon in 2001, while observing and conducting interviews at one of these schools, I was invited to listen to a group of these children of the lake rehearsing for a school program. This public high school had been holding classes in a much-better equipped local madrasah after having been forced to abandon its own building as a result of a recent *rido*. Their current location worried some teachers too, however, as Philippine troops reportedly passed frequently along the road on their way to the recent battles at Camp Bushra and back again carrying truckloads of looted household goods. The concrete building sat at the edge of a field of emerald green rice between the dark gray waters of Lake Lanao and heavily forested mountain range known locally for its profile of the "Sleeping Lady" and near, the teachers claimed, the site of one of the first mosques to be built in the Philippines. The children, a group of young girls dressed in blue school uniforms and blue hijab, exhibited a fairly typical, giggling mixture of shyness and curiosity when asked to perform for a visitor. Nevertheless, they sang with enthusiasm on their teacher's cue: *We sing here like birds in the wilderness / birds in the wilderness / birds in the wilderness. We sing here like birds in the wilderness / waiting for the others to come.* Then, improbably, they launched into a rendition of the Swedish pop group Abba's song, "I Have a Dream."

Their songs, rather innocently and movingly, captured much of the current predicament of the children of the lake. For, as far as many of their Filipino countrymen are concerned, they do inhabit a wilderness populated by uncivilized, dangerous savages. About the only non-Maranao Filipinos to visit the area are the soldiers of the Philippine armed forces who man the numerous checkpoints along the roads and pursue the mujahidin of the locally popular MILF, an occurrence so frequent over the past 30 years that the surrounding area is described as "Vietnam" by some locals. But, at the same time there was genuine hope in their songs, hope that inspires families to continue to send their children to school despite chronic problems and dubious prospects and a continuing faith in education that inspires some Maranao educators to experiment with locally inspired alternatives to the centralized national policies that have been formulated by outsiders and handed down for implementation in Lanao for a century.

Decolonizing Minds? The Resurgence of Islamic Identity in the Southern Philippines

As discussed at greater length in Chapter 2, Islam has been a central cultural feature of 13 ethno-linguistic groups in western Mindanao, the Sulu Archipelago, and southern Palawan for centuries. For a variety of reasons, it has been most highly developed among the Tausug, Maguindanao, and Maranao, who together comprise more than 90 percent of the five million or more Muslim inhabitants of the Philippines and were, with the exception of the Maranao, the first to adopt Islam.[6] While the underlying culture and languages of these Islamicized groups are quite clearly related to the cultures and languages of other Filipinos, and while Muslim Filipinos themselves remain relatively fragmented along ethno-linguistic lines as well as internally by class, education, and so on, Islamic identity has long constituted a marker of profound difference between Islamicized and Christianized inhabitants of the Philippine Archipelago.[7] Thus, Muslim Filipino relations with the Philippine government and the Christianized majority have to be read simultaneously at two levels: at the level of interaction between the government of the Christianized majority and a Muslim minority sharing both a common faith and a common history of resistance to outside domination and at the level of individual and community strategies of acceptance, accommodation, subversion, and rejection, which reveal the complexity of Muslim responses to integration efforts without negating the salience of the Muslim–Christian dichotomization of Philippine society. The stream of postcolonial theory that draws upon Hegelian-Marxist inspired analyses of relations between colonizer and colonized, oppressor and oppressed reflected in the internal colonial model is essential to understanding the first of these levels.[8] The parallel stream of postcolonial theory that draws upon the insights of Fanon, Foucault, Derrida, and others, to analyze both the complexity of psychological responses to oppression as well the fluidity of power characterizing class, gender, and other relations within communities and which can explain the occasional local reversal of power relations between Muslims and Christians within an overarching context of majority domination, is essential to understanding the second.[9]

Social identity theory also lends important insight into the complexity of Muslim Filipino responses to colonial and postcolonial exercises in domination through integration. It suggests that such dichotomization of identity between Muslim and Christian is at least partially a result of the individual's need to "partition the world in comprehensible units" and to attach emotional significance to membership in such social units. This sense of belonging is further strengthened and distinctions clarified by comparison to out-groups. Moreover, where the categorization is perceived to be of especial importance to the members, the sense of identification and differentiation may be particularly strong.[10] There is, perhaps, no more compelling basis for categorizing oneself than in terms of one's relation to the divine and all that relation is believed to require. Moreover, when such identify formation occurs within a colonial context marked by centuries of political and economic subordination, cultural denigration, and military conflict, such dichotomization of identities can become a profound cultural fault line defining the borders of a struggle between the majority and minority communities over their desires to maintain distinct identities in opposition to the creeping cultural and political hegemony of the majority. This helps to explain the continuing deployment on both sides of the Muslim–Christian dichotomy to talk about the social, cultural, and political problems of Mindanao despite the widely acknowledged fact that it is not, fundamentally, a religious conflict.

The assertion and strategic deployment of a Bangsamoro/Islamic identity rooted in a common faith and a more or less similar historical experience is real, though ephemeral, for it does not guarantee Muslim solidarity in the Philippines or prevent the cooperation of many Muslim Filipinos with the Philippine government, nor does it entirely prevent cooperation and friendship across religious differences. For, as both postcolonial and critical theorists have long argued, colonial and postcolonial relations of inequality do not prevent members of subordinated groups from subscribing to the aims of the majority, nor do they prevent some members of the dominant majority from standing in genuine solidarity with the subordinated minority.[11] This is particularly true in the political context of an imperfect, but nevertheless democratic, Philippine society profoundly influenced by the American ideology of individual social mobility through education that, while it might be disparaged as a tokenism that simply serves to maintain the status quo by co-opting the talented within subordinated groups, nevertheless represents a possibility for some members of Muslim Filipino communities. Even so, religious identity has long been and continues to be the marker of a profound and dangerous fault line in Philippine society.

Though Islam has a long history in the Philippines, the resurgence and reinforcement of Islamic identity as a categorical distinction within Philippine society has been one of the major sociopolitical phenomena of the Philippines over the last 30 years.[12] Beginning in the 1950s, as government-sponsored migration of Christian Filipinos from Luzon and the Visayas to Mindanao put increasing pressure on Muslims' ownership of land, and accelerating in the 1970s as the resulting tensions erupted into armed conflict, Islamic identity has risen as an increasingly important factor in Philippine society, politics, and education.[13] During this time, more and more Muslim Filipinos have traveled to the Middle East to make the *haj* and to pursue an education in centers of Islamic learning in Egypt, Saudi Arabia, and Pakistan. Meanwhile, Islamic societies in the Middle East have sent money and missionaries in support of their beleaguered Muslim brethren in the Philippines.[14] As the Muslim Philippines has become more closely integrated into the Muslim world, Filipino Muslim culture has been increasingly influenced by the Middle East, adopting modes of dress, values, and religious expressions more in keeping with what is often believed to be the "purer" Islam of the Middle East and increasingly at odds with aspects of traditional culture.

One of the most striking evidences of this influence has been the growth of the *Jama'at al Tabligh* in the 1990s and early 2000s. Founded in

Hindu-dominated India in 1927 by Muhammad Ilyas, the Tabligh sought to prevent the corruption of India's Muslim minority by instituting a radical break with surrounding society by urging its followers to a strict imitation of the life and behavior of the Prophet Mohammed.[15] To physically mark this separation, members grow their beards, wear a distinctive white garment called a *djellaba*, and rigorously follow Islamic rituals and prohibitions. Kepel (1994) describes the Tabligh as yet another manifestation of the movement toward re-Islamization from below after the widespread disappointment of Islamist movements with Arab nationalism in the 1950s and 1960s. The Moro Islamic Liberation Front's establishment of functioning Islamic communities in western Mindanao was another example of this "re-Islamization from below" meant to answer the social needs of Muslims "at sea in an atmosphere of rapid modernization" and seeking "a way of rebuilding an identity in a world that has lost its meaning and become amorphous and alienating."[16] Fundamentally, then, the Tabligh seems to be a response to assimilative pressures manifested in a conscious assertion of a purely Islamic and thus oppositional—in the context of a majority Christian society—identity.

The Tabligh first appeared in Muslim Mindanao in the early 1970s with the establishment of the Shubba'an al-Muslimen Tableegh in Lanao, just as the secessionist movement of the Moro National Liberation Front was reaching its height.[17] Organized into teams, called *jama'ah*, members function as a "roving madrasah" propagating Islam by their example and through informal education in mosques and other settings. Ten years after the establishment of the first *jama'ah*, a second was established in Lanao, and by the late 1980s as many as 20 were in existence in Muslim communities throughout the Philippines.[18] By 2000, there were reportedly 20,000 Tabligh in the province of Basilan alone, with even more in Lanao del Norte. Though the Tabligh is widely thought to be apolitical and harmless in the Philippines, it has reportedly been influential in Basilan politics.[19] Whether the Tabligh is intentionally political or not, its efforts are likely to have profound political effects to the extent that it is successful in refashioning Islamic identity in Mindanao along fundamentalist lines drawn positively on the model of the Prophet and negatively in opposition not only to the larger Christian society but to the Western-oriented sectors of Filipino Muslim society as well. Its rapid growth in the southern Philippines since the mid-1980s points to an apparently influential, little noticed informal educational movement redefining Muslim Filipino identity as a rejection of integration with the Filipino mainstream in favor of integration into the more fundamentalist manifestations of *dar-ul Islam*. Thus it represents one steam of contemporary Muslim Filipino response to the integration policies of the Philippine state.

A second, closely related stream of response is expressed in the proliferation of *madaris*, Islamic schools, in the southern Philippines.[20] As discussed in Chapters 1–3, Islamic education has been a feature of Muslim Filipino society since the introduction of Islam in the late fourteenth century. For much of this history, however, the inculcation of Islamic doctrine was largely a function of individual learned men teaching small groups of individuals in association with a mosque or what the American colonial regime called *pandita* schools. The imposition of American colonial rule, however, profoundly impacted indigenous educational institutions by introducing a more modern, secular system of education along with social, political, and economic structures premised on the types of knowledge disseminated in such schools and offering the prospect of social, political, and economic advancement for those who possessed such knowledge. In short, colonial education introduced a radically different regime of truth supportive of Western political domination and weakening, though by no means eradicating, traditional ontological and epistemological frameworks. Thus, colonial rule dichotomized religious and secular education, tradition and modernity in ways quite similar to the experience of other colonized Muslim societies, introducing a tension between Western-educated and traditionally educated segments of Muslim societies.[21]

The 1950s saw the establishment and expansion of some of the earliest formal *madaris* in the Lanao capital of Marawi City as Western-educated Muslim political figures encouraged the establishment of Islamic schools in an effort to consolidate their political power as intermediaries between local Muslim populations and the state and as missionaries from Egypt, Pakistan, Indonesia, and other Muslim countries increasingly traveled to the southern Philippines.[22] Since the early 1970s, the number of *madaris* has mushroomed from a mere handful to the thousands of schools, reflecting a similar pattern of dramatic growth in Pakistan, India, and Europe.[23] This rapid growth reflects both the efforts of local Muslims as well as the assistance of Muslim states undergoing their own Islamization movements reemphasizing *madrasah* education. By the late 1980s, the Ministry of Muslim Affairs listed approximately

1100 *madaris* throughout the country. However, according to Boransing, Magdalena, and Lacar (1987), if small, less formally organized schools were included, the total number could be in the neighborhood of 2000. Moreover, roughly half of the *madaris* they reported on as well as half of the total enrollment in the *madrasah* system was concentrated in Lanao del Sur and Marawi City.[24]

Though there is a long and illustrious tradition of learning within Islam, *madrasah* education was eventually reduced historically throughout much of the Middle East to the inculcation of religious traditions and dogma as other subjects were gradually subordinated in favor of the transmission of revealed, a priori knowledge thought to be contained in the Qur'an. Its traditional reliance on social elites and the state for support made the *madrasah* a central institution in the creation of a strong religious, cultural, and political identity in often-diverse Muslim societies.[25] As was the case with the Philippines, colonization seriously challenged these identities and the role of Islamic education in forging them, splitting colonized societies between tradition and modernity and creating a dichotomization that many are still struggling to overcome. According to Talbani (1996), traditionalists have responded to this dichotomization by reasserting the *madrasah's* role in defending and transmitting intact received knowledge of Islam. This includes the "Islamization of knowledge" in secular academic disciplines to ensure their conformity to Islam.[26] Other Muslim societies have attempted to integrate secular curricula into the *madaris* in order to ensure that students receive a religious education as well as a modern education that will enable them to attend universities and function in a modern, technological world.[27]

These somewhat contradictory trends of conservation and accommodation are reflected in contemporary Philippine *madaris* as well. Traditionally, of course, they have taught the principles of Islam and the performance of its rites, the Qur'an, the life and teachings of the Prophet, Islamic jurisprudence and theology, Islamic ethics, and Arabic language.[28] The legacy of the colonial dichotomization of Muslim Filipino society, however, has meant that such traditional Islamic education represented a dead-end in terms of social and economic mobility within the larger Philippine society. As a result of this, a number of Muslim Filipino educators began in the 1980s to call for the integration of government-approved curricula into the curricula of the *madaris*.[29] While the government offered limited support for such efforts, which the Department of Education in the Autonomous Region in Muslim Mindanao attempted to implement, progress was hindered by constitutional restrictions that prevented direct support to religious schools, the material poverty of most *madaris* and their constituents who can ill-afford the trained teachers and materials necessary for the effort, and the fears of some Muslims that the integration effort might lead to increased government interference in Islamic education.[30]

Private groups had, in some respects, more success in this matter. In 1995, for instance, a group of ulama involved in *madrasah* education in Lanao del Sur joined forces with the Ranao Council, an association of Western-educated Muslim academics at Mindanao State University to create the Ibn Siena Integrated School in Marawi City. According to the school's published brochure, it offered the basic requirements of the public school curriculum as well as the traditional Islamic curriculum of the *madaris* in order to, citing the Muslim educational scholar Ismail Al Faruqi, resolve "the present dualism in Muslim education, its bifurcation into Islamic and secular systems. The two systems," he is quoted as saying, "must be united and integrated, and the emergent system must be infused with the spirit of Islam."[31] Within five years of its establishment, the school had grown to an enrollment of 2000 students from kindergarten through high school and was making plans to expand to offer college-level courses. Moreover, its success had inspired the establishment of similar schools in the area.[32]

It is plausible to read such efforts to "integrate" *madaris* as an educational effort designed to strengthen Islamic identity while eschewing what some see as the more fundamentalist tendencies of the traditional *madrasah* or the Tabligh. Some proponents of the reform, in fact, see it as a mechanism that can enable Muslim Filipinos to more fully participate in Philippine society while retaining their religious identity. According to Foucault (1971), however, institutions like schools are "means of maintaining or modifying the appropriateness of discourses with the knowledge and power they bring with them," discourses which constitute a regime of truth and the social-political power it authorizes.[33] The *madrasah* schools, even the integrated *madaris*, encode a regime of truth quite different from that encoded in secular government schools or Catholic schools. Thus, they represent at the very least, a profound sense of dissatisfaction, if not outright rejection, among some Muslims of the educational alternatives offered to Muslim Filipinos by mainstream society.

Coordinates of Maranao Identity

As educated members of their respective communities, teachers are intimately aware of the social forces at work in Filipino Muslim society, responding to and at times shaping those forces. And as agents of the state, they are perhaps uniquely positioned to experience first hand the tensions between these evolving local identities and the authorized identities encoded in state educational policies and curricula. Therefore, teachers as social agents and schools as social locations occupied by the most vulnerable and valued members of any society can offer unique insight into the relationship between evolving socio-religious identities and the continuing legacy of colonial and neocolonial education. As I have asserted, however, this relationship must be read at two levels: at the microlevel of individual, local responses of acceptance, accommodation, subversion, or rejection and at the macrolevel of broad sociopolitical relations of inequality, marginalization, and oppression between the majority and the minority.

Because of this complexity, assertions of Islamic identity among teachers interviewed in Lanao del Sur, as well as among other Muslims in the province, convey a variety of different but interrelated levels of meaning that are intimately connected to an equally interrelated complex of purposes that collectively constitute Islamic identity in Lanao. At the most basic, and perhaps important level, when a Maranao teacher says "I am Muslim" she is making a straightforward statement of religious affiliation. She is asserting the Islamic profession of faith—"there is no God but Allah, and Mohammed is his messenger"—a belief that the Holy Qur'an is the word of God as revealed to Mohammed, and her adherence to the five pillars of Islam: the profession of faith, the *haj*, the daily prayers, giving alms or *zakat*, and the fast in Ramadan.[34] In the language of social identity theory, she is expressing the value significance of her membership in a defined social group that literally and figuratively renders the world comprehensible to her.

At the same time, particularly in the Philippine context, that assertion also announces her location on one side of the cultural divide marked Muslim–Christian in the Philippines, thus reinforcing her sense of identity by distinguishing it from the overarching out-group labeled Christian. In this sense it is not necessarily an assertion of religious belief—the individual may or may not be devout in their religious practice or may not practice it at all—but rather a broad marker of cultural affiliation beyond the ethno-linguistic group of Maranao, Tausug, Maguindanao, and others to the wider community of Filipino Muslims and beyond that to the worldwide Islamic community. Therefore, to assert Islam as one's faith also carries political and cultural overtones regarding one's relationship to the cultural and political mainstream of Philippine society and one's likely loyalty in the struggle to preserve Muslim religious and cultural identity in the face of the threat of cultural assimilation and continued political subordination. It is, to an extent, an acknowledgment of one's marginalization from that mainstream. This level of assertion of Islamic identity is epitomized in some individuals' claim to be Muslim or Maranao, but not Filipino.

Social identity theory also holds that individuals have "an upward directional drive which leads us to compare ourselves to others who are similar or slightly better than ourselves on relevant dimensions."[35] Thus the claim "I am Muslim" in the Philippine context also asserts one's recognition of a regulative moral ideal understood and articulated in religious terms. Muslim Filipinos often make the distinction between a good Muslim and a bad Muslim, a true Muslim and not a real Muslim. A good Muslim is spiritual, follows the teachings of the Qur'an, is non-violent, honest, and does not engage in the corruption and violence that so often mars Philippine society, both Muslim and Christian. Those who are corrupt, engage in violence, and so on are often said to be not real Muslims. Thus, the assertion of an Islamic identity marks one's articulation of and relationship to a moral ideal expressed in explicitly Islamic terms.

These levels of meaning of the assertion of an Islamic identity are interrelated, not distinct, and one may be asserting any one or all three at the same time depending upon the context and one's purpose. For instance, deploying the distinction between a true Muslim and not a real Muslim signals one's fealty to a regulative moral ideal articulated in Islamic terms and gives one a moral yardstick by which to judge one's own behavior as well as the behavior of others. Thus, it provides both a direction and a goal for ethical development toward which the ordinary Muslim, with all of his or her imperfections, strives. In addition, quite apart from the hope for a better future embodied in belief in an afterlife, the conception of the good Muslim provides a framework for cultural critique and social transformation.[36] It offers hope for those on this side of paradise who find themselves living in a world marred by violence, oppression, corruption, and hopelessness, which government and other secular institutions have heretofore been powerless to redress. "If Muslims will be good Muslims," it is often said in Mindanao, "and Christians will be good Christians, then we will have no more problems." This is clearly one of the reasons behind the growth of the Tabligh as well as the widespread admiration many Muslim Filipinos feel for its members.

Assertion of an Islamic identity also serves to lay claim to a sense of individual and collective dignity by a proud people whose experience of poverty, oppression, violence, and corruption tends to rob them of their human dignity. It also serves to distinguish them from those outgroups—the Christians, the Filipinos, and the West—whom many perceive as being responsible for the indignities they suffer. They are not the poor, uneducated, uncivilized, backward people their Christian fellow citizens so often portray both in their attempts to condemn and to assist the Moros. They are Muslims, part of *dar-ul Islam*, and heirs to a civilization whose learning, sophistication, and accomplishments rival that of any other civilization in the world. Thus, the claiming of an Islamic identity is both an assertion of one's dignity and an expression of resistance to those forces that would rob one of that dignity.

The strengthening sense of a more or less common Islamic identity has not, by any means, erased the significance of ethno-linguistic identity and diversity among Muslim Filipinos, however. Due to the long history of Islam in the southern Philippines, religious identity is closely intertwined with cultural identity. For some Islamicized groups, for instance the Maranao, to be a Maranao is to be a Muslim.[37] However, the resurgence of Islamic identity among the Maranao for instance, particularly an Islamic identity articulated increasingly within the framework of what is perceived to be a purer Islam imported from the Middle East, has created some tension with traditional culture.[38] Some traditional cultural practices that have formed part of Maranao cultural life for centuries have been gradually abandoned as un-Islamic. Other aspects of culture, the Maranao's *maratabat* for instance, continue in spite of their perceived contradiction of the conception of the good Muslim because they are so central to the group identity and cohesion of Maranao society and because they reinforce the other manifestations of Islamic identity discussed earlier. *Maratabat*, a Maranao value system that places the acquisition and maintenance of social status for oneself and one's clan above almost all other considerations, engenders a pride and a willingness to use violence in defense of that pride that is at odds with the ideals of humility, non-violence, and so on embodied in their conception of the good Muslim.[39] However, *maratabat* is also one of the cultural forces that have helped to preserve the Maranao as a culture and a Muslim people in the face of centuries of often violent colonial and postcolonial oppression.

Thus, while cultural identity as Maranao, Tausug, Maguindanao, and so on remains relatively strong, Islam, which has always been a salient feature of group identity among Muslim Filipinos, seems to have become increasingly salient as a positive marker of group affiliation as Muslim Filipinos, part of *dar-ul Islam*, and as a negative distinction of oneself from membership in the perceived oppressive majority: Christian Filipinos.[40] And since, according to teachers and others, "Islam is a complete way of life," this growing salience of Islamic identity certainly influences education. Among the Maranao, for instance, there appears to be no sense of identity that is not intertwined with or encompassed by religious identity. They are not separable and cannot be bracketed out of certain aspects of life and embraced in others. Any effort to do so is seen as a violation of one's faith. Any effort by outsiders to impose such a separation on them is perceived as an attack on their Islamic identity that should be resisted.

While local culture has always been and remains a key coordinate of Maranao social identity and Islam appears to be a more and more dominant feature of that identity, many—perhaps most—still assert their citizenship within the Philippine state as an aspect of their identity.[41] Thus, whether in a practical recognition of political reality or in a principled claim of their rights and duties as citizens, many claim identity as Muslims, as Maranao, and as Filipinos. Even among those most assertive of a Bangsamoro identity and political independence the frequently expressed goal of "independence … or genuine autonomy" as an outcome of the struggle suggests, at the very least, a practical recognition that they are and are likely to remain citizens of the Philippines. More significantly, the majority of individuals and groups in Mindanao critical of government policy toward the Muslim minority deploy their critiques and advocate for reform within the framework of Philippine political structures and citizenship.[42] This ambiguous relationship with the Philippine state, moreover, is not particularly new but, rather, has been a characteristic of Muslim Filipino relations with both the colonial and postcolonial Philippine states for at least a century.[43] It exists, and has existed, side by side with active resistance to state authority when that authority has been perceived as threatening to the first two coordinates of Maranao identity. Thus, educational policy is deployed and can only be understood in Lanao in a complex context of microlevel acceptance, accommodation, subversion and resistance and macrolevel relations of domination and subordination, centralization and marginalization.

ISLAMIC IDENTITY AND PUBLIC EDUCATION IN LANAO DEL SUR

As discussed in Chapter 3, the ideology of Philippine nationalism has figured prominently in the formulation of educational policy since at least the commonwealth period. In a nation comprising thousands of islands inhabited by hundreds of different ethno-linguistic groups and colonized for more than 300 years, it is perhaps inevitable that Philippine education would be and continues to be very concerned with inculcating a sense of national identity in Filipino schoolchildren.[44] This nationalist agenda has grown out of the perception of many Filipino intellectuals that the lack of national identity left the country vulnerable to Spanish and American imperialism and that what many see as a continuing weak sense of national identity threatens national fragmentation and makes the country vulnerable to neocolonial political and economic exploitation.[45] However, the concern with national identity has not entirely blinded political and cultural leaders to the diversity within Filipino society or the need to respect that diversity, in rhetoric if not always in action.

In the early 1970s, the Ministry of Education under Ferdinand Marcos authorized the teaching of Arabic as a second language and its use as a medium of instruction in schools that desired to do so.[46] This modest concession to Muslim concerns about Philippine government hostility toward them took place within the context of the MNLF rebellion and the government's efforts to blunt criticism from Muslim countries over its treatment of Filipino Muslims. The lack of trained teachers and resources, however, severely limited the practical impact of the move. Later, after the overthrow of the Marcos regime and the reestablishment of democratic government in 1986, the Autonomous Region in Muslim Mindanao was created, ostensibly providing a measure of local autonomy to the four predominately Muslim provinces of Tawi-tawi, Sulu, Maguindanao, and Lanao del Sur. The agreement included devolution of authority over schools in the ARMM to a regional Department of Education, Culture, and Sports. For the first time in almost 100 years,

Muslims ostensibly had policy-making authority over the public schools in the four provinces of the Autonomous Region.[47]

The ARMM however proved a political and administrative disappointment due to its continued financial dependence on the Philippine government as well as internal political infighting and corruption. Many Muslims in the region dismissed it as a false autonomy. Consequently, the DECS-ARMM had limited success in changing or improving public education in the region. A foreign-funded effort to Islamize textbooks in the 1990s, for instance, failed to produce or disseminate adequate numbers of textbooks sensitive to the Islamic identity of the local inhabitants because of the disappearance of funds meant for their publication and other controversies.[48] Today, they are extremely difficult to find. Thus, the ARRM experience seems to confirm postcolonial critiques of such grants of limited local autonomy within the context of an internal colonial relationship as a mechanism for maintaining the status quo.[49] While there have been such modest efforts at educational transformation for Muslim Mindanao—including many individuals in both Muslim and Christian communities who are working sincerely to improve relations between them—many Muslim teachers doubt the sincerity of the Philippine government because they see so little change in the conditions of their schools.

Though there has been some recent discussion of decentralization, the Philippine educational system remains highly centralized, with decisions on policy, curricula, textbooks, and so on made at the Department of Education in Manila.[50] Given the history of such centralization and the material poverty of the country, particularly in the remote, impoverished regions like Muslim Mindanao, the textbook becomes all-important. The textbook is the curriculum. It contains the academic content that has been authorized by the Department of Education, which the local students will be expected to demonstrate familiarity with while taking the standardized tests that determine admission to universities. Teachers have no control over the selection of texts; these are selected either by the Department of Education or, as in the case of the schools in Lanao del Sur studied here, by central administrators in charge of the schools. In many cases, even course syllabi are prepared by central administrators and distributed to teachers to be implemented. It is, as one informant called it, a *lutong makao* curriculum, "a cooked curriculum": it is cooked in Manila and the teachers simply serve it to the students.[51]

One result of the legacy of colonial and postcolonial centralization is a kind of idolatry regarding books. The civilization discourse underpinning colonial educational policy required that the locus of educational decision-making shift from families and local communities to the central government. The nationalist discourse underpinning educational policy-making after independence required the same sort of centralization. Authorized knowledge was determined by those with the authority to decide and disseminated via the printed text. Access to publication, and thus control of content, was largely controlled by the same community of authorities, particularly when it came to the curriculum of schools. This constituted a profound shift in epistemic authority. Prior to the imposition of colonial rule in Muslim Mindanao, decisions about what knowledge was of most value—epistemic authority—were made in local communities on the basis of the traditions, values, and perceived needs of those communities. Knowledge was a cultural construct emerging from the experience of local communities. The emerging idolatry of the text in colonial and later postcolonial education transferred epistemic authority to books written from within a different set of epistemological assumptions and emerging from the traditions, values, and perceived needs of different cultural communities. Thus, the gap between the authorized knowledge contained in the book and local knowledge objectifies the official ignorance of local people while at the same moment the shift to English—and later Pilipino—renders them illiterate and speechless.

This shift in epistemic authority also radically transforms conceptions of the educated person and the social status that concept carries. The implicit educational values of the *Darangen* explored in Chapter 2 suggested a conception of the educated person as one intimately familiar with the history, values, and traditions of Maranao culture. Moreover, the epic's oral cultural origins strongly imply the necessity of continually demonstrating one's status as an educated person through daily behavior in conformity to ideals contained in Maranao history, values, and traditions. The introduction of Islam profoundly changed local culture of course and introduced a profound veneration for a book—the Qur'an—but the process of Islamization was a voluntary adaptation of traditional culture to a new faith. Furthermore, while the epistemic content of the conception of the educated person changed somewhat, it remained an ideal that could only be demonstrated through correct behavior. The epistemic authority of the *lutong makao* curriculum and the authorized textbook establishes an ideal of the educated person measured by one's acquisition of alien knowledge and certified by external authorities rather than the norms of one's community.

The effects of both shifts are profound. The shift in epistemic authority and the transformation of ideals of the educated person dichotomized Maranao society between tradition and Islam and secular modernity. The effects of this dichotomization can be seen in the gradual loss of Maranao traditions—something experienced by almost all indigenous communities in the process of development—and in the split between Islamic and public education. Such splits sap cultural power of education rooted in local experience and oriented toward local aspirations. At the individual level, it tends to create among those defined as ignorant and backward by authorized knowledge a condition the African-American sociologist W.E.B. DuBois called "second sight."

> Born with a veil and gifted with second-sight in this American world—a world which yields him no true self consciousness, but only lets him see himself through the revelation of the other world. It is a peculiar sensation, this double consciousness, this sense of always looking at one's self through the eyes of others, of measuring one's soul by the tape of a world that looks on in amused contempt and pity. One ever feels his twoness ...[52]

This painful condition often seeks resolution in conformity to authorized ideals and thus a turning away from one's identity or the violent rejection of those authorized ideals in favor of others that are seen as enhancing the sense of self-worth implicit in traditional ideals. The majority, however, struggle desperately to reconcile the two, a struggle which often leads to an obsession with credentials and widespread cheating.

Moreover, given the material poverty of the region, the academic nourishment of the *lutong makao* curriculum cooked in Manila is often inadequate. In all but one of the fifteen schools examined for this study, there were only enough textbooks on hand to supply the teachers. Children had no textbooks at all. With nonexistent school libraries and hours of difficult travel from cities, teachers have very little access to instructional material with which to supplement the text. Trapped between the expectations of centralized authority, standardized tests, and a dearth of supplemental instructional materials, teachers rely almost exclusively on the textbook provided them. Thus, teachers are reduced to what they call "spoonfeeding"—copying material from the textbook onto the blackboard so students can in turn copy the material into their notebooks to memorize and reproduce on tests—a particularly impoverished form of banking education that, even under the best material conditions, functions to preserve unequal, dichotomous social relations of subject-object, colonizer-colonized.[53] Consequently, widely used instructional methods, dictated both by the impoverished conditions and professional climate within which teachers work, help perpetuate the oppressive social relations characteristic of the internal colonial model. This idolatry of the book, when combined with the inability of centralized authority to provide them to rural schools, often means that teaching grinds to a halt because the lack of books is understood as the lack of access to authorized knowledge, and teaching is conceived as the one-way transmission of that knowledge to students. The libraries of many schools in Lanao del Sur, for instance, contain row upon row of old textbooks that are deemed "obsolete" because they do not reflect up to the minute Department of Education goals even as teachers complain about the lack of books for their students. This is perhaps the most debilitating effect of the idolatry of the book.

When it is successful in actually reaching students, the *lutong makao* curriculum, enshrined in government authorized textbooks, is perhaps the most important mechanism by which schools in Lanao del Sur and, indeed, throughout the Philippines help to sustain an unequal and alienating status quo. Critical educational theorists, for example, argue that schools often function as "agents of cultural and ideological hegemony" through their control of cultural capital deployed as a filtering device to maintain relations of domination and subordination within a society. This "selective tradition" embodied in school curricula privileges the "cultural capital of a particular class and then act[s] as if all children had equal access to the attitudes, skills, and linguistic competencies that enable achievement of that ideal."[54]

Unfortunately, Muslims and their history, culture, and contributions to Philippine history are largely absent from the selective tradition embodied in most Philippine textbooks. This absence has been a feature of Philippine textbooks since at least the 1930s when the textbooks written by Camilo Osias, discussed in Chapter 3 were first published. More contemporary analyses suggest things have not changed all that much since Osias's tenure. Content analyses of elementary and secondary textbooks in use in the late 1980s and early 1990s revealed that fully half of the 38 textbooks studied contained no reference to or mention of Muslims at all. Of those that did include some mention of Muslim Filipinos, most contained no more than one or two paragraphs to a couple of pages. Furthermore, as with the Osias texts, much of the information included was either erroneous or insulting to Muslims.[55]

The 15 high schools providing the empirical foundation for discussion in Chapter 4 of contemporary Muslim Filipino dissatisfaction with public education are not administered directly by the Department of Education; therefore, they have been given the opportunity to select different texts, though the content of those texts must meet with Department of Education approval.[56] The Muslim Filipino officials with administrative responsibility for these schools selected textbooks published by the Phoenix Publishing House because, in their opinion, the series was most inclusive of Muslim Filipinos and least offensive. However, a survey of the Social Studies, English, and Values Education textbook series suggest that problems found in earlier content analyses of commonly used Philippine textbooks remain problematic.

High school students in the Philippines, for instance, take a sequence of social studies courses that include Philippine History and Government, Asian History, World History, and Geography. It is in this curriculum that one would expect, therefore, to find an acknowledgment of Filipino Muslim's history, culture, and contributions to contemporary Philippine society. On this point, the series' text for Philippine History and Government, *Kasaysayan at Pamahalaang Pilipino*, seems to support the administrator's assertion that the series is the most inclusive of Muslim Filipino history.[57] This text provides a reasonably substantial, thorough, and positive treatment of the Islamization of the southern Philippines as well as the long history of Muslim Filipino resistance to Spanish attempts to extend their colonial domination in Mindanao. However, Muslim Filipinos disappear from the narrative of Philippine history in this text after 1898 except for a sentence acknowledging that a legacy of the Moro-Spanish wars is a wall between Muslims and Filipinos. The section concludes with the statement that, in the minds of Muslim Filipinos they were not then, nor are they now, nor will they ever be Filipinos. While the author, a former Secretary of the Department of Education, Culture, and Sports, has clearly intended to do justice to Muslim Filipino history and to contemporary feelings of alienation, the text leaves unaddressed the twentieth-century history of Muslim–Christian relations and inadvertently suggests that any lingering hostility is the unfortunate legacy of nineteenth-century history rather than the more recent government policies and events. The texts for Asian History and World History, while containing nothing particularly negative about Islam, do not make up for this silence since they address a broader history further away from Philippine experience.[58] Thus, despite obviously good intentions, students of these texts could easily come away with the notion that the grievances of Muslim Filipinos are historically and geographically remote from contemporary concerns.

At the time, the fieldwork for this study was conducted Phoenix published two series for use in high school English courses. Both reportedly conformed to Department of Education guidelines and used literature to teach language as it is, in the opinion of the editors, "the major vehicle for values development" and one of the last opportunities students would have to "read writings that record man's understanding of man in relation to himself, to nature, to society, and his Creator."[59] Here again, editors made some effort to be inclusive: the texts include folktales from a number of different cultures, including some Middle Eastern Muslim cultures. However, these are overwhelmed by the number of overtly Christian stories from the Bible, images of Santa Claus, and other manifestations of majority culture. Moreover, the selections with Middle Eastern cultural origins are folktales about genii, magic carpets, and other such venerable stereotypes of Arab culture rather than stories that offer some understanding of contemporary Muslim societies. There is no evidence in any of the four texts that Muslims existed or exist in the Philippines. One Maranao poem translated by an American missionary is so stripped of cultural references that there is nothing recognizably Maranao about it but its label.[60] This exclusion is reinforced by the editors' assertion that "Filipino is the language of the home and the community."[61] Such a statement ignores the fact that Filipino is not the language of the home for the majority of Filipinos and implies that the majority who speak Cebuano, Illongo, Maranao, Tausug, or some other dialect are not quite Filipinos.

The second English series, *English Communication Arts and Skills*, parallels the social studies series by focusing on Philippine literature in the first year, Asian and African literature in the second, American, British, and Philippine literature in the third, and world literature in the fourth.[62] It reflects a clear attempt to be more inclusive in its selections. Readers are introduced to a variety of Filipino, American, British, Chinese, Japanese, as well as other European, Middle Eastern, and Asian literary selections. The editors also include more Filipino Muslim folktales as well as a brief account of traditional Tausug life written from the perspective of a Tausug girl.[63] Readers of the series, however, will see far more selections from American and British—even Chinese and Japanese—sources than from Filipino Muslim societies. And while they will learn about early Indian influences on the *Darangen*, the reading selections are almost exclusively folklore; thus, they tend to depict Muslim Filipinos as historically and geographically remote, exotic Others rather than fellow citizens of the contemporary world. This sense of separation is compounded by language referring to them, their and they and using terms such as Mohammedan and Moro or calling attention to the number of wives Muslim men might have and slavery, the very sorts of things that characterized General John J. Pershing's discussion of Muslim Filipinos almost a century before. The literary selections, as well as the language used to discuss them, represent Muslim Filipinos as outsiders see them rather than how they see themselves. Thus, the texts offer them, in DuBois's (1969) terms, an exercise in second sight.

Phoenix Publishing also had two series of textbooks for Values Education in print in 2000–2001 that were based on the values framework issued by the Department of Education and intended for use in Philippine public and private schools.[64] The first series claims to offer an account of *the* Filipino, *the* Filipino psyche, and *the* Filipino way of life in order help students achieve the goal of becoming a *true* Filipino (emphasis added).[65] Thus, they are deeply essentialist, deploying the authors' normative conception of Filipino identity rather than engaging students in an exploration of what such an identity might be or the variety of ways in which it might be expressed. This conception of Filipino identity is deeply nationalistic and religious. The texts encourage a patriotism and faith in God consistent with the Department of Education Values Education program and the primary goals of Philippine education stretching back to the commonwealth period. They also promote a concern for social justice, human rights, the environment, as well as understanding of adolescents' individual and social development. In these respects, the texts are quite impressive. Moreover, in the sections that most explicitly address religious faith, the authors have attempted to include Islam as one among a number of world religions embodying different, legitimate expression of faith in God, though the vast majority of material is explicitly Christian. There is, however, nothing that suggests Islam might have a greater claim on students' awareness than say, Buddhism or Confucianism. Moreover, the images, the examples, the scenarios on gender relations or dating, the names of the children, the psychological theories on adolescent development deployed are all clearly drawn from middle class, Western, Christian models. These models, along with the explicitly normative intent of these texts, powerfully reinforce the message of the *civilization-development discourse*, discussed in Chapters 1–3, that has shaped colonial and postcolonial relations with Muslim Filipinos since the beginning of the twentieth century: your culture and values are deviations from the norm/modernity. You can keep your religion, but to be a *true* Filipino you should be like us in all other respects.

Thus, while some few authors and publishers have attempted to include more of Filipino Muslim history and culture in recent textbooks, it remains extremely limited and continues to portray Filipino Muslims as either irrelevant artifacts of early Philippine history or rebels threatening the peace and stability of the country.[66] In this way, the curriculum, even where it includes material on Muslim Filipinos, engages in the intellectual construction of the Muslim Other in ways that reinforce popular biases and "divide the world" in ways that justify and perpetuate the marginalization of Filipino Muslims.[67] Attempts to sympathetically portray the lived culture and experience of contemporary Muslim Filipinos in ways that might acknowledge the dignity of Muslims and help eradicate the strong bias against them held by many Christian Filipinos are largely absent or ineffective. Thus, the *lutong makao* curriculum falls short of a fundamental ethical principle: the idea that the child should see herself in the curriculum and learn to see through others' eyes.[68] Some contemporary textbooks still available and in use continue to portray the Philippines as the "only Christian nation in Asia" ordained by God to bring Christianity to the rest of the continent.[69] Such texts are no doubt intended for use in private schools. But with up to 30 percent of all secondary school students enrolled in private schools in the late 1990s, texts with a fundamentalist Christian point of view can have a powerful effect of popular attitudes toward Muslim Filipinos.[70] Such attitudes, whether explicitly articulated or not, are widespread and leave the Muslim Filipino with little doubt as to where he or she stands in Philippine society: at best an exotic but historically and culturally irrelevant Other, at worst a deviant and violent threat to the Filipino norm.

In spite of a few good faith efforts to craft more inclusive texts for use in schools, many teachers in Lanao del Sur recognize the continuing bias of available textbooks, complaining that the textbooks, and thus the curriculum, that they are able to serve to their students do not adequately or accurately portray the history, culture, and lives of Muslim Filipinos. This gap between good intentions and reality in the province is due to a number of factors. Perhaps the most important of these is the centralization of educational decision-making in Manila. Given Manila's preeminence in terms of social and political power and in higher education, the cultural milieu in which policies are formulated and decisions made is dominated by the cultural values and academic perspectives of people largely educated and residing in Manila. Thus, the cultural capital of the colonized margins is subordinated to the cultural capital of the colonizing metropolis. And such perspectives are hardly neutral. Through the colonial period, the commonwealth, the postwar republic, and the Marcos dictatorship the educational opportunities made available to Muslim Filipinos by the state reflected what those in power thought good for Muslim Filipinos rather than what they thought good for themselves and their children. Even though the restoration of democracy under Corazon Aquino eventually led to a political settlement with the MNLF, the crucial role of the Catholic Church in Aquino's victory helped to foster a sense of Filipino nationalism even more closely tied to Catholic Christianity than it had, perhaps, ever been before. The presence in the Department of Education central offices of a Catholic chapel in 2000–2001 symbolizes the depth of that influence.

Adding to the factors that conspire to produce cultural bias in Philippine textbooks and curricula—in spite of the good intentions of many individual officials—is the relative dearth of Muslim writers, particularly Muslim writers with the Manila-centered academic credentials deemed most credible by the Christian-dominated educational establishment. Thus, even the most well-intentioned efforts to write more inclusive textbooks are handicapped because they are written by non-Muslim, urban academics with little direct knowledge or experience of Muslim culture and history and who themselves are products of a Philippine mainstream that has long neglected or stereotyped Muslims. The instances discussed above in which textbook authors use labels such as Mohammedan or Moro, refer to *them* in ways that rhetorically reinforce long-held assumptions about Muslim Filipino deviance, assume that folklore accurately represents contemporary Muslim Filipino experience, or deploy normative ideals of identity and behavior based on the experiences and values of a Westernized, Christian, middle class offer evidence of the continuing failure of even well-intentioned textbook writers to enable Muslim Filipino children to see themselves in the curriculum.

Finally, even where modest efforts have been made to craft a more inclusive curriculum there is virtually no impact on the classroom in provinces like Lanao del Sur. The material poverty is so severe that most often even teachers do not have the most up-to-date textbooks. They frequently make do with whatever they happen to own themselves or whatever they can find. In none of the 15 schools in western Mindanao visited for this study did children have their own textbooks. School libraries typically consisted of shelves full of rotting textbooks deemed obsolete by the teachers. Other reading materials were rare and generally unavailable to children for fear that they would be damaged or not returned. The few books written on Muslim Filipinos are unavailable in most of the urban bookstores even if teachers could afford them on their meager salaries or had the time for the long and frequently difficult trips it would take to reach them. And given the history of bureaucratic centralization and top-down management in Philippine education, teachers are not prepared or encouraged to design their own curricula in response to local needs, experiences, or aspirations. The end result is the *lutong makao* curriculum that is finally served to Muslim children is both insufficient—most students have little direct access to it—and nutritionally inadequate—containing little in the way of nourishment of the cultural identity of Muslim children. The result is Muslim children who are both academically and culturally starved in their public schools.

The Legacy of Colonial Education

The combination of factors tending to reinforce in-group identity—a strong and growing sense of Islamic identity coupled with the traditional cultural and familial pride embodied in *maratabat*—and factors reinforcing a sense of exclusion—the practical invisibility of Muslims in the curriculum and the continuing material poverty of the province and its schools contributes to a strong sense of alienation from the Philippine mainstream and dissatisfaction with public schools. The situation constitutes something of a standoff between an indigenous community that is culturally strong—though politically weak—and a weak state lacking the cultural or political muscle to enforce its authorized norms at the local level. The ensuing dissatisfaction in many ways confirms a long tradition of Maranao mistrust of public schools as agents for the Christianization of their children. For many years after the introduction of public schooling in Mindanao in the early part of the twentieth century, many Maranao defied American blandishments and compulsory education laws because they feared the schools would alienate their children from their culture and their religion.[71] It was not until, perhaps, the 1970s that significant portions of the school-age population in Lanao del Sur participated in public education. Even today school participation, promotion, and graduation rates are among the lowest in the country while drop out rates, poverty, illiteracy, infant morality rates, and so on are among the highest.[72] Much of this is due to the material poverty of the region, but it also reflects a sense of alienation from the institutions of a Philippine mainstream that, as one teacher said vehemently, "doesn't give a damn about us."

This sense of alienation from a social and educational mainstream that is perceived as unwilling or incapable of respecting the unique Islamic cultural identity of its Maranao citizens exacerbates the negative consequences of the material poverty that plagues so many, not just Muslim-dominated, areas of the Philippines. It contributes to a widespread sense of futility and hopelessness that contributes to high rates of absenteeism among students and leads some teachers to neglect their responsibilities. In most rural communities in Lanao del Sur, for instance, a position at the local school represents the only opportunity for steady professional employment in the area. Caught between the desperate need for a job and a sense of futility engendered by material poverty, neglect, and alienation from the Philippine mainstream, some teachers do no more than is necessary to keep their positions. While such behavior is widely perceived as evidence of laziness or lack of professionalism, it might also be read as a form of psychological resistance to an internal colonial system that demands the loyalty and participation of the colonized while offering little in the way of cultural, economic, or existential security in return.[73] At the very least it represents a method of coping with the seemingly impossible demands of an official discourse that offers education as the route to individual success and societal improvement while failing to provide the material resources and conditions necessary to meet these goals. In spite of such difficulties, however, the Maranao have not been robbed entirely of their faith in education. Many teachers and students struggle gamely on, making the most of what they have. A few succeed, but not enough to transform social, economic, and educational conditions of the province.

Critical analyses of classical colonialism highlight the cultural and psychological price often paid by those enjoying such success.[74] The fact that they are so notable underscores their relative rarity and raises the suspicion that such successes serve more to reinforce the myth of the permeability of the colonizer-colonized boundary and to enlist apparently successful individuals of such marginalized communities in the effort to reconcile those communities and their aspirations to the status quo.[75] In a public educational system dominated by the cultural values of the Christian mainstream that has largely neglected the history, culture, and faith of Muslim Filipinos, the route to academic and social success lies largely through the terrain of an alien culture that frequently looks upon Muslims with suspicion. Survival, let alone acceptance, in that mainstream often means surrendering many aspects of one's cultural and religious identity in order to fit in.[76] Thus, academic and social success in the mainstream often comes at the price of alienation from one's cultural and religious roots, of acquiring a "second sight" by learning to see oneself "through the revelation of the other world" and thus to measure "one's soul by the tape of a world that looks on in amused contempt and pity."[77] Preservation of those cultural and religious roots has come at the price of cultural, political, and economic marginalization. From the perspective of psycho-cultural analyses of education, such schooling fails in one of its primary functions, which is to nurture the self-esteem of children by helping them find a sense of identity through their participation in the "distributed intelligence" and meaning-making processes of their cultural community.[78]

This dilemma has long been epitomized by the educational choice that the Maranao have had to make. Maranao parents have learned through their own hard experience that one of the officially sanctioned routes to a materially better life lies through education. After initially rejecting public schools, they later embraced them and send their children to them in the hope that they will achieve success within the dominant society as engineers, doctors, lawyers, and so on. They have recognized, however, that those same schools offered a curriculum that ignored, where it did not openly disparage, their cultural and religious values. Therefore, in an effort to resist pressures to assimilate and preserve their unique religious identity, they send their children to the *madaris* on the weekends to learn Arabic and Islam. Thus, many Maranao parents send their children to school seven days a week in a desperate attempt to ensure a better future for their children while retaining their identity as Muslims. In recent years, middle-class Maranao parents who have recognized the difficulty that trying to follow two systems has placed on their children have started so-called integrated schools that endeavor to combine the Western education of the public schools with the education of the Islamic schools.[79] Enrollment in the first of these schools has mushroomed since its inception in 1995, testifying to the perceived need among the Maranao for an education that honors and respects their identity as Muslims, yet provides opportunities for success in the secular world.[80] Such schools provide a glimpse of the kind of schools Maranao parents want to provide for their children in contrast to the kinds of schools the Philippine mainstream has decided is good for them. Currently, the Department of Education in the ARMM is pursuing an effort to reform *madaris* along similar lines. However, the option embodied in such schools remains limited, for the most part, to those who can afford them. The vast majority of Maranao schoolchildren lack the resources to do so and are consigned to impoverished, dilapidated public schools serving them a "cooked curriculum" that does not meet their needs and ignores the most deeply held aspect of their cultural identity—their faith.

Educational Responses and the Moro Problem

The sense of an identity rooted both in local culture and Islam and separate from the rest of the Philippines has long presented a challenge to colonial and postcolonial Philippine governments bent upon forming a unified Philippine state ruled from Manila. Since at least the beginning of the twentieth century, public education has been deployed as a tool for dealing with this challenge.[81] Both American and Filipino governments saw education as the means of bringing Muslim Filipinos into conformity with ideals of civilization, citizenship, and modernity premised on the norms of white, Western, Christian political and cultural values. This *civilization-development discourse* was deployed via policies designed to integrate Muslim Filipinos into the Philippine body politic without in any way transforming the relations of power and privilege existing in that body politic. Thus integration meant, in fact, the marginalization and subordination of Muslim Filipinos within the status quo. This effort was the dominant theme in Philippine educational policy toward Muslim Filipinos for the past century.

During the American colonial regime, public schools were introduced into recently pacified Muslim areas with the avowed aim of bringing the uncivilized tribes, as they were termed in official documents of the time, up to the level of civilization of the remainder of the country so that they could be effectively and safely integrated into an independent Philippine society.[82] While pursuing this goal, much of Mindanao and Sulu were administered by American military and civilian governors separately from the rest of the Philippines until 1920. The yardstick of civilization used in this effort, however, was an American, Christian ideal.[83] Thus, even though American policy claimed to honor the constitutional ideal of separation of church and state, the model of civilization used effectively excluded Islamic and local cultural identity from that ideal. The policy of integration, to the extent that it was successful, required Muslim Filipinos to set aside their religion and their culture as the price for admission into the mainstream. Most Muslim Filipinos rejected integration at such a price and refused to send their children to government schools.

With independence in 1946, the Philippines in effect inherited the colonial mantle passed down from the Spanish to the Americans, continuing the effort to integrate Muslim Filipinos through the traditional policies of educational development and military suppression and thus continuing the Muslim–Christian, colonized-colonizer dichotomy in what was ostensibly a postcolonial period. The problems of Muslim Filipino society and the tensions between it and the mainstream were seen as a consequence of the material poverty of the region and the lack of access to quality education. Thus, by the mid-1950s efforts were made to expand access to public schools among Filipino Muslims and to establish a state university in the area.[84] Implicit in this approach was the assumption that the Moro Problem was a result of the economic and cultural backwardness of Muslim Filipinos; in short, it continued the civilizing mission of American educational policy in order to facilitate the exploitation of the economic resources of Muslim Mindanao for the betterment of a Philippine society of which Muslims were, theoretically, a part. To be sure, material poverty, lack of access to education, and cultural impediments were and are factors in the marginalization of Filipino Muslims within Philippine society. And improved access to education has made a difference in the material prosperity and social mobility of many Muslim Filipinos and helped diffuse some of the mistrust between Muslims and Christians that has long fueled the conflict. However, the conflict and its underlying tensions remain, often organized and expressed by the most educated members of Muslim Filipino society.[85] This is due in part to the widely held perception that integration into the mainstream requires assimilation to an ideal that is modeled on the culture and values of the Christian majority. Thus, the price of integration and acceptance into the mainstream is often the sacrifice, or at least subordination, of that which makes one most different from the mainstream: a strict adherence to Islam.

The creation in 1990 of the Autonomous Region in Muslim Mindanao and the devolution of some authority over education to a regional office of the Department of Education suggested a different approach to educational policy designed to mitigate Muslim–Christian tensions: autonomy.[86] Ostensibly, this autonomy project gave greater decision-making authority to Muslim educators and local political leaders who theoretically had a better understanding of the needs and interests of their fellow Muslims. In actual practice, however, most Muslim teachers interviewed for this study argued that autonomy had done little or nothing to change conditions in their schools. The larger political and economic problems that led to what many Muslims called—and which the internal colonial model anticipates—a false autonomy have tended to thwart whatever efforts toward educational reform that may have been attempted.[87] Thus, the reality of the autonomy policy was that conditions were largely the same in schools while, to some extent, national educational leaders could absolve themselves of much of the responsibility for those conditions.

Implicit in the move toward even false autonomy was some recognition that an integration policy cooked with the best of intentions in Manila by an urban, educated, Christian elite had largely failed to integrate the vast majority of Muslim Filipinos into the mainstream of the Philippine body politic or to diffuse historic tensions between Muslim and Christian communities. This limited move toward decentralization came as a result of the recognition that Muslim Filipinos have a distinct culture that is worthy of respect, that the educational needs of that culture should be met, and that Muslim educators are the best ones to determine how those needs should be met. Left undisturbed in such a policy, as it was in the autonomy policy, was the assumption that the Moro Problem was the Moro's problem: the problem lay with Muslim Filipinos. If poverty and violence continues, it is their fault. Their American colonial masters tried to solve it for them and failed. Their Christian "brothers" tried to solve it for them and failed. Now Muslim Filipinos were given some leeway to solve their own problems, albeit without the latitude and resources necessary to succeed.

This conception of the problem posed by Islamic identity in the Philippines and Philippine education failed to recognize the role of the cultural and religious biases of the mainstream in the problem and the need for schools all over the country, not just those in the Muslim–Christian contact zone in Mindanao, to offer an education that challenges those biases. Thus, the social mainstream into which Muslim Filipinos were to be integrated continued to be defined by the fundamental assumptions and biases of Christian Filipinos, causing Muslim Filipinos to experience such integration as, in fact, assimilation, which they have resisted at the cost of their lives and treasure for more than three centuries. In the context of such an educational approach to integration/assimilation that tended to reinforce hierarchical dominant-subordinate relations, such resistance was then interpreted as evidence of continuing ignorance and backwardness, which called forth a greater effort for education and development in response.

Alternative Educational Responses to the Moro Problem

Viewed from the secularist, social science perspective of contemporary Western education, the problem of Islamic identity in Philippine education appears to be an instance of the dangerous mingling of sacred and secular that many modern societies guard against through legal restrictions on church-state relations. From such a perspective, championed by the American colonial regime and at least nominally adhered to in the Philippine political system, the emphasis on religion as a marker of in-group and out-group boundaries reifies and further radicalizes dichotomous Muslim–Christian, colonized-colonizer relations in ways that effectively divide the nation into two. According to this view, Muslim Filipinos who insist that their religious beliefs guide all public and private aspects of their lives tend to alienate their Christian fellow citizens. Moreover, many Christian Filipinos are unaware of the manner in which their religious and cultural values shape assumptions about behavior, history, society, civic participation, and education in ways that offend and alienate their Muslim fellow citizens. From this point of view a strict separation of church/mosque and state, like that practiced in the United States for instance, would be a better solution to the problem of religious identity in Philippine society and education.

This was, in fact, the approach attempted by American colonial officials. After three centuries of unapologetic mingling of church and state under Spanish rule, American colonial policy professed a strict adherence to the principle of church-state separation as key to earning the trust of Muslim Filipinos and integrating them with the rest of the country.[88] And American policy was somewhat successful in this regard even though it could never fully mask the widely held belief that Islam was an impediment and Christianity an asset to civilization. Bracketing out religious identity from cultural identity and decisions about education policy was an extremely difficult enterprise, even for these educated Americans steeped in a political tradition that had long struggled to do just that. It was an enterprise, however, that was and is problematic for many Muslims.

The ideal of the separation of church and state represents a principle to which the modern Philippine government aspires as well. The 1986 Philippine Constitution states that "the separation of church and state shall be inviolable" and that "no law shall be made respecting an establishment of religion, or prohibiting the free exercise thereof."[89] This is, of course, word for word the same language as that enshrined in the First Amendment of the US Constitution. Elsewhere in the Philippine constitution, however, the nation's schools are charged with the spiritual development of schoolchildren, a charge that was interpreted in the Department of Education Values Education Program as a charge to foster faith in God.[90] While such a charge is probably not, on its face, offensive to Muslims, it does open the door to a greater involvement of religion in education than is the case in the United States.

From the secular perspective of contemporary Western education, however, the failure of first the American and later Filipino attempts to effectively separate religious bias from political and educational decision-making is not a failure of the principle of separation but a failure in the strict application of the principle. While a stricter application of the principle might help diffuse tensions, the principle itself remains problematic for many Muslims here who understand Islam to be a way of life where separation of the sacred and secular into different spheres is impossible. Such a separation may be perceived as a denial of the significance and relevance of a core aspect of Filipino Muslim identity, an invitation to participate as citizens cut in half: Filipino, but not Muslim in any meaningful way. Thus, the very basis of the principle of separation contradicts a tenet of their faith as many understand it and its enforcement is likely to be experienced not as neutrality but rather as hostility toward their faith. To the extent that this is true, it would suggest that the only response of a religiously neutral Philippine state and system of education would be to allow Muslims to create their own parochial schools.

This has been an option long exercised by Muslim Filipinos. Islamic education predated public school in Mindanao by centuries and continues to exist side-by-side with public schools today. Scholars of Muslim Filipino history have suggested that a tutorial system of learning existed for centuries in the southern Philippines while Western travelers as early as the seventeenth century describe schools that instructed children in literacy and Islam.[91] By the early twentieth century, American colonial officials noted what they called *pandita* schools, relatively small groups of students studying under a local Muslim scholar along the lines of the Indonesian *pondok pesantren*.[92] The first formal *madaris* emerged after World War II and have proliferated over the past 30 years in conjunction with Islamicization movements and a renewed interest in *madrasah* education in other parts of the Muslim world.[93] Their formal curricula have tended to focus on Arabic language as well as Islam. By some accounts, their total enrollment approaches the total enrollment of Christians and Muslims in the public schools of the region.[94] This healthy enrollment—particularly among the poorer classes in Muslim Mindanao—is a testament to Muslim families' effort to find ways to nurture their children's Islamic identity outside the confines of the public school.

However, children's simultaneous participation in two different systems of education is difficult for them and their families. For instance, their participation in both systems of education requires Muslim children to negotiate their education through as many as five different languages in an impoverished educational system hard-pressed to meet the challenge of bilingual education for the children of the mainstream.[95] Thus, language policy alone helps insure a social stratification with Muslim and other language minority children at the bottom. And even if the madrasah is the only appropriate venue for explicitly religious instruction, it does not absolve the public school of its ethical obligations to be sensitive to and inclusive of the religious and cultural identity of its students even as it correctly eschews religious indoctrination.

The establishment of so-called integrated schools that attempt to combine a traditional public school curriculum with the religious instruction of the traditional madrasah represents an Islamic counterpart to the Catholic parochial schools that have for so long been a prominent feature of Philippine education. The Ibn Siena Integrated School, for instance, was established in 1995 by a consortium of local *ulama* and Muslim academics from the nearby state-run university and grew quickly to a total enrollment of 2000 students within five years. This private school offers a combination of *madrasah* and public school curricula in an attempt to bridge the gap between their identity as Muslims and their status as Filipino citizens and ensure their future prospects as Filipino Muslims. As of 2001, however, the curricula did not include an emphasis on the regional cultural identity of its students. The success of Ibn Siena has inspired or coincided with the establishment of similar schools, such as the Shariff Kabunsuan College in Cotabato City or the Philippine School for Advanced Integrated Education, with branches in several communities and the aspiration of establishing an Islamic university in the region.[96] Given the recent establishment of these schools, there is little more than anecdotal evidence of their success or failure in meeting their goals. However, while such schools may well offer a better chance at social mobility while affirming children's self-esteem as Muslims and offer a relatively homogenous and thus comfortable cultural climate as Maranao, they represent an option available only to the middle classes, who can afford it. Moreover, even widespread access to such Muslim parochial education is still subject to the flaws inherent in the autonomy policy discussed above: it leaves untouched the ignorance and biases of the Christian mainstream that in part fuel tensions between the two communities. It fails to challenge the assumption that the Moro Problem is the Moro's problem. And in failing to do so, it fails to address the problem of social fragmentation and marginalization even as it honors the Islamic identity of its students.

While many Muslim teachers criticize what they see as Christian bias in the school curricula cooked for them in Manila, they do not call for the strict exclusion of all mention of religion from Philippine schools. Nor do they want Islam to dominate the public schools. They want to be included, to have the history and culture and heroes and accomplishments, and religious beliefs of Muslim Filipinos acknowledged and included as more than a historical relic or a rebellious threat to national integrity. However, this is a goal that cannot be accomplished by attempting to bracket off that which is most distinctive about them—their religious identity—from their cultural identity. Their plea for inclusion is a plea for the public school and its curriculum to recognize them and the children they teach for who they are—Filipino citizens *and* Muslims—with a distinctive culture worthy of the respect and understanding of their fellow citizens. While almost no citizen, certainly no Filipino educator, would dispute this fact, and while good faith efforts toward this goal have been made by both Christian and Muslim educators, these Muslim teachers still feel that they and their children are third-class citizens in Philippine society and public education.

Despite the best of intentions, the centralization of educational decision-making in what many see as the Christian-dominated imperial metropolis perpetuates existing biases and robs teachers of the local flexibility to adapt their teaching to local culture. A curriculum for all Filipinos more inclusive of the culture and religion of Filipino Muslims, even while it rejects religious indoctrination, would teach the Christian mainstream a greater understanding and respect for their Muslim fellow citizens and help them interrogate their own complicity in the more than three century Moro Problem. Such a curriculum would also honor the Islamic identity of the teachers and students of the lake and thus harness their fierce pride in who they are—Muslims and Maranao—and offer them spiritual, intellectual, and psychic sustenance in their effort to achieve greater economic and social mobility as Filipino citizens and to attain their moral ideal of being good Muslims. Such a de-centered and therefore non-colonizing curriculum would not pose any one cultural or religious identity as the Filipino norm and thus contribute to the liberation of both Muslim and Christian Filipinos from the dichotomous relations of the colonial legacy.

NOTES

1. Abuza, *Militant Islam in Southeast Asia*, 91–95.
2. Ibid., 89.
3. Ibid., 110–112.
4. Villaluz, "The Lake's Scientific and Socio-Economic Importance," in Saber and Madale, *The Maranao*, 4.
5. Republic of the Philippines, *Lanao del Sur Provincial Profile*, 4.
6. Majul, *Muslims in the Philippines*; Gowing, *Mandate in Moroland*.

7. Kamlian, *Bangsamoro Society and Culture*, 115–122; Bentley, "The Evolution of Muslim–Christian Relations," 127–187; Rasul, "Muslim–Christian Relations at the Grassroots Level," 137–156; Schlegel, "Muslim–Christian Conflict in the Philippine South," 20–26; Filipinas Foundation, *Philippine Majority-Minority Relations and Ethnic Attitudes*, 117–207.
8. For instance, Memmi, *The Colonizer and the Colonized*; Freire, *Pedagogy of the Oppressed*; Liu, "Internal Colonial Model," in Brydon, ed., *Postcolonialism*.
9. Fanon, *Black Skin, White Masks*; Foucault, *The History of Sexuality, Vol. 1*; Young, *Postcolonialism: An Historical Introduction*, 395–426.
10. Abrams and Hogg, "An Introduction to the Social Identity Approach," in Abrams and Hogg, eds., *Social Identity Theory*.
11. See, for instance, Memmi, *The Colonizer and the Colonized*; Freire, *Pedagogy of the Oppressed*.
12. Bauzon, *Liberalism and the Quest for Islamic Identity in the Philippines*.
13. George, *Revolt in Mindanao: The Rise of Islam in Philippine Politics*.
14. McKenna, *Muslim Rulers and Rebels*.
15. Muhammad Khalid Masud, "Introduction," in Muhammad Khalid Masud, *Travelers in Faith*; Kepel, *The Revenge of God*, 34–35.
16. Kepel, *The Revenge of God*, 35, 187.
17. Boransing, et al., *The Madrasah Institution in the Philippines*, 27.
18. Ibid.
19. Vitug and Gloria, *Under the Crescent Moon*, 209–210.
20. Boransing, et al., *The Madrasah Institution*.
21. Donald Malcolm Reid, "Educational Institutions," in John L. Esposito, *The Oxford Encyclopedia of the Modern Islamic World*, 412.
22. Mastura, "Assessing the Madrasah as an Education Institution," 6–15. See also McKenna, *Muslim Rulers and Rebels*, 200–203.
23. Mona Abaza, "Madrasah," in John L. Esposito, *The Oxford Encyclopedia of the Modern Islamic World*, 13–16.
24. Boransing, et al., *The Madrasah Institution in the Philippines*, 59, 62.
25. Nimat Hafez Barazangi, "Religious Education," in Esposito, *The Oxford Encyclopedia of the Modern Islamic World*, 406–411; Talbani, "Pedagogy, Power and Discourse: Transformation of Islamic Education," 66–82.
26. Talbani, "Pedagogy, Power and Discourse."
27. Abaza, "Madrasah," 15–16.
28. Boransing, et al., *The Madrasah Institution*, 7.
29. See, for instance, Damonsong-Rodriquez, *A Madrasah General Education Program for Muslim Mindanao*.
30. Mastura, "Assessing the Madrasah"; Pandapatan, "Madrasah System of Education in the Philippines."

31. "Primer," *Ibn Siena Integrated School* (Marawi City: ISIS Foundation, n.d.).
32. Macmood Maguindanao, Ali Macarambon, and Malawi Panambulan, personal interview, February 2001.
33. Michel Foucault, *L'ordre du discours* (Paris: Gallimard, 1971), cited in Talbani, "Pedagogy, Power and Discourse."
34. Isma'il R. Al Faruqi, *Islam*, 19–34.
35. Abrams and Hogg, *Social Identity Theory*, 3.
36. Philosopher of religion Cornel West argues that this is one function of all religious faiths. See West, *The American Evasion of Philosophy*, 211–242.
37. Disoma, *The Meranao: A Study of Their Practices and Beliefs*, 1–3.
38. Ibid.; Nagasura T. Madale, interview with the author, July 10, 1999.
39. Riemer, "Maranao Maratabat and the Concepts of Pride, Honor, and Self Esteem," 125–180; Saber, Tamano, and Warriner, "The Maratabat of the Maranao," in Saber and Madale, *The Maranao*.
40. Disoma, *The Meranao*; Majul, *Muslims in the Philippines*; Gowing, "How Muslim Are the Muslim Filipinos?" in Gowing and McAmis, *Muslim Filipinos*.
41. Bauzon, *Liberalism and the Quest for Islamic Identity*, 151.
42. See, for instance, Muslim, *The Moro Armed Struggle in the Philippines*; Coronel-Ferrer, *Peace Matters: A Philippine Peace Compendium*; Santos, Jr., *The Moro Islamic Challenge: Constitutional Rethinking of the Mindanao Peace Process*.
43. See Gowing, "How Muslim Are the Muslim Filipinos?" McKenna, *Muslim Rulers and Rebels*; Abinales, *Making Mindanao*.
44. *Constitution of the Republic of the Philippines*, Article XIV, Sec. 3(2); Department of Education, Culture, and Sports, Bureau of Secondary Education, *Manual of Information on Secondary Education*, 35; Licuanan, "A Moral Recovery Program: Building a People—Building a Nation," in Dy, *Values in Philippine Culture and Education*.
45. Constantino, *Neocolonial Identity and Counter Consciousness*.
46. Hassoubah, *Teaching Arabic as a Second Language*, 7.
47. Tamano, *Educational Visions for Muslim Mindanao*.
48. Salipada Saud Tamano, former Regional Secretary, DECS-ARMM, interview with the author, June 10, 2000; Vitug and Gloria, *Under the Crescent Moon*, 74–102.
49. Liu in Brydon, *Postcolonialism*, 1353.
50. For an account of the history of that centralization see Douglas Foley, "Colonialism and Schooling in the Philippines," in Altabch and Kelly, *Education and Colonialism*, 33, 53.
51. I am grateful to Dr. Malawi Panambulan, special assistant to the Assistant Vice Chancellor for Academic Affairs at Mindanao State University, for this description. Interview with the author, November 16, 2000.

52. DuBois, *The Souls of Black Folk*, 45.
53. Freire, *Pedagogy of the Oppressed*, 57–74.
54. Apple, *Ideology and Curriculum*, 32–33.
55. Bula, "Muslims in the Philippine Public Elementary and Secondary School Textbooks," 122–196.
56. The national agency in charge of education in the Philippines recently changed its name from the Department of Education, Culture, and Sports to the Department of Education.
57. Gonzalez, Sta. Ana-Rankin, and Hukom, eds., *Kasaysayan at Pamahalaang Pilipino*.
58. Radford, *World History*.
59. Gill, *Phoenix English for Secondary Schools, Fourth Year*, xvi.
60. Ibid., 45–47.
61. Gil, *Phoenix English for Secondary Schools, First Year*, xv.
62. Serrano and Lapid, *English Communication Arts and Skills*.
63. Serrano and Lapid, *English Communication Arts and Skills Through Philippine Literature*, 145–148.
64. Guerrero and Castano, eds., *Values Education I: A True Filipino*, v; Pedrajas, *Values Education II: A Concerned Filipino*; Palma-Rallos, *Breakthrough*; Tuvilla, *Person for Others, Community Builder and Steward on Earth*.
65. Guerrero and Castano, *A True Filipino*, v.
66. Rodil, "Remarks on Textbooks Used by a Private School in Iligan for Grades 3, 5 and 6." Unpublished manuscript; Salic, "A Content Analysis of Instructional Materials in Philippine History."
67. For an account of curriculum as a tool for colonial domination see Willinsky, *Learning to Divide the World: Education at Empire's End*.
68. Martin, *The Schoolhome*.
69. Zaide, *Philippine History and Government*, 241.
70. Republic of the Philippines, *1999 Philippine Statistical Yearbook* (Manila: National Statistical Coordination Board, 1999), Sec. 10–11.
71. Isidro, "Education in the Muslim Regions," in Isidro and Saber, *Muslim Philippines*, 95.
72. National Statistical Coordination Board, *1999 Philippine Statistical Yearbook*, 10/1–10/24; *Lanao del Sur Provincial Profile* (Manila: National Statistics Office, 1990); Tadem, "The Political Economy of Mindanao: An Overview" in Turner, May, and Turner, *Mindanao: Land of Unfulfilled Promise*, 7–30.
73. On the psychological resistance to colonialism see Franz Fanon, *A Dying Colonialism*, trans. Haakon Chevaliar, 63.

74. Fanon, *Black Skin, White Masks*.
75. Abrams and Hogg, *Social Identity*; Gandhi, *Postcolonial Theory*, 20–21. For an example of the mediating role of such "successful" individuals in the Filipino Muslim context see Saber, "Marginal Leadership in a Culture-Contact Situation."
76. After the latest round of heavy fighting between the MILF and Philippine government, newspapers reported Muslim men and women in Manila abandoning religiously conspicuous dress in order to avoid undue attention from police and security personal. On the impact of education on family relationships among Muslims see Lacar, "Familism Among Muslims and Christians in the Philippines," 42–65.
77. DuBois, *The Souls of Black Folk*, 45.
78. Bruner, *The Culture of Education*, 1–44.
79. Damonsong-Rodriguez, *A Madrasah General Education Program for Muslim Mindanao*.
80. Macmood Maguindanao, former chair, Board of Trustees and Ali Macarambon, former vice president, Ibn Siena Integrated School, Marawi City, interview with the author, February 13, 2001.
81. Gowing, *Mandate in Moroland*; Cameron, "The Schools of Moroland," Reyes and Rodriguez, eds., *Journal on National Integration*; Isidro, *The Moro Problem: An Approach Through Education*.
82. Bliss, "The Government of the Moro Province and Its Problems"; Jones, "Our Mandate Over Moroland," 609–615.
83. General John Pershing, American military governor of the Moro Province wrote: "An endeavor is being made to bring them up to womanhood under the elevating moral influence of the American Christian woman." Pershing, *The Annual Report of the Governor of the Moro Province for the Fiscal Year Ended June 30, 1913*, 32.
84. Isidro, *Muslim–Christian Integration*.
85. For instance, Nur Misuari, chairman of the Moro National Liberation Front was a former professor of political science at the University of the Philippines and Hashim Salamat, chair of the Moro Islamic Liberation Front is an Islamic scholar educated in Egypt. See Vitug and Gloria, *Under the Crescent Moon*.
86. Milligan, "Religious Identity, Autonomy, and National Integrity," 435–448.
87. Liu in Brydon, *Postcolonialism*, 1353.
88. Gowing, *Mandate in Moroland*.
89. *Constitution of the Republic of the Philippines*, Article III, Sec. 5.
90. Ibid., Article XIV, Sec. 3.2; *Values Education for the Filipino: 1997 Revised Version of the DECS Values Education Program* (Manila: UNESCO National Commission of the Philippines Education Committee, 1997), 10.

91. Pandapatan, "Madrasah System of Education in the Philippines."
92. Cameron, "Schools of Moroland"; Abaza, "Madrasah" in Esposito, *The Oxford Encyclopedia*.
93. Abaza, "Madrasah" in Esposito, *The Oxford Encyclopedia*; Boransing, et al., *The Madrasah Institution*.
94. Pandapatan, "Madrasah System of Education."
95. Children in Lanao del Sur, for instance, learn to speak Maranao at home, English and Pilipino in public schools, Arabic in the madrasah, and often learn Cebuano, the dialect spoken by the majority of their Christian neighbors.
96. Maguindanao and Ali Macarambon, personal interview.

CHAPTER 6

Reclaiming an Ideal: The Islamization of Education in Muslim Mindanao

Almost four hundred years of Muslim resistance to Spanish and later American colonization left a bitter legacy of animosity and mistrust between the Muslim minority and Christian majority in the Philippines.[1] Throughout the twentieth century, successive colonial and postcolonial governments deployed secular educational policy as a primary tool in their effort to heal that social rift.[2] Those efforts largely failed, however, to fully integrate Muslim Filipinos into the national mainstream or to prevent the outbreak of an Islamic secessionist movement that has since gone on for more than three decades and taken on disturbing international ramifications.[3] As the twentieth century came to a close, however, the government of the Philippines began to allow a measure of local political and educational autonomy in Muslim Mindanao. This provided Muslim educators with a new freedom to conduct policy experiments mapping out possible alternatives to the educational dualism offered Muslim communities wracked by religious and political conflict through much of the twentieth century. These new policies aimed to heal the alienation of Muslim Filipinos described in Chapter 4.

Reclaiming an Ideal: The Islamization of Education in Muslim Mindanao

This history of conflict and enforced integration into a social mainstream shaped by centuries of anti-Muslim bias and a clearly Western, Christian-oriented conception of modernity is the backdrop against which recent efforts to Islamize education in Mindanao must be understood. From the beginning of the twentieth century, the cornerstone of Philippine educational policy for its Muslim minority was integration. The underlying assumption of this policy was that the dichotomization of Philippine society between Muslims and Christians was an unfortunate legacy of Spanish colonization. This mistrust was no longer justified in a postcolonial state in which everyone was an equal citizen. It was largely perpetuated, however, by the backwardness and ignorance of the Muslims. The integration policy assumed that a unified curriculum, common textbooks and unified policies, combined with efforts to increase Muslim Filipinos' access to secular public education, would gradually resolve Muslim–Christian tensions.

From the early 1950s on, this resulted in efforts to expand secular public schools and establish a government university in the Muslim regions.[4] At about the same time, the government created the Commission on National Integration, an agency intended to provide a broad range of development assistance but which put most of its efforts into the provision of college scholarships for Muslim youth.[5] A highly centralized national Department of Education administered these policies. These efforts failed, however, to head off the eruption of the armed secessionist movement in the early 1970s. Many of the CNI scholarship recipients never finished their education.[6] Some of those who did, such as Moro National Liberation Front Chairman Nur Misuari, turned up as leaders in the secessionist movement.[7]

The overthrow of the Marcos dictatorship and reinstitution of elite democracy in 1986 created a political rupture within which new possibilities for Muslim Filipinos began to take shape. The new administration of Corazon Aquino, tending to see lingering communist and Islamist insurgencies as artifacts of the Marcos dictatorship, was sympathetic to Muslims' claims of oppression and relatively willing to acknowledge the historical legacy of Christian Filipinos' biases in furthering that oppression. While this new openness did not go so far as to interrogate the extent to which new policies perpetuated those biases, it did create a climate in which decentralization and local autonomy could be seriously entertained as viable political responses to the conflict.[8]

This new climate led to the creation of the Autonomous Region in Muslim Mindanao in 1990. The act creating the ARMM charged its regional government with the creation and maintenance of a public educational system that would teach "the rights and duties of citizenship and the cultures of the Muslims, Christians and tribal peoples in the region to develop, promote and enhance unity in diversity."[9] It also went on to require Arabic language instruction for Muslim children, to require schools to "develop consciousness and appreciation of one's ethnic identity," and to give the autonomous government the power to regulate the *madaris*. Responsibility for the educational measures delineated in the act was devolved to a Regional Department of Education, Culture and Sports in 1991. Thus, by the mid-1990s the legal and policy frameworks were in place to, theoretically, allow Muslim Filipinos to determine the content and direction of their education for the first time since losing their independence to the United States at the beginning of the century.

Muslim Filipino educators quickly seized upon this new freedom to Islamize education in the ARMM.[10] Their efforts led to private and public initiatives in Muslim Mindanao, initiatives that were supported in some cases by the national Department of Education for Muslim children residing outside the region.[11] These initiatives involved the Islamization of education in the region. Though the geographic concentration of Muslims in western Mindanao and the growth in the numbers of Muslim schoolteachers since the 1970s meant that many Muslim children attended majority Muslim schools taught by Muslims and located in Muslim communities, the centralization of policy-making in Manila ensured that curricula did not reflect, and at times conflicted with, local values.[12] Centralized testing policies enforced teacher compliance with this curriculum; those who chose to deviate from it jeopardized their students' already slim chances for social advancement. Thus, the new autonomy to design curricula that reflected local values represented a significant shift in direction policy-wise; however, at the same time it represented an effort to reclaim an historical ideal: the madrasah as a center of learning of both revealed and acquired knowledge.

The Integrated *Madrasa*

Both shifts reflected an intensification of Islamic identity in the broader Muslim community, which in turn reinforced the age-old problem of securing an education for children who are both Muslim and Filipino and inspired the development of what became known locally as integrated *madaris*, essentially Islamic parochial schools.[13] These schools attempted to resolve the dilemma of choosing between an Islamic and a public education for Muslim Filipino children by combining key elements of the *madrasa* curriculum with the subjects required by the Department of Education in Manila. Where they were successful in doing so and acquiring official government recognition, their graduates were theoretically able to sit for national examinations and earn admission to public and private universities.

Early efforts at *madrasah* integration began in the private sector among middle-class Muslim professionals. One of the better known of these new integrated *madaris* was the Ibn Siena Integrated School in the Islamic City of Marawi. The school was established in 1994 by two groups representing the dual educational systems existing in Muslim Mindanao: the Ranao Council, consisting of Western-educated academics at the nearby Mindanao State University, and the Markazoshabab Al Muslim Fil Filbin, an organization of local *ulama* and religious leaders in Lanao del Sur, products of the growing transnational ties between the Filipino Muslim community and the Muslim communities of the Middle East, North Africa, and South Asia.

Ibn Siena was created in response to the perception of both groups that the public schools were failing to meet the needs of Muslim children. While some of these perceived failings were academic, the primary perceived shortcoming of the public schools was moral. While the Values Education Program put into effect at the time by the national Department of Education for the public schools was perceived as good, it was deemed inadequate by many Muslim educators because it was not grounded in the ethical and epistemic values of the knowledge revealed in the Qur'an, even though it was conveyed by Muslim teachers to Muslim students in Muslim communities. In a social climate plagued by drug smuggling, kidnapping, and other crimes, as well as by armed insurgency, there is a widespread assumption that only Islam can offer an ethical system with the historical and cultural resonance in local communities to counter the short-term payoffs of such illegal activity.

According to one former administrator of Ibn Seina, "You cannot just recruit educated people to go to the mountains."[14]

The curriculum of Ibn Siena, therefore, includes study of the Qur'an, the *hadith*, and the *sunna* as well as Islamic history and values and the Arabic language. It also included secular curricula required by the Philippine Department of Education, including English-language instruction. Its objective was to produce graduates who are "a Muslim engineer, a Muslim doctor, or a Muslim lawyer."[15] This meant professionals who have the knowledge and skills necessary for economic advancement and social status within Philippine society but who also possess the knowledge of Islam and commitment to their religion required of a "good Muslim." Ibn Siena sought to transform both the reality and the perception of Muslim Filipinos, who are often perceived by their fellow Filipinos as dangerous and backward and by their fellow Muslims as ignorant of Islam. Implicit in the goal was the assumption that the existing *madrasa* and public school systems had failed to achieve this, thereby contributing to a dire socioeconomic and political predicament that was perceived to be, at least partly, the result of a moral failure on the part of Muslims.

The rapid growth of Ibn Siena suggests that many in Lanao del Sur shared this analysis of Muslim Filipinos' social predicament and agreed with the school's response to it. Incorporated in 1994, Ibn Siena opened its doors in 1995 with 153 students; the following year 800 students were enrolled; and by 2000 more than 2000 students were enrolled in kindergarten through high school.[16]

The Shariff Kabungsuan College in Cotabato City represented another model of the integrated *madrasa*. As with Ibn Siena, the director's articulation of Shariff Kabungsuan's purpose was grounded in a moral discourse centering on Islam. "It is our moral obligation," she claimed, "to educate our people," and "we feel that Muslim children are morally safe in an Islamic school."[17] And, as with Ibn Siena, this perceived "morally safe" haven was being created within a social context plagued by material poverty, crime, political instability, and violence. In contrast, the system of public education was viewed as not offering a comparable moral security because it did not operate from within a moral framework of Islamic values.

The public education system, with some justification, was also perceived as corrupt, bureaucratic, inefficient, and staffed by overburdened teachers who, because they are asked to accomplish so much with so little, often retaliate by shirking their responsibilities.[18] Shariff Kabungsuan, therefore, purported to offer both an ethical and epistemic alternative to public education. While it offered ostensibly secular subjects such as mathematics, science, social studies, and English, which were required for Department of Education recognition and for the academic mobility of its pupils, the moral significance of these subjects was rendered meaningful within the framework of knowledge revealed in the Qur'an, the *hadith*, and the *Sunna* of the Prophet Muhammad.

This is the heart of the integrated *madrasa* and constitutes the crucial distinction between it and either government or other private schools. Because government schools are, ostensibly, secular, this revealed knowledge is ignored; therefore, the acquired knowledge represented in secular subjects either lacks a morally meaningful context or has a moral context that involves the Christian values held by the Manila-based educational bureaucrats who shape national curricula and policy. Both options are deeply problematic for many devout Muslim Filipinos. Shariff Kabungsuan attempted to ease this burden and resolve the dichotomization of revealed and acquired knowledge in the public schools by offering both curricula in the same school through teachers who were trained, to a significant extent, in Shariff Kabungsuan.

Ibn Siena and Shariff Kabungsuan were not the first or the only schools in Muslim Mindanao to attempt to offer both Islamic and secular curricula. Nor are they particularly unique theoretically or practically; they were, essentially, Islamic versions of the Catholic parochial schools that have long been a part of the educational landscape in the Philippines, albeit without the institutional structure and history of Catholic education. They offered evidence, however, of an ongoing sense of the inadequacy of government-sponsored "secular" education to meet the needs of Muslim children. Moreover, as entirely local initiatives, they could be read as alternatives that reflect the desires of local populations. As such, they suggested a growing desire for educational opportunities that would inculcate an appropriate mix of revealed and acquired knowledge, a truly Islamic education for the children of Muslim Mindanao that would enable them to be, first, good Muslims and, second, good citizens of the Philippine Republic.

Project Madrasa Education

Private initiatives to integrate Islamic and secular education such as Ibn Seina and Shariff Kabunsuan roughly coincided with the establishment of the Autonomous Region in Muslim Mindanao and the devolution of some authority over educational policy-making to a regional Department of Education, creating spaces for new voices and perspectives on educational reform in Muslim Mindanao. In some instances, these new perspectives enjoyed rhetorical, if not significant material, support from the national Department of Education and the then Office of the Undersecretary for Muslim Affairs.

Some of the most prominent of these voices at the time were the products of the transnational Islamist movements that had increasingly influenced Muslim Mindanao since at least the 1970s. Their perceived superior knowledge of Islam and often-lengthy sojourns in the wider Muslim world give them status within the local Muslim community as individuals who embodied, to a greater degree than most, an ideal with profound cultural resonance: the good Muslim. Thus, they were seen as especially well qualified to reshape local education in the spaces opened up by decentralization and multiculturalism in order to bring it into greater conformity with that ideal. Two particularly prominent examples of this phenomenon were Mahad Mutilan, a highly respected Muslim scholar educated at Al Azhar University in Egypt and founder of Ompia, an Islamically oriented political party, and Mawlana Faisal, a locally respected leader of the Jema'at al Tabligh, a transnational Islamic *da'wah* movement then enjoying increasing prominence in Muslim Mindanao.[19]

While serving as vice-governor and secretary of the Department of Education in the ARMM in 2003, Mutilan launched Project Madrasah Education, an effort simultaneously to infuse aspects of the public school curriculum into the *madaris* and to Islamize public education in the ARMM. While not an entirely new initiative—former ARMM DepEd Secretary Salipada Tamano had attempted a similar effort in the late 1990s—the political climate of the mid-2000s seemed somewhat more conducive given national support for madrasah integration from the office of Undersecretary for Muslim Affairs Manaros Boransing. Mutilan appointed Mawlana Faisal to serve as director of the project and assembled a team of Western-educated Muslims and local *ulama* educated in the Middle East to design and implement PME.[20]

Thus, decentralization and the rhetoric of multiculturalism enabled, for perhaps the first time in the educational history of the region, an attempt to resolve the dualism that had characterized education in Muslim Mindanao throughout the twentieth century. This dualism presents a dilemma for Muslim Filipino families and students. The public educational system has been perceived as indifferent, if not actually hostile, to their Islamic identity.[21] Thus, children who attend only public schools are widely believed to have an inadequate education as Muslims. On the other hand, children who attend Islamic schools are not prepared with the knowledge, academic skills, and civic identity necessary for higher education in the Philippines or social and economic advancement in the mainstream of society: "These Muslims who study in the madrasah are virtual foreigners in their own country," one Muslim educational official stated, while those who study only in the Philippine educational system "are Muslim in name, but they do not know their religion."[22] PME sought to create a more or less unified, Islamized vision of education for Muslim Mindanao.

Mutilan's approach to educational reform in the ARMM was premised on an analysis of the Mindanao problem that differed somewhat from that of many other observers, most of whom had tended to emphasize poverty, underdevelopment, cultural bias, and the colonial legacy as root causes of the conflict. Mutilan, in contrast, argued that these were also problems in other provinces of the Philippines and that the "main factor is religion," the long colonial and postcolonial effort to subordinate, if not eradicate, Islam in the southern Philippines and Muslim Filipinos' struggle to retain Islam as the core of their religious and cultural identity.[23] The solution to the problem was to allow both sides to cultivate an identity that was attractive to them.

> Supposing you invite me to eat lunch, and you want me to enjoy eating with you in this. What are you going to do? You prepare me the food I like. And you eat your food that you like. Give me the one I like when I eat with you ... enjoying together ... on the same table. After eating we become all satisfied and stronger; we can work together for the preservation of our people.[24]

Mutilan's explicitly multiculturalist metaphor was precisely the opposite of the centralized *lutong makao* curriculum that had long dominated educational fare in Muslim Mindanao for more than a century.

Mutilan asserted that the extension of the Arabic language and Islamic values would, perhaps paradoxically, mitigate Muslim Filipinos' suspicion of and hostility toward the Philippine government: "If that will be implemented religiously, the Muslims will feel that this is their government. This is not the same as previous governments. This is a government that is not only going to preserve and defend our culture and faith but even struggle for its flourishing and development. So this is our government. So they will behave and stop resisting."[25]

Project Madrasah Education had three goals: (1) To infuse Islamic values and Arabic language instruction into the curricula of all public schools in the ARMM in order to produce graduates who are good Muslims capable of success in the wider society as professionals and citizens, (2) To standardize the curricula of madaris in the ARMM and integrate subject matter such as science, mathematics, social studies, and English into their curricula in order to enable madrasah students to function socially and economically in the wider society or to pursue higher education in the Philippines if they so choose, and (3) To establish pilot schools in each of the provinces of the ARMM in order to establish and develop models of the sort of integrated, educational system envisioned by the leaders of PME.[26] The conceptual center upon which this integration was based was "Islamization."

To achieve the first of these goals, a group of *ulama* was assembled to collaborate with educators from the ARMM Department of Education to prepare curricula and textbooks in both Islamic values and Arabic for dissemination to public schools in the region. The *ulama* involved in PME, all of whom were graduates of Islamic universities in Saudi Arabia and Kuwait, clearly understood the relationship between revealed and acquired knowledge in Islam.[27] However, "Islamization" was left largely undefined conceptually, so its practical application remained somewhat nebulous. It could, for instance, have involved the application of a "semantic structure" of concepts and values revealed in the Holy Qur'an and articulated in the language of Islam (Arabic) as a framework within which all other subjects—acquired knowledge—are rendered meaningful, thus suggesting a much more radical reorientation of education.[28] Or it could have been seen as the mere addition of secular subjects into the already packed madrasah curriculum and the addition of an Islamic studies course in the public school curriculum.

The second initiative involved the so-called integration of the *madaris*.[29] Ever since the introduction of government education under the American colonial regime Islamic education, though respected and supported within the Filipino Muslim community, represented a social and economic dead end for Muslims as citizens of the Philippine state. The vast majority of *madaris* focused almost exclusively on religious instruction, thus students who attended them did not receive instruction in those subjects that would enable them to attend universities or compete for positions in the larger society. Even those *madaris* that did offer such instruction were often not recognized by the government or were of such poor quality that their graduates were equally handicapped. Thus, graduates of the *madaris*, some of whom do go on to receive an advanced Islamic education in the Middle East, were employable only as poorly paid teachers in Islamic schools. This contributes to a sense of exclusion, frustration and discrimination that has radicalized many.

The aim of *madrasah* integration, therefore, was to encourage and support *madaris* to expand their curricula to include subject matter taught in the public schools. This would enable those integrated *madaris* to seek government recognition and thus be eligible for limited public support under the Fund for Assistance to Private Education. It would also, theoretically, afford those students who chose a *madrasah* education a measure of social mobility through the acquisition of knowledge and skills necessary to transfer to public schools, attend government universities, or to seek employment in the national economy. The PME, therefore, was intended to standardize the religious curriculum of these independent *madaris* and infuse the government-approved, secular curriculum into their programs to facilitate their students' access to the mainstream of Philippine education and society. The *madaris* would retain, however, their identity as institutions that render acquired knowledge meaningful by interpreting it in light of the revealed knowledge contained in the Qur'an.[30] In effect, these reforms aimed to integrate what for centuries had been two separate systems of education: government education and Islamic education. Thus, the century-long search for an approach to education that would enhance the prospects of peace between Muslims and Christians shifted from the long-held faith in secularization to Islamization.[31]

The third and least well-articulated objective of the project involved the establishment of pilot integrated *madaris* in each of the provinces of the Autonomous Region. These institutions were intended to serve as laboratories in which curricula and methods could be developed and their effectiveness demonstrated prior to dissemination to participating *madaris*.³² Interviews with PME staff at the time left unclear how the pilot integrated *madaris* would differ from existing private integrated *madaris*, such as the Ibn Siena Integrated School in Marawi or Shariff Kabungsuan College in Cotabato City, other than the presence of ARMM Department of Education control over the pilot schools. By the mid-2000s, this aspect of PME had seen the least progress toward realization.

Ultimately, the objectives of PME were to make public schools in the Autonomous Region more attractive to Muslim families by better reflecting the religious and cultural values of local communities and to improve the education offered in the *madaris* by (*a*) standardizing the Islamic curriculum and (*b*) infusing government-required secular curricula. Doing this, it was hoped, would not only improve the education of Muslim Filipino children but also transform the relationship between the Muslim community and the Philippine government. In this effort, the promoters of PME had the apparent support of the national Department of Education.³³

Educating for Peace and Reconciliation in the Second Decade of the Twenty-First Century

The Philippines' faith in education as a tool for mitigating the continuing conflict in Muslim Mindanao continued largely undimmed in the second decade of the twenty-first century. As discussed in previous chapters, explicit peace education efforts were a feature of the early years of the Mindanao State University in the 1970s and expanded to other institutions, particularly Catholic institutions such as the Notre Dame University in Cotabato City, in the 1980s and 1990s. These were, and are, noble efforts by sincere and passionate advocates of peace in a region that suffers from endemic conflict to this day.

These efforts have been encouraged and supported by a series of government proclamations and legislation over the last 20 years. In 2001, for instance, Executive Order Number 3 *Defining the Policy and Administrative Structure for Government's Comprehensive Peace Efforts* called for the "building and maintenance of a climate conducive to peace advocacy and peace education programs." This was followed in 2004 with Proclamation Number 675 designating September as Peace Consciousness Month and in 2005 with the development of two volumes of Peace Education Teaching Exemplars by DepEd and the Office of the Presidential Advisor on the Peace Process with the assistance of UNICEF. In 2006, Executive Order 570 ordered the institutionalization of peace education in the basic education and teacher education curricula of the nation's schools and universities. And in 2016 Republic Act 10908 required the integration of Muslim Filipino history into school curricula as an integral part of the history of the Philippine nation and its people. The Peace and Development Roadmap and the 2017–2022 Philippine Development Plan of the administration of President Rodrigo Duterte called for the mainstreaming of peace education and the achievement of a just and lasting peace.[34] There is no shortage of rhetorical support for peace in the Philippines, though there is an apparent shortage in implementation and follow-through.

The last ten years have largely seen however a continuation of the policy initiatives begun in the first decade of the century under the rubric of "integration." The fundamental ideas animating these policies could, in fact, be traced back as far as the Marcos administration in the 1970s and the early years of the Aquino administration in the late 1980s. One of these ideas was the offering of Arabic language instruction and the teaching Islamic values within the framework of the existing Values Education Program where both were deemed desirable by local families. Though such efforts to appease Muslim parents' demands for an educational experience for their children that supported and reflected their religious beliefs were envisioned as early as the Marcos administration, significant efforts along these lines did not take place until 2005–2006 when the administration of President Gloria Macapagal-Arroyo initiated the Arabic Language and Islamic Values Education (ALIVE) Program.[35]

ALIVE permitted and encouraged Arabic language instruction and the inculcation of Islamic values within the framework of the existing Values Education Program in those schools inside and outside the ARMM where the presence of Muslim students warranted it. The enrollment threshold to offer ALIVE was as low as 15 students; however, actual implementation depends upon the judgment of school administrators and the support of local government. The practical result is that ALIVE is offered in 1660 schools nationwide, with the vast majority of these located in the ARMM and predominately Muslim communities in Mindanao, though other areas, such as Quezon City in Metro Manila, have offered the program where it enjoys the support of local officials and educational administrators.[36]

Like so many other well-intentioned educational efforts in the Philippines, however, ALIVE has been hampered by the lack of the material and human resources necessary to fully realize the intentions of its authors. For instance, there is a dearth of educators with the knowledge of Islam, the expertise in curriculum development, and a sophisticated understanding of children's moral development necessary to develop texts and other instructional materials to support the program: Educators trained in curriculum development or child psychology have no understanding of Islam and Islamic values while those equipped with this knowledge typically do not have an understanding of curriculum development of children's moral development.[37]

In order to address the shortage of qualified teachers for the ALIVE program, the Department of Education implemented the Accelerated Teacher Education Program with support for the Australian Agency for International Development. This program provided financial support for madaris teachers with at least a high school diploma to earn a degree in education and thus be eligible to sit for the teacher licensure examination, a requirement to teach in the public schools. Unfortunately, the passing rate for participants in the program was low, less than 10 percent, since most lacked the general education background assessed by the examination. Moreover, the program ended after only six years when the international funding ended.[38]

This shortage of teachers is compounded by reports of possible bias in the hiring of teachers. Teachers are hired locally. Those who are appropriately licensed and qualified to teach in the public schools are then ranked by the local hiring officials in order of qualifications and other criteria. Prospective ALIVE teachers are reportedly ranked consistently at the bottom of these lists. It is impossible to know whether this is a result of inferior academic backgrounds of candidates who have not had the same educational opportunities as other candidates, or if ALIVE is seen as a low priority by school administrators more focused on core academic subjects, or if there is bias against hiring Muslim teachers in predominately non-Muslim schools. In all likelihood, all three factors may play a role. The upshot is that the ALIVE program, a laudable policy response to the concerns of Muslim families and students, is not implemented as widely or effectively as intended.

The policy of of madrasah integration continued into the second decade of the century as well, overseen in the ARMM by the Bureau of Madrasah Education and outside the ARMM by the national Department of Education. Under the madrasah integration policy, madaris could earn Department of Education accreditation by applying for a permit to operate, as with any other private educational institution, which requires them to prove ownership of land and buildings that meet DepEd requirements. They are also required to have licensed teachers to offer a curriculum that complies with the basic education requirements of the Department of Education; namely, mathematics, science, English, and social studies. Those madaris that meet the criteria for accreditation qualify for an annual 5000 peso (US$ 95.00) per student subsidy to help pay the salaries of those teachers delivering instruction in DepEd required subjects.[39]

While these requirements seem fairly straightforward, they have proved to be a difficult burden for most madaris in the country. Many cannot afford to hire teachers of these subjects who can meet DepEd certification standards. Where they can, those teachers often leave when they are able to find more lucrative jobs in urban areas or public schools. Thus, the shortage of teachers is compounded by high turnover rates. Moreover, many Philippine madaris are comprised of a small group of students meeting after school or on the weekends at the home of the teacher. Others, while they may have larger enrollments and a more formal organizational structure, nevertheless have poor physical facilities due to their reliance on tuition from relatively poor families. The result is that many madaris cannot meet DepEd requirements for suitable buildings, licensed teachers, or mandated curricula.[40]

Because of these hurdles, of the 2000 or so madaris claimed by former Undersecretary for Muslim Affairs Manaros Boransing in the late 1980s, only 89 were accredited by DepEd as of 2016. That number dropped to 59 in 2017 after an outbreak of fighting in Marawi, and then rose again to 86 in 2018. Meeting accreditation standards was further complicated by the implementation of nation-wide reforms expanding the Philippine education system to include mandatory kindergarten and grades 11 and 12 in order to bring the system into conformity with international standards. These reforms added to the challenges madaris faced to earn DepEd accreditation by expanding the class levels and subjects requiring qualified teachers and curricula to comply with basic education standards. Thus, in 2018 the Department of Education was providing per pupil subsidies for something over 18,000 madaris students nationwide, or approximately 200 students per accredited madrasah.[41]

The progress of madrasah integration was further hampered by the resistance or simple lack of interest of madaris owners and operators. While the idea of madrasah integration was gaining some traction in Muslim Mindanao in the 1990s, it began to gain national attention and advocacy after the September 2001 terrorist attacks on the United States amid a growing awareness of the national security threats posed by Wahhabi influences on Islamic education in the Philippines during the 1990s. Thus, the promotion of madrasah education occurred within, in part, a national security framework that demanded greater scrutiny and control of unregulated Islamic schools. Moreover, anti-money laundering and anti-terrorism measures put into place after 9/11 severely restricted the flow of money from Saudi Arabia and other wealthy Muslim countries into the Philippines which had been a major source of support for Philippine madaris. As a result, some madaris were forced to close.[42] In this climate, many madaris owners saw integration as, at best, an impossible, even if desirable goal, and at worst an unwarranted and undesirable effort by a historically hostile government to control them. Others were more concerned with external accreditation from Muslim countries such as Saudi Arabia or Malaysia or did not want to "water down" their curricula by adding secular subjects.[43]

This reluctance on the part of school operators points to the need for addressing the professional development of madaris leaders. To this end, the National Commission on Muslim Filipinos helped to create a national organization of madaris owners and operators.[44] However, their development has received even less systematic attention that the development of madaris teachers. Thus, what appear to be well-intentioned policies designed to improve madrasah education are rendered largely ineffective because, some critics contend, they were developed without a realistic understanding of the conditions and constraints within which madaris operate. Therefore, seemingly reasonable criteria are, in practice, virtually impossible hurdles because the technical support necessary to move from where they are to where everyone would like them to be is missing. The result is that significant progress toward madrasah integration is severely constrained.

Finally, widespread effective improvements in the education of Muslim Filipino children are hamstrung by forms of corruption and mismanagement that have long plagued Philippine education. Ghost teachers and schools and inflated enrollments siphon already limited funds away from academic functions. And, in some instances, funds that have been allocated to support schools never reach them. Thus, well-intentioned policies are ineffectively implemented and the dichotomization of education that has long characterized the experience of Muslim Filipino children continues.

Ambiguities of Islamization

Efforts to "Islamize" education in Mindanao and thus make it more palatable to Muslim Filipinos also suffered from a lack of conceptual clarity on the meaning of "Islamization." Was Islamization achieved by merely adding more courses to the already extensive curricula of the madaris or offering Arabic language and Islamic values to the menu of public schools?

Islamization of education is one aspect of a broader "Islamization of knowledge" (IOK) movement, an expression coined at The First World Conference on Muslim Education held in 1977 in Mecca.[45] Since its inception, it has grown into "one of the most important intellectual movements of the 20th century in the Muslim world."[46] Early key figures in the IOK movement such as Maurice Bucaille, Seyyed Hossein Nasr, Ziauddin Sardar, and Ismail Raji al-Faruqi have led an effort to Islamize science by demonstrating the "complete agreement [of the Qur'an] with modern scientific data,"[47] thus preserving the subordination of acquired to revealed knowledge in Islam from the dichotomization of sacred and secular knowledge in modern Western science.[48] According to Nasr, knowledge has its roots in the sacred; therefore, the desacralization of knowledge in modernity represents a falling away from knowledge rather than a surer road toward it.[49]

While this body of scholarship is characterized by a variety of voices and perspectives, it articulates a broadly common diagnosis of the root cause of the "malaise of the ummah" as well as a common response in the call to Islamize academic disciplines and education at all levels.[50] This body of scholarship accounts for what it sees as the failure of the Muslim world to keep pace with the West in terms of social, economic, and political progress and the continuing colonization of the Muslim mind by Western conceptions of modernity and paradigms of scientific, cultural, and political thought.[51] This epistemic neo-colonialism leads Muslim intellectuals into the trap of orienting intellectual endeavors by ideals that are fundamentally at odds with an Islamic worldview which positions Muslim intellectual production as an imitation of Western models and alienates Muslim intellectuals from their rich intellectual heritage. They argue, in effect, that Muslim intellectual production has been uprooted from the soil that nourished its great achievements of the past—Islam—which constitutes the only context in which it can truly flourish in a manner that is organically connected with that past and thus accomplished on its own distinct terms.[52]

This epistemic alienation, they argue, is reflected in and reproduced by a dualistic system of education in the Muslim world that has tended to maintain colonial educational systems which separate revealed and acquired knowledge, a separation rejected in Islam.[53] According to Abaza, the IOK movement "represents a disguised battle on 'difference' between competing intellectuals (local against western experts, but also divergent interests and ideological orientations within the local context) over the bargaining about who 'knows better' the 'reality,'" thus constructing "a clear divide between Islam and the West in centering it around the question of faith."[54]

Though there are significant differences within the IOK movement, there is broad agreement on the need to define a uniquely Islamic epistemology that reconciles the relationship between revealed and acquired knowledge and develops methods of inquiry that are grounded in that theory of knowledge and which can be applied to the task of rethinking academic disciplines from an Islamic perspective.[55] For some scholars, this means systematically weeding out fundamental secular assumptions that are built into the very fabric of modern academic disciplines. For others, it simply means recognizing them for what they are—assumptions—and clarifying their differences with an Islamic worldview, thus clearing the way for inquiry from within the fundamental tenets of that worldview. The goal of both, however, is nothing less than the decolonization of the Muslim mind. A co-requisite of this agenda is the reconciliation of the dualism of educational institutions serving Muslims at all levels, that is, Islamization of education.

As is to be expected of any broad and ambitious intellectual movement, there are a variety of voices and a number of key figures within the IOK movement.[56] Ismail Raji al-Faruqi, one of the most important founders of this movement, established the International Institute for Islamic Thought to further the IOK movement. He developed a 12-point plan which took as its starting point the mastery of modern academic disciplines and stressed the revision and production of textbooks to reflect an Islamic worldview.[57] That agenda has been criticized by others for paying insufficient attention to the prior epistemic re-orientation that must be accomplished before any transformation of the academic disciplines or revision of textbooks along Islamic lines can take place, a priority implicit in the very label of the movement: IOK.[58]

Given that implicit priority, I will briefly review the perspective of one of the most prominent exponents of the epistemology-first approach to Islamization, Syed Muhammad Naquib al-Attas, as illustrative of one direction that Islamization of education in Muslim Mindanao might take before turning to a critic of the IOK movement, Fazlur Rahman, whose ethics-oriented conception of Islamization represents, I will argue, a more practical and likely course of Islamization of education in Muslim Mindanao.

Al-Attas's Concept of Education in Islam

Syed Muhammad Naquib al-Attas is widely considered to be one of the most important contributors to the IOK movement.[59] Through his wide-ranging and prolific scholarship as well as his founding of the International Institute for Islamic Thought and Civilization in Kuala Lumpur, al-Attas has been instrumental in launching an ambitious, collaborative scholarly agenda aimed at the Islamization of a wide range of academic disciplines.[60] Al-Attas argues that the fundamental problem facing Muslim education is confusion regarding correct knowledge. Thus, the problem is first epistemological and then it is a problem of the transmission of correct knowledge that is education.[61]

Western knowledge, "tainted" by the values of Western civilization, is characterized by and productive of in the Muslim world a dualism of sacred and secular inconsistent with Islamic values and therefore productive of secularization of the Muslim world. "The epistemological weapons they use to bring about the de-Islamization of the Muslim mind," al-Attas writes, "are invariably the same, and these are – apart from the underlying principles of secular philosophy and science that produced and nurtured them – anthropology, sociology, linguistics, psychology and the principles and methods of education."[62] The consequence is confusion and the loss of a proper sense of order, a moral leveling inevitably manifested in disorder, a characteristic of injustice, which must be replaced by a correct sense of the hierarchy of knowledge and a social order based upon it, which is a characteristic of justice. This confusion is reflected in and perpetuated by the modern university, which is premised on the legitimization of doubt and conjecture as the epistemological tools of scientific inquiry.[63] Finally, because lower education necessarily takes its pattern from the university, a similar dualism and confusion characterize it as well.

Al-Attas's response to such problems is to re-establish knowledge on secure, stable and true foundations. All knowledge, in keeping with Islamic belief, comes from God. It is revealed to humanity in two "books": the Holy Qur'an, as revealed to the Prophet Muhammad, and the "book of nature." The first is the source of revealed knowledge, and the second is the source of acquired knowledge, the product of intellectual inquiry into the workings of the natural world by individual human beings.[64] These are not separate types of knowledge, but different expressions of the same underlying truth. Since the former is a direct revelation from the divine, the second—acquired knowledge—is, inasmuch as human beings are susceptible to mistakes, necessarily subordinated to it. A correct understanding of acquired knowledge is necessarily consistent with a correct understanding of the revealed knowledge since they are both expressions of the same underlying truth. According to al-Attas, "a thing, like a word, is in reality ultimately a sign or a symbol that is inseparable from another thing not equally apparent, in such wise that when the former is perceived the other, which cannot be perceived … is known."[65]

Knowledge, therefore, as al-Attas defines it, is the arrival of the soul at the meaning of a thing. The meaning of a thing means the right meaning of it, and what is considered to be the right meaning is in this context determined by the Islamic vision of reality and truth as projected by the Qur'anic conceptual system.[66] Right meaning can be achieved via the "scientific" method of *tafsir*—"the science of exegesis and commentary"—and *ta'wil*—"an intensive form" of the former.[67] These methods differ from Biblical hermeneutics in that there is no room for learned guess or conjecture; no room for interpretation based upon subjective readings, or understandings based merely upon the idea of historical relativism as if semantic change had occurred in the conceptual structures of the words and terms that make up the vocabulary of the sacred text.[68] This critical difference between *tafsir* and hermeneutics is possible because, since Arabic is the language in which God chose to reveal the Qur'an and generations of scholars have meticulously preserved the original meaning of words and concepts, the Arabic of the Qur'an has a "scientific structure" in that it has a "definitive aspect that characterizes science" which, al-Attas argues, is missing in other languages.[69] Thus, it is possible, through *tafsir* and *ta'wil* to establish the "semantic field" within which the right meaning and coherent interrelationship of key concepts, such as education, can be determined. These key concepts are "all the Arabic terms that are interrelated in meaningful pattern, projecting a worldview that is distinctively Qur'anic."[70]

Arabic was "Islamized," as are other languages and disciplines, through "the Qur'anic reorganization and reformation of the conceptual structures, semantic fields, vocabulary and basic vocabulary" of the language.[71] The truth of the Qur'an is revealed in this semantic structure. And "when the truth of the matter is revealed to man and recognized by him, it then becomes incumbent upon him to guide his conduct so as to conform with that truth." Truth, then, is "suitableness to the requirements of the proper places of things," adherence to which is a precondition of justice.[72] Failure to arrive at right meaning is erroneous and causes confusion and injustice. To justify deviation from the right meaning in relativistic terms is a misleading foreign element, like the concepts of dualism, humanism, secularism, and tragedy, that must be isolated from "every branch of the rational, intellectual and philosophical sciences" as justice is to be preferred over injustice.[73]

This epistemic cleansing is, according to al-Attas, Islamization, "the liberation of man first from magical, mythological, animistic, national-cultural tradition, and then from secular control over his reason and his language."[74] Islamization of science, then, means to read the book of nature through the lens of this semantic structure. Islamization of education would mean to ensure that the transmission of this truth, conveyed in the right meaning of key concepts within their correct semantic structure, is conducted in a fashion appropriate to the developmental level of the learner but consistent with the truth of the Islamic worldview contained in the Qur'an and delineated in the coherence of these key concepts. So, the concept of education peculiar to Islam, according to al-Attas, is "recognition and acknowledgment, progressively instilled into man, of the proper places of things in the order of creation, such that it leads to the recognition and acknowledgment of the proper place of God in the order of being and existence."[75]

Al-Attas's approach to Islamization manifests two philosophical assumptions of considerable antiquity: a foundational epistemology and a correspondence theory of truth. Truth is a quality of symbols or statements that correspond to the underlying, objective reality of being and existence as a creation of God. To know is to recognize this truth, thus knowledge rests upon the secure foundation of truth. Anything that deviates from this truth is, by definition, error. And where the stakes are as profound as one's proper relationship to the eternal and divine, the difference between truth and error is no small matter. Thus, education is centrally and, most importantly, a problem of the transmission of right meanings of key truths and the ability to read all aspects of human experience through the lens of these truths. According to this perspective, human preferences and social, cultural, or historical context are irrelevant to this truth.

Though this perspective has certain affinities with some Western theories of knowledge and truth—Platonism and positivism, for instance—al-Attas is quite correct in his claim that it has been under attack by modern intellectuals: In fact, many Western intellectuals would argue that it has been quite thoroughly undermined in the last century or so of philosophical inquiry.[76] And one of the key questions in this assault has been the question of the significance of history.

Fazlur Rahman and the Historical Contextualization of Islamization

Fazlur Rahman shared al-Attas's concerns for the intellectual revitalization of the Muslim world and the educational reforms necessary to enable and sustain that revitalization. While al-Attas focused on the establishment of right meaning of key concepts in order to correctly understand and apply the conceptual framework of Islamic truth, Rahman focused on understanding the Qur'an in its totality as a coherent expression of a fundamental worldview.[77] While al-Attas saw Islamization as first an epistemological problem, Rahman saw it as, first and foremost, an ethical problem. It was on this basis that Rahman critiqued the IOK movement and its key figures like Isma'il Raji al-Faruqi. Though he shared many of the movement's concerns and objectives, his approach was radically different.[78] "The feeling is that the modern world has been developed and structured upon knowledge which cannot be considered Islamic," Rahman wrote. "Actually, what we should be saying is that the modern world has misused knowledge; that there is nothing wrong with knowledge, but that it has simply been misused ... The question to be posed then, is: how to make man responsible?"[79]

For Rahman, the central concern of the Qur'an is the conduct of man. According to Rahman, the intellectual stagnation of the Muslim world began long before colonialism.[80] The early companions of the Prophet made decisions based on their understanding of the totality of the Qur'an and since no individual verse or text is conclusive, it must be understood in the context of the whole Qur'an.[81] Subsequent generations of scholars increasingly took an "atomistic" approach that focused on the meaning of particular words or verses in order to derive laws for the proper conduct of Muslims. Commentaries replaced original texts as curricular material, and commentaries were written on commentaries, giving rise to a new type of scholar: One of encyclopedic knowledge with nothing new to say and who assumed that whatever can be known is known rather than seeing inquiry as a way of producing new knowledge. "And so it came to pass that a vibrant and revolutionary religious document like the Qur'an was buried under the debris of grammar and rhetoric."[82]

Thus, according to Rahman, the cause of intellectual stagnation was not political disintegration or the destruction of the Caliphate but this uncreative method of interpretation. Colonialism exacerbated this problem by introducing conceptions of modernity, intellectual inquiry, and education which developed in an alien historical and cultural context, often eliciting either a conservative, uncritical embrace of tradition or an uncritical embrace of Western intellectual and educational models divorced from local tradition and culture.[83] Newly independent Muslim states tended to perpetuate colonial educational systems since they were seen as critical to the development of technological expertise necessary for economic development and maintenance of newly formed social hierarchies. But these models and systems were "not organically related to the traditional cultures of those developing societies," and thus were largely ineffective. According to Rahman, "education, to become more meaningful, has to be effectively integrated with the basic cultural values. ... This can be done in Muslim societies only by linking it with some higher purpose and with a concretely formulated and stated goal."[84] That higher purpose is embodied in Islam; therefore, effective integration of modern approaches to inquiry and education require their articulation from within an Islamic worldview.

This worldview, according to Rahman, is fundamentally moral rather than legalistic.[85] It is concerned with acting in the world in accordance with the will of God. Rahman quotes a hadith: "The Prophet said that real and true belief is that a person, who, when he sees something wrong, changes it with his hands; if he cannot change it with his hands, then he must speak out; and, if he cannot speak out about it, he must dislike it with his heart; but that is the weakest form of belief." This cannot be achieved by using the Qur'an like a manual because "for the most part it consists of moral, religious, and social pronouncements that respond to specific problems confronted in concrete historical circumstances."[86] It can be achieved, however, via a hermeneutical method of reading the Qur'an which would allow one to arrive at a sufficient understanding of its message so that one who wants to live by it could do so coherently.

This hermeneutical method involves first understanding Qur'anic precepts in the context of their "occasions of revelation," the sociohistorical context of the specific problem to which the precept responds. These specific responses can be generalized to distill a coherent sense of the general moral-social principles communicated in the Qur'an, which can then be applied to understanding the problem of moral action in the current sociohistorical context. This is not, however, a call to read the Qur'an for literal answers to current problems but rather it should be an effort to understand the general principle underlying a particular response to a specific context as a guide for action in a different sociohistorical context where a different answer may well be more consistent with the underlying principle than the original response given the different context of the present. In this fashion, individual behavior need not be identical to behavior in the Qur'an in order to remain morally consistent with Qur'anic moral principles; indeed, it should differ to the extent that the current sociohistorical context differs from the sociohistorical context of the "occasions of revelation." Thus, moral consistency need not be purchased at the price of dismissing the significance of history.[87]

Rahman's hermeneutic method requires direct engagement with the Qur'an itself as well as critical inquiry into the past and the present simultaneously. Its historicity necessarily eschews any final, definitive interpretation of the Qur'an; therefore, it foregrounds the necessity of continual discussion and debate in the formation of temporary consensus which will, in turn, give way to new interpretations. The knowledge of the Qur'an claimed by any one individual or group at any particular time is provisional and subject to reinterpretation given the different circumstances; however, the moral principles derived from the Qur'an and used as a guide for conduct by devout Muslims remain constant. Thus, Rahman's approach to Islamization stresses moral consistency over epistemological certainty. "We must not get enamored over making maps and charts of how to go about creating Islamic knowledge," Rahman wrote. "Let us invest our time, our energy and money in the creation, not of propositions, but minds."[88]

Rahman's pragmatism differs significantly from al-Attas's epistemic foundationalism in their implications for education. Al-Attas's approach to Islamization of education emphasizes the transmission of right meaning from one generation to the next whereas Rahman's approach emphasizes a method whereby communities of learners are engaged in the collaborative interpretation of provisional meaning. Al-Attas offers propositions; Rahman offers method. Al-Attas offers a recipe for how to think by defining the conceptual framework through which thought encounters subject matter; Rahman offers an invitation to think. "My plea, therefore, is that we create thinkers, those who have the capacity to think constructively and positively. We cannot lay down rules for them to think."[89]

Theoretical and Practical Achievements of Islamization

Thus, Islamization can mean more than the simple addition of courses that seems to have marked efforts to integrate Muslim Filipino education in the first two decades of the twenty-first century. It could mean a more or less radical reconception of education for Muslim Filipinos that could go in the direction of reinforcing the fundamentalist tendencies inherent in the Wahabi influences of the late 1990s and early 2000s or it could take a more pragmatic moral direction that may have affinities with aspects of Filipino culture, both Christian and Muslim. The direction it takes likely depends on which side most clearly articulates a conception of the Islamization of education that resonates with Muslim Filipinos and marshals the resources necessary to bring that vision to reality.

Making good on the potential inherent in these public policy and private educational experiments has been, as have virtually all educational efforts in Muslim Mindanao, severely hampered by endemic poverty, continued financial dependence on the central government, corruption and infighting within the ARMM, and the lingering habits of a century of educational centralization.[90] Through the first two decades of the twenty-first century, however, officials of the Department of Education at both the national level and in the ARMM have begun to articulate policies responsive to the charge to teach Muslim culture, develop consciousness of one's ethnic identity and "adopt an educational framework that is meaningful, relevant and responsive to the needs, ideals and aspirations of the people in the Region."[91] The general intent of these policies was the Islamization of education in the Autonomous Region.

After a century of colonial and postcolonial government efforts to subordinate Islamic identity to national identity and to dismiss it as irrelevant to educational development in the southern Philippines, Muslim educational leaders in the ARMM were working to place that identity at the heart of a program of educational reforms they thought necessary for the social and economic development of Muslim Mindanao. Their aspirations came across clearly in interviews conducted in the mid-2000s through the metaphors deployed by Muslim Filipino educators to describe both the problems of public education and the promise of the Islamization of education in Muslim Mindanao. Many of these metaphors revolved around food, sustenance, and growth. The government-approved curriculum was described as a *lutong makao* curriculum, a term that, while it refers loosely to Chinese cooking, is meant to convey the image of a menu settled and prepared elsewhere and merely served to captive diners, whether it suited their tastes or not.[92] Combined with the dilapidated facilities, lack of books, low graduation and college entrance rates, and other indices of educational poverty in the government schools of Muslim Mindanao, the metaphor painted a critical picture of educational malnutrition, of schools feeding students on a curricular diet many find unpalatable in quantities inadequate for their intellectual sustenance.

Mahad Mutilan's plea to "prepare me the food I like. And you eat your food that you like. ... [Then] we can work together for the preservation of our people" is illustrative of the demand at the time for curricular fare that catered to the academic tastes of Muslim Filipinos, as did Mawlana Faisal Abdullah's metaphor of the mango seed:

> If a small boy of four or five finds a mango seed in the road, he will throw it away. But a young man who finds it will plant it because he knows he might even become a millionaire from its fruit. That is the difference of knowledge between the child and the young man. How much more would an agriculturist know? And the scientist might know even more. Who knows? He might even be able to develop a medicine from that mango. It is the same with the Qur'an.[93]

The Mawlana's metaphor not only emphasizes the possibility of growth in one's of knowledge in Islam; its use of a ubiquitous item of household trash and roadside debris—a discarded mango seed—draws attention to the unlimited potential for intellectual growth in content as local and homely as the mango, an almost universally enjoyed item in the local diet.

Such metaphors were particularly evident in descriptions of Shariff Kabungsuan College by its founder and director. The school was built on soil that was trucked into fill a swampy site. Where they had the resources to place fill dirt, they built school buildings and planted—interestingly—mango and other trees. Where they lacked the resources to displace the water, they planted rice and made fishponds. The produce of these endeavors was given to supplement the meager income of teachers, who were themselves "grown" locally inasmuch as they are trained in the school itself to teach the integrated curriculum.[94] Taken together, these metaphors point to the perceived importance of local responses to local needs in local conditions—decentralization—and the perceived inefficiency of externally determined responses to imagined local needs in order to achieve others' purposes—excessive centralization.

Another theme common to interviews conducted with Muslim Filipinos in the mid-2000s was a concern with morality and moral safety. While there was criticism of government failures, oppressive military policies, majority bias, and neocolonial interference from the United States, much of the blame for the problems of crime, drug smuggling, kidnapping, violence, and terrorism in local communities was attributed to the moral failings of the people themselves.

> America is not our enemy. ... Our enemy is Satan, who tries to take us from the right path. ... [W]hat is happening to the Muslims is because of the deviation of the Muslim from the right path. ... Lots of groups, they believe that what is happening now to the Muslims, for example, the attacking of Afghanistan by your [the United States] ... they say, oh, imperialism, we will try to fight them. ... For us, the Tablighi, what is happening to the Muslims is a form of punishment from God. ... God has many soldiers: the fire, the volcano, the tidal wave, the rat, the earthquake. ... So, the message of Tabligh is, if problems are there, check yourself.[95]

While it is unlikely everyone agrees with this individual's analysis of the problems that plague Filipino Muslim society, most recognize a significant degree of moral responsibility on the part of Muslim Filipinos for these problems. And the response is, rather uniformly, the need to struggle toward an ideal conception of the good, an ideal articulated in the discourse of Islam. The belief that "if Muslims will only be good Muslims then all of their problems would be solved" is a common theme. And, significantly, this faith in faith reprises the key element in the food metaphors discussed above, for the concept of the Good Muslim idealizes the unlimited potential of a central feature of local identity in response to local needs and local aspirations.

These two themes—sustenance and morality—constitute an implicit critique of the education offered to Muslim Filipinos by successive colonial and postcolonial governments. Beyond the obvious and widely acknowledged absence of resources, the bureaucratic inefficiency and corruption, and the cultural biases of textbooks and curricula was the absence of a locally meaningful purposefulness that could offer existential and spiritual sustenance for Muslim schoolchildren. This suggests that, even if the material problems that plague Philippine education were miraculously solved, it will still fall short of Muslim Filipinos' needs if it remains silent—on constitutional grounds—regarding students' moral purpose as Muslims or substitutes some alternative ideal—the majority's Christian ideals, say, or Filipino identity—in its place. These themes help to explain the phenomenon of Islamization which rose to prominence in the spaces opened up by the decentralization of educational decision-making in Muslim Mindanao.

While new in terms of formal policy, Islamization of education in Muslim Mindanao was merely the latest channel of a powerful current that has run through the history of Muslim Mindanao: the consolidation and spread of Islam. Despite centuries of pressure, Islam has been and remains a central element of cultural and religious identity in Mindanao and the Sulu Archipelago. These trends appear, in fact, to signal an intensification of that identity as Filipino Muslim educators use the space created by decentralization to strengthen the Islamic character of society in Muslim Mindanao and to project it into private and public, formal and non-formal education in the region in the sociohistorical context of the first two decades of the twenty-first century. At the same time, the trend toward decentralization as a key element of democratic educational reform created the space for Muslim educators to begin to reclaim an old ideal: a thoroughly Islamized education.

Such a development is likely viewed with some alarm by Western observers who assume that secularization is crucial to educational development, particularly in the current international political climate, where Islamization is often seen as synonymous with radicalization. But in the peculiar context of Muslim Mindanao—where both real and imagined threats to Muslims' religious identity have conspired with endemic poverty, cultural bias, and political manipulation to fuel Islamist insurgencies and thus create conditions hospitable to even more radical foreign elements—there is perhaps something to the locally common notion that many of their problems can be solved by being better Muslims. This may not be just naive faith, but an assertion that the orienting ideals and the motive energy capable of resolving the problems of Muslim Mindanao are to be found in the spiritual, intellectual, and cultural resources of Muslim Filipinos themselves, not in the imported ideals of civilization, Filipino identity, or modernity enacted in the educational policies of successive colonial and postcolonial governments, however well-intentioned.

Notes

1. Majul, *Muslim Filipinos*.
2. Milligan, "Democratization or Neocolonialism"; Milligan, "Faith in School."
3. Vitug and Gloria, *Under the Crescent Moon*.
4. Isidro, *The Moro Problem*.
5. Clavel, *They Are Also Filipinos*.
6. Ibid.
7. Majul, *Muslim Filipinos*; Vitug and Gloria, *Under the Crescent Moon*.
8. Brilliantes, "Decentralization in the Philippines"; Tanggol, "Regional Autonomy and Social Development."
9. Republic of the Philippines, "Republic Act 6734."
10. Tamano, *Educational Visions for Muslim Mindanao*.
11. Mutilan, *Leading a New Beginning at DepEd ARMM*; M. Boransing, personal communication, July 7, 2004.
12. Bula, "Muslims in the Philippine Elementary and Secondary Textbooks"; Pascual-Lambert, "The Need for Minorities in Curriculum and Textbook Reforms"; Rodil, "Remarks on Textbooks."
13. Milligan, "Teaching Between the Cross and the Crescent Moon"; Damonsong-Rodruigez, *General Education Program for Muslim Mindanao*.

14. Macmood Maguindanao, interview by the author, Marawi City, Philippines, March 22, 2001.
15. Ali Macarambon, interview by the author, Marawi City, Philippines, March 22, 2001.
16. C. Derico, personal communication, June 27, 2004.
17. Cabaybay Abubakar, interview with the author, June 2004.
18. Chua, *Robbed*; Cabaybay Abubakar, interview with the author, June 2004.
19. Masud, *Travelers in Faith*; Milligan, "Reclaiming an Ideal."
20. Mahad Mutilan, interview by the author, Marawi City, Philippines, July 5, 2004; Aida Hafiza Macada-ag, interview by the author, Marawi City, Philippines, June 23, 2004.
21. Bula, "Muslims in the Philippine Elementary and Secondary Textbooks"; Madale, "Educating the Muslim Child"; Milligan, "Teaching Between the Cross and the Crescent Moon."
22. Manaros Boransing, Undersecretary of Education for Muslim Affairs, Department of Education, personal communication, July 7, 2004.
23. Mahad Mutilan, interview by the author, Marawi City, Philippines, July 5, 2004.
24. Ibid.
25. Ibid.
26. Aida Macada-ag, Project Consultant, PME, personal communication, June 23, 2004; Mahad Mutilan, former Secretary of Education, ARMM, personal communication, 5 July 2004.
27. Ulama [pseud.], interview by the author, July 12, 2004.
28. Al-Attas, *The Concept of Education in Islam*.
29. Aida Hafiza Macada-ag, interview by the author, Marawi City, Philippines, June 23, 2004.
30. Ibid.
31. Saligoin, "Open Learning System for Public Schools and Madaris"; Abdullah, "Madrasah Education in the Philippines"; Ghazi, "To Change Madrasah Education"; Boransing, "Modernization and Development of the Madrasah Institution."
32. Aida Hafiza Macada-ag, interview by the author, Marawi City, Philippines, June 23, 2004.
33. Manaros Boransing, interview with the author, June 2004.
34. Estonillo, "Existing Government Policies on Peace Education."
35. Darwin Absari, interview with the author, Manila, Philippines, November 15, 2018.
36. Mita Parocha, interview with the author, Manila, Philippines, November 21, 2018.
37. Ibid.
38. Ibid.

39. Ibid.
40. Darwin Absar, interview with the author, Manila, Philippines, November 15, 2018.
41. Mita Parocha, interview with the author, Manila, Philippines, November 21, 2018.
42. Darwin Absar, interview with the author, Manila, Philippines, November 15, 2018.
43. Ibid.
44. Laman Piang, interview with the author, Manila, Philippines, November 21, 2018.
45. Abaza, "Some Reflections on the Question of Islam in the Social Sciences."
46. Haneef, *A Critical Survey of Islamization of Knowledge*, 1.
47. Bucaille, *The Bible, the Qur'an and Science*.
48. Stenberg, *The Islamization of Science*.
49. Nasr, *Knowledge and the Sacred*.
50. Al-Attas, *The Concept of Education in Islam*; Al-Faruqi, *Islamization of Knowledge*; Haneef, *A Critical Survey of Islamization of Knowledge*.
51. Al-Attas, *The Concept of Education in Islam*.
52. Nasr, *Islamic Life and Thought*.
53. Ibid., Hashim, *Educational Dualism in Malaysia*.
54. Abaza, "Some Reflections on the Question of Islam in the Social Sciences," 301, 307.
55. Abaza, "Debates on Islam and Knowledge"; Al-Attas, *The Concept of Education in Islam*; Al-Faruqi, *Islamization of Knowledge*.
56. Abaza, "Debates on Islam and Knowledge"; Haneef, *A Critical Survey of Islamization of Knowledge*; Stenberg, *The Islamization of Science*.
57. Al-Faruqi, *Islamization of Knowledge*.
58. Haneef, *A Critical Survey of Islamization of Knowledge*.
59. Ibid.
60. Wan Mohd, *The Educational Philosophy and Practice of Syed Muhammad Naquib al-Attas*.
61. Al-Attas, *The Concept of Education in Islam*.
62. Ibid., 12.
63. Ibid.
64. Ibid.
65. Ibid., 18.
66. Ibid.
67. Ibid., 4–5.
68. Ibid.
69. Ibid., 2.
70. Ibid., 8.

71. Ibid., 10.
72. Ibid., 20.
73. Ibid., 5.
74. Ibid., 45.
75. Ibid., 21.
76. Phillips and Burbules, *Postpositivism and Educational Research*.
77. Rahman, *Islam and Modernity*.
78. Abaza, "Some Reflections on the Question of Islam and the Social Sciences."
79. Rahman, "Islamization of Knowledge," 4.
80. Rahman, *Islam and Modernity*.
81. Ibid.
82. Ibid., 37.
83. Ibid.; Tibawi, *Islamic Education*.
84. Rahman, *Islam and Modernity*, 89–90.
85. Ibid.
86. Rahman, "Islamization of Knowledge," 5.
87. Rahman, *Islam and Modernity*.
88. Rahman, "Islamization of Knowledge," 10.
89. Ibid., 11.
90. Chua, *Robbed*; S. Tamano, personal communication, July 12, 1999; Chua, 1999; A.H. Macada-ag, personal communication, June 23, 2004; Darwin Absari, personal communication, November 21, 2018.
91. Republic of the Philippines, "Republic Act 6734."
92. Malawi Panambulan, interview with the author, November 2000.
93. Mawlana Faisal Abdullah, interview by the author, Marawi City, Philippines, June 28, 2004.
94. Cabaybay Abubakar, interview with the author, June 2004.
95. Salic Ayoong Mala, interview by the author, Binidayan, Lanao del Sur, Philippines, July 6, 2004.

CHAPTER 7

Understanding the Past, Navigating the Future: Theorizing a Way Forward for Mindanao

The preceding chapters have attempted to lay out as thoroughly as possible the history of Muslim Mindanao from the precolonial period to the present, paying special attention to the place of education and educational policy in that history. As promised in the introduction to this work, postcolonial theory provided the theoretical framework for this historical analysis. I will not rehearse here the argument made in the introduction for postcolonial theory as an appropriate lens through which to interpret the educational history of Muslim Mindanao. It is perhaps enough to state the obvious: The Philippines was colonized for more than 300 years. The independent Philippine state is a postcolonial state. Moreover, the concepts of neocolonialism and internal colonialism articulated within postcolonial discourse are useful constructs for understanding the relationship between the Philippine state and its dominant Christian majority with the minority—predominately Muslim—communities of Mindanao.

However, while postcolonial theory clearly has its uses is understanding the educational experience of Muslim Mindanao, I do not believe it offers sufficient theoretical resources for navigating the future, for charting a way forward for education in Muslim Mindanao that has some hope of breaking out of the colonial and neocolonial ruts that have largely kept education in Muslim Mindanao on the same path for most of the last century. In this chapter, therefore, I will attempt to clarify the shortcomings of postcolonial theory for this task and argue for a pragmatic alternative that can provide, with crucial adjustments to be detailed in the next chapter, a useful theoretical framework for a way forward that reflects the religious identity and historical experience of Muslim Filipinos and offers direction to their aspirations for a better educational future for their children.

Understanding Mindanao: The Uses and Shortcomings of Postcolonial Theory

Postcolonial theory is an indispensable analytical tool for understanding the continuing legacy of colonialism, a fundamental prerequisite for any attempt to transform inequitable socioeconomic conditions in postcolonial societies such as the Philippines. Young describes postcolonial theory as a "theoretical creole," conceptually and methodologically diverse, yet coherent in its emergence "out of the continuing reverberations of the political and cultural history of the struggle against colonialism and imperialism."[1] Thus, postcolonial theory involves the critical reexamination of the history of colonialism, the political, economic, and cultural discourses supporting it, the ontological, epistemological, and psychological effects of those discourses on particular cultural communities, the forms of resistance these forces elicited in colonized societies, and the lingering effects that continue to shape the lives of marginalized groups in ostensibly independent nation-states. However, postcolonial theory goes beyond sociohistorical analysis to deploy a mode of "activist writing" intended not only to critique but to intervene in and transform oppressive political, cultural, and economic relations within and between nation-states. It is both an analytical and a political project.

> The overall political project of postcolonial critique remains coherent and urgent. First, investigating the extent to which not only European history but also European culture and knowledge was part of, and instrumental in, the practice of colonization and its aftermath. Second, identifying fully the means and cause of continuing international deprivation and exploitation, and analyzing their epistemological and psychological effects. Third, transforming those epistemologies into new forms of cultural and political production that operates outside the protocols of metropolitan traditions and enable resistance to, and transformation of, the degradatlion and material injustice to which disempowered peoples and societies remain subjected.[2]

The historical and contemporary critique I have offered here of the use of educational policy to manage relations with Islamized ethnic minorities in the southern Philippines represents an attempt to address the first and second of these goals. While I will explore in this final chapter one possible response to the third, the articulation of "new forms of cultural and political production" in the effort to resist and transform the legacies of injustice that still plague Muslim Filipinos is, in the end, a project for Muslim Filipinos.

Historically grounded in and inspired by the anticolonial struggles of previous generations, postcolonial critique draws heavily on Marxist analyses of the relationship between colonialism and the development of capitalism. Marxist thought provided a theoretical understanding of the political and economic workings of imperialism as well as a vision of futures free from colonial domination. Such analyses and visions framed many anticolonial struggles throughout the twentieth century.[3] While subsequent history has done much to undermine Marxism as a political and economic philosophy for governing, it remains a useful lens through which to examine the relationship between economic inequity and culture within and between states. In the case of the Philippines, for instance, such perspectives reveal the country's continuing neocolonial dependence on the United States and the ways that dependence helps to create the conditions for the internal colonization of Muslim Filipinos.

Marxist thought has been critical to the history of resistance to neocolonial subordination to US political and economic interests in the Philippines as well as the local political bureaucracies that have served those interests as well as their own.[4] This dialectical encounter between the forces of political-economic oppression and resistance on the part of the oppressed, however, has betrayed some in the nationalist camp to deploy dichotomized, essentialist conceptions of nationalist identity in opposition to colonialist identities. Marxist analyses, though indispensable, have contributed to this construction of dogmatic, opposing identities that obscure the fluidity of complex power relations within and between the categories of oppressor and oppressed. Such dualistic thinking often fails to capture the nuances of power or the variability of strategies of resistance in, say, gender or majority–minority relations, sexual orientation, or the fluidity of power among shifting subjective positions.

Since, at least, the publication of Edward Said's *Orientalism* (1978), however, postcolonial critics have increasingly drawn on the ideas of poststructuralists such as Michel Foucault and Jacques Derrida for insight into the circulation of power in societies via ever-evolving discursive structures, which are inscribed not only in official political structures and high culture but popular culture as well.[5] Deploying deconstructive readings of history, social relations, and products of culture such as fiction and travel writing against the grain, postcolonial criticism attempts to examine "the ways in which a particular kind of discourse was developed in order to describe, represent, and administer the colonial arena."[6]

The postmodernist contribution to postcolonial theory shifts the ontological and epistemological terrain upon which critiques of colonialism can take place. Through much of the colonial and postcolonial eras, colonial domination and neocolonial development have been rationalized by conceptions of reality and knowledge production that explained existing inequities as reasonable consequences of natural conditions. The developing science of the time, coincident in many respects with the spread of colonialism, posited a realist ontology, a theory that reality existed "out there" separate from and unaffected by the mind of the knower. In order to have knowledge of this reality, and thus be in a position to predict and control it to the fullest extent possible, the knower must seek an objective encounter with that reality free of any biases, desires, opinions, or other preconceived ideas in order to know that reality as it really is rather than how we imagine it to be. Thus, knowledge is founded upon direct acquaintance with the essence of reality. Progress is defined as the increasing ability to manipulate and control that reality for human purposes.

The deployment of this sort of foundationalist epistemology and essentialist ontology to the encounter with other races and cultures provided a scientific rationale for colonialism.[7] Colonial rule, this rationale suggested, was not a result of the illegitimate and immoral domination of one people by another but a natural result of the superiority of one and the inferiority of the other. This same science, moreover, provided the rationale for what should be done with these inferior peoples: The civilization and development discourses underpinning educational policy in the colonial and postcolonial Philippines are simply applications of the scientific theory of evolution and progress to the administration of subject peoples.

In a sense, Marxism simply offered an antithetical orienting ideal waiting at the end of the road of progress that was revealed in a more "scientific" account of history. Though the ontological and epistemological assumptions remain roughly the same, the orienting ideal is different, thus it functions usefully and powerfully as a critical alternative to Western, capitalist justifications for colonialism. But the postmodern theories of reality and knowledge production informing contemporary postcolonial theory are anti-essentialist and anti-foundationalist.[8] Pragmatist and postmodernist accounts of reality start with the realization that we can have no encounter with reality unmitigated by theory: We cannot step outside of our identities defined in terms of gender, race, class, culture, history to compare our observation from that position to observations from a position not defined by those characteristics. We cannot get at the essence of reality.

Knowledge claims, therefore, are not founded upon their correspondence with reality as it really is, but are rather imperfect, contingent, and revisable assertions from specific subject positions. Their "truth" is determined by their usefulness in achieving the knower's purposes or by their coherence with other knowledge claims previously found useful.[9] Knowledge, then, is not something discovered but rather something constructed, and it is judged not simply on its correspondence with reality but by the ethical consequences of the purposes it serves. One consequence of this is the idea that there is no single truth to which only the properly trained have privileged access, but rather that there have been and are competing regimes of truth created and sustained by discursive practices which respond to and create power and are shot through with ethical consequences.

The old truths that justified colonialism and imperialism, therefore, are social constructs, fictions subject to deconstructive readings that reveal their discursive production of power, compose counter-narratives productive of their own oppositional power, and interrogate the ethical ramifications of both. In this way, postcolonial analysis attempts a more nuanced understanding of the hybrid identities and complex responses of diversely situated colonized subjects. But it seeks such understanding in order to enable resistance to and transformation of inequitable power relations. According to Young (2001), "postcolonialism's central preoccupation is with the politics of the 'fourth world' still colonized within many officially decolonized countries."[10]

In this effort it focuses its attention on the "subaltern," a term borrowed and revised from Antonio Gramsci and used to name groups disempowered and marginalized on the basis of gender, ethnicity, language, religion, caste, or race.[11] The concept of the subaltern, along with poststructuralist insights into the nature of social power, highlights the distinctive, yet complex, set of responses by diverse Muslim Filipino communities to the hegemony of the Christian majority. The creative tension of the Marxist and poststructuralist currents in postcolonial theory makes it possible to attend to that complexity without obscuring the fact that it occurs within a broader historical discourse of colonizer-colonized relations in which both Muslim and Christian Filipinos are victims.

While postcolonial theory is an indispensable analytical tool for understanding the intended and unintended effects of educational policy in managing relations between the Filipino mainstream and the Filipino Muslim minority, it is, I argue, insufficient by itself in articulating a philosophical framework for a way forward. After the postcolonial critique, what sort of constructive alternatives are possible? The Marxist vein of postcolonial theory, of course, has historically articulated a political alternative, but the credibility of that alternative has been severely undermined by the collapse of communism around the world. And, while Marxist thought has inspired revolutionary struggle in the Philippines through much of the twentieth century, it has never captured the imagination of the vast majority of Filipinos and is anathema to the religious sensibilities of Muslim Filipinos.

The poststructuralist vein of postcolonial theory would appear to offer even less in terms of a positive philosophical framework for rethinking educational policy in Muslim Mindanao. It is often criticized as politically impotent in that its emphasis on the fluidity, ubiquitousness, and positionality of power undermines both the assignment of responsibility for the misuse of power and the possibility of political alliances in resistance to such misuse: It is not entirely clear who the oppressors and the oppressed are. Any political alliance of the disempowered becomes a new assertion of power productive of its own inequities and open to new deconstructive analyses. We must turn, I think, elsewhere for guidance on constructive alternatives while continually deploying postcolonial analysis of such alternatives in a hermeneutic of skepticism and hope that might enable us to move forward without repeating the mistakes of the past.

Understanding Mindanao: Postcolonial Liberalism

In his book *Postcolonial Liberalism* (2002), Duncan Ivison develops an example of the sort of hermeneutical framework I have in mind here for finding a way forward. In this work, Ivison confronts the challenge to liberal democracies posed by the claims of indigenous peoples living within such societies. How can liberal democracies respond to the claims of indigenous people regarding group rights, ownership of land, the preservation of native cultures, compensatory justice, and other issues that flow from conceptions of personhood, history, and the relations of individuals to nature and to community radically different from those espoused by liberalism? Given the historical and contemporary facts of indigenous people's experience in settler colonies—appropriation of land, genocidal violence, cultural destruction, poverty, political and social marginalization—how can liberal democracies possibly avoid responding to such claims? Ivison's project is not to determine whether or how such claims should be answered, but rather to suggest a framework within which such claims might be discussed.

> The idea is to craft a conceptual and discursive framework within which the argument between indigenous and non-indigenous peoples can be carried out on a more satisfactory footing than has hitherto been the case ... What postcolonial liberalism aspires to is articulating a space within liberal democracies and liberal thought in which these Aboriginal perspectives and philosophies can not only be heard, but given equal opportunity to shape (and reshape) the forms of power and government acting upon them.[12]

The goal is to seek a mutually acceptable path between assimilation and separatism, a reconciliation between the two that enables indigenous peoples to feel at home in a world that is no longer alien to them.[13]

Ivison starts with a broad conception of liberalism as a "complex of evolving discourses" that nevertheless shares some common concerns: the search for appropriate moral limits on the authority of governments and the need to deal with the fact that people disagree on many aspects of what constitutes a good life.[14] Reconciling these concerns has given rise in liberalism to ideals such as the notion that state authority should rest on some agreed upon justification, that the state should be neutral in treating the claims of different constituents, the equality of individual members of society, and the freedom of those individuals to pursue their own well-being as they understand it.[15]

Liberalism, however, has come under severe attack by postcolonial critics.[16] Postmodern philosophical perspectives on the nature of social power, for instance, call into question the very possibility of neutrality as envisioned in liberal political philosophy as well as the notion that state authority can be or ever has been justified by the shared consensus of the governed. Postcolonial theorists have also criticized liberalism's complicity in colonialism, arguing that it contributed to the assumptions of cultural superiority underpinning the colonial civilization discourse and that economic liberalism lay at the heart of capitalism and thus imperialism. Ivison sums up postcolonial theory's challenge to liberalism in four areas: First, as I have tried to show in this account of Muslim Filipino experience in the twentieth century, liberalism's appeal to abstract principles simply obscures the ways those principles serve the interest of some at the expense of others. Second, its appeal to moral individualism makes it incapable of adequately understanding or responding to the rights of indigenous communities, such as Muslim and non-Muslim ethnic groups in Mindanao, as intermediate levels of association between the individual and the state or understanding supra-national identities such as the Muslim *ummah* (Merry and Milligan, 2010). Third, because of this individualistic focus, liberalism's conception of justice is too narrow to account for historical injustice or differing conceptions of rights by indigenous or supra-national groups. And finally, liberal conceptions of pluralism underestimate the complexity and fluidity of individual and social identities. Thus, the structures, procedures, and values liberalism proposes to respond to that diversity are inadequate.[17] Ivison argues, however, that at the very same time postcolonialists dismiss liberalism, they appeal to liberal ideals such as individual freedom, democracy, justice, and equality.[18]

Ivison develops his conception of postcolonial liberalism as an attempt to reconcile the ideals of liberalism with what he sees as the justifiable criticisms of liberalism by postcolonial theorists. The first step in this reconciliation is the acknowledgment of historical injustice and the recognition that such injustices are not merely historical events but on-going influences on the nature of contemporary experience for indigenous and non-indigenous peoples. Their consequences continue to reverberate in the contours of contemporary relations of power and privilege. Therefore, we have a moral obligation to address historical injustice not simply for what happened in the past but for the contemporary problems it engenders in the present.[19]

Ivison's vision of postcolonial liberalism eschews the notion that liberal democracy can only take shape around an a priori conception of justice, say, to which all members of the society agree and upon which social institutions and the machinery of government can be erected. He takes seriously the challenge of postmodern epistemology that any such consensus is inevitably partial and self-interested and that claims otherwise are simply attempts to hide that fact. Instead of placing an imaginary consensus or illusory neutrality at the center of society he places the inevitability of disagreement and positionality at the heart of postcolonial liberalism. The emphasis, then, shifts from the achievement of some final consensus to the nature of ongoing dialogue and debate and revisable, contingent agreements as a "modus vivendi," a way of living or conducting oneself that enables complex, mutual coexistence within postcolonial liberal democracy.[20] Rather than determining what the outcome of such dialogues will be, postcolonial liberalism focuses on members' rights to develop the capabilities necessary to participate as full and equal participants in social debates.

We have an outline now of the normative shape of postcolonial liberalism: complex mutual coexistence between indigenous peoples and the state, grounded in a discursively legitimated set of dynamic *modi vivendi* on constitutional essentials and institutional arrangements that help to secure and promote people's basic capabilities.[21]

Seen through the lens of Ivison's postcolonial liberalism, the articulation of educational policy targeting Muslim Filipinos in the service of the civilization discourse of American colonialism and conceptions of development and Filipino identity in the postcolonial is problematic in several ways. Educational policy in both eras posited a priori, essentialized ideals of civilization, modernity, and Filipino identity and then deployed education as a tool to socially engineer Muslim Filipinos, and all Filipinos for that matter, to fit those ideals. Because the civilization and development discourses were premised on assumptions of Muslim Filipinos' lack of civilization, savagery, ignorance, and underdevelopment, they could not, of course, be expected to play a role in defining what civilization, development, or Filipino identity might mean for them. Despite the noble rhetoric that characterized the language of educational policy in both eras, policy-making and implementation were, at best, paternalistic and, at worst, oppressive. Either way it generally denied the capacity of Muslim Filipinos to participate intelligently in deliberations about their experience and future.

Moreover, by claiming the sole authority to establish ideal ends, the sociopolitical elite effectively defined capability to participate in such deliberations on the part of individual Muslims here and there by their proximity to the capabilities of those in power. In short, those individual Muslims who shared the interests and ideals, the training and the language of those in power were allowed marginal roles in the deliberations. Those who did not had nothing to offer. Education, in effect, was and is an instrument of violence against Muslim Filipinos.

The emphasis on capabilities in Ivison's postcolonial liberalism, however, suggests a role for education as one means by which societies deliberately set about equipping their citizens with the capabilities necessary to participate as full and equal partners in social deliberations. But this seems uncomfortably close to the very civilization and development discourses criticized here. How might it be possible to conduct educational policy-making and practice in such a way that it develops the capacities of its constituents without falling into the repressive routines of colonial pedagogy?

In the remainder of this chapter, I attempt to emulate Ivison's strategy in reconciling liberal ideals with postcolonial criticism in search of a way forward between the extremes of assimilation and separatism for indigenous peoples in liberal democracies. I explore a philosophical perspective that seems closely related to Ivison's articulation of postcolonial liberalism—the pragmatism of John Dewey—and which has the added advantage of including a well-developed theory of education. It is subject, however, to many of the same criticisms from postcolonial theory as Ivison's liberalism. I argue that it is possible to reconcile the two and articulate a "conceptual and discursive framework" for educational policy-making and practice that steers a course between assimilation and separatism in education and acknowledges the religious identity of Muslim Filipinos.

Pragmatism: A Modus Vivendi for Muslim Mindanao?

Pragmatism is widely considered a distinctively American contribution to world philosophy. In some key respects its origins lie in the thought of the American essayist, poet, and philosopher Ralph Waldo Emerson, who, in the first half of the nineteenth century was engaged in his own postcolonial project; namely, the relationship between political independence and cultural independence or, in more contemporary idiom, the problem of transcending cultural neocolonialism.[22] In the process, Emerson called for a radical break with history—"We have listened too long to the courtly muses of Europe"—and extolled the power of the ordinary individual to transform conditions through the power of his personality.[23] These ideas were picked up and elaborated upon by Charles Sanders Peirce and William James, who explored the power of scientific method as a tool for the critical examination and transformation of environing conditions and further popularized the heroic potential of the individual. Pragmatism flowered in the work of John Dewey in the first half of the twentieth century as Dewey sought an understanding of the individual's relationship with the past, with nature, and with social communities that acknowledged the way each shaped and constrained individual experience without entirely determining that experience. Dewey's work, in short, was an exploration of the philosophical import of democracy.[24]

By the second half of the twentieth-century pragmatism was, according to Rorty (1982), widely regarded as an outdated, provincial movement by contemporary philosophers.[25] Just a few years later, however, West (1989) was announcing "a small-scale intellectual renascence … occurring under the broad banner of pragmatism" as a result of the work of Richard Rorty and other contemporary pragmatists.[26]

> The distinctive appeal of American pragmatism in our postmodern moment is its unashamedly moral emphasis and its unequivocally ameliorative impulse. In this world-weary period of pervasive cynicisms, nihilisms, terrorisms, and possible extermination, there is a longing for norms and values that can make a difference, a yearning for principled resistance and struggle that can change our desperate plight.[27]

Yet, pragmatism is not a recipe to be crudely applied as a solution to social problems. It is saddled with its own negative baggage that must be critically engaged; however, it does provide theoretical resources that offer crucial insight into the processes by which we come to identify and search for contingent solutions to social problems.

> Its common denominator consists of a future-oriented instrumentalism that tries to deploy thought as a weapon to enable more effective action. Its basic impulse is a plebian radicalism that fuels an antipatrician rebelliousness for the moral aim of enriching individuals and expanding democracy. This rebelliousness, rooted in the anticolonial heritage of the country, is severely restricted by an ethnocentrism and a patriotism cognizant of the exclusion of peoples of color, certain immigrants, and women yet fearful of the subversive demands these excluded peoples might make and enact.[28]

In invoking pragmatism as a useful philosophical resource for tentatively theorizing an approach to education that might avoid the flaws of Philippine educational policy as applied to Muslim Filipinos, I am all too aware of the contradictions West describes. The Emersonian celebration of individual creativity and independence contributed to an ideal of the rugged individual that encouraged the expropriation of Native American lands and underpins capitalism. Peirce's and Dewey's encouragement of scientific thinking as a way of intelligently directing experience coincided with the social Darwinism that inspired the civilization discourse which, in turn, provided the moral rationale for American colonialism in the Philippines. Dewey himself, in fact, often used the language of civilization and savagery to describe the difference between "advanced" and "primitive" societies.[29] Moreover, turning to the only distinctively American philosophy for this purpose smacks of the very sort of imposition of American ideologies on Philippine educational experience that I have criticized throughout this book.

However, while there are rather conspicuous silences on the part of many of the pragmatists on the racism and colonialism that were rampant in the first half of the twentieth century, some, like William James, were vocal critics of American imperialism and others, such as Dewey, clearly articulated political philosophies that were antithetical to imperialism. I would argue, therefore, that pragmatism is no more alien to Philippine experience than the Marxist philosophies that have inspired Filipino intellectuals' criticism of neocolonialism and the revolutionary struggle against dictatorship and oppression. It is no more alien than the French poststructuralism that informs Indian intellectuals' accounts of postcolonial theory. The question is not necessarily the geographical or cultural source of a philosophical idea but whether or not it contributes to a better understanding of particular problems and the search for acceptable solutions.

Does pragmatism offer a conceptual and discursive framework within which educational policies can be articulated that are sensitive to local conditions yet avoid the pitfalls criticized in previous chapters? Given the "myopic blindnesses" and "debilitating weaknesses" of pragmatism, it cannot do so without critical assistance.[30] But I do not believe that the invaluable critical insights of postcolonialism offer an adequate theoretical framework for reconstructing more hopeful educational alternatives. However, the creative synthesis of pragmatism and postcolonialism can capitalize on the strengths and compensate for the weaknesses of both.

For instance, postcolonial theory's emphasis on socioeconomic exploitation and power can highlight such criticisms that are latent in pragmatism. And pragmatism's ameliorative impulse may help give that same impulse in postcolonialism a more practical expression. For, ultimately, this is what I argue is essential to any postcolonial theory of education: Critical analysis is necessary, but insufficient. Practical responses are necessary. It should help lead to a better way of doing things.

Pragmatism and Education

Among the pragmatist philosophers, John Dewey's thought is the most logical place to look for the resources necessary to the development of a theory of postcolonial pragmatism relevant to the educational problems of ethno-religious minorities trapped in internal colonial and neocolonial relations with national majorities and international benefactors. First of all, Dewey's thought represents in many respects the fullest flowering of pragmatism. Second, his life-long preoccupation with bringing philosophy to bear on the identification and solution of social problems led Dewey to the most significant and sustained engagement with educational theory of any philosopher in the pragmatic tradition. Though he was by no means a Marxist, elements of Dewey's philosophy reveal a consistent socialist critique of capitalist excesses and their corrosive impact on individual freedom and the possibilities of democracy: Cornel West has described him, perhaps a bit hyperbolically, as "the American Hegel and Marx."[31] Moreover, Dewey's articulation of a thoroughly historicized and contingent theory of knowledge anticipates critical insights of postmodern epistemologies. Thus, Dewey's thought includes elements that resonate in important ways with the two key elements of contemporary postcolonial theory—Marxism and poststructuralism—which come together in a theory of education reflective of a radical democratic ideal. Though Dewey wrote very little about colonialism, he is, I argue, an implicit postcolonial educational theorist.

Dewey's philosophy was intimately connected to a socialist conception of democracy in which democracy was not simply a matter of the machinery of politics but "a mode of associated living, of conjoint communicated experience" inimical to the "barriers of class, race, and national territory which kept men from perceiving the full import of their activity" and which demanded "the extension in space of the number of individuals who participate in an interest so that each has to refer his own action to that of others, and to consider the action of others to give point and direction to his own."[32] Thus, democracy was not simply about the negative freedom of individuals from external constraints but rather a quality of the relationships among free individuals in social relationships. And those social relationships included economic as well as political relationships. Thus, democracy as a "mode of associated living" was an ideal applicable to the factory and the distribution of wealth as well. Dewey wrote, "A democracy of wealth is a necessity."[33]

> In the degree in which men have an active concern in the ends that control their activity, their activity becomes free or voluntary and loses its externally enforced and servile quality, even though the physical aspect of behavior remain the same. In what is termed politics, democratic social organization makes provision for this direct participation and control: in the economic region, control remains external and autocratic.[34]

The failure to extend democracy from the political realm to the economic—not as in the bourgeois liberalism that justified unfettered individual competition but in provision for the fullest and freest participation of individuals in society—represents, in effect a failure of democracy. The "distortion and stultification of human personality by the existing pecuniary and competitive regime give the lie to the claim that the present social system is one of freedom and individualism in any sense in which liberty and individuality exist for all."[35]

Dewey was reluctant to too closely associate his position with the existing socialist movements of his day, arguing that "in 'democratic socialism' democratic should apply to socialism when attained not merely to the method of attaining it."[36] He was, in other words, concerned that the determinism in Marxist thought led to the articulation of a social ideal in which democracy as a mode of communal living requiring constant reconsideration of the status quo was no longer required or welcome. Marxism posited an end to history and thus an end to thinking. Dewey was also uncomfortable with Marxists' insistence on the inevitability of violent class struggle as the moving force of the law of history. "The issue is not whether some amount of violence will accompany the effectuation of radical change of institutions. The question is whether force or intelligence is to be the method upon which we consistently rely and to whose promotion we devote our energies."[37]

Dewey chose to rely on and promote intelligence as the method of effecting radical change, thus his emphasis on the democratization of education not just in terms of access but at the level of theory. Thus, Dewey rejected the dogmatism of Marxist thought as as much a threat to democracy as corporate liberalism, yet he remained a socialist in his critical understanding of the antidemocratic nature of corporate capitalism.

> One may hold that if there is to be genuine and adequate democracy there must be a radical transformation of the present controls of production and distribution of goods and services, and may nevertheless accept the criticisms to be made [of Marxism]—indeed may make or accept the criticisms *because* one believes the transformation is required.[38]

In this, Dewey's thought anticipates the current predicament of postcolonialism and other critical movements attempting to deploy Marxist critiques of socioeconomic inequality amidst the general collapse of faith in Marxism as a political ideology.

Dewey's philosophy, as a philosophy of process, rejects the search for secure foundations for knowledge claims either in the forms of pure reason or the data of sensory experience. Thus, he rejects idealism—both religious and rationalistic—and empiricism. In so doing he broke with the one of the central projects of Western philosophy, which had, since the Enlightenment been concerned with bridging the gap between a conception of reality as fixed and immutable inherited from the Greeks and a theory of knowledge as correspondence between knowledge claims and that reality with newer empiricist theories that knowledge must be a product of sensory experience. These two forms of foundationalist epistemology both posited a spectator theory of knowledge: Knowledge, once acquired, was ideally final and unaffected by the actions of the knower.[39] If we could arrive at such knowledge secured by its correspondence with the essence of reality—Truth—then it would theoretically be possible to organize ourselves in conformity to that truth.

Instead of searching for an a priori conception of reality or truth upon which to found a philosophical system, Dewey starts with the concept of experience. Unlike the empiricists, however, who conceived of experience as a passive reception of sensory stimuli, Dewey conceived of experience as both an undergoing and a doing: The individual both received stimuli from her environment, but also acted upon that environment and experienced the consequences of that action. Thus, Dewey's conception of experience is active and experimental.[40] Mind is an achievement of the intelligent direction of this interaction between the organism and the environment; therefore, it is individual since the interaction of different individuals, though alike in terms of biological and cognitive endowments, takes place at particular times and places and in pursuit of particular ends.[41] The individual's actions become intelligent, rather than merely habitual or instinctual, with the intervention of thought, a process by which the individual draws upon prior experience to effect a successful resolution of a problem in current experience. This fund of prior experience Dewey calls knowledge: It is what has worked in the past in achieving desired ends. It is, however, contingent, always open to revision on the basis of new experience.[42]

This fund of prior experience is not limited to the experience of the individual. Through verbal communication the individual has access to the accumulated knowledge of his community, to the experience of elders and others that can enhance the individual's power to resolve problems and render his actions even more intelligent. Through symbolic communication—writing—the individual has even greater access to the accumulated experience and knowledge of an ever-widening community of inquirers across time and space.[43] This knowledge remains contingent, revisable, a storehouse of the collected experience of human communities, which is, ideally, constantly being reevaluated, trimmed, or added to by the ongoing experience of members of the community. Knowledge claims are not adjudicated on the basis of their correspondence with an essential reality, but on the basis of their usefulness in achieving socially desirable ends, ends that are shaped by ethical values that are themselves subject to reevaluation and reinterpretation in light of experience.[44]

A consequence of Dewey's theory of knowledge is the recognition that knowledge is historically and culturally contingent, a social construct. It exposes and eschews the foundationalist pretensions of traditional epistemology as well as the essentialist ontological myths that have been used for generations to convince the disempowered that the particular status quo they happened to find themselves in was something more than the construct of the powerful. Thus, it reveals how what we take to be social reality is susceptible to the discursive operations of power that manufacture regimes of truth that privilege some at the expense of others.[45] However, it is also open to potential revision in ways that are resistant to such regimes of truth. In this way, Dewey's thought anticipates one of the key insights of poststructuralist philosophies, the way power creates knowledge and truth.

> Dewey and Foucault make exactly the same criticism of the tradition. They agree, right down the line, about the need to abandon traditional notions of rationality, objectivity, method and truth. They are both, so to speak, "beyond method."
>
> We should see Dewey as having already gone the route Foucault is traveling, and as having arrived at the point Foucault is still trying to reach—the point at which we can make philosophical and historical reflection useful to those, in Foucault's phrase, 'whose fight is located in the fine meshes of the webs of power.'[46]

For Dewey, the construction of man-made regimes of truth that attempt to fix conceptions of knowledge and reality in configurations beneficial to those in power constitutes an "undesirable society" that "internally and externally sets up barriers to free intercourse and communication of experience." A desirable society, on the other hand, is one "which makes provisions for participation in its good of all its members on equal terms and which secures flexible readjustment of its institutions through interaction of the different forms of associated life."[47] A democratic society, therefore, is one in which the members have the freedom and capacity to participate most fully in the ongoing social inquiry and debate shaping the direction of that society. Though Dewey and Foucault, according to Rorty, are "trying to do the same thing," Dewey did it better because "his vocabulary allows room for unjustifiable hope, and an ungroundable but vital sense of human solidarity."[48]

Dewey's hope is, according to West (1989) a manifestation of an "overly optimistic theodicy" of American pragmatism, a faith in the possibilities of human intelligence and solidarity to transform what "we would have … otherwise."[49] This transformation can be brought about, not by revolutionary violence, but by developing and disseminating more widely the capacity of individuals to bring their own intelligence to bear on the problems of society. It requires as well the setting aside of dogmatic absolutisms—such as Marxist dystopia and all fundamentalisms, religious or otherwise—that constitute impediments to thought. In this way, Dewey hopes democracy as a mode of associated living can permeate not only the political, but the cultural, economic, and aesthetic realms of human experience as well.[50] Dewey's ideal of democracy is that of a participatory aesthetic in which all individuals are allowed and able to participate in the creation and recreation of society.

> The ideal ends to which we attach our faith are not shadowy and wavering. They assume concrete form in our understanding of our relations to one another and the values contained in these relations. We who now live are parts of a humanity that extends into the remote past, a humanity that has interacted with nature. The things in civilization we most prize are not of ourselves. They exist by grace of the doings and sufferings of the continuous human community in which we are a link. Ours is the responsibility of conserving, transmitting, rectifying and expanding the heritage of values we have received that those who come after us may receive it more solid and secure, more widely accessible and more generously shared than we have received it. Here are all the elements of a religious faith that shall not be confined to sect, class, or race. Such a faith has always been implicitly the common faith of mankind. It remains to make it explicit and militant.[51]

The achievement of this vision of democracy required philosophers and other intellectuals to quit their ivory towers and self-appointed roles as adjudicators of truth and beauty to assume the role of organic intellectuals, cultural critics who bring intellectual tools as simply one more contribution among many to the common social and political struggle to realize a more democratic society. For Dewey, one of the key weapons and sites of this struggle was education.

Dewey's philosophy was, in broad terms, a philosophy of education. In fact, he defined philosophy as the general theory of education.[52] The concept of experience, therefore, is as central to his philosophy of education as it is in his more general philosophy. According to Dewey, we learn through experience, through the perpetual doing and undergoing of our interaction with the environment. The result of this interaction, our memories of previous experience, is the knowledge that is brought to bear in the intelligent direction of future experience. Our environment, of course, includes others in families and communities, so our experience includes interactions with others, which produces learning and knowledge. This is the means by which communities sustain themselves over time.[53] There can be, therefore, no end to education other than more education, no externally imposed purpose other than to keep open the possibility of continued learning and growth. The external imposition of predetermined, a priori ends constitutes an impediment to experience and thought likely designed to serve the interest of those designing the ends rather than the interests of the learner.[54]

This does not mean, however, that all experiences are educative. Some are miseducative. They lead the learner down dead ends that block the possibility of further growth. One might, for example, see the adoption of a fundamentalist religion or the acquisition of expertise in carrying out terrorist acts as experiences that produce learning. However, they would be, in Dewey's view miseducative in that they would tend to block future growth: The fundamentalist is convinced that he possesses the truth and need not inquire further and the terrorist may well wind up dead. Educative experiences, on the other hand, can be distinguished by two criteria: continuity and interaction. Continuity refers to the fact "that every experience both takes up something from those which have gone before and modifies in some way the quality of those which come after."[55] An educative experience, therefore, is one which is sufficiently familiar to the learner to be meaningful, yet sufficiently novel that it requires the learner to use thought—the method of intelligence—to resolve the perplexity or doubt embodied in the experience. Thus, the experience opens onto new experiences and new possibilities for growth. If it fails the first half of this criterion, it is meaningless to the learner; if it fails the second, it is mere routine that does not open onto new experience. The criterion of interaction draws attention to the fact that any experience is shaped both by internal, psychological factors, and external, social factors.[56] For an experience to be educative, therefore, it must also account for the individuality of the learner as well as the social context in which the learner has his experience.

In order to elicit thought, an educative experience must be meaningful to the learner; it must involve ends that are of interest to the learner. And these ends are inevitably influenced by the prior experience of the learner and the social context in which those experiences have taken place. The achievement of these ends poses a problem for the learner, a problem which requires her to reflect on previous experience, to draw on what she has learned about the experience of others, to mentally rehearse likely solutions to the problem, to put one possible solution into effect, and to evaluate the consequences of that experiment. If that solution does not achieve the desired end, she repeats the process. If it does, she stores that experience away and moves on until she encounters other doubts, perplexities, or problems. This is the method of intelligence.

This is "the only freedom of enduring importance ... freedom of observation and of judgment exercised in behalf of purposes that are intrinsically worth while."[57]

The freedom to frame and execute his own purposes does not mean that the learner is free to do anything. Because he is immature, the learner alone cannot judge the experiences that are likely to lead to the fullest exercise of his freedom as an adult in his community. On the other hand, the ends-in-view of the learner cannot be ignored without sacrificing internal motivation for external imposition. The task of the teacher is to make use of the ends-in-view of the learner to help him achieve the ends-out-of-view that the teacher, from her adult experience, knows are essential to participating fully in the life of the community.[58] Traditional education, according to Dewey, has been characterized by the imposition of ends derived from the experience or interests of the powerful rather than the interests of the learner. It requires, therefore, the exercise of power, coercion, and control in order to secure conformity to purposes that are different from or contrary to those of the learner.[59] In short, traditional education is a form of violence. What Dewey termed progressive education, on the other hand, was not focused on the achievement of some predetermined end, but rather emphasized the development of the individual's capacity to utilize her own intelligence in the interest of shared purposes and thus participate fully and freely in the ongoing discourses of democratic community.

Seen in light of Dewey's philosophy of education, the education of Muslim Filipinos enacted by American colonial educators and their postcolonial Filipino heirs represents yet another instance of this traditional education. It imposed ends, in the form of conceptions of civilization, development, and Filipino identity, which represented the interests and goals of those in power rather than the interests and goals of Muslim Filipinos. In so doing it violated the criteria of educative experiences discussed above. The failure to adequately include Muslim Filipinos' histories, cultures, and contemporary lives in textbooks and curricula represents a violation of the principles of continuity and interaction. The knowledge and intelligence the child has acquired through her experiences with her local environment and community are less likely to be useful in a setting defined by the experiences and goals of others. Thus, she is immediately handicapped in the full use of her intelligence. The imposition of externally defined goals, no matter how benevolent the intentions, sets up a tension between the purposes of those in power from the purposes of the local communities. Thus, the Muslim Filipino child is robbed of some of the motive power of interest. Cut off from local experience and local purposes, education is alien. Force is required—constabulary officers, compulsory attendance laws, official exhortations, entrance examinations, and insults—in order to achieve any level of compliance. When such methods are successful, the result is often assimilation. When they are not, the result is the sort of alienation described in Chapter 4.

I am arguing here that Dewey's pragmatic philosophy of education offers a useful starting point in the effort to frame a conceptual and discursive structure within which an approach to education might be devised to enable Muslim Filipino students to steer a path between assimilation and alienation. I am not, however, arguing that Dewey's conception of education is sufficient in and of itself. Dewey's long professional career encompasses the entire period of American colonization in the Philippines, a colonization that saw such levels of violence in the initial suppression of Filipino resistance that it drew congressional hearings. The invasion and colonization of the Philippines caused an intense public debate over the morality of American imperialism, and American colonial policy was a regular subject in the popular press, as was the resistance of the so-called Moros. Yet Dewey, a philosopher who was apparently committed to a variety of progressive causes, apparently wrote nothing on the topic. These were also years when American racism against African-Americans was particularly virulent. Yet, one does not find the sort of explicit and forceful engagement with such topics one might expect from the philosopher of American democracy. In fact, one frequently encounters the very dichotomization of civilization and savagery to mark the direction of social progress found in the rhetoric of American colonial officials in the Philippines. Perhaps it is unreasonable to expect any single figure to have written on all topics worthy of attention, but given the contours of his philosophy, it is difficult to see how he missed these.

While it is important to acknowledge Dewey's silences and shortcomings, it is equally important to recognize that they do not necessarily negate the relevance of his philosophy to minority education in postcolonial settings. His use of the rhetoric of civilization and savagery can be, must be in the overall context of his philosophy, read as belief in the desirability of cultural transformation and a faith that such transformation could be in the direction of greater freedom and democracy. And that direction need not be defined by the status quo of white, Euro-American culture.

Between 1919 and 1921, for instance, Dewey traveled and lectured widely in China, developing in the process an abiding interest in the democratic development of that country.[60] He was highly critical of America's imperialistic tendencies in relations with China, arguing that China should be left alone to chart her own course with only such involvement from the outside as would help bring about "ends which are helpful to others as will call out and make effective their [developing nations] activities."[61] Thus, his conception of just relations between nations was analogous to his conception of just relations between individuals: to resist the temptation to impose purposes from without—imperialism—in favor of assisting others, where necessary, in developing the capacity to pursue their own ends. This is a crucial difference between Dewey's theory of social progress and the civilization-development discourses animating the colonial and postcolonial education of Muslims in the Philippines.

Finally, pragmatism is not a traditional philosophy in the sense of asserting foundational truths or knowledge claims that logically determine conclusions. West, in fact, describes pragmatism as an *evasion* of philosophy. It is rather a process, a method, a modus vivendi. Though Dewey's articulation of pragmatism exhibits an unmistakably American accent, this is due to the fact that this was the sociohistorical context in which he was writing. The core tenets of pragmatism—a future-oriented experimentalism in the pursuit of democratically determined moral ideals that yield historically and culturally contingent knowledge claims which are judged by their usefulness to the realization of those ideals—can just as easily be expressed in a Philippine cultural idiom as an American. This was something recognized, I think, by the Chinese and Turkish contemporaries of Dewey that sought to translate his ideas into their own sociohistorical contexts. I see no insurmountable obstacles to a comparable translation of the pragmatic modus vivendi into the sociocultural context of Muslim Mindanao. However, if we are to salvage the powerful democratic arguments of Deweyan pragmatism, as well as its deep insights into the educational implications of democracy, and turn them to the task of theorizing a way forward for Muslim Mindanao, we must address Dewey's skepticism—one might say hostility—regarding supernatural religion and the likely reception of pragmatic epistemology by faithful Muslims who see the Qur'an as the unquestionable source of secure knowledge. This is the task of the final chapter.

NOTES

1. Young, *Postcolonialism: An Historical Introduction*, 69.
2. Ibid.
3. Ibid., 6.
4. See Constantino, *Neocolonial Identity and Counter Consciousness*.
5. Young, *Postcolonialism: An Historical Introduction*, 415.
6. Ibid., 392.
7. Ania Loomba, *Colonialism/Postcolonialism*, 115–118.
8. Ivison, *Postcolonial Liberalism*, 40–41.
9. For a fuller account of these arguments see Cornel West, "The Politics of American Neo-Pragmatism," in Rajchman and West, *Post-Analytic Philosophy*; Code, *What Can She Know?*
10. Young, *Postcolonialism: An Historical Introduction*, 59.
11. Ibid., 354.
12. Ivison, *Postcolonial Liberalism*, 1.
13. Ibid., 7.
14. Ibid., 16.
15. Ibid., 5, 16–18.
16. Ibid., 24.
17. Ibid., 47–48.
18. Ibid., 30.
19. Ibid., 105–106.
20. Ibid., 84–88.
21. Ibid., 140.
22. See, for instance, Ralph Waldo Emerson, "The American Scholar," "The Poet," and "Experience," in Whicher, *Selections from Ralph Waldo Emerson*, 63–79, 222–240, 254–273.
23. Emerson, "The American Scholar," 79.
24. See West, *The American Evasion of Philosophy*.
25. Rorty, *Consequences of Pragmatism*, xvii.
26. West, *The American Evasion of Philosophy*, 3.
27. Ibid., 4.
28. Ibid., 5.
29. See, for instance, John Dewey, *Democracy and Education*, 47–48, 211–214.
30. West, *American Evasion*, 5.
31. Ibid., 69.
32. Dewey, *Democracy and Education*, 87.
33. Coughlan, *Young John Dewey*, 91 cited in West, *American Evasion*, 80.
34. Dewey, *Democracy and Education*, 260.
35. Cited in Westbrook, *John Dewey and American Democracy*, 431.

36. Ibid., 430.
37. Ibid., 470.
38. Ibid., 473.
39. Dewey, *Democracy and Education*, 291–293; Biesta and Burbules, *Pragmatism and Educational Research*, 18–21.
40. Dewey, *Democracy and Education*, 266–275.
41. Ibid., 295; Biesta and Burbules, *Pragmatism and Educational Research*, 36.
42. Dewey, *Democracy and Education*, 340.
43. Biesta and Burbules, *Pragmatism and Educational Research*, 42–50.
44. Dewey, *A Common Faith*, 51.
45. See, for example, Code, *What Can She Know?*
46. Rorty, *Consequences of Pragmatism*, 204, 207.
47. Dewey, *Democracy and Education*, 99.
48. Rorty, *Consequences of Pragmatism*, 208.
49. West, *American Evasion*, 101; Dewey, *A Common Faith*, 45.
50. Dewey, *Art as Experience*.
51. Dewey, *A Common Faith*, 87.
52. Dewey, *Democracy and Education*, 331.
53. Ibid., 1–22.
54. Ibid., 100–101.
55. Dewey, *Experience and Education*, 35.
56. Ibid., 38–42.
57. Ibid., 61.
58. Ibid., 61–65.
59. Ibid., 17–23.
60. Westbrook, *John Dewey*, 240–260.
61. Cited in Westbrook, *John Dewey*, 252.

CHAPTER 8

Prophetic Pragmatism: Toward a Bangsamoro Philosophy of Education

It has been now more than 120 years since the US Army landed in the Philippines in the vanguard of a westward imperial expansion that had itself begun little more than a century before. Americans arrived in the Philippines fired, in part, by a missionary zeal for a colonial *mission civilisatrice* intended to, in President McKinley's words, "educate the Filipinos, and uplift and Christianize them, and by God's grace do the very best we could by them, as our fellow men for whom Christ died."[1] Their tools for this divine mission would come to include "high powered rifles, Stokes mortars, and gas bombs" and the mythology of the "little red schoolhouse": the first to subdue Christian and Muslim Filipinos' aspirations for independence and the second to convince them, and ourselves, that it was for their own good.[2] Thus, where Spain left most of the Philippines with a legacy of Christian piety, the US colonial legacy to the Philippines was a deep faith in education as a tool for social transformation and a moral cover for political oppression.

The United States deployed these tools throughout the Philippines, including the Islamized regions of Mindanao and the Sulu Archipelago where, from 1903 to 1920, Americans governed the "fearful" Moros separately against the day their Christian Filipino pupils in self-governance would possess the skills necessary to administer this most unruly of classrooms in the imperial schoolhouse that was the Philippine Islands. When that day came in 1920, Filipinos took up the mantle of the American *mission civilisatrice* as well as the Americans' tools—military might and education—to fulfill that mission. For the subsequent decades of colonial rule, commonwealth government, and independence, Filipinos would continue to deploy these tools in the service of a sense of national identity and economic security that required the assimilation and subordination of a recalcitrant Muslim minority and its territory into the infrastructure of an emerging Philippine state. This effort became, unintentionally, a century-long experiment in the use of educational policy as a tool for the mitigation of ethno-religious conflict in a culturally and religiously divided postcolonial state.

This experience is, of course, deeply relevant to the history, current practice, and future of Philippine education. However, that experience should be of interest to educators in other countries as well. It is, for instance, at one level a manifestation of the almost universal problem of balancing unity and diversity in multicultural societies: How can educational policy be deployed in such a way that it fosters the sense of common identity necessary for the preservation of the state while adequately respecting the diversity of cultures and individuals comprising that state? Inasmuch as this is a challenge faced by many other societies, there is something to be learned from this experience.

But the Philippine experience offers even more insight into contemporary educational problems because it brings to the fore the unique challenges posed by a resurgent Islam and neocolonial power relations within and between independent states. For instance, Muslim minorities in Russia, India, China, the former Yugoslavia, Europe, and the United States are struggling—peacefully and, at times, violently—to preserve and assert their identity as Muslims against social forces that, in their view, threaten that identity. Even in majority Muslim countries such as Indonesia, Egypt, or Saudi Arabia, there is a widespread sense that these same modernist and postmodernist social forces threaten Islam and require faithful Muslims to engage in *jihad* against them.[3] Recent decades have seen Americans embark yet again on what many have seen as new neo-imperial adventures in Afghanistan and Iraq, adventures marked by the familiar deployment of images of Afghan schoolgirls and soldiers rebuilding bombed-out Iraqi schoolhouses to justify, in part, military actions. We would do well to attend to the lessons of earlier efforts among the Muslims of the southern Philippines and its postcolonial legacy.

The Continuing Past: Education and Conflict in a New Century

It is, of course, important to acknowledge the very real accomplishments of Philippine education in the colonial and postcolonial eras as well as the progressive intentions of the vast majority of those engaged in it. Almost every year of the past century saw increases in the access to schooling of an ever-growing school-age population of Christian and Muslim Filipinos. And over those years, many thousands of Filipino and American teachers worked hard in difficult conditions to teach millions of children to read and write, to develop skills in agriculture and industry, and to improve the living conditions of their students and their communities.[4] Many of them worked with great dedication and skill on behalf of Muslim Filipino children.[5] Moreover, the last decade or two has seen an increasing awareness of Muslim Filipino contributions to national culture and greater efforts to see to it that those contributions are reflected in school curricula and textbooks.

And, even if the accomplishments of Philippine education have fallen short of the great needs of the Filipino people, it is equally important to acknowledge the enormous impediments against which that success should be measured. Four centuries of colonization so distorted indigenous ways of thinking and living that it is extremely difficult to discover what they were prior to colonization or what they might have been without it. As Albert Memmi, Franz Fanon, Chinua Achebe, Nadine Gordimer, Edward Said, and a host of more recent postcolonial writers have shown, colonization robbed the colonized of the freedom to guide their own cultural development along lines consistent with indigenous values and traditions, forcing instead a pattern of social, psychological, and intellectual development warped by the pressures of the colonial encounter.[6] The long period of economic exploitation, moreover, left a neocolonial dependence on the American colonizer in particular, which influences Filipino economic, cultural, and political values to this day.[7] On top of this colonial legacy, the postcolonial Philippine experience of Japanese invasion and occupation, Muslim and communist insurgencies, dictatorship and endemic poverty has thrown up even more impediments to the success of Philippine education. It is this colonial and postcolonial legacy, in the context of the rich cultural and religious diversity of the Philippine Archipelago, which must bear a significant portion of the blame for the animosity between Muslim and Christian Filipinos that continues to plague Philippine society to this day.

My purpose here, therefore, has not been to belittle the accomplishments nor impugn the motives of Filipino educators past or present who have attempted to serve their Muslim fellow citizens. Rather, my purpose has been to argue that behind the real and pervasive impediments to the successful implementation of Philippine educational policy for the Muslim minority lies a network of fundamental assumptions and biases shaped by the colonial experience, which has undermined the attempt to use educational policy as a tool for mitigating tensions with Muslim Filipinos.

Of course Muslim–Christian relations in the southern Philippines are far more complex than can be captured in any crudely dichotomous account of Filipino oppression and Muslim resistance. Those relations have run the gamut from friendship to open hostility just as Muslim Filipino responses to government policy have been marked by active cooperation, grudging acceptance, deliberate subversion, and outright resistance depending upon the policy and the particular circumstances of the moment. Muslim Filipino relations with the Philippine mainstream today are no less complex, ranging from enthusiastic participation in the government to armed attacks against its interests.

That said, it is nevertheless reasonable to conclude that the educational policies deployed by successive colonial and postcolonial Philippine governments to integrate and thereby reconcile Muslim Filipinos to the mainstream of Philippine society have failed. In the early 1970s, for instance, after more than 50 years of reliance on education as the primary mechanism for Muslim integration, more than 65 percent of Muslim Filipino respondents to a Filipinas Foundation survey identified themselves as Muslims rather than Filipinos. Almost 40 percent reported unfavorable views of Western education while 55 percent refused to give an opinion. The Filipinas Foundation's report concluded that there was "an embarrassing lack of concern on the part of both the national government and private sector to understand Muslims as Filipinos."[8] Four years later another Filipinas Foundation analysis of majority–minority relations found that 78 percent of Christian respondents expressed hostile or indifferent attitudes toward Muslims while 82 percent of Muslim respondents expressed similar attitudes toward Christians. Muslims ranked ninth of nine ethnic groups in terms of reported desirability. "The principal single trait ascribed to this group [Muslims] is that of treachery," the Foundation reported.⁹ This negative bias was also found in content analyses of newspaper depictions of Muslims in the 1970s and 1980s that found that Muslims were typically categorized as rebels, terrorists, killers, and outlaws. In the late 1990s, Tolibas-Nunez reported: "the perceptions and understandings that Muslims and Christians have of each other lack objectivity and are colored by strong biases and prejudices; but especially strong are the biases Christians have of Muslims."¹⁰

Over the last twenty years Mindanao has seen the spectacle of Abu Sayyaf abductions and beheadings, the "all-out war" of President Joseph Estrada against the MILF in 2000, bombings in Manila and Mindanao, the inclusion of the Mindanao conflict in the US-led war on terrorism, the declaration of a "state of lawlessness" in Basilan by President Gloria Macapagal-Arroyo in 2001, and outbreaks of renewed fighting in 2003 and 2008. In 2013, the three-week "Siege of Zamboanga" saw the MNLF occupy portions of the city before being driven out by the Philippine military, but not before more than 200 people were killed and another 100,000 displaced.¹¹ In 2017, this tragic litany of conflict seemed to reach its zenith in the terrible siege of Marawi, when approximately 1000 militants affiliated with the Maute Group, with the assistance of Islamic State fighters from overseas, launched an attack on the Islamic City of Marawi that led to five months of house-to-house fighting, the longest period of urban combat the Philippine military had experienced since World War II. 6000 members of the Philippine armed forces used artillery and aerial bombardment on the urban center of the city, leaving well over a thousand militants, soldiers and civilians dead, a million Mindanaoans displaced, and the city in a state reminiscent of scenes from the Syrian civil war. Martial law was imposed across Mindanao and continues in effect as of late 2018.¹²

Even as the armed conflict between the government of the Philippines and Muslim secessionist groups periodically erupted into spasms of open combat, more garden variety forms of violence continued to trouble the region. In 2009, for instance, political violence reached a new low with 58 individuals massacred—the largest single loss of working journalists in history—in a dispute between rival political clans in Maguindanao.¹³ And throughout Muslim Mindanao, the age-old practice of *rido*—clan conflict—resulted in levels of violence that many claimed to be worse than the armed conflict between the MILF and the Philippine government.

The 2016 *Report of the Transitional Justice and Reconciliation Commission* strongly suggests that Muslim–Christian perceptions are no more positive today than they were in 1997 or 1971. After more than 210 listening sessions with 3000 community members and officials throughout Mindanao, they found "a prejudice that is deeply embedded in the psyche of Philippine society at large and, particularly, among many civil servants."[14] This prejudice, and the legacy of historical injustices suffered by so many Muslim Filipinos, has led to the persistence of a "perception of Moro 'otherness'…both as internalized self-awareness on the part of the Moros themselves and as an imposed identity marker by the State and the majority population."[15] This general lack of mutual sympathy or understanding, along with the continued lack of socioeconomic development in Muslim communities, demonstrates that educational policy as a primary tool in the integration and development of Muslim Filipinos and the mitigation of Muslim–Christian tensions has not been the panacea many earlier observes had hoped it might be.

The central question, then, is why did the policy of integration through education fail? The short answer is that it was never really a policy of integration. It was, rather, a policy of assimilation through education pursued by colonial and postcolonial education officials. The key challenge of Philippine history has been the problem of creating a modern, unified nation-state out of a rather arbitrarily drawn colonial geography, of harmonizing the diverse notes of dozens upon dozens of languages and cultures. This has been a tall order: to bring all those different voices to sing, so to speak, from the same page. And the success of both colonial and postcolonial governments in this effort should not be minimized. Spain convinced, or forced, most Filipinos to sing along to the tune of Catholic Christianity, and the United States taught them the show tunes and rock and roll of American popular culture. But the so-called Moros refused to sing along. Like the young Muslim girls described in Chapter 4 singing "in the wilderness," they had their own song to sing.

National harmony implies a process of mutual accommodation in which all parties are called upon to make adjustments and both parties have a say in the nature of those adjustments. This has never been the case in Muslim Mindanao. As demonstrated in Chapter 2, the colonial administration of Muslim Filipinos deployed an imperialistic pedagogy founded on essentialist notions of modern civilization. Muslim Filipinos were not asked for their ideas about a Moro modernity.

They were expected to conform themselves to the ideals of the Americans' civilization discourse. Those who could not or would not were relegated to the margins of the social, political, and economic mainstream. Those who actively resisted were suppressed, often through military force. As demonstrated in Chapter 3, American essentialism was replaced by Filipino nationalist essentialism in the Commonwealth and postcolonial periods. Here, Muslim Mindanao was governed for the economic benefit of the political center and Muslim Filipinos were expected to conform themselves to a "true" Filipino identity composed of the values of the Christian political-intellectual elite in Manila. Those who could not or would not were branded ignorant and relegated to the socioeconomic margins. Those who actively resisted were suppressed, often through military force. The message to Muslim Filipinos was, if I can stretch my metaphor just a bit further, "sing like us or be silenced."

Thus, the real choices offered to Muslim Filipinos in the colonial and postcolonial eras were assimilation and subordination, alienation and marginalization, or silence. Despite more than a century of noble rhetoric about education and uplift, the implicit assimilation-subordination agenda of colonial and postcolonial policy for Muslim Filipinos frequently became quite explicit in public pronouncements. For instance, Moro Province Governor Tasker Bliss wrote in 1906 that the purpose of the Moro Province was to put the Moro on "all fours" with the Filipinos, "because the Filipino already has the highest form of religion, already has considerable culture, and is friendly to the government."[16] In the same year, he wrote in a special number of the *Mindanao Herald*: "the exercise of their customs and religion will not be interfered with unless contrary to law or repugnant to the usages of civilized nations."[17] More than 60 years later Clavel (1969), in his officially sanctioned review of the work of the Commission on National Integration, offered a remarkably similar agenda for Muslim Filipino "integration."

> If the minorities are to become active members of the national community, they should abandon, as the price they have to pay, their backward ways and adopt those that are in consonance with modern living. Inevitably, they have to observe some values upheld by the majority group…in the process of helping them attain a higher degree of civilization, they have to discard some of their traditional values and customs. It is suggested that they retain those [values and customs][that] do not constitute a barrier to national progress and an irritant to their relations with one another or with the members of the majority group.[18]

Integration in both instances meant the abandonment of whatever those in power found repugnant or irritating in Muslim Filipino culture and conformity to a cultural model epitomized by modern, Western-oriented, Christian Filipinos. Whatever the label put on it, this was assimilation. Effectively, successful integration meant the eradication of distinctive Muslim Filipino cultural identities.

Romanticized, popular accounts of the history of US involvement in Philippine education credit Americans with the introduction of an American-style system of public education designed to educate the masses for productive citizenship.[19] While there may be a legitimate historical case to be made for the American introduction of a public educational infrastructure with the goal of providing universal schooling, the historical circumstances differed radically from that of US educational experience. Schooling in the United States grew somewhat haphazardly in response to local initiatives and needs over a century or more, evolving into systems of mass education in some states by the mid-nineteenth century. By the time of the US colonization of the Philippines, public education was a fixture in American society. Having grown, however, from the bottom up, there was a strong tradition of local control. The Progressive Era of the early twentieth century saw increasing efforts to use education to address social problems; however, there was little centralization of policy-making beyond the level of state governments. The growth in the role of the national government in educational policy is a phenomenon of the last few decades of the twentieth century.[20]

Thus, while the organizational structures, curricular models, and the goals of US colonial education in the Philippines might have appeared almost identical to those in the United States, their effect, and the experience of them, would have been quite different. For white Americans, it was a system that had to one degree or another grown out of their own historical experience and was oriented toward participation in their own society. Transplanted to the Philippines it became an exercise in radical social engineering on a grand scale. The introduction of a system that had grown over time from the bottom up became in the Philippine context a top-down model of educational decision-making. A system that could somewhat plausibly—for white Americans—claim democratic purposes in the US context became imperialistic in effect when transplanted to the Philippine context.

Nationalist historians of Philippine education are quite correct in seeing through the benevolent rhetoric of American colonial education to its role in supporting US imperialism in the Philippines and pointing out how the naïve acceptance of that rhetoric supports a continuing neocolonial relationship with the United States.[21] They often fail to see, however, how the continuation of a centralized, top-down educational bureaucracy in the service of an essentialist nationalism shifted the inequitable power relations of colonialism from the American-Filipino encounter to the majority Filipino-minority Filipino encounter. The effort to rescue Filipinos from neocolonialism by appealing to an essentialized nationalist identity is achieved at the expense of an internal colonialism for Muslim Filipinos and other cultural minorities.

In 2016, the Transitional Justice and Reconciliation Commission affirmed this reading of the failure of misguided educational policies to achieve their hoped-for impact on the conflict when it cited biased historical narratives enshrined in school texts, the pursuit of a policy of assimilation resulting in a failure of the state to manage diversity, as well as a history of injustice as contributing factors in the continuation of the conflict. "The TJRC came to the conclusion that these issues are the result of three interlocking phenomena—violence, impunity, and neglect—which, in turn, are rooted in the imposition of a monolithic Filipino identity and Philippine State by force on multiple ethnic groups in Mindanao and the Sulu archipelago that saw themselves as already pre-existing nations and nation-states."[22]

Despite the apparent failure of past educational policies intended to mitigate conflict in Mindanao and elsewhere, the TJRC's recommendations include educational strategies, including community-based human rights education, the creation of a Bangsamoro Center for History, Culture, and Arts, the writing of new history textbooks that include Muslim history as an integral part of the history of the Philippines, more research on the diversity of Mindanao and Sulu, culturally sensitive educational materials, and strengthening the Islamic education and madrasah system as integral parts of the national system of education.[23]

Faith in education springs eternal. But in fairness, what other tools are there? Of course, inclusive economic development, redress for past injustices, effective delivery of social services, and impartial administration of the rule of law are all important mechanisms for addressing the underlying causes of this most intractable of conflicts in Muslim Mindanao. But surely formal education is one tool—perhaps the tool *par excellence*—that modern democratic societies use to bring about desirable social change. As John Dewey (1916) argued in *Democracy and*

Education, education is the primary means societies have not only to reproduce themselves, but to reimagine themselves in ways more consistent with their own ideals.[24] Therefore, the failure of education to solve the conflict in Mindanao—surely an excessive burden for any one social institution—does not mean that education failed in all instances—it surely contributed to the social amity and progress that does exist between and for many Muslim and Christian Filipinos. Rather, it means that the tool was not used as effectively as it might have been. It suggests that we learn from our past failures and try again. The alternative is despair.

The Bangsamoro Opportunity

In late 2018 new opportunities to try again presented themselves. After 17 years of negotiation between the MILF and the government of the Philippines, the parties reached a Framework Agreement on the Bangsamoro in 2012. This was followed in 2014 by a Comprehensive Agreement on the Bangsamoro. Though delayed and almost derailed in 2015 by an unintended encounter between the MILF and the Philippine National Police Special Action Force that led to the deaths of 44 policemen, these agreements finally led to the passage in the Philippine Congress of RA 11054, The Organic Law for the Bangsamoro Autonomous Region in Muslim Mindanao, which was signed into law by President Rodrigo Duterte on July 27, 2018.[25]

The Bangsamoro Organic Law establishes the Bangsamoro Autonomous Region in Muslim Mindanao as a replacement for the old ARMM on the territory of the ARMM as well as selected areas outside of the ARMM that voted to join the new region in a plebiscite held in January 2019. Its Preamble reads

> Imploring the aid of Almighty God, in recognition of the Bangsamoro people and other inhabitants in the autonomous region in Muslim Mindanao to establish an enduring peace on the basis of justice, balanced society and asserting their right to conserve and develop their patrimony, reflective of their system of life as prescribed by their faith, in harmony with their customary laws, cultures and traditions, within the framework of the Constitution and the national sovereignty as well as the national integrity of the Republic of the Philippine, and the accepted principles of human rights, liberty, justice, democracy, and the norms and standards of

international law, and affirming their distinct historical identity and birthright to their ancestral homeland and their right to chart their political future through a democratic process that will secure their identity and posterity, and allow genuine and meaningful governance, the Filipino people, by the act of the Congress of the Philippines, do hereby ordain and promulgate this Organic Law for the Bangsamoro Autonomous Region in Muslim Mindanao.[26]

The new law establishes the Bangsamoro Autonomous Region as a democratic, secular autonomous government under the umbrella of the Philippine Constitution and guarantees the religious liberties of all its citizens, both Muslim and non-Muslim.[27] Crucially, it asserts a new Bangsamoro sociopolitical identity which includes not only the Muslims, but the indigenous peoples and settler groups that currently populate the region.[28] Thus, the burden of forming a common sociopolitical identity from a diverse collection of ethno-religious groups with a history of conflict and tensions will be shared for the first time in its history by the Philippine state with the new Bangsamoro Autonomous Region. And one of the tools delegated to them to achieve this goal is education.

The Bangsamoro Organic Law delegates authority over education in the autonomous region to the Bangsamoro government and charges it with establishing and maintaining an "integrated system of quality education…relevant and responsive to the needs, ideals, and aspirations of the Bangsamoro people."[29] It further charges the Bangsamoro government with supervising and regulating private schools, supervising and improving madaris education and Islamic studies, integrating Islamic values and Arabic studies into the curricular of the public schools in the region, establishing a tribal university, preserving and transmitting Moro history and culture, and promoting science, technology, and research. In addition, the Bangsamoro Parliament "shall assign the highest budgetary priority to education, health, and social services."[30]

Thus, while the national government will provide financial and other assistance to the Bangsamoro government through a block grant and provisions on internal revenue collection and continue to bear responsibility for education and other services for Filipino citizens—Muslim and non-Muslim—outside the region, the Bangsamoro Autonomous Region will henceforth bear a primary responsibility for developing and promulgating educational policies and practices designed to foster the peace and development of the region and its residents. The central question now is what will the Bangsamoro government do with this autonomy? Will they learn from the mistakes of the past and realize the potential of education to bring about a more peaceful and prosperous society, or will they repeat those mistakes? Old habits are, after all, difficult to break.

But, as John Dewey argued, habits are not necessarily bad things; they are in fact behavioral routines that have proved useful in accomplishing past purposes. When we discover that a particular routine no longer satisfies our purposes, we experience that discovery as a problem. We ask, "Why isn't this working? What should I do differently." The problem causes us to investigate the conditions that may have led to the problem and to reflect upon possible solutions, new plans of operation that might solve it. But of course we cannot know whether this new plan of operation will solve the problem until we put that plan into effect and observe the results. If it works, we go on our way; if it doesn't, the problem requires more thought. This, according to Dewey, is how we think.

This is, essentially, the structure of this book: I have argued that American and later Filipino educators have deployed educational policies and practices that may have worked in the education of the white majority in the United States or the Christian majority in the Philippines, but they have not, by and large, worked effectively in satisfying the educational aspirations of Muslim Filipinos. This is the problem. I have tried to investigate as thoroughly and objectively as I could the historical and contemporary circumstances of the problem of education in Muslim Mindanao in order to develop an alternative theoretical understanding of it. I have concluded that the major cause of the failure of previous educational plans of operation was not the ignorance or backwardness of Muslim Filipinos—as claimed by both American and Filipino observers in the past—but rather their fundamentally assimilative character, that they failed to adequately account for and respect the distinctive religious and cultural identities of Muslim Filipinos, identities that they have fought fiercely to preserve and pass on to their children. What remains, then, is the consideration of an alternative plan of operations, a new way forward.

An alternative way forward, however, requires a theoretical framework for action that matches the new theoretical understanding of the problem. In the remainder of this chapter, I will attempt, therefore, to describe a theoretical framework for educational policy and practice in Mindanao that reflects and respects the worth and dignity of Muslim Filipinos' religious and cultural values as resources in an approach to education that may be more likely to achieve social justice and create a brighter future for their children. If Muslim Filipino educators find that framework persuasive, it will be up to them to put it into practice and test its practical results.

Prophetic Pragmatism: A Philosophy of Education for Muslim Mindanao?

As discussed in the previous chapter, the contemporary pragmatist philosopher and organic intellectual Cornel West views pragmatism—and Dewey—as necessary, but insufficient to the articulation of a philosophy of social engagement adequate to the promise and pitfalls of multicultural democracy. According to West, "Dewey is the culmination of the tradition of American pragmatism," who brings a modern historical consciousness to philosophy, a sense of the "radical contingency and variability of human societies, cultures and communities."[31] Dewey's philosophy is centered on process, on the process of free and open inquiry and the widest possible dissemination of the capacity for it in pursuit of democratically shared ends. Thus, he short-circuits totalizing narratives that would confine thought and creative purpose to channels defined by preordained beginning or ends or supposedly iron laws of history or nature. Thus, Dewey shifts the grounds of philosophy from the search for indubitable truths to engagement in the struggle to bring about a more just society. "After him [Dewey], to be a pragmatist is to be a social critic, literary critic, or a poet—in short, a participant in cultural criticism and cultural creation."[32] This aspect of Dewey's thought is indispensable to West's project as well.

West argues that the tradition of pragmatism is "in need of a more explicit political mode of cultural criticism," one that "promotes a more direct encounter with the Marxist tradition of social analysis" for its insight into the deep structures of the social and economic forces that create and sustain inequality and oppression.[33] Such an encounter highlights Dewey's criticisms of the antidemocratic tendencies of capitalism and his calls for fundamental social, cultural, political, and economic change. According to West, "Dewey put forward a powerful interpretation of socialism that … highlights a conception of social experimentation which … embraces the idea of fundamental economic, political, cultural, and individual transformation." Yet, West is doubtful of Dewey's faith in members of the educated, professional classes as historical agents of his notion of gradual social change. He is also profoundly troubled, however, by the political, cultural, and moral failures of Marxist political regimes. He proposes, therefore, a revision of pragmatism—prophetic pragmatism—that attempts to build "on the best of the Jefferson-Emerson-Dewey and Rousseau-Marx-Gramsci legacies."[34]

West's prophetic pragmatism shares with the poststructuralist philosophy of Foucault a "preoccupation with the operations of power"; however, he faults Foucault for concentrating only on the ways "human beings are constituted into subjects" via discourses, for failing to attend to the "operations of power in economic modes of production and nation-states," and for devaluing moral discourse. Like Foucault, West writes, "prophetic pragmatists criticize and resist forms of subjection, as well as types of economic exploitation, state repression, and bureaucratic domination. But these critiques and resistances, unlike his, are unashamedly guided by moral ideals of creative democracy and individuality."[35] Thus, like postcolonial theory, West's prophetic pragmatism draws upon both Marxist theory and poststructuralism, but he finds them both inadequate to the task of providing a way forward in the search for a more just and humane social order. As I have proposed here, he looks to pragmatism for assistance in that project.

A major shortcoming of pragmatism, however, is its "overly optimistic theodicy"—or theory of evil—its failure to adequately address the inescapable reality of the tragic, "the irreducible predicament of unique individuals who undergo dread, despair, disillusionment, disease, and death *and* the institutional forms of oppression that dehumanize people."[36] This failure to attend to the tragic—seen perhaps in Dewey's relative silence on racism and colonialism—tinges the optimism of the pragmatic tradition in the possibilities of social progress with a hint of naïveté. Moreover, the pragmatists' transformation of the philosophical vocation to that of engaged cultural critic suggests that what is required is more than a philosophical account of the tragic. What is required is an understanding of how ordinary people cope with it.

> The culture of the wretched of the earth is deeply religious. To be in solidarity with them requires not only an acknowledgment of what they are up against but also an appreciation of how they cope with their situation. This appreciation does not require that one be religious; but if one is religious, one has wider access into their life-worlds. This appreciation also does not

entail an uncritical acceptance of religious narratives, their interpretations, or, most important, their often oppressive consequences. Yet to be religious permits one to devote one's life to accenting the prophetic and progressive potential within those traditions that shape the everyday practices and deeply held perspectives of most oppressed people.[37]

The truth of this observation is borne out by the reemphasis of Islamic identity in the southern Philippines in response to decades of poverty, socioeconomic marginalization, cultural erosion, and political violence. West's critical insight here represents something of a challenge, however, for both pragmatism and postcolonial theory. Dewey, for instance, seemed to view supernatural religion as an impediment to thought, as one of those "barriers to free intercourse and communication of experience" characteristic of "an undesirable society."[38] His hope for social progress was at least partly premised on the possibility of emancipating the "religious function in experience" from the dead weight of supernatural religion. This could only be accomplished, he felt, "through the surrender of the whole notion of special truths that are religious by their own nature, together with the idea of peculiar avenues of access to such truths."[39] This clearly has not happened among "the wretched of the earth," which also reveals a significant blind spot in postcolonial theory illustrated by the field's treatment of "the most widely known anti-colonial leader of all time," Mahatma Gandhi.

> Gandhi's anomalous position brings out the extent to which, as a result of its Marxist orientation, an absolute division between the material and the spiritual operates within postcolonial studies, emphasizing the degree to which the field is distinguished by an unmediated secularism, opposed to and consistently excluding the religions that have taken on the political identity of providing alternative value-systems to those of the west—broadly speaking, Islam and Hinduism. Postcolonial theory, despite its espousal of subaltern resistance, scarcely values subaltern resistance that does not operate according to its own secular terms.[40]

This cultural blind spot in both Deweyan pragmatism and postcolonial theory suggests profound consequences for the possibility of either discourse moving out of the realm of intellectual debate among relatively privileged academics in order to bring about the radical social transformations both espouse. West suggests that it is a recipe for political impotence.

> Since the Enlightenment in eighteenth-century Europe, most of the progressive energies among the intelligentsia have shunned religious channels. And in these days of global religious revivals, progressive forces are reaping the whirlwind. Those of us who remain in these religious channels see clearly just how myopic such an antireligious strategy is. The severing of ties to churches, synagogues, temples and mosques by the left intelligentsia is tantamount to political suicide; it turns the pessimism of self-deprecating and self-pitying secular progressive intellectuals into a self-fulfilling prophecy.[41]

West situates himself philosophically within the tradition of pragmatism of which John Dewey is such a central figure while rejecting the antireligious strains within pragmatism argued by Dewey in *A Common Faith* (1934) in order to reclaim the historical role of progressive, prophetic religious voices.[42] West wants to assert the great good that has been and can be accomplished in the name of religious faith. So, his prophetic pragmatism comprises three distinct elements: the tradition of the Hebrew prophets—the prophets shared by Jews, Christians, and Muslims—pragmatic epistemology and progressive Marxism.

In the prophetic tradition so central to his African-American spiritual heritage—a heritage shared by Muslims and Jews—West sees the figure of the prophet as the man or woman who holds the community to account for the moral ideals it claims to embody. The prophet says, in effect, this is what God ordains and you are called to, but this is how you behave. Prophecy, according to West, in not fortune telling or predicting the future, it is an ethical critique of the shortcomings of society in light of its shared ideals and a warning of the consequences of those moral failures. In the image of the prophet, West finds a model for the social critic and advocate of social justice that remains in connection with the religious traditions that still move most people in the world.

At the same time, West recognizes the long history and ever-present danger of strongly held religious beliefs degenerating into the terrible certainty of absolutism and fundamentalism, the certainty that I am right and you are wrong, that I alone know God's will which is so often used to justify repression, control, and even violence. To counter this West draws on the epistemic presuppositions of pragmatism: the idea that all knowledge claims are provisional, contingent, subject to change and that truth is a matter of coherence, consistency of beliefs rather than an external, independent reality accessible only to the privileged few. Contra

Dewey, West is essentially arguing that one need not give up one's faith in the transcendent or even the belief that the Truth is there in one's religious tradition; rather, one must surrender the arrogance of certainty. I must be open to the possibility that I might be wrong, thus I need the voices and perspectives of others to correct me when I err.

Finally, mindful of the historical tendency of some religious expressions to justify the existence of present injustice and evil with the promise of rewards in heaven, West draws on the intellectual and political tradition of progressive Marxism as perhaps the most effective analytical tool for understanding economic injustice. He recognizes though that Marxist thought too has its absolutist, fundamentalist strains that have been used to justify some of the worst repression and political violence the world has ever seen. Like prophetic religion, Marxist thought is powerfully useful and dangerous. How do we harness the power while mitigating the danger? The answer, West implies, is in that simple recognition embodied in pragmatist epistemology: the recognition that I could be wrong.

West looks to the examples of figures like Mahatma Gandhi and Martin Luther King, Jr. as prototypical prophetic pragmatists who demonstrated the antiracist, anti-imperialist, anti-oppressive potential of religious traditions while eschewing the fundamentalist currents of both faith traditions that have instituted their own oppressions and continue to do so today. He illustrates this potential in discussion of the significance of Afro-American Protestant Christianity to his own political struggle, a tradition that provides him with the existential sustenance to go on in the face of the tragic. That tradition teaches that we are made in the image of God, yet we are fallen. This "Christian dialectic of human nature" highlights the incomparable dignity of individual human beings as well as their utter fallibility and calls them to struggle for the realization of ideal ends they know cannot be realized on this side of paradise.[43] Thus, the temptation to declare premature success in the attainment of those ideals is tempered by the realization of human fallibility and any such claims subject to critical comparison against those ideals. It is, in a sense, pragmatism dressed in the traditional mythic robes of Christianity.

West is careful not to limit his articulation of prophetic pragmatism to Christianity alone, however. It can be and has been articulated within a variety of religious and secular traditions. Gandhi, for instance, is an obvious example. Dewey, perhaps, manifests a secular version of it. The discussion in Chapter 5 of Fazlur Rahaman's historicization of enduring Islamic moral principles, the way the ideal of the good Muslim is deployed in Muslim Filipino discourse to provide a moral framework for social and self-criticism as well as an orienting ideal for moral development, and even the efforts of the *ulama* involved in Project Madrasah Education to reconcile Bloom's taxonomy of educational objectives with their own understanding of the Prophet Muhammad's teachings all suggest a prototypical *Islamic* prophetic pragmatism. They are examples of faithful Muslims experimenting within the contingencies of history to articulate plans of operation that will be useful to the realization of Islamic ideals. While West does not name the Islamic Gandhi or King or Dewey, his articulation of prophetic pragmatism embraces the possibility.

> Prophetic pragmatism worships at no ideological altars. It condemns oppression anywhere and everywhere, be it the brutal butchery of third-world dictators, the regimentation and repression of peoples in the Soviet Union and Soviet-bloc countries, or the racism, patriarchy, homophobia, and economic injustice in the first-world capitalist nations. In this way, the precious ideals of individuality and democracy of prophetic pragmatism oppose all those power structures that lack public accountability, be they headed by military generals, bureaucratic party bosses, or corporate tycoons. Nor is prophetic pragmatism confined to any preordained historical agent, such as the working class, black people, or women. Rather, it invites all people of goodwill both here and abroad to fight for an Emersonian culture of creative democracy in which the plight of the wretched of the earth is alleviated.[44]

PROPHETIC PRAGMATISM AND THE EDUCATION OF MUSLIMS IN POSTCOLONIAL PHILIPPINES

A *prophetic* pragmatism in the context of Mindanao, inspired by but not imitative of West's articulation of prophetic pragmatism from within his own spiritual and cultural context, would foreground the ideals of all Mindanaoans as providing the inspiration and moral framework for conceptions of a good life worth pursuing and passing on to their children, recognizing that for many, perhaps most, these ideals will be articulated in the language of Islam. For Christians it may be Christianity, for indigenous groups it may be their own spiritual traditions, for the non-religious it may be other ethical traditions. Whatever the case, it is these traditions that give direction to moral progress, that provide the yardstick by which we measure our shortcomings and thus recognize injustice, that offer us the existential sustenance to cope with the inevitable tragedies of life while sustaining hope that life can and will be more than tragedy. Thus, prophetic pragmatism in Muslim Mindanao will be distinctively Islamic.

However, just as West recognizes the danger of religious belief degenerating into fundamentalisms that are themselves oppressive, prophetic pragmatism in Muslim Mindanao will have to guard against the very real possibility that intolerant, divisive expressions of Islam occupy the spaces opened up for local interests by policies allowing educational autonomy. The *lutong makao* curriculum cooked in Manila may be replaced with a *lutong makao* curriculum cooked in Saudi Arabia or Kuwait. West's articulation of prophetic pragmatism relies on pragmatism's conception of knowledge as historically and culturally contingent to short circuit the attraction toward fundamentalism and absolutism that is present in virtually all religions. It seems to me, however, that the religious belief that there is such a thing as timeless, objective Truth and that it is revealed, say, in the Qur'an or Bible is not easily surrendered because it rests on faith and trust, not evidence. So I am not at all confident that pragmatist epistemology can do for an *Islamized* prophetic pragmatism in Muslim Mindanao what it does for West. If it cannot, does this leave Mindanao prey to extremism, that terrible certainty into which claims to know—whether religious or secular—so often slips, thus justifying both real and symbolic violence?

Perhaps not. For I believe at the bottom of both pragmatist epistemology and scientific method is an ethic of humility, an *epistemic* humility, a small voice that says this is what I think the evidence shows, but I could be wrong. And though I am not a scholar of religion, especially Islam, I suspect that there is a similar ethic of humility in our religious traditions, a call to discern the Truth and the will of God as revealed in the holy scriptures to the best of our ability while acknowledging our imperfections and our inability to truly comprehend the mind of God, a voice that says, "I'm doing my best. This is what I believe, but I'm just a man. I could be wrong."

Epistemic humility, I suggest, is the functional equivalent of pragmatist epistemology. The ethic of epistemic humility diffuses the disagreements among people of different faiths or people of faith and secularists over conceptions of God, the existence of the transcendent, etc. The principle of epistemic humility leaves space for you to seek the Truth in whatever tradition you find meaning in, to embrace it, to share it with others, to order your life around it. But it reminds us that the world and the will of God are vast things, that we are fallible, limited human beings who, whatever our intellectual gifts, can never fully comprehend it all. And that sense of limitation, of fallibility, and of incompleteness opens us up to the voices and the gifts of others. We need them because their knowledge and understanding and gifts may aid us in our own search for truth, and we may help them in theirs.

Thus, prophetic pragmatism in Mindanao might be characterized by a dialectic oriented on one end by conceptions of the good life articulated in religious (or non-religious) terms and grounded on the other by the humble recognition that, as imperfect, fallible human beings, we all fall short of that ideal. And in between these two poles a culture of restless, pragmatic experimentalism might flourish, judging current policies and practices against the ideals they are intended to realize and searching for better alternatives when they fall short of realizing them. Spiritual ideals—Islamic, Christian, indigenous, secular—epistemic humility, pragmatic experimentalism: These are the three coordinates of a prophetic pragmatism in Muslim Mindanao.

Each element is indispensable. Without a clear moral compass, a moral compass that for most of humankind comes from religious faith, pragmatism risks degenerating from mere practicality to expediency. Corruption lies at the end of that road. But without the epistemic humility of pragmatism, religious belief risks calcifying into absolutism and fundamentalism. Extremism lies at the end of that road. And without the pressing project of social justice, the never-ending quest to put moral idealism and pragmatic experimentalism in the service of those who "experience dread, despair, disillusionment, disease and death, *and* the institutional forms of oppression that dehumanize people" on this side of paradise, then faith is the opiate Marx said it was.

What are the practical consequences of rethinking education in Muslim Mindanao through the conceptual and discursive structures of prophetic pragmatism? The first and most important consequence is the realization that these consequences cannot be entirely determined from the perspective of a cultural outsider. The effort to do so, the effort to determine the direction that another society will take, was and is a hallmark of imperialism. Key insights of pragmatism—the cultural and historical contingency of knowledge and the importance of freedom of inquiry in assuring a more just society—teach us that philosophy is a form of cultural criticism, thus a philosophical scheme cannot be worked out separately from the context for which it is intended and then applied to that context. Rather, pragmatism is a philosophy that attempts to describe a process by which the members of a society work out indigenous conceptions of a more just and democratic social order. Thus, the content, character, and direction of that society must be worked out by its members, not well-intentioned outsiders.

That does not mean, however, that only cultural insiders are authorized to speak. Or, to put it in the context of the tense history of Philippine–American relations, that the American observer can have nothing legitimate to say about Muslim education in the Philippines. What is a cultural insider in this case? Is a well-educated, urban, Christian Filipino an insider authorized to speak about the education of Muslims in rural Mindanao because she shares a common citizenship? Is an assimilated, educated Muslim Filipino authorized to speak because he shares a common cultural and religious heritage but not current cultural or class values? Is a Muslim from the Middle East an outsider unauthorized to speak? One of the central arguments of this book has been the idea that key defects in Philippine education policy regarding the needs of Muslim Filipinos are legacies of American colonialism. This is, therefore, in many respects as much American history as Filipino or Filipino Muslim history. Postmodern insights into the constructedness and fluidity of identity suggest that each of us occupies a more or less unique and constantly shifting subject position. To claim that one is only authorized to speak about the position one occupies is to reduce all writing to biography. And there is real reason to doubt that even biography is epistemically privileged.

> It [is] a mistake to think of somebody's own account of his behavior or culture as epistemically privileged. He might have a good account of what he's doing or he might not. But it is not a mistake to think of it as morally privileged. We have a duty to listen to his account, not because he has privileged access to his own motives but because he is a human being like ourselves.[45]

This is what I have attempted to do in this book, to—metaphorically and literally—listen as carefully and faithfully as I could to Muslim Filipinos' accounts of their own cultural and educational experience, something that has not, from what I have seen, been done as comprehensively as I have tried to do here in the existing Philippine literature on Muslim education or the American literature on Philippine education. Whether it has been done well, or well enough, is someone else's call. Rorty's account of what we owe others is a description of attentive, mutually respectful conversation. My account of the shortcomings of Philippine education policy is offered in just that spirit, as an entry in a conversation rather than a complete, closed, or final accounting of reality. It is a response, in essence, to 20 years of listening to Filipino and Muslim Filipino accounts of their own cultural and educational experience in the historical record, contemporary scholarship, observation, and literal conversations: This is what *I* hear. This is what *I* think it might mean. It takes its impetus from the Deweyan insight that the communication of experience allows individuals to draw upon a potentially infinite range of human experience in the search for solutions to present problems. We have something to learn from the conversation.

In this spirit, and this spirit only, I am willing to hazard a few conjectures about what prophetic pragmatism might mean for Muslim–Christian relations in the Philippines and for Muslim Filipino education. Clearly, at the broader level of cultural criticism prophetic pragmatism demands a relentless and uncompromising critique of the economic exploitation, political injustice, and cultural repression perpetrated either by foreign institutions or Filipino elites so common to contemporary Philippine society. Leftist nationalists have courageously and eloquently sustained this line of critique since at least the late 1960s. However, this frequently inspiring expression of Filipino nationalism, emerging out of the colonial and neocolonial encounter with the United States, has all too often posited an essentialized nationalism in contradiction to American imperialism. In so doing, it has frequently failed to interrogate its own complicity in the internal colonization of Muslim Filipinos via constructs of the "true Filipino" that leave out Muslim Filipino experience even as it hews to the boundaries of the colonial state. Marxist theory has long been central to the nationalist critique. The poststructuralist perspectives within both postcolonial theory and prophetic pragmatism will offer critical insight into the problem of nationalist essentialism.

Philippine cultural criticism is no stranger to the importance of religion to the wretched of the earth either. The Catholic Church in particular has played a key role in inspiring courageous critique of socioeconomic injustice during the Marcos dictatorship and today, drawing on the deep religiosity of Filipinos to marshal them to the struggle for a more humane society. The danger is that this religiosity can too easily ignore the pragmatic elements of religious figures like Mahatma Gandhi and Martin Luther King, Jr. and slip into forms of fundamentalism or religious identity politics that threaten to exacerbate existing ethno-religious tensions. Politically powerful charismatic groups within Catholicism and certain Protestant denominations who seek to use the strength of their numbers to enhance the existing Christian biases of Philippine government and society are examples of this danger. Islamic fundamentalism in Mindanao is another. There are, however, initiatives such as the Bishop-Ulama Conference and other nonformal groups devoted to interfaith dialogue that offer a tenuous, but hopeful third way. West's prophetic pragmatism envisions just such strategies and offers a powerful philosophical framework for conceiving their work.

While Dewey's philosophy demonstrated the fallacy of attempting to separate education from its broader cultural context, educational policy has been the central concern of this book. In turning to education, however, I am mindful of West's criticism of Dewey's selection of historical agents—educators, in essence—who he sees as perhaps too invested in and beholden to state bureaucracies and the economic elites controlling them to ever risk assuming the role in radical democratic change Dewey envisioned for them. And I am mindful of my own critique in previous chapters of the excessive faith in education of colonial and postcolonial educators.

My critique, however, was of the belief that education could cover up for bad social policy, that you could hide oppression and marginalization behind the benevolent mask of the schoolteacher and expect the victims of that oppression to be fooled. But in response to West's critique of Dewey, I would ask, what else is there? It is a mistake, of course, if we conceive education narrowly as schooling. However, if we see education broadly, as Dewey did, as "that reconstruction or reorganization of experience which adds to the meaning of experience, and which increases ability to direct the course of subsequent experience" then education includes all those efforts to transform society via dialogue and the dissemination of information, including schools.[46] The only alternative to education, as one early American observer of Mindanao astutely observed, is violence. However, we must also be attuned to the fact that education can itself be a form of violence, a fact largely missed, I have argued, by American and Filipino educational policy makers.

In the realm of educational policy, it seems to me that a prophetic, pragmatic examination of Philippine colonial and postcolonial education from the perspective of Filipino Muslims demands a radical shift from centralization to localization, from elite imposed ends to ends that emerge from the purposes of local communities. Dewey's criteria for an educative experience—continuity and interaction—require attention to the experience of individual children in interaction with the particular cultural communities in which they live. What is the experience of *this* Maranao girl, this little bird in the wilderness, and how does her culture shape, without necessarily defining, the interests that motivate her toward her own ends? What curriculum, methods, ends-in-view will help her develop her capacity to frame and execute *her* purposes? To demand, as colonial and postcolonial education has done, her conformity to ends determined by the interests of political elites far removed geographically, culturally, and economically from the milieu she occupies is to perpetrate violence upon her. An approach to education framed within the conceptual and discursive structure of prophetic pragmatism would endeavor to free this bird, not crush her.

Prophetic pragmatism suggests a switch in curricular fare from the *lutong makao* curriculum precooked in Manila and served in Oliver Twist portions in Muslim Mindanao. It suggests that the curriculum should be "cooked" in the kitchens of the schools the children occupy by the teachers and parents who instruct them and in accordance with the "nutritional" needs of *these* children. The Department of Education might establish nutritional guidelines, but decisions about how those guidelines will be met ought to be made locally. Teachers might be authorized to use their intimate knowledge of individual children along with their adult experience of the wider world those children are preparing to enter to draw on local, national, or international experience communicated in textbooks, on the Internet, or the words of locally respected elders to fashion a curriculum that helps this child move from where he is to where he and his community want him to be.

The various policies and initiatives examined in Chapter 5 which seek to Islamize education in Muslim Mindanao represent a positive step in the direction of pragmatic experimentation. They represent an attempt to try something new. But to truly try something new, as opposed to simply announcing a new policy, that something new has to be faithfully implemented and evaluated to judge its effectiveness. But the evidence suggests thus far that these initiatives have not been as effectively implemented as their proponents might hope. The ALIVE program is not implemented in all schools where the presence of Muslim children would warrant it, and where it is implemented it suffers from a shortage of qualified teachers. Moreover, due to a lack of understanding of Arabic and of Islam in the DepEd, as well as literal interpretations of church-state separation in the Philippine Constitution, DepEd leaves the content of ALIVE to "experts" on these topics, some of whom are reportedly injecting intolerant, *salafi* interpretations of Islamic values into the courses, thus undermining the very purpose of the program.

Likewise the effort to integrate and accredit the madaris has fallen short of intentions. With less than 10% of the madaris in the country currently accredited—many of those that are accredited are large, established madaris that have always offered a broad curriculum—it suggests that the criteria for accreditation are unattainable for most madaris or that the vast majority of madrasah operators have other reasons for eschewing integration. After centuries of overt hostility toward Muslims in the Philippines, they may be, understandably, deeply suspicious of the government's newly found interest in helping them. Overcoming that suspicion may require a multi-generational effort to build trust and capacitate new generations of Muslim Filipino educators to make effective use of the autonomy envisioned in these policy changes to realize a better future for Muslim children.

To realize the potential of pragmatic experimentation to arrive at more inclusive plans of operation that move us toward the realization of our moral ideals, prophetic pragmatism in Muslim Mindanao will have to take seriously the cultural and educational politics of pragmatism: Do not block the road of inquiry. Do not put up artificial barriers to the free and unfettered exchange of ideas. This suggests a form of multiculturalism in the curriculum that goes beyond the zoological approach that conceives of multicultural curriculum as a collection of this cultural specimen and that cultural specimen between the covers of a book. Prophetic, postcolonial pragmatism envisions multiculturalism as the ability and freedom to engage in discussion and debate over social purposes, whatever their source. Fundamentalisms, whether Islamic, Christian, or secular, are, of course, major impediments to such a vision.

Such changes, however, will likely require a radical shift in the way teachers are trained and their roles conceived. Teachers' education should liberate them from their bondage to textbooks and "precooked" curricular materials even as it teaches them to use such materials as part of an ensemble of materials including their own knowledge of the subject at hand, professional judgment, familiarity with local culture, and insight into the needs of individual students in a creative and flexible balance of individual needs, local conditions, and instructional goals. While most teacher education programs may claim to teach such skills and educational officials to value them, the prevalence of "spoonfeeding"—what Freire called "banking methods"—utterly belies such claims.[47] Teachers might be trained to approach their task as art rather than a bureaucratic functionary, as a form of improvisational performance rather than the mechanical, even if faithful, reproduction of the authorized knowledge contained in textbooks and precooked curricula.

To achieve this, teachers might also learn to eschew the subject–object, master–slave relationship between teachers and students characteristic of colonial and neocolonial education in favor of a subject–subject relationship governed by an ethic of love. By this I do not mean the sentimental and often shallow love of children that teachers often claim as their motivation for teaching, nor do I mean the oppressive love that manifests itself in the impulse to shape the child's identity in conformity to some alien ideal for their own good. I mean rather the love of individuals as inevitably imperfect beings endowed—by their Creator, if you like—with infinite worth and dignity and the ability to struggle toward the realization of ideals that they themselves have a hand in shaping. Such love requires more than support and encouragement, however. It also requires careful analysis and courageous critique of the forces—both within the individual and within society—that impede the individual's realization of his or her fullest potential.

Prophetic pragmatic teachers and educational leaders would be deeply suspicious of idolatry—whether in the form of nationalist essentialism, religious fundamentalism, or neocolonial "development"—as adequate organizing principles for schools in a multicultural, religiously diverse democracy. They would be critical, and self-critical, of social and individual impediments to human flourishing. And they would be inspired and directed by ethical ideals—contingent and imperfectly understood as they may be—which flow from diverse religious, cultural, and secular sources. They would approach their task in a spirit of creative, improvisational, yet disciplined composition of ethical, aesthetically pleasing, and meaningful lives by and with their students. Such a conception of education constitutes a more open, tolerant, and creative response to the challenge of providing democratic education for Muslim

Filipinos—indeed all Filipinos—than the cultural imperialism, essentialist nationalism, and functionalist developmentalism heretofore offered them by American colonialism and its postcolonial Filipino heirs.

LESSONS FROM MUSLIM FILIPINO EDUCATIONAL EXPERIENCE

The examination of Philippine educational policies from the perspective of Muslim Filipinos via the lens of prophetic pragmatism offers more than a critique of these policies. For I would argue that the shortcomings revealed are applicable equally—if not in precisely the same ways—to education in many other multicultural, religiously diverse democracies, including the United States. Almost from its inception, debates over the role of religious diversity and schooling have been a recurring feature of public discourse on education.[48] For the past 30 years or more, conservative fundamentalist and evangelical Christians have challenged public schools on a variety of issues arising out of the conflict between their religious identity and the values and direction of schools. Rising immigration into the United States from the developing world has led to a growing religious diversity to which schools are challenged to respond. This increase of diversity includes a rapidly growing Islamic population. Given the current tensions arising from the so-called war on terrorism, it is an open question whether the United States will handle its internal relations with Muslims any better than the Philippines has. It certainly has not done so in its international relations with the Muslim world.

Therefore, the examination of Muslim Filipino educational experience raises a number of interesting questions. Can schools afford to ignore religious identity or remain silent, as is so often the case, on religious differences and their impact on culture, the arts, and politics? In school systems that claim to respect cultural diversity is it possible or desirable to separate religious identity from cultural identity? Is such a separation possible only for those who are either in the majority or for whom religion is unimportant? Does the assumption that the sacred and secular are separable for everyone constitute a form of cultural violence against some students? How does religious faith interact with learning?

On the other hand, how can schools take religious identity into account without violating constitutional principles, or appearing to take sides in religious debates, or being torn asunder by the explosive mix of religion, culture, and politics that is fragmenting so many societies? The experience of Muslim students and their teachers in the southern

Philippines suggests that neither silence, nor the dominance of one group over another, nor educational balkanization are adequate answers. Democratic, multicultural education for religiously diverse societies must find ways of accounting for religious identity in ways that respect the identity, aspirations, and rights of all its constituents.

The examination of Filipino Muslim educational experience can offer invaluable resources, as Dewey's theory of experience predicts, for thinking through this challenge in other national contexts. While many of the specific tensions between Islamic identity in Mindanao and Philippine public education are unique to that particular context, the general question of how public schools interact with religious communities, particularly minority religious communities, is an issue faced by many school systems around the world. In Indonesia, India, Israel, the former Yugoslavia, and a variety of other countries the powerful mix of religious and cultural identity fuels social tensions that often lead to violence and threaten national fragmentation. Such social conflicts inevitably involve schools in one way or another and challenge educators to respond. Those responses, however, may exacerbate these tensions or mitigate them. Current US efforts to assist in the reconstruction of educational systems in Afghanistan and Iraq will require local and American educators to face this challenge posed by ethno-religious differences without slipping into the well-worn ruts of educational imperialism.

The kind of social conflicts examined here, as Dewey knew, inevitably manifest themselves in education and thus set a problem. "It is the business," he wrote, "of an intelligent theory of education to ascertain the causes for the conflicts that exist and then, instead of taking one side or the other, to indicate a plan of operations proceeding from a level deeper and more inclusive than is represented by the practices and ideas of the contending parties."[49] That has been the goal of this inquiry. I conclude it, therefore, in the hope that the effort it embodies to bring the perspectives of postcolonial theory and prophetic pragmatism to bear on the challenges of providing democratic education to Muslim minorities has furthered that aim.

Notes

1. Cited in Karnow, *In Our Image*, 128.
2. Hayden, "What Next for the Moro?" 636; Hayden, "Americanizing the Moros," 260.

3. See Kepel, *The Revenge of God*; Marty and Appleby, *The Glory and the Power*; Abuza, *Militant Islam in Southeast Asia*.
4. See, for instance, Pecson and Racelis, *Tales of the American Teachers*; Lardizabal, *Pioneer American Teachers and Philippine Education*; Sibayan, *The Long Ago Teacher*.
5. Lloyd G. Van Vactor, "Four Decades of American Educators in Mindanao and Sulu," 225–252.
6. Memmi, *The Colonizer and the Colonized*; Fanon, *Black Skin, White Masks*; Achebe, *Things Fall Apart*; Gordimer, *July's People*; Said, *Orientalism*.
7. See Constantino, *Neocolonial Identity and Counter Consciousness*.
8. Filipinas Foundation, *An Anatomy of Philippine Muslim Affairs*, 116–117, 192.
9. Filipinas Foundation, *Philippine Majority–Minority Relations and Ethnic Attitudes*, 122, 139, 158.
10. Tolibas-Nunez, *Roots of Conflict*, 43, 84.
11. *Report of the Transitional Justice and Reconciliation Commission*.
12. Punongbayan, "AFP, PNP Back Another Year of ML."
13. *Report of the Transitional Justice and Reconciliation Commission*.
14. Ibid., 25.
15. Ibid., 22.
16. Bliss, *Annual Report of Brigadier General Tasker H. Bliss, U.S. Army, Governor of the Moro Province: April 16, 1906 to August 27, 1906* (Manila: Bureau of Printing, 1906), 81.
17. Bliss, "The Government of the Moro Province and Its Problems," *The Mindanao Herald* (February 3, 1909), 6.
18. Clavel, *They Are Also Filipinos*, 71.
19. Morris, *The American Contribution to Philippine Education*, 3.
20. See Button and Provenzo, Jr., *History of Education, and Culture in America*.
21. See, for instance, Estioko, *History of Education: A Filipino Perspective*.
22. *Report of the Transitional Justice and Reconciliation Commission*, xvii.
23. Ibid.
24. Dewey, *Democracy and Education*.
25. Republic of the Philippines, "Republic Act 11054."
26. Ibid., 27.
27. Ibid., Article IX, Sec. 5.
28. Ibid., Article II, Sec. 1.
29. Ibid., Article IX, Sec. 16.
30. Article XII, Sec. 16, 18, 19, 21.
31. West, *American Evasion*, 70–71.
32. Ibid., 71.
33. Ibid., 212–214.

34. Ibid., 223.
35. Ibid., 223–226.
36. Ibid., 226, 228.
37. Ibid., 233–234.
38. Dewey, *Democracy and Education*, 99.
39. Dewey, *A Common Faith*, 33.
40. Young, *Postcolonialism*, 338.
41. West, *American Evasion*, 234.
42. Dewey, *A Common Faith*.
43. West, *Prophesy Deliverance!* 15–20.
44. West, *American Evasion*, 235.
45. Rorty, *Consequences of Pragmatism*, 202.
46. Dewey, *Democracy and Education*, 76.
47. Freire, *Pedagogy of the Oppressed*.
48. See, for instance, Fraser, *Between Church and State*.
49. Dewey, *Experience and Education*, 5.

BIBLIOGRAPHY

Abaza, M. "A Note on Henry Corbin and Seyyed Hossein Nasr: Affinities and Differences." *Muslim World* 90, no. 1/2, p. 91 (Spring 2000).
———. *Debates on Islam and Knowledge in Malaysia and Egypt: Shifting Worlds.* New York: Routledge Curzon, 2002.
———. "Some Reflections on the Question of Islam and Social Sciences in the Contemporary Muslim World." *Social Compass* 40, pp. 301–321.
Abdullah, M.F. "Madrasah Education in the Philippines." Paper presentation. Second Conference on the Unification and Development of Madrasah Education, Marawi City, Philippines, May 31–June 1, 2003.
Abinales, Patricio N. *Making Mindanao: Cotabato and Davao in the Formation of the Philippine Nation-State.* Manila: Ateneo de Manila University Press, 2000.
Abrams, Dominic and Hogg, Michael. Eds. *Social Identity Theory: Constructive and Critical Advances.* New York: Harvester Wheatsheaf, 1990.
Abuza, Zachary. *Militant Islam in Southeast Asia: Crucible of Terror.* London: Lynne Rienner, 2003.
Achebe, Chinua. *Things Fall Apart.* New York: Anchor Books, 1994.
Adams, David Wallace. *Education for Extinction: American Indians and the Boarding School Experience, 1875–1928.* Lawrence: University of Kansas Press, 1995.
Ahmad, Aijaz. "The War Against the Muslims." In Gaerlan, Kristina and Stankovitch, Mara. Eds. *Rebels, Warlords and Ulama: A Reader on Muslim Separatism and the War in the Southern Philippines.* Quezon City: Institute for Popular Democracy, 2000.

Al-Attas, Syed Muhammad Naquib. Ed. *Aims and Objectives of Islamic Education*. Jeddah, Saudi Arabia: Hodder & Stoughton, 1992.

———. *The Concept of Education in Islam*. Kuala Lumpur, Malaysia: International Institute for Islamic Thought and Civilization, 1999.

Aldana, Benigno. *The Educational System of the Philippines*. Manila: University Publishing, 1949.

Al Faruqi, Isma'il R. *Islam*. Niles: Argus Communication, 1984.

———. *Islamization of Knowledge: General Principles and Work Plan*. Herndon, VA: International Institute for Islamic Thought, 1997.

Altbach, Philip G. and Kelly, Gail P. Eds. *Education and Colonialism*. New York: Longman, 1978.

"Americanizing the Moros." *The New Republic* 65 (January 21, 1931).

Anderson, Benedict. *Imagined Communities*. Pasig City: Anvil Publishing, 2003.

Angeles, Vivienne S.M. "Islam and Politics: Philippine Government Policies and Muslim Responses, 1946–1976." Ph.D. diss., Temple University, 1986.

Ante, Jose. "Muslim–Christian Integration in the Notre Dame Schools of Sulu." *Solidarity* 5, no. 3 (March 1970).

Apple, Michael W. *Ideology and Curriculum*. New York: Routledge, 1990.

Arong, Jose Roberto T. "Schooled in Conflict: The Impact of Education and Culture on Ethno-Religious Conflict in Southern Philippines." Ph.D. diss., Stanford University, 1976.

Bain, David Howard. *Sitting in Darkness: Americans in the Philippines*. Boston: Penguin, 1984.

Baradas, David B. "Ambiguities in Maranao Social Rank Differentiation." *Philippine Sociological Review* 21, no. 3–4 (July–October 1973).

Barrows, David Prescott. "The Memoirs of David Prescott Barrows." *Bulletin of the American Historical Collection* 23, no. 3 (July–September 1995).

Bauzon, Kenneth E. *Liberalism and the Quest for Islamic Identity in the Philippines*. Manila: Ateneo de Manila University Press, 1991.

Bazaco, Evergisto. *History of Education in the Philippines (Spanish Period, 1565–1898)*. Manila: University of Santo Tomas Press, 1953.

Bentley, G. Carter. "The Evolution of Muslim–Christian Relations in the Lanao Region, Philippines." *Dansalan Quarterly* 3, no. 3 (April 1982).

Biesta, Gert J.J. and Burbules, Nicholas. *Pragmatism and Educational Research*. Lanham: Rowman and Littlefield, 2003.

Bliss, Tasker H. *Annual Report of Brig. General Tasker H. Bliss, U.S. Army, Governor of the Moro Province, 1906*. Manila: Bureau of Printing, 1906.

———. *The Annual Report of the Governor of the Moro Province for Fiscal Year Ended June 30, 1907*. Manila: Bureau of Printing, 1907.

———. *The Annual Report of the Governor of the Moro Province for the Fiscal Year Ended June 30, 1908*. Zamboanga: The Mindanao Herald Publishing, 1908.

———. "The Government of the Moro Province and Its Problems." *The Mindanao Herald: A Decennium Issue* (February 3, 1909).
Bloom, Benjamin. Ed. *Taxonomy of Educational Objectives: The Classification of Educational Goals*. New York: Longman, 1964.
Board of Educational Survey. *A Survey of the Educational System of the Philippine Islands*. Manila: Bureau of Printing, 1925.
Boransing, Manaros. "Modernization and Development of the Madrasah Institutions in Philippines." Paper presentation. Second Conference on the Unification and Development of Madrasah Education, Marawi City, Philippines, May 31, 2003.
———. "Oplan Bangsa Pilipino." *FAPE Review* (May 1982).
Boransing, Manaros, Magdalena, Frederico V., and Lacar, Luis Q. *The Madrasah Institution in the Philippines: Historical and Cultural Perspectives*. Iligan City: Toyota Foundation, 1987.
Brands, H.W. *Bound to Empire: The United States and the Philippines*. New York: Oxford University Press, 1992.
Brilliantes, A. "Decentralization in the Philippines: An Overview." *Philippine Journal of Public Administration* XXXI, no. 2, pp. 131–147.
Brownell, Atherton. "Turning Savages into Citizens." *Outlook* 96 (December 24, 1910).
———. "What American Ideas of Citizenship May Do for Oriental Peoples: A Moro Experiment." *Outlook* 81 (December 23, 1905).
Bruckner, Pascal. *The Tears of the White Man: Compassion as Contempt*. New York: The Free Press, 1986.
Bruner, Jerome. *The Culture of Education*. Cambridge: Harvard University Press, 1996.
Brydon, Diana. Ed. *Postcolonialism: Critical Concepts in Literary and Cultural Studies*. London and New York: Routledge, 2000.
Bucaille, M. *The Bible, the Qur'an and Science: The Holy Scriptures Examined in the Light of Modern Knowledge*. Paris: Seghers, 1986.
Bula, D. "Muslims in the Philippine Public Elementary and Secondary School Textbooks: A Content Analysis." *Dansalan Quarterly* 10, no. 3–4 (April–July 1989).
Bullard, R.L. "Preparing Our Moros for Government." *Atlantic Monthly* 97 (March 1906).
———. "Road Building Among the Moros." *Atlantic Monthly* 92 (December 1903).
Bureau of Education. *Bulletin No. 6-1904, Report of Industrial Exhibits of the Philippine Schools at the Louisiana Purchase Exposition*. Manila: Bureau of Printing, 1904.

———. *Bulletin No. 7-1904, Courses of Instruction for the Public Schools of the Philippine Islands Prescribed by the General Superintendent of Education, Manila, P.I., June 15, 1904.* Manila: Bureau of Printing, 1904.

———. *Twenty-Seventh Annual Report of the Director of Education.* Manila: Government of the Philippine Islands Department of Public Instruction, 1926.

Button, H. Warren and Provenzo, Eugene F. *History of Education and Culture in America.* Englewood Cliffs: Prentice-Hall, 1983.

Cameron, Charles R. "Charles R. Cameron Papers." Xavier University Museum and Archives, Cagayan de Oro, Philippines, July 20, 1907.

———. "The Schools of Moroland." *The Mindanao Herald: A Decennium Issue* (February 3, 1909).

Carpenter, Frank W. *Report of the Governor of the Department of Mindanao and Sulu (Philippine Islands), 1914.* Washington: Bureau of Insular Affairs, War Department, Government Printing Office, 1916.

Caulkins, Glenn Whitman. "Public Education in Mindanao-Sulu Philippine Islands Under the American Regime." M.A. thesis, University of Washington, 1934.

Che Man, W.K. *Muslim Separatism: The Moros of the Southern Philippines and the Malays of Southern Thailand.* Manila: Ateneo de Manila University Press, 1990.

Chua, Yvonne T. *Robbed: An Investigation of Corruption in Philippine Education.* Quezon City: Philippine Center for Investigative Journalism, 1999.

Clavel, Leothiny S. *They Are also Filipinos: Ten Years with the Cultural Minorities.* Manila: Bureau of Printing, 1969.

Code, Lorraine. *What Can She Know? Feminist Theory and the Construction of Knowledge.* Ithaca: Cornell University Press, 1991.

Coedes, G. *The Indianized States of Southeast Asia.* Honolulu: University of Hawaii Press, 1968.

Constantino, Renato. *Neocolonial Identity and Counter Consciousness: Essays on Cultural Decolonisation.* London: Merlin Press, 1978.

———. *The Philippines: A Past Revisited, Vol. 1.* Quezon City: Foundation for Nationalist Studies, 1975.

Constitution of the Republic of the Philippines, 1986.

Cook, Katherine M. "Public Education in the Philippine Islands." *Bulletin 1935, No. 9, U.S. Department of the Interior, Office of Education.* Washington: U.S. Government Printing Office, 1935.

Coronel, Delia. Ed. *The Darangen, Vol. 1–8.* Cebu: Jose Clavano, 1986.

Coronel-Ferrer, Miriam. Ed. *Peace Matters: A Philippine Peace Compendium.* Manila: University of the Philippines Center for Integrative and Development Studies/Peace, Conflict Resolution and Human Rights Program, 1987.

Coughlan, Neil. *Young John Dewey: An Essay in American Intellectual History.* Chicago: University of Chicago Press, 1973.
Damonsong-Rodriguez, Lolita Junio. *A Madrasah General Education Program for Muslim Mindanao.* Marawi City: Mindanao State University Office of the Vice-Chancellor for Research and Extension, 1992.
Department of Education and Culture. *A Year of Progress Under Martial Law.* Manila: Department of Education and Culture, 1973.
Department of Education, Culture, and Sports. *Manual of Information on Secondary Education.* Manila: Department of Education, Culture and Sports, Bureau of Secondary Education, 1993.
———. *Values Education for the Filipino.* Manila: Department of Education, Culture and Sports, 1997.
Dery, Luis Camara. *The Kris in Philippine History: A Study of the Impact of Moro Anti-Colonial Resistance, 1571–1896.* Quezon City, 1997.
Dewey, John. *A Common Faith.* New Haven: Yale University Press, 1934.
———. *Art as Experience.* New York: Perigee Books, 1934/1980.
———. *Democracy and Education.* New York: Free Press, 1916/1966.
———. *Experience and Education.* New York: Collier Books, 1938/1963.
Disoma, Esmail R. *The Meranao.* Marawi City: Mindanao State University Office of the Vice Chancellor for Research and Extension, 1999.
"District of Lanao." *The Mindanao Herald: A Decennium Issue* (February 3, 1909).
DuBois, W.E.B. *The Souls of Black Folk.* New York: Signet, 1969.
Dumarpa, Jaime. "An Exploratory Study of Maranao Muslims' Concepts of Land Ownership: Its Implications for the Mindanao Conflict." *Dansalan Quarterly* VI, no. 1 (October 1984).
Dy, Manuel B. *Values in Philippine Culture and Education.* Washington: Council for Research in Values and Philosophy, 1994.
Elevazo, Aurelio O. and Elevazo, Rosita A. *Philosophy of Philippine Education.* Manila: National Bookstore, 1995.
Elevazo, Aurelio O. and Villamor, Fortunata C. *Educational Objectives and Policies in the Philippines, 1900–1972.* Manila: Division of Educational Planning, 1973.
Esposito, John L. Ed. *The Oxford Encyclopedia of the Modern Islamic World.* New York: Oxford University Press, 1995.
Esteban, Rolando C. "Amaipacpac: 19th Century Maranao Hero." *Dansalan Quarterly* 18, no. 1–2 (January–June 1998).
Estioko, Leonardo R. *History of Education: A Filipino Perspective.* Manila: Logos Publications, 1994.
Estonillo, Ernest. "Existing Government Policies on Peace Education." Presentation. Al Qalam Institute for Islamic Identities and Dialogue in Southeast Asia, Davao, Philippines, November 6, 2018.

Evans, A. "Understanding Madrasahs." *Foreign Affairs* 85, no. 1, pp. 9–14.
Fanon, Franz. *A Dying Colonialism*. New York: Grove Press, 1965.
———. *Black Skin, White Masks*. New York: Grove Weidenfeld, 1967.
Filipinas Foundation. *An Anatomy of Philippine Muslim Affairs*. Manila: Filipinas Foundation, 1971.
———. *Philippine Majority–Minority Relations and Ethnic Attitudes*. Makati: Filipinas Foundation, 1975.
Finley, John P. "The Development of the District of Zamboanga." *The Mindanao Herald: A Decennium Issue* (February 3, 1909).
Foreman, John. *The Philippine Islands*. Manila: Filipiniana Book Guild, 1906/1980.
Foster, Philip. "The Educational Policies of Postcolonial States." In Anderson, Lacelles and Windham, Douglas M. Eds. *Education and Development*. Lexington: Lexington Books, 1982.
Foucault, Michel. *The History of Sexuality, Vol. I*. New York: Vintage Books, 1990.
Francisco, Juan R. "Sanskrit in Maranao Language and Literature." *Mindanao Journal* 1, no. 1 (July–September 1974).
Fraser, James W. *Between Church and State: Religion and Public Education in Multicultural America*. New York: St. Martin's, 1999.
Freire, Paulo. *Pedagogy of the Oppressed*. New York: Continuum, 1990.
Gandhi, Leela. *Postcolonial Theory: A Critical Introduction*. New York: Columbia University Press, 1998.
George, T.J.S. *Revolt in Mindanao: The Rise of Islam in Philippine Politics*. Kuala Lumpur: Oxford University Press, 1980.
Ghazi, A. "To Change Madrasah Education: Continuity and Change." Paper presentation. Institute for Islamic Studies, University of the Philippines, Manila, Philippines, October 2003.
Gill, Avelina J. *Phoenix English for Secondary Schools, First Year*. Quezon City: Phoenix Publishing House, 1997.
———. *Phoenix English for Secondary Schools, Fourth Year*. Quezon City: Phoenix Publishing House, 1998.
Gleeck, Lewis E. *Americans on the Philippine Frontiers*. Manila: Carmelo & Bauermann, 1974.
Gonzales, Bro. Andrew, Sta. Ana-Rankin, Lilia, and Hukom, Adelaida N. Eds. *Kasaysayan at Pamahalaang Pilipino*. Quezon City: Phoenix Publishing, 1999.
Gordimer, Nadine. *July's People*. New York: Quality Paperbacks, 1992.
Government of the Philippine Islands Department of Public Instruction, Bureau of Education. *A Statement of Organization, Aims and Conditions of Service in the Bureau of Education*. Manila: Bureau of Printing, 1911.

———. *Sixteenth Annual Report of the Director of Education, January 1, 1915–December 31, 1915*. Manila: Bureau of Printing, 1915.

———. *Nineteenth Annual Report of the Director of Education, January 1, 1918–December 31, 1918*. Manila: Bureau of Printing, 1919.

———. *Twenty-First Annual Report of the Director of Education, January 1, 1920–December 31, 1920*. Manila: Bureau of Printing, 1921.

———. *Twenty-Second Annual Report of the Director of Education, January 1, 1921–December 31, 1921*. Manila: Bureau of Printing, 1922.

———. *Twenty-Third Annual Report of the Director of Education, January 1, 1922–December 31, 1922*. Manila: Bureau of Printing, 1923.

———. *Twenty-Seventh Annual Report of the Director of Education, 1926*. Manila: Bureau of Printing, 1927.

———. *The Philippine Islands: Information for Americans Thinking of Entering the Philippine Teaching Service*. Manila: Bureau of Printing, 1925.

Gowing, Peter G. *Mandate in Moroland: The American Government of Muslim Filipinos, 1899–1920*. Quezon City: New Day, 1983.

———. "Moros and Indians: Commonalities of Purpose, Policy and Practice in American Government of Two Hostile Subject Peoples." *Dansalan Research Center Occasional Papers* 6 (January 1977).

Gowing, Peter G. and McAmis, Robert. *Muslim Filipinos*. Manila: New Day, 1974.

Gripaldo, Rolando M. "Quezon's Philosophy of Philippine Education." *The Technician* 3, no. 2 (December 1990).

Guerrero, Juanita S. and Castano, Paulina M. *Values Education I: A True Filipino*. Quezon City: Phoenix Publishing House, 1999.

Guingona, Teopisto. "Historical Survey of Policies Pursued by Spain and the United States Toward the Moros in the Philippines." Unpublished manuscript, 1943.

Hall, G. Stanley. *Educational Problems, Vol. II*. New York: D. Appleton & Co., 1911.

Haneef, M.A. *A Critical Survey of Islamization of Knowledge*. Kuala Lumpur: International Islamic University of Malaysia.

Hashim, Rosnani. *Educational Dualism in Malaysia: Implications for Theory and Practice*. Kuala Lumpur: The Other Press, 2004.

Hassoubah, Ahman Mohammad H. *Teaching Arabic as a Second Language in the Southern Philippines*. Marawi City: Mindanao State University Research Center, 1983.

Hayden, Ralston. "Americanizing the Moros." *The New Republic* 65 (January 21, 1931).

———. "What Next for the Moro?" *Foreign Affairs* 6 (July 1928).

Hing, L.K. *Education and Politics in Indonesia, 1945–1965*. Kuala Lumpur: University of Malaya Press, 1995.

Hoyt, Ralph W. *Annual Report of Colonel Ralph W. Hoyt, 25th United States Infantry, Governor of the Moro Province for the Fiscal Year Ended June 30, 1909.* Zamboanga: Mindanao Herald Publishing, 1909.
Isidro, Antonio. *Education in the Philippines.* Manila: University of the Philippines Press, 1939.
———. *Muslim–Christian Integration at the Mindanao State University.* Marawi City: Mindanao State University Research Center, 1968.
———. *The Philippine Education System.* Manila: Bookman, 1949.
Isidro, Antonio and Saber, Mamitua. "Education of the Muslims." *Solidarity* 4, no. 3 (1969).
———. *Muslim Philippines.* Marawi City: Mindanao State University Research Center, 1968.
———. *The Moro Problem: An Approach Through Education.* Marawi City: Mindanao State University Research Center, 1979.
Ivison, Duncan. *Postcolonial Liberalism.* Cambridge: Cambridge University Press, 2002.
James, Gavin. "The Role of Education in ASEAN Economic Growth: Past and Future." In Wong, Tai-Chee and Singh, Mohan. Eds. *Development and Change: Southeast Asia in the New Millennium.* Singapore: Times Academic Press, 1999.
Jones, O. Garfield. "Our Mandate Over Moroland." *Asia* 20 (July 1920).
Kamlian, Jamail A. *Bangsamoro Society and Culture: A Book of Readings on Peace and Development in the Southern Philippines.* Iligan City: Iligan Center for Peace Education and Research, 1999.
Karnow, Stanley. *In Our Image: America's Empire in the Philippines.* New York: Ballantine Books, 1989.
Kepel, Gilles. *The Revenge of God: The Resurgence of Islam, Christianity and Judaism in the Modern World.* University Park: The Pennsylvania State University Press, 1994.
Lacar, Luis Q. "Familism Among Muslims and Christians in the Philippines." *Philippine Studies* 43 (First Quarter 1995).
Lardizabal, Amparo Santamaria. *Pioneer American Teachers and Philippine Education.* Quezon City: Phoenix Press, 1991.
Laubach, Frank. "A Literacy Campaign Among the Moros." *The Moslem World* 23 (January 1933).
———. "Moslems Under the American Flag." *Missionary Review of the World* 54 (May 1931).
L.B., Lieut. "The Regular and the Savage." *Lippencott's Magazine* 74 (December 1904).
LeRoy, James A. "The Moro and Pagan Question." *Independent* 54 (July 24, 1902).
Loomba, Ania. *Colonialism/Postcolonialism.* New York: Routledge, 1998.

Lucman, Datu Norodin Alonto. *Moro Archives: A History of Armed Conflicts in Mindanao and East Asia.* Quezon City: FLC Press, 2000.

Madale, Abdullah T. "Educating the Muslim Child: The Philippine Case." In Salazar, Z.A. Ed. *The Ethnic Dimension: Papers on Philippine Culture, History and Psychology.* Cologne: Counseling Center for Filipinos, Caritas Association for the City of Cologne, 1983.

———. "Educational Implications of Moro History." *Mindanao Journal* 3, no. 1 (July–September 1976).

———. "Ghost Schools and the Maranaw." *Philippine Journal of Education* 36, no. 6 (February 1957).

Madale, Nagasura T. "A Socio-Cultural Analysis of Radia Indarapatra: A Maranao Folk Narrative." Ph.D. diss., University of the Philippines-Diliman, 1981.

———. Ed. *The Muslim Filipinos: A Book of Readings.* Quezon City: Alemar-Phoenix Publishing, 1981.

Majul, Cesar Adib. *Muslims in the Philippines.* Quezon City: University of the Philippines Press, 1999.

Mallat, Jean. *The Philippines: History, Geography, Customs.* Manila: National Historical Institute, 1846/1994.

Mangadang, Musur M. "The Educational Problems of the Muslims in Lanao." M.A. Thesis, Arellano University, 1957.

Manoga, L.B. *The Da'wah Tabligh Movement in Selected Cities of Mindanao: Towards an Alternative Filipino Values Education Framework.* Unpublished doctoral diss., Mindanao State University, Marawi, Philippines, 2002.

Martin, Jane Roland. *Reclaiming a Conversation: The Ideal of the Educated Woman.* New Haven: Yale University Press, 1985.

———. *The Schoolhome: Rethinking Schools for Changing Families.* Cambridge: Harvard University Press, 1992.

Marty, Martin and Appleby, R. Scott. *The Glory and the Power: The Fundamentalist Challenge to the Modern World.* Boston: Beacon Press, 1992.

Mastura, Datu Michael O. "Assessing the Madrasah as an Educational Institution: Implications for the Ummah." *FAPE Review* (May 1982).

Masud, Muhammad Khalid. Ed. *Travelers in Faith: Studies of the Tablighi Jama'at as a Transnational Islamic Movement for Faith Renewal.* Leiden: Brill, 2000.

Maybury-Lewis, David. *Indigenous Peoples, Ethnic Groups and the State.* Boston: Allyn & Bacon, 2002.

McKenna, Thomas M. *Muslim Rulers and Rebels: Everyday Politics and Armed Separatism in the Southern Philippines.* Manila: Anvil Publishing, 1998.

Mednick, Melvin. "Encampment of the Lake: The Social Organization of a Moslem-Philippine (Moro) People." *Research Series No. 5, Philippine Studies Program.* Department of Anthropology, University of Chicago, 1965.

Memmi, Albert. *The Colonizer and the Colonized*. New York: Orion Press, 1965.

Mignolo, Walter D. *Local Histories/Global Designs: Coloniality, Subaltern Knowledges, and Border Thinking*. Princeton: Princeton University Press, 2000.

Milligan, Jeffrey Ayala. "Democratization or Neocolonialism? The Education of Muslims Under U.S. Military Occupation, 1903–1920." *History of Education* 33, no. 4, pp. 451–467.

———. "Faith in School: Educational Policy Responses to Ethno-Religious Conflict in the Southern Philippines, 1935–1985." *Journal of Southeast Asian Studies* 36, no. 1, pp. 67–86.

———. "Islam and Educational Policy Reform in the Southern Philippines. *Asia Pacific Journal of Education* 28, no. 4, pp. 369–381.

———. "Islamization or Secularization? Educational Reform and the Search for Peace in the Southern Philippines." *Current Issues in Comparative Education* 7, no. 1, pp. 1–8. Retrieved from http://www.tc.columbia.edu/cice/articles/jm171.htm:1-8.

———. "Postcolonial Pragmatism? Ethno-Religious Conflict and Education in Postcolonial Spaces." *Philosophy of Education*, pp. 287–295.

———. "Prophetic Pragmatism? Post-Conflict Educational Development in Aceh and Mindanao." *Diaspora, Indigenous and Minority Education: An International Journal* 3, no. 4, pp. 245–259.

———. "Reclaiming an Ideal: The Islamization of Education in the Southern Philippines." *Comparative Education Review* 50, no. 3, pp. 410–430.

———. "Religious Identity, Autonomy, and National Integrity: Implications for Educational Policy from Muslim–Christian Conflict in the Philippines." *Islam and Christian–Muslim Relations* 12, no. 4 (October 2001).

———. "Rethinking the Ideal of the Educated Person: An Alternative from the Maranao-Filipino Oral Epic 'Darangen'." *Journal of Thought* 35, no. 3, pp. 67–79.

———. "Teaching Between the Cross and the Crescent Moon: Islamic Identity, Postcoloniality and Public Education in the Southern Philippines." *Comparative Education Review* 47, no. 4, pp. 468–492.

———. "The Prophet and the Engineer Meet Under the Mango Tree: Leadership, Education and Conflict in the Southern Philippines." *Educational Policy* 24, no. 1, pp. 28–51.

Ministry of Education and Culture (MEC). *Annual Report 1980 (Regional Offices)*. Manila: Ministry of Education and Culture, 1980.

———. *Report on Educational Development in the Seventies*. Manila: Ministry of Education and Culture, 1979.

Ministry of Education, Culture and Sports (MECS). *Annual Report 1983*. Manila: Ministry of Education, Culture and Sports, 1983.

———. *Annual Report 1984*. Manila: Ministry of Education, Culture and Sports, 1984.
Morris, Greta N. Ed. *The American Contribution to Philippine Education, 1898–1998*. Manila: USIA Regional Service Center, 1998.
Muslim, Macapado Abaton. *The Moro Armed Struggle in the Philippines: The Non-violent Autonomy Alternative*. Marawi City: Mindanao State University College of Public Affairs, 1994.
Mutilan, Mahad. *Leading a New Beginning in DepEd ARMM*. Cotabato City: Department of Education, Autonomous Region in Muslim Mindanao, Philippines, 2003.
Nasr, Syed Hussein. *Islamic Life and Thought*. Albany: State University of New York Press, 1981.
———. *Knowledge and the Sacred*. Albany: State University of New York Press, 1989.
National Statistical Coordination Board. *1999 Philippine Statistical Yearbook*. Makati: National Statistical Coordination Board, 1999.
———. "Administrative Policies Towards the Muslim in the Philippines: A Study in Historical Continuity and Trends." *Mindanao Journal* 3, no. 1 (July–September 1976).
Navarro, Josefina N. "Curricular Directions in the New Society." *Educational Directions in the New Society*. Manila: Philippine Association of School Superintendents, 1973.
Ocampo, R. "Decentralization and Local Autonomy: A Framework for Assessing Progress." *Philippine Journal of Public Administration* XXXV, no. 3, pp. 191–204.
Ono, Y. "The Process of Integrating Islamic Education into Public Education in the Philippines." Paper presentation. 13th World Congress of Comparative Education Societies, Sarajevo, Bosnia and Herzegovina, September 2007.
Osias, Camilo. "Notes on Education." Unpublished report to the President of the Philippines, September 16, 1940.
———. "Speeches on Education." Manila: Unpublished manuscript, 1963.
———. *The Philippine Reader, Books II–VII*. Boston: Ginn & Company, 1932.
Osterhammel, Jurgen. *Colonialism: A Theoretical Overview*. Princeton: Markus Wiener Publishers, 1997.
Palma-Rallos, Ma. Zilpha. *Breakthrough*. Quezon City: Phoenix Publishing House, 1999.
Pandapatan, Abdulrahim-Tamano M. "Madrasah System of Education in the Philippines." *Muslim Education Quarterly* 3, no. 1 (Autumn 1985).
Partridge, G.E. *Genetic Philosophy of Education: An Epitome of the Published Educational Writings of President G. Stanley Hall of Clark University*. New York: Sturgis and Walton, 1912.

Pascual-Lambert, N. "The Need for Minority Identities in Textbooks and Curriculum Reform." *The Mindanao Forum* XII, no. 1, pp. 97–103.

Pecson, Geronima T. and Racelis, Maria. Eds. *Tales of the American Teachers in the Philippines*. Manila: Carmelo & Bauermann, 1959.

Pedrajas, Teresita P. *Values Education II: A Concerned Filipino*. Quezon City: Phoenix Publishing House, 1999.

Pershing, John J. *The Annual Report of the Governor of the Moro Province for the Fiscal Year Ended June 30, 1913*. Zamboanga: Mindanao Herald Publishing, 1913.

Phillips, Denis C. and Burbules, Nicholas. *Postpositivism and Educational Research*. Lanham: Rowman & Littlefield, 2000.

Pratt, Mary Louise. *Imperial Eyes: Travel Writing and Transculturation*. New York: Routledge, 1992.

"Primer." Marawi City: Ibn Siena Integrated School Foundation, n.d.

Punongbayan, Michael. "AFP, PNP Back Another Year of ML." *The Philippine Star* XXXIII, no. 130 (Tuesday, December 4, 2018), pp. 1, 3.

Radford, Josefa L. Quirante. *World History*. Quezon City: Phoenix Publishing House, 2000.

Rahman, Fazlur. *Islam and Modernity*. Chicago: University of Chicago Press, 1982.

———. "Islamization of Knowledge: A Response." *American Journal of Islamic Social Sciences* 5, no. 1, pp. 3–11.

Rajchmann, John and West, Cornel. *Post-Analytic Philosophy*. New York: Columbia University Press, 1985.

Rasul, Jainal D. "Muslim–Christian Relations at the Grassroots Level." *Dansalan Quarterly* 5, no. 3 (April 1984).

Report of the Transitional Justice and Reconciliation Commission. Manila: Transitional Justice and Reconciliation Commission, 2016.

Republic of the Philippines. *Lanao del Sur Provincial Profile*. Manila: National Statistics Office, 1990.

———. "Organic Law for the Bangsamoro Autonomous Region in Muslim Mindanao, Republic Act. No. 11054," 2018.

———. "Republic Act 6734: Organic Act for the Autonomous Region in Muslim Mindanao." Manila, Philippines, 1990.

Reyes, Alice H. and Rodriguez, Artemio S. Eds. *Journal on National Integration*. Quezon City: Commission on National Integration, 1968.

Riemer, Carlton L. "Maranao Maratabat and the Concepts of Pride, Honor, and Self Esteem." *Dansalan Quarterly* 8, no. 4 (July 1987).

Rodil, Rudy B. "Ancestral Domain: A Central Issue in the Lumad Struggle for Self Determination in Mindanao." In Turner, Mark, May, R.J., and Turner, Lulu R. Eds. *Mindanao: Land of Unfulfilled Promise*. Quezon City: New Day, 1992.

———. "Remarks on Textbooks Used by a Private School in Iligan for Grades 3, 5 and 6." Unpublished manuscript, 2000.

Rorty, Richard. *Consequences of Pragmatism*. Minneapolis: University of Minnesota Press, 1982.

Saber, Mamitua. "Introduction." In Coronel, Delia. Ed. *The Darangen, Vol. I*. Cebu: Jose Clavano, 1986.

———. "Marginal Leadership in a Cultural-Contact Situation." *Mindanao Journal* 18, no. 1–2 (July–October 1991).

Saber, Mamitua and Madale, Abdullah T. Eds. *The Maranao*. Manila: Solidaridad, 1975.

Saber, Mamitua and Tamano, Mauyag M. "Decision-Making and Social Change in Rural Moroland." *Mindanao Journal* 12, no. 1–4 (July 1985–June 1986).

Said, Edward. *Orientalism*. New York: Vintage, 1979.

Saleeby, Najeeb M. "Studies in Moro History, Law and Religion." *Ethnological Survey Publications, Vol. IV, Part I*. Manila: Bureau of Printing, 1905.

———. *Sulu Reader for the Public Schools of the Moro Province*. Zamboanga City: Mindanao Herald Press, 1905.

———. "The Moro Problem: An Academic Discussion of the History and Solution of the Problem of the Government of the Moros of the Philippine Islands." *Dansalan Quarterly* 5, no. 1 (October 1983) (Original date of publication 1913).

Salgado, Geoffrey. "Development Policies for Muslim Mindanao in the Pre-Martial Law Period (1955–1971)." *The Mindanao Forum* 9, no. 1 (June 1994).

Salic, Basher D. "A Content Analysis of Instructional Materials in Philippine History: Towards Utilization of Muslim History in Social Studies I." M.A. thesis, University of the Philippines, 1990.

Saligoin, M.I. "Open Learning System for Public Schools and Madaris." Paper Presentation. First Madrasah Conference, General Santos City, Philippines, October 16, 1997.

Santos, Jr., Soliman M. *The Moro Islamic Challenge: Constitutional Rethinking of the Mindanao Peace Process*. Manila: University of the Philippines Press, 2001.

Sarangani, Datumanong A. "Islamic Penetration in Mindanao and Sulu." *Mindanao Journal* 1, no. 1 (July–September 1974).

Schlegel, Stuart. "Muslim–Christian Conflict in the Philippine South." *Mindanao* (July–September 1986).

"Schoolyear 76–77 Sees More Reforms in RP's Educational System." *New Philippines* 41, no. 2 (May 1976).

Schwartz, Karl. "Filipino Education and Spanish Colonialism: Towards an Autonomous Perspective." *Comparative Education Review* 15, no. 2 (June 1971).

Serrano, Josephine B. and Lapid, Milagros G. *English Communication Arts and Skills Through Philippine Literature*. Quezon City: Phoenix Publishing House, 2000.

Sibayan, Bonifacio P. *The Long Ago Teacher: Reflections on Philippine Education*. Quezon City: Phoenix Publishing House, 1995.

Soriano, Liceria B. "Our Moro Problem and the Community School in Mindanao." *Philippine Journal of Education* 32, no. 5 (1953).

Spencer, Herbert. *Education: Intellectual, Moral and Physical*. New York: D. Appleton & Co., 1914.

Spivak, Gayatri Chakravorty. "Can the Subaltern Speak?" In Nelson, C. and Grossbert, L. Eds. *Marxism and the Interpretation of Culture*. Urbana: University of Illinois Press, 1988.

Spring, Joel. *The Cultural Transformation of a Native American Family and Its Tribe, 1763–1995*. Mahwah: Lawrence Erlbaum Associates, 1996.

Stenberg, L. *The Islamization of Science: Four Muslim Positions Developing an Islamic Modernity*. Lund, Sweden: Novapress, 1996.

Stenhouse, P. "Ignoring Signposts on the Road: Da'wa, Jihad with a Velvet Glove." *Quadrant* 51, no. 6, pp. 40–47.

Suzuki, Mary Bonzo. "American Education in the Philippines, the Early Years: American Pioneer Teachers and the Filipino Response, 1900–1935." Ph.D. diss., University of California-Berkeley, 1991.

Talbani, Aziz. "Pedagogy, Power and Discourse: Transformation of Islamic Education." *Comparative Education Review* 40, no. 1 (February 1996).

Tamano, Mayug M. "What of Education in the Muslim Provinces?" *Philippine Journal of Education* 38, no. 3 (September 1959).

Tamano, Salipada Saud. *Educational Visions for Muslim Mindanao*. Cotabato City: Regional Department of Education, Culture and Sports, Autonomous Region in Muslim Mindanao, 1996.

———. "The Educational Problems of the Muslims in the Philippines." M.Ed. thesis, Ain Shams University, Cairo, United Arab Republic, 1971.

Tanggol, S.D. "Regional Autonomy and Social Development: Some Notes on Muslim Mindanao." *Philippine Journal of Public Administration* XXXIV, no. 1, pp. 1–24.

Tawagon, Manuel R. "The Darangen as a Pre-Islamic Oral Tradition." *Dansalan Quarterly* 17, no. 3–4 (July–December 1997).

———. "The Pengampong: Multiple Sultanates of Lanao." *Mindanao Journal* 16, no. 1–4 (July 1989–June 1990).

"Terror in Jolo." *Time* 38 (December 1, 1941).

Thomas, Ralph Benjamin. "Muslim But Filipino: The Integration of Philippine Muslims, 1917–1946." Ph.D. diss., University of Pennsylvania, 1971.

Tibawi, A.L. *Islamic Education: Its Traditions and Modernization in the Arab National Systems*. London: Luzac, 1979.

Tolibas-Nunez, Rosalita. *Roots of Conflict: Muslims, Christians, and the Mindanao Struggle.* Makati City: Asian Institute of Management, 1997.
Torrance, Arthur Fredric. "The Philippine Moro: A Study in Social and Race Pedagogy." Ph.D. diss., New York University, 1917.
Townsend, Henry Schuler. "Civil Government in the Moro Province." *Forum* 36 (July 1904).
Turner, Mark, May, R.J., and Turner, Lulu Respall. Eds. *Mindanao: Land of Unfulfilled Promise.* Quezon City: New Day Publishers, 1992.
Tuvilla, Ma. Victoria. *Person for Others: Community Builder and Steward on Earth.* Quezon City: Phoenix Publishing House, 1999.
Van Vactor, Lloyd G. "Education for the Maranaos: A Perspective on Problems and Prospects." *Dansalan Research Center Occasional Papers* 9 (January 1978).
———. "Four Decades of American Educators in Mindanao and Sulu." *Mindanao Journal* 8, no. 1–4 (July 1981–June 1982).
Vitug, Marites Danguilan and Gloria, Glenda M. *Under the Crescent Moon: Rebellion in Mindanao.* Quezon City: Ateneo Center for Social Policy and Public Affairs/Institute for Popular Democracy, 2000.
Walters, O.W. *Early Indonesian Commerce: A Study of the Origins of Srivijaya.* Ithaca: Cornell University Press, 1967.
Wan Mohd, W.N.D. *The Educational Philosophy and Practice of Syed Muhammad Naquib al-Attas.* Kuala Lumpur: International Institute of Islamic Thought and Civilization, 1998.
Watson, Keith. *Education in the Third World.* London: Croom Helm, 1982.
West, Cornel. *Prophesy Deliverance! An Afro-American Revolutionary Christianity.* Philadelphia: Westminster Press, 1982.
———. *The American Evasion of Philosophy: A Genealogy of Pragmatism.* Minneapolis: University of Minnesota Press, 1989.
Westbrook, Robert B. *John Dewey and American Democracy.* Ithaca: Cornell University Press, 1991.
Whicher, Stephen E. *Selections from Ralph Waldo Emerson.* Boston: Houghton Mifflin, 1960.
Willinsky, John. *Learning to Divide the World: Education at Empire's End.* Minneapolis: University of Minnesota Press, 1998.
Wilson, Fiona. "In the Name of the State? Schools and Teachers in an Andean Province." In Hansen, Thomas Blom and Stepputat, Finn. Eds. *States of Imagination: Ethnographic Explorations of the Postcolonial State.* Durham: Duke University Press, 2001.
Wood, Leonard. *First Annual Report of Major General Leonard Wood, Governor of the Moro Province.* Zamboanga City: Mindanao Herald Publishing, 1904.

———. *Third Annual Report of Major General Leonard Wood, U.S. Army, Governor of the Moro Province, July 1, 1905 to April 16, 1906.* Zamboanga City: Mindanao Herald Publishing, 1906.

Young, Robert J.C. *Postcolonialism: An Historical Introduction.* Oxford: Blackwell Publishers, 2001.

Zaide, Gregorio F. and Zaide, Sonia M. Eds. *Documentary Sources of Philippine History, Vol. 6–7.* Manila: National Bookstore, 1990.

Zaide, Sonia M. *Philippine History and Government.* Quezon City: All Nations Publishing, 1999.

INDEX

A
absentee rates, 144
Abu Bakr, 28, 37
Abu Sayyaf, 5, 142, 243
Abuza, Zachary, 142
Achebe, Chinua, 241
adat, 27, 28, 30
aesthetic intelligence, 34
Afghanistan, 142, 208, 240, 266
African–Americans, 2, 57, 159, 235, 254
agama, 27, 50
agricultural education, 70, 88
    aims of, 75
agricultural plantations, 59
Aguinaldo, Emilio, 107
Al Faruqi, Ismail, 151
alienation, 111, 120, 121, 125, 127, 135, 141, 148, 160, 161, 166–168, 172, 183, 199, 235, 245
alim, 37
Alonto Report, 115
Altbach, Philip, 17
Althusser, Louis, 11

Amai Pakpak, 43
American education, aims of, 90
American educators, in key posts, 85
American schooling, resistance to, 56, 81–83
anonen a rawaten, 27
anticolonial resistance, 11
anti-imperialism, in U.S., 57
Aquino, Benigno, 127
Aquino, Corazon, 16, 127, 165, 184
Arabic language instruction, 123, 185, 191, 194
Arnold Primer, 74
Asalan i Gibonen, 33
assimilation/integration model, 11
assimilation
    failure of, 247
    versus separatism, 221, 224
Autonomous Region in Muslim
    condition of schools, 171
    Department of Education in, 130, 151, 156, 169, 171, 185, 189, 191, 193, 195, 206

© The Editor(s) (if applicable) and The Author(s), under exclusive license to Springer Nature Singapore Pte Ltd. 2020
J. A. Milligan, *Islamic Identity, Postcoloniality, and Educational Policy, Islam in Southeast Asia*, https://doi.org/10.1007/978-981-15-1228-5

devolution of policy authority to, 156, 171, 189
establishment of, 128, 131, 189
infant mortality in, 24
life expectancy in, 24
literacy in, 24
maternal mortality in, 24
Mindanao, 24, 128, 134, 141, 143, 151, 156, 171, 185, 189, 248, 249
autonomy policy
as experiment, 132, 134
failure of, 171
false, 171
limitations of, 134

B
Bacon Bill, 84
bangsa, 27, 50
bangsamoro, 50, 131, 146, 155, 247–250
homeland for, 131
Bangsamoro Liberation Organization, 5
banking methods, 264
Bantogen, 31, 32, 34
barangay, 40
Barracuda, 121
Barrows, David Prescott, 58
Bazaco, Evergisto, 47
Bembaran, 36
Beowulf, 31
bin Laden, Osama, 142
Bishop-Ulama Forum, 261
Blackshirts, 121
Bliss, Tasker, 38, 60, 63, 70, 73, 80–82, 120, 245
boarding schools, 70, 73, 76, 77, 91
Board of National Education, 112
Bonifacio, Andres, 88, 107
book of prophecy, 34

Boransing, Manaros, 150, 189, 196
Borneo, 26, 28, 121
Boroboro sa Ragat, 35, 36
bride price, 76
Bruckner, Pascal, 18
Bud Dajo, Battle of, 81
Bureau of Education, 68, 69, 72, 85, 89
Bureau of Non-Christian Tribes, 61, 83, 92, 110, 116
Bush, George W., 142

C
Cameron, Charles R., 39, 68–70, 73, 77, 99, 101
Camp Abubakar, 131, 142
Camp Bushra, 131, 139, 142, 144
Caraga, 44, 48
Carpenter, Frank W., 38, 79, 81, 83, 98, 100–102
Catholicism, 41, 108, 261
influence of, 3, 47
Caulkins, Glenn, 90
census, Spanish of 1818 and 1866, 48
centralization of education, 110, 134, 165, 176, 209
Chapman, King, 86
Charles II, 46
Charles IV, 46
Chechnya, 1
China, 1, 236, 240
Chirino, Father Pedro, 45
Christian dialectic of human nature, 255
Christian Filipinos, attitudes toward, 8, 30, 43, 44, 46, 49, 65, 67, 69, 72, 74, 75, 83–86, 91, 92, 95–97, 109, 110, 114, 126, 130, 133–135, 141, 147, 155, 164, 172, 220, 242, 246, 248

Muslims, 8, 30, 44, 69, 72, 84–86, 89, 92, 97, 108, 110, 126, 133, 134, 141, 164, 170, 175, 184, 242, 248
Christianization, 42, 45, 48
Christian–Muslim dichotomy, 10
Chu-po, 26
church-state separation, 107, 108, 173, 263
Civilian Home Defense Forces, 122
civilization discourse, 89, 90, 92, 96, 115, 119, 120, 124, 126, 158, 222, 223, 226, 245
  and development, 126, 218, 223, 224
  and modernity, 119, 169
  evolutionary continuum in, 64
civilization policy, 43, 61, 64
civilization-savagery dichotomy, 115
civilized/non-civilized tribes, 61
class, 2, 5, 7, 8, 10, 13, 18, 29, 38, 46, 47, 108, 144–146, 160, 164, 174, 196, 219, 228, 252
Clavel, Leothiny, 118, 119, 136, 137, 210, 245, 267
Code of Civic and Ethical Principles, 107
cognatic kinship, 27
colonial education, 12–14, 45, 94, 133, 149, 158, 199, 204, 246
  Christianization of, 47, 166
  Hispanicization of, 47, 48
  legacy of, 4, 6, 26, 48, 190, 241
colonialism, 2, 6–11, 13, 16, 18, 25, 55, 56, 67, 80, 168, 179, 204, 215–219, 222, 226, 227, 247, 252, 259
  and education, 3, 25, 204, 215, 240
  and pedagogy, 12, 58, 67, 224
  criticism in U.S., 208

colonial policy, 11, 46, 55–57, 63, 65–68, 77, 78, 80, 81, 83, 95, 115, 117, 132, 173, 235
  instruments of, 115
colonization, 4, 5, 7, 11, 14, 18, 23, 25, 26, 37, 40, 84, 117, 128, 150, 183, 198, 217, 235, 241, 246, 260
  of minds, 7
  role of military might, 239
color-line, 2
Commissioner for Mindanao and Sulu, 116
Commission of Public Instruction, 46
Commission on National Integration (CNI), 116–119, 121, 125, 141, 184, 245
  corruption in, 125
  education division, 117
  objectives of, 117
Communist Party of the Philippines, 16, 122, 127
compulsory education laws, 82, 167
conflict, ethnic and religious, 3
continuity, criterion of, 233
Corregidor, 121
Cotabato, 29, 48, 62, 85, 87, 91, 111, 121, 175
  literacy in, 39, 49
  resistance in, 43
cotta, 93, 94
critical theory, 147
cultural capital, 160, 165
cultural criticism, Philippines, 260
cultural intelligence, 34
cultural minorities, U.S. education of, 56
cultural oppression, resistance to, 56
cultural subordination, 10
culture, similarities of, 1
curriculum
  academic, 88, 159

agricultural, 71, 88
as authorized knowledge, 158, 160, 264
Christian bias in, 175
hidden, 74, 77, 79, 80, 82, 83; aims of, 74; anti-Islamic, 151, 193
high school, 88, 151, 161, 195
in classroom, 166
in *Darangen*, 33
in Moro Province, 72–74
lutong makao, 157–160, 164, 166, 190, 207, 257, 262
Muslim views of, 172, 240
of public schools in *madaris*, 123, 129, 175, 192
of Spanish schools, 46–48
rationalization, in *madaris*, 129
unification of, 110, 112, 125–127, 184
Cusicanqui, Silvia Rivera, 9, 20

D

Dampier, William, 37
Darangen, The
concept of educated man in, 32, 34, 35
concept of educated person in, 32–34, 36
concept of educated woman in, 35
concept of uneducated person in, 35
educational values in, 31, 49, 158
teaching in, 35
dar-ul Islam, 141, 149, 154, 155
identification with, 141
Darwin, Charles, 12
Darwinism, social, 60, 80, 118, 226
Datu Alamada, 81
Datu Tawantawan uprising, 114
Datu Utto, 43
deconstruction, 218–220
deculturalization, 74, 76

Department of Education, Culture and
bureaucracy in, 130
corruption in, 130
creation of Regional, 129
dependency of Regional, 128–130, 134, 156, 171, 185, 189
Regional, 128–130, 134, 156, 185
Sports, 130
Department of Mindanao and Sulu, 38, 57, 61, 69, 79, 81, 83, 85, 93, 100, 116, 128
Department of Public Instruction, 67, 68
Derrida, Jacques, 146, 217
development, 5, 13, 26, 30, 59, 66, 67, 83, 89–91, 96, 111, 116, 119, 123, 172, 186, 191, 193, 195, 197, 210, 217, 223, 234, 236, 244, 256, 264
postcolonial, 13
Dewey, George, 56, 57
Dewey, John
and Marxism, 227–229
conception of democracy, 227
conception of experience, 230
critique of imperialism, 236
educational philosophy of, 227, 232, 234; and postcolonial education, 235, 236
educative experience, concept of, 233, 234, 262; criterion of continuity, 233, 234; criterion of interaction, 233, 234
in China, 236
intelligence, freedom of, 229, 231, 234
method of intelligence of, 233
miseducative experience, 233
spectator theory of knowledge, 229
difference, religious versus racial, 65
diversity, 14, 112, 154, 156, 222, 240, 241, 247, 265

cultural, in Philippines, 23, 106, 134, 265
geographic, in Philippines, 23, 106, 134
linguistic, in Philippines, 23, 106, 134
Diwata Ndaw Gibon, 31, 33, 35
djellaba, 148
drop out rates, 87, 88, 167
  Lanao del Sur, 167
DuBois, W.E.B., 2, 159, 163

E
economic dependency, 9, 10
Economic Development Corps, 111
educated person, concept of, 32, 34, 36, 50, 51, 158
  Maranao conception of, 32, 34, 35, 50, 51, 158, 159
education
  administration, 46, 58, 67, 85, 86, 128, 134, 218, 247
  American purposes in, 75
  and assimilation, 115, 120, 172, 224, 235, 240, 244, 245, 247
  and autonomy, 5, 127, 132, 134, 141, 171, 175, 183, 250, 257
  and democracy, 229, 235, 236, 248, 264
  and internal colonialism, 6, 215, 247
  and Islamic identity, 143, 145, 147, 151, 155–157, 172, 174, 186, 190, 207, 266
  as instrument of civilization, 67
  centralization of, 110, 134, 165, 176, 206
  decentralization of, 134, 157, 171, 189, 190, 209
  expansion of system, 13, 46, 67, 68
  faith in, 105, 112, 115, 120, 125, 130, 133–135, 143–145, 167, 193, 239, 247, 261
  first public primary, 46
  growth of, 1903-20, 68–70, 87
  history of, 32, 45, 55, 166, 188, 215, 246
  industrial, 70, 71, 73, 74, 88
  in Philippines, 3, 5, 7, 11, 14, 16, 17, 19, 25, 32, 36, 37, 45–47, 49, 55, 56, 68, 70, 85, 89, 107, 112, 125, 129, 133, 143, 150, 169, 170, 172, 183, 188, 190, 191, 193, 195, 197, 207, 215, 236, 239, 246, 247, 250, 259, 260, 266
  Islamic, in Philippines, 37, 150, 188, 197
  Islamization of, 36, 129, 184, 185, 198–200, 202, 206, 207, 209
  moral, 34, 47, 70, 112, 123, 186–188, 209, 256, 263
  multicultural, 135, 189, 190, 240, 265, 266
  nationalism in, 47, 106, 107, 110, 112, 123, 126, 156, 247, 265
  objectives, resistance to, 81, 82
  of Muslim girls, 70, 76, 89
  philosophy of, 31, 227, 232, 234, 235, 251
  policy, 2, 3, 5–7, 11, 13–15, 17–19, 26, 32, 47, 56, 70–72, 74, 75, 98, 105–108, 110, 112, 118, 120, 123–126, 128–130, 132, 135, 152, 156, 158, 169–171, 173, 183, 184, 189, 210, 217, 218, 220, 223, 224, 226, 240, 242, 244, 246, 247, 249, 250, 259–261, 265; American aims in, 72, 75; and colonial policy, 46, 55, 56, 67, 68, 75, 80, 95, 115, 245; and ethno-religious

tensions, 5, 14, 105, 135; and identity, 7, 10, 108, 110, 112, 134, 135, 152, 156, 173, 210, 223, 240, 244; and Muslim Filipinos, 6, 11, 14, 18, 32, 56, 70, 72, 75, 82, 123, 135, 170, 171, 183, 210, 220, 223, 226, 234, 244, 245, 250, 259, 265; and religious faith, 107, 112, 123; civilization-development frame, 126; in Autonomous Region, 128, 141, 157, 171, 189, 249; in Commonwealth, 5, 105–107, 156, 240; in Lanao del Sur, 144, 156; in Moro Province, 68, 70, 72, 82, 141, 245; in New Society, 123; Philippines, goals of, 123, 163, 246; postcolonial, 3, 6, 7, 11, 13, 14, 17, 132, 134, 155, 158, 183, 184, 210, 215, 218, 220, 223, 224, 226, 240, 242, 244, 245, 261, 262; problems in, 2, 105, 112, 129, 130, 133, 134, 144, 145, 161, 170, 171, 207, 209, 210, 227, 246; resistance to, 14, 56, 81, 82, 94, 115, 135, 155, 156, 183; U.S., 6, 14, 15, 55, 56, 70, 75, 185, 246, 250, 265; vocational, 71, 72, 112
progressive, 119, 202, 234, 241, 246
role in ethno-religious conflicts, 3, 15, 26, 32, 115, 132, 135, 143, 144, 240
Spanish, 45, 47, 48; Muslims in, 6, 25, 36, 37, 45, 48–50, 183, 184; policy, 3, 6, 15, 47, 106, 170
traditional, 26, 28, 31, 50, 75, 90, 92, 149, 150, 170, 204, 234

values, 14, 15, 25, 27, 30, 31, 36, 37, 49, 50, 107, 129, 133, 158, 163, 173, 186, 188, 193, 194, 249; indigenous, 30; of Muslim Filipinos, 11, 49, 50, 90, 133, 161, 172, 250; precolonial, 25, 31, 49; pre-Islamic, 25, 30, 31, 36
Education Decree of 1863, 46
Emerson, Ralph Waldo, 224, 237, 252
encampments of the lake, 27
encomienda system, 40
enrollment
  1866, 48
  1870, 48
  Caraga, 48
  Christian, 48, 68–70, 74, 82, 87, 164, 174
  Davao, 48, 87
  decreases, 87
  grades, 68, 69, 87, 88
  growth, 68, 69, 87, 151, 187
  in Moro Province, 68, 69
  Maranao, 69, 94
  Misamis, 48
  Muslim, 70, 82, 87, 93, 174, 175
  Surigao, 48
  Yakan, 69
epistemic authority, 158, 159
essentialism, 245, 260, 264
  American, 245, 250
  Filipino nationalist, 245
  ontology, 218, 230
Estrada, Joseph, 141, 243
ethnicity, 7, 113, 219
evolutionary theory, 12, 59
extended family, 49, 50, 75, 76, 124

F
Fanon, Franz, 7, 146, 177, 180, 241
farm schools, 75, 85, 88

feudalism, 40, 60
Filipinas Foundation, 118, 124, 137, 138, 242, 267
Filipinization, policy of, 67, 68, 79, 83, 85, 97
Filipino identity, emergence of, 4
Foucault, Michel, 7, 17, 20, 146, 151, 178, 217, 231, 252
foundationalist epistemology, 218, 229
four ways of doing good, 34, 35
Freire, Paulo, 126, 138, 179, 264, 268
Fugate, James R., 90, 91
Funan, 26

G
Gandhi, Leela, 6, 7
Gandhi, Mahatma, 20, 253, 255, 261
gas bombs, 81, 239
gender, 7, 8, 10, 18, 35, 77, 96, 146, 164, 217, 219
genealogy, 17, 31, 34, 115
genetic psychology, 80
gobirno a sarawang tao, 27, 95, 125
good Muslim, conception of, 153–155, 209
Gordimer, Nadine, 241, 267
Gramsci, Antonio, 11, 219, 252
Guingona, Teopisto, 83, 99

H
hadith, 37, 187, 188, 204
haj, 79, 147, 152
Hall, G. Stanley, 59, 99
Hashim, Salamat, 131, 180, 212
Hawaii, 55, 96
Hayden, Joseph Ralston, 92, 93, 99, 101–104, 266
Hegel, Georg Wilhelm Friedrich, 7, 227
Hindu civilizations, 26

Hispanicization, 47, 48
home economics, 88
homestead policy, 59
House Committee on National Minorities, 114
Hukbalahap, 111
Human Development Index, 24

I
Ibn Siena Integrated School, 151, 175, 180, 186, 193
identity
 Bangsamoro, 50, 146, 155, 249
 cultural and religious, 40, 50, 96, 132, 168, 209
 Filipino, 4, 11, 40, 64, 74, 83, 87, 96, 106–108, 110, 112, 114, 133, 135, 148, 155, 156, 163, 165, 173, 176, 209, 210, 223, 234, 240, 245–247, 250, 265
 intra-ethnic, 50
 Islamic, 29, 64, 97, 131, 143, 145–148, 151–157, 166, 172, 174–176, 186, 190, 207, 253, 266; among teachers, 152, 155, 176; assertion of, 133, 148, 153, 154; problem of, 172, 175, 186, 190; resurgence of, 145, 147, 154
 national, 3, 13, 23, 107, 108, 110, 118, 126, 134, 135, 156, 207, 240
 religious, 40, 50, 56, 74, 82, 96, 108, 116, 127, 132, 147, 151, 154, 155, 168, 173, 176, 209, 210, 216, 224, 261, 265, 266
Ilaga, 121
Iliad, 31
Ilyas, Muhammad, 148

imperialism, 2, 6, 7, 18, 91, 95–98, 108, 216, 217, 219, 222, 236, 258, 265, 266
   United States, 6, 14, 56, 67, 77, 80, 85, 91, 96, 122, 156, 226, 235, 247, 260
Indanan School for Moro Boys, 90
independence, 1, 2, 4, 6–8, 10, 24, 37, 56, 83, 84, 91–93, 95, 106–109, 111, 117, 126, 128, 143, 155, 158, 170, 185, 224, 226, 239, 240
   disagreements over, 83
   struggle for, 4, 106, 107, 131
India, 1, 26, 31, 148, 149, 240, 266
Indian Bureau, 58
Indianization, 26
Indians, 26, 58, 59, 84, 91, 163, 226
Indian Wars, 4, 59
Indonesia, 1, 24, 26, 29, 149, 240, 266
infantilization discourse, 96
instructional methods, 160
insurgents, Filipino, 56
integrated *madaris*, 151, 186, 192, 193
integration
   and Islamic schools, 123
   as assimilation, 11, 133, 171, 172, 244
   as marginalization, 169
   failure of, 125
   Muslim attitudes toward, 91, 124, 172
integration policy, 149, 171, 184, 196
   assumptions of, 134, 184
   failure of, 125
interaction, criterion of, 233
internal colonialism, 6, 8, 9, 11, 25, 215, 247
Iraq, 240, 266
ironworking, 73

Islam
   adoption by Maranao, 31, 50
   American attitudes toward, 77
   Americans knowledge of, 38, 51, 64
   and proto-nationalist identity, 30
   bias against, 79
   cultural influence of, 26, 30, 40
   defense of, 82
   introduction in Mindanao, 50, 149, 167
   sense of threat to, 1, 78, 97, 197, 240
   spread of, 28, 41, 50, 209
Islamic law, 28
Islamic schools, 78, 79, 113, 114, 123, 129, 133, 149, 169, 187, 190, 192, 197
Islamization
   from above, 131
   from below, 131, 148
   of knowledge, 150, 198, 200, 208
Islamized ethnic groups, 4, 24
Ivison, Duncan, 220–224, 237

J

Jabidah Massacre, 121
jama'ah, 148
James, William, 225, 226
Jamiatul Philippines Al-Islamia, 114
Japanese invasion, 93, 94, 241
Japanese occupation, resistance to, 5
Jemaah Islamiyah, 142
jihad, 44, 122, 240
Jolo, 44, 90, 91, 94, 126
Jones Act, 83
Jones Law, 110, 117, 141
juramentado, 43, 61, 81, 94, 102, 116, 136

K

Kamilol Islam Institute, 114
Kamilon rebellion, 114
kampilan, 34, 50
kataba, 38
Kepel, Gilles, 19, 131, 138, 148, 177, 267
King, Martin Luther, Jr., 255, 261
kinship, 27, 28, 30, 42, 49, 50
kirim, 31
kolintang, 34
kris, 94
Kuder, Edward M., 86

L

Lacar, Luis, 52, 138, 150, 180
Lake Lanao, 29, 43, 48, 82, 143, 144
  description of, 143, 144
  geography of, 143, 144
lamin, 33
Lanao, 14, 25, 43, 82, 85–87, 91, 93, 94, 111, 113, 121, 145, 148, 149, 152, 156
  resistance in, 14, 43, 156
Lanao del Sur, 15, 115, 116, 120, 128, 131, 143, 150, 152, 156, 157, 160, 164, 166, 167, 181, 186, 187
  poverty in, 166
land of promise, 23
land ownership, 59, 75, 111, 121
language policy, 13, 74, 174
Laubach, Frank, 86, 103, 104
Law of recapitulation, 59
Law of the Indies, 41
Legazpi, Miguel Lopez de, 41
Letter of Instruction No. 71-A, 123
Leyte, 42
liberalism, 221–224, 228, 229
  postcolonial critiques of, 220–222
Libya, 122

literacy rates, 24, 39
  Samal, 39
  Sulu, 39
Liu, John, 9–11, 20
Loomba, Ania, 6, 18, 20, 21, 237
Lumad, 23, 24
Luzon, 42, 43, 46–48, 59, 75, 92, 97, 106, 108, 111, 147

M

Macapagal-Arroyo, Gloria, 143, 194, 243
Madale, Abdullah, 51, 124, 138
Madali, 32
madaris
  enrollment in, 150, 196
  growth of, 149
  parents choice of, 168
madrasah, 37, 149–151, 174, 175, 186, 190, 192, 197, 247, 263
  education, history of, 247
  education in Lanao, 151
  integration, 189, 195–197
  reconciliation of, 129, 130
  system, 129
Magdalena, Frederico, 52, 150
Magsaysay, Ramon, 111
Maguindanao, 14, 29, 30, 37, 41–43, 45, 49, 50, 74, 128, 131, 145, 153, 155, 156, 243
  Islamization of, 29
  Spanish inroads in, 42
  sultanate, 41, 42
Mahabharata, 31
Majapahit, 26
Majul, Cesar, 19, 29, 41, 52, 53, 121, 137, 176, 210
makatib, 38
makhdumin, 28, 37
Malabang, 29
Malaysia, 24, 26, 121, 142, 197

Malay sultanate structure, 27
Maranao, 14, 15, 25–32, 34–36, 38, 42, 43, 48–51, 69, 89, 92–94, 116, 143–145, 152–156, 158, 159, 162, 166–169, 175, 176, 181, 262
  Islamization of, 30, 50, 155
  resistance of, 28, 43, 116, 155
maratabat, 33, 49, 50, 154, 155, 166
Marawi City, 114, 115, 149–151
  destruction of schools, 93
Marcos, Ferdinand, 16, 121–123, 125, 127, 128, 156, 165, 184, 194, 260
Marcos dictatorship, demise of, 125
Maria Cristina, Queen Regent, 47
Marquardt, W.W., 89
martial law, 122, 127, 243
Martin, Jane Roland, 31, 102, 127
Marxism, 2, 7, 217, 218, 227–229, 254, 255
  influence in Philippines, 7, 217
Masiu, 82
Mastura, Datu Michael, 52, 53, 136, 177
McKinley, William, 239
medium of instruction, 73, 123, 156
Memmi, Albert, 7, 11, 241, 267
migration
  of Christian Filipinos, 10, 43, 75, 97, 147
  policy, 59
military pacification, 115
Military Training Act, 94
Mindanao
  American administration of, 68, 81, 95
  Christianization of, 48, 167
  cultural influences, 26, 30
  economy, 5
  ethnic segmentation, 30
  history of, 26, 28, 157, 161, 190, 209, 215
  Islamization of, 28, 29, 37, 129, 184, 198, 200, 207, 209, 210
  natural resources, 24, 84, 106
  population density, 59, 75
  poverty, 24, 157, 206, 207, 210
  U.S. aid for, 79, 142, 143, 248
  western colonization of, 26
Mindanao Herald, 245
Mindanao Independence Movement (MIM), 121, 122
Mindanao Problem, 14, 190
Mindanao State University, 116, 123, 144, 151, 178, 186, 193
Mindanao-Sulu Mohammedan Students Association, 86
Ministry of Education, 156
Ministry of Muslim Affairs, 149
Misamis, 44, 48
missionaries, 28
  Arabian, 29
  Muslim, 28, 29, 114, 147, 149
mission civilisatrice, 239
Misuari, Nur, 122, 127, 131, 132, 137, 180, 184
modus vivendi, 223, 224, 236
Monroe Commission Survey, 89
Moors, 30, 98
Moro Islamic Liberation Front (MILF), 5, 131–133, 141–143, 145, 148, 180, 243, 248
  renunciation of terrorism, 243
Moro National Liberation Front (MNLF), 5, 16, 122, 123, 125, 127, 128, 131, 132, 137, 148, 156, 165, 180, 184, 243
Moro Problem
  as Filipino problem, 130
  as pedagogical problem, 67, 95

Philippine government response, 5, 109, 115
resurgence of, 114
revisioning of, 127
Moro Province, 38, 39, 57, 59–65, 67–74, 77–79, 81, 82, 89, 93, 99, 101, 116, 120, 128, 141, 142, 245
Moros, 4, 23, 30, 39, 41, 42, 44, 45, 56, 58, 60, 61, 64, 78, 84, 86, 92–94, 97, 98, 108, 120, 154, 235, 239, 244
Moro Wars, 40–42, 44, 50
mosala, 34
Mount Basak, Battle of, 81
Muhammad, Prophet, 27, 49, 188, 201, 256
mujahideen, 5, 132–134, 142
multiculturalism, 189, 190, 263
Murphy, Governor-General, 92
Muslim–Christian, 1
 attitudes, 92, 242
 dichotomization of society, 4, 146
 relations, 7–10, 15, 25, 44, 56, 126, 129, 161, 172, 242, 260
 tensions, 59, 83, 84, 111, 125, 133, 171, 184, 244
Muslim education, 5, 6, 89, 113, 124, 151, 190, 198, 200, 207, 259, 260, 266
 abroad, 190
 precolonial, 49
Muslim Filipinos
 and government schools, 113, 133, 151, 170
 armed resistance of, 80, 93
 attitudes toward independence, 10, 37, 84, 92, 111, 126, 185, 239
 Commonwealth policy, 97, 245
 depiction of, 243
 gender relations, 8, 18, 76, 77
 influence of Middle East on, 114, 147, 162, 186, 259
 marriage, 76, 77
 modernization of, 49, 65, 70, 169, 210, 223
 portrait of, 62, 67
 precolonial, 49
 resistance, 38, 41, 42, 64, 79–82, 89, 94–96, 116, 161, 242
 resistance to U.S., 38, 64, 80–82, 96
 respect for, 49, 64, 129, 171, 250
 self identification of, 49
 U.S. education of, 6, 17, 56, 70, 72, 74, 76, 82, 83, 169, 234, 250, 259
 view of Christians, 91, 164, 172
Muslim majority provinces, 24
Muslims
 Bornean, 42
 conversion of, 43, 76
 marriage, attempts to change, 76
 teachers, percentage of, 86
Muslim students, college readiness, 116

N

Nandy, Ashis, 6
National Academy of Education, 16
National Council of Education, 110, 112
National Cultural Minorities, 119, 120
national identity, 3, 13, 23, 107, 108, 110, 118, 126, 134, 135, 156, 207, 240
nationalism, 1, 2, 88, 107, 108, 110, 112, 122, 123, 126, 127, 148, 156, 247, 260, 265
 Christian foil, 126
 essentialism, 245, 260, 264
 Filipino, 4, 47, 106, 165, 260
 Moro, 122, 165

nationalists, 1, 2, 40, 47, 50, 110, 124, 126, 131, 158, 217, 245–247, 260, 264
national spiritual reconstruction, 106, 108
Native Americans, 55, 57, 58, 62, 119, 226
neocolonialism, 8, 16, 215, 224, 226, 247
New People's Army, 16, 122, 127
New Republic, The, 93
New Society, 123
newspapers, depiction of Muslims, 243
New York, 142

O
Odyssey, 31
Office of the President, 116
orientalism, 56, 115, 217
orientalist discourse, 56, 98
Osias, Camilo, 88, 103, 106, 110, 135–137, 160, 161
Other, 18, 61, 62, 95, 96, 115, 164

P
Pagan and Mohammedan Tribes, Bureau of, 61
pagtamat, 39
Palawan, 142, 145
Panay, 42, 45
pandita, 37, 49, 149, 174
pandita schools, 37–40, 48, 49, 83, 149, 174
Papal Bull of 1537, 41
paternalism, 91
peace talks, with MILF, 127, 141, 142
pedagogical imperialism, 77, 80, 85, 91, 95–98
aims of, 67, 91

Peirce, Charles Sanders, 225, 226
pengampong, 27
People Power Revolt, 127
Pershing, John J., 62, 66, 76–79, 81, 83, 99–103, 120, 163, 180
Philippine Readers, 88, 103
Philippine revolution, 43
Philippines
  armed forces, expansion of, 10, 115, 121, 122, 142, 145, 243
  colonization by Spain, 4, 25, 41, 184
  Commonwealth, 85, 86, 92, 97, 105–107
  Constabulary, 81, 83
  Constitution, 112, 129, 173, 249, 263
  education, 3, 5, 7, 11, 14, 16, 17, 19, 37, 45–47, 49, 55, 56, 67, 107, 112, 113, 123, 125, 130, 133, 156, 163, 166, 169, 172, 175, 188, 190–193, 195–197, 207, 209, 218, 239–241, 246, 259, 260, 262, 265, 266;
  accomplishments of, 241;
  impediments, 170, 241, 242;
  U.S. influence on, 17
  government, Muslim policy, 44, 70, 92, 108, 109, 114, 117, 121, 133, 155, 242
  History and Government, 161
  Islamization in, 29, 36, 161
  Legislature, establishment of, 83, 84, 110
  madaris, trends, 114, 149, 150, 192, 196, 197
  Republic, declaration of, 57
Philippines School for Advanced Integrated Education, 175
Phillip II, 41
Phoenix Publishing House, 161
physical intelligence, 34

Piang, Datu Gumbay, 84, 91
pilgrimage, to Mecca, 78
pioneer discourse, 58, 59, 61, 86, 116
political dependency, 10
political-economic subordination, 74
polygamy, 61, 62, 76
pondok pesantren, 174
population, 1866, 48
postcoloniality, 3, 7
Postcolonial Liberalism, 220, 237
postcolonial liberalism, 222–224
postcolonial pragmatism, 224, 253, 263
   and Philippine education, 226, 227
   prophetic, 252, 256, 260, 262, 263, 266
postcolonial state, 8, 11, 215
postcolonial theory
   and Marxism, 7, 227
   and poststructuralism, 7, 226, 227, 252
   and pragmatism, 224, 226, 227, 252, 253, 260, 266
   and prophetic pragmatism, 252, 260, 266
   and religion, 219, 253
   and the fourth world, 219
   as analytical tool, 216, 220
   insufficiency of, 220, 227
poststructuralism, 7, 226, 227, 252
pragmatism
   optimistic theodicy of, 231, 252
   postcolonial, 227, 252, 253, 263, 266
   prophetic, 251, 252, 254–258, 260–266
precolonial culture, 25, 31, 49
Princess Paramata Gandingan, 32, 34
Puerto Rico, 96
Pulangi River, 29

Q
Quezon, Manuel, 94, 106–109, 124
Quezon Code, 107, 108
Quirino, Elpidio, 111
Qur'an, 26, 37, 64, 76
   and education, 26, 37, 45

R
race, 7, 10, 30, 47, 56, 58, 59, 71, 88, 219
race pedagogy, 67
racism, among American soldiers, 57
Radia Indarapatra, 26, 27, 49
Rajah Baguinda, 28
Ramadan, 152
Ramayana, 26, 31
Ramos, Fidel, 131, 132
Ranao Council, 151, 186
religious bias, 65, 172, 173
religious freedom, guarantees of, 108
religious identity, and schools, 40, 176, 265
religious orders, 40, 45, 107
Republic Act 1387, 115
Republic Act 1888, 116
resettlement policies, 23
resistance, 1, 5, 7, 11, 28, 38, 41–43, 55–57, 64, 79–83, 89, 90, 93–96, 98, 111, 115, 116, 122, 126, 132, 135, 141, 145, 154–156, 161, 167, 172, 197, 216, 217, 219, 220, 235, 242, 252
   psychological, 7, 167, 179
   to U.S. forces, 43, 57
rido, 143, 144, 243
Rizal, Jose, 47, 88, 107
Rorty, Richard, 225, 231, 237, 238, 260, 268
Roxas, Manuel, 111

S

Sabah, 121
sagayan, 33
Said, Edward, 12, 20, 99, 115, 136, 217, 241
Saleeby, Najeeb, 39, 53, 65, 68, 73, 74, 77, 100, 102
salsila, 27
Samar, 42
Sanskrit, 26, 37
Santo Tomas, University of, 47
Sayana, 32–35
Sayid Alawi Balpaki, 28
schools
  as civilizing agents, 70, 86, 170
  catechism, 45–48
  growth of, 68–70, 87, 133, 149
  intermediate, 14, 72
  Islamic, 78, 79, 113, 114, 123, 129, 133, 149, 169, 187, 190, 192, 197
  Koranic, 37, 45
  libraries, Lanao del Sur, 160, 166
  locations in Moro Province, 69
  material poverty of, 151, 166, 187
  Mindanao and Sulu, 37, 38, 47, 67, 69, 70, 79, 80, 87
  pandita, 37–40, 48, 49, 83, 149, 174
  state of, 83
secessionist movement, 5, 16, 121, 122, 131, 135, 148, 183, 184
  casualties in, 5
  expansion of, 135, 148, 183
second sight, 159, 163, 168
September 11, 2001, 142
shariah, 28, 30
Sharif al-Hashim, 37
Sharif Auliya Makhdum, 28
Shariff Kabunsuan College, 175
Sharif Muhammad Kabungsuwan, 29
Shubba'an al-Muslimen Tableegh, 148
slavery, 61, 62, 75, 76, 163
Sleeping Lady, 144
social Darwinism, 60, 80, 118, 226
social identity theory, 146, 152, 153
social intelligence, 33
Society of Jesus, 46
South China Sea, 26
Southern Philippines Development Authority, 125
Spain
  arrival in Philippines, 36, 56
  colonial rule, 3, 11, 40–42, 45
  colonization of Philippines, 4, 25, 41, 183, 184
  sovereignty claims, 43
Spanish–American War, 4, 16, 55, 56
Spencer Postdoctoral Fellowship, 16
Spivak, Gayatri Chakravorty, 17, 19, 21
spoonfeeding, 159, 264
Srivijaya, 26
Stokes mortars, 51, 81, 239
students, spiritual development of, 129, 173
subaltern, 219, 253
Sufism, 29
Sultan of Sulu, 26, 57
Sulu, 4, 26, 28, 29, 37, 39, 41–44, 48, 57, 68, 72, 74, 80–88, 90, 94–97, 105, 114, 115, 121, 128, 143, 156, 170, 247
Sulu Archipelago, 4, 26, 28, 29, 37, 41, 43, 56, 106, 145, 209, 239, 247
Sulu Reader, 39
Superintendent of Public Instruction, 39, 65, 69, 70, 90

T

Tabligh, Jama'at al, 148, 151, 154, 189
  as informal education, 148
  in Basilan, 148
taritib, 28, 30
tarsila, 28, 37
Tausug, 30, 43, 49, 50, 74, 94, 145, 153, 155, 162, 163
  Islamization of, 30, 50, 145, 155
  resistance of, 43
Tawagon, Manuel, 28, 51, 52
Tawi-tawi, 28, 128, 156
teachers
  absenteeism, 167
  as historical agents, 252, 261
  as prophetic pragmatists, 264
  Christian Filipino, 69, 72, 82, 86, 93, 96
  in Moro Province, 64, 67–69, 72, 82, 89
  methods, spoonfeeding, 159, 264
  Muslim Filipino, 38, 56, 64, 69, 72, 80, 86, 96, 123, 130, 155, 165, 166, 185, 188, 197, 241
  relations with students, 264
  training of, 46, 112
Ternate, 29
textbooks
  absence of Muslims, 209
  and epistemic authority, 158
  as curriculum, 113, 125, 157, 158, 160, 164–166, 184
  Asian and World History, 161, 162
  Christian bias in, 108
  critiques of, 157
  cultural relevance of, 124
  essentialism of, 250
  high school English, 162
  idolatry of, 158, 160
  inclusion of Islam, 161, 162, 164, 165
  Islamization of, 191, 200
  portrayal of Muslims, 164, 165
  selection of, 157
theory of knowledge, 199, 227, 229, 230
third worldism, 18
Tolibas-Nunez, Rosalita, 139, 243, 267
Torrens system, 75
Treaty of Paris, 57
tribal communities, 23
Tripoli Agreement, 122, 128

U

ulama, 38, 44, 151, 175, 186, 189, 191, 256
ummah, 27, 198, 222
United States
  attention to Mindanao, 142, 197
  colonization of Philippines, 4, 7, 183, 235, 246
  Constitution, 79, 107, 173
  displacement of Spain, 50
  Fulbright Program, 16
  imperialism, 6, 14, 56, 57, 67, 77, 80, 91, 96, 122, 156, 226, 235, 247, 260
  Institute of Peace, 16
  invasion of Philippines, 4, 235
  Peace Corps, 15
  pedagogy of imperialism, 14, 67
unity and diversity, problem of, 240
University of the Philippines, 122, 137, 180
ustadh, 38
Uti, 82

V

Values Education Program, 129, 194
verbal eloquence, 33, 34

Vietnam, 26, 145
Visayas, 42–44, 46–48, 59, 75, 92, 97, 147

W
war on terrorism, 1, 5, 243, 265
Washington, D.C., 54, 142
Watson, Keith, 17, 20, 21
West, Cornel, 98, 178, 225–227, 231, 236–238, 251–257, 261, 267, 268
  critique of pragmatism, 227, 252
  on John Dewey, 227, 254
Weyler, Governor-General Valeriano, 43
wild tribes, 60

Wilson, Fiona, 13, 19, 21
Wood, Leonard, 57, 59, 64, 67, 73, 82, 92, 99–103, 120
woodworking, 73

Y
Young, Robert J.C., 216, 219, 237, 268
Yugoslavia, 1, 240, 266

Z
zakat, 152
Zamboanga, 42, 44, 48, 66, 69, 81, 82, 87, 91, 99, 115, 243

GPSR Compliance

The European Union's (EU) General Product Safety Regulation (GPSR) is a set of rules that requires consumer products to be safe and our obligations to ensure this.

If you have any concerns about our products, you can contact us on

ProductSafety@springernature.com

In case Publisher is established outside the EU, the EU authorized representative is:

Springer Nature Customer Service Center GmbH
Europaplatz 3
69115 Heidelberg, Germany

www.ingramcontent.com/pod-product-compliance
Lightning Source LLC
LaVergne TN
LVHW011006250326
834688LV00004B/94